THE
CHINESE
OF
AMERICA

THE
CHINESE
OF
AMERICA

Jack Chen

Harper & Row, Publishers, San Francisco
Cambridge, Hagerstown, Philadelphia, New York
London, Mexico City, São Paulo, Sydney

1817

THE CHINESE OF AMERICA. Copyright © 1980 by Jack Chen.
All rights reserved. Printed in the United States of America. No part
of this book may be used or reproduced in any manner whatsoever
without written permission except in the case of brief quotations
embodied in critical articles and reviews. For information address
Harper & Row, Publishers, Inc., 10 East 53rd Street, New York, NY
10022. Published simultaneously in Canada by Fitzhenry & Whiteside,
Limited, Toronto.

FIRST EDITION

Designed by Jim Mennick

Library of Congress Cataloging in Publication Data

Chen, Jack, 1908–
    The Chinese of America.

    Includes index.
    1.   Chinese Americans—History.   I.   Title.
E184.C5C458   1980   973'.04951   80–7749
ISBN 0-06-250140-2

80 81 82 83 84 10 9 8 7 6 5 4 3 2 1

Contents

Tables, Graphs, and Maps

Preface

The bosom of America is open to receive not only the opulent
and respectable stranger but the oppressed and persecuted of
all nations and religions; whom we shall welcome to a
participation of all our rights and privileges, if by decency and
propriety of conduct they appear to merit the enjoyment.

GEORGE WASHINGTON, 1783

THE PEOPLING and building of America by
immigrants from many lands is one of the epics of world history. Native
American Indians, English, French, Germans, Spaniards, Irish, Italians,
Japanese, Latin Americans, Chinese, whites, blacks, and many others have
made this land what it is—a dynamic, vital conglomerate of peoples—a "nation
of nations," in Walt Whitman's phrase—a still-evolving experiment to better
the human condition.

These men and women were indeed pioneers in the largest sense, and,
while paying tribute to those of other nations who fashioned and are fashioning
this new nation, this book's purpose is to tell the Chinese story as an integral
part of that history, with its ups and downs, its blemishes and its beauties,
its tragedies and triumphs.

I wish to thank the Chinese Culture Foundation of San Francisco for
sharing its facilities. Its members and those of the Chinese Historical Society
of America generously gave advice and made material available to me. Special
thanks must go to Mr. Him Mark Lai for his invaluable comments and to
Marie Cantlon of Harper & Row. Any shortcomings in the book are mine
alone.

JACK CHEN
San Francisco, 1980

Introduction

I AM a traveling type of man. I find it astonishing that a person can live happily for a lifetime in one place. After I have been for several years in a city, I get restless. When I first arrive in a place, my sensations of it are exciting and vivid. I see it with a heightened consciousness. As time goes by, I see less and less of it. Gradually I grow self-centered, seeing more of what is already inside my head and only intermittently becoming vividly aware of the sights and sounds "out there." And then I want to move, to have my senses stimulated by new sights and sounds and experiences.

It is a small world, but big for us as individuals. I have only a few score years to live in it, and I feel that I had better get moving before it is too late to see this heritage of ours. So I pick up my belongings and am off. I never feel "alien." I belong to that growing number of people who after arriving in a new country soon begin speaking of "us." I identify with the people around me, and life quickly furnishes innumerable good reasons why I should. So I suppose I am the stuff out of which immigrants are made.

By 1970, after living in China for twenty years, longer than I have lived in any other country at a single stretch, it was time to leave. My wife and my young son were also eager to travel. With invitations to lecture at Harvard, Cornell, Yale, Stanford, and a number of other American universities and to address Washington's prestigious Asia Society and New York's Council on Foreign Relations, and with a few hundred dollars worth of travelers' checks in my pocket, I booked a seat on an American Airlines jet from Hong Kong and flew across the 7,000 miles of the Pacific in the wake of half a million or so other Chinese who had made the journey before me in pursuit of happiness.

I did not realize it at the time, but I was a typical new immigrant: a middle-class intellectual, supremely self-assured that all I needed to succeed was tucked away in my head conveniently near my tongue, and quite convinced that the world was my oyster.

At the time, I rationalized it all quite neatly: my wife and I would see America; perhaps we would stay. We had solid reasons for the move. I had already seen the world and America, but my wife, a budding writer, needed to broaden her horizons and find a publisher. It would be good to give my son a taste of American education. I had occupied my position in the magazine I worked for, *Peking Review,* for so long that I felt it was time I vacated a space for the younger generation's promotion. Those whom I supported in the Cultural Revolution had come out on top, and I did not like saying, "I told you so." We also hoped that, at a time when it was sorely needed, we might be able to pass on something of what we knew about China to the Americans, who were eager to find out more about the mysterious New China after a twenty-year gap in communications.

I felt that Washington was slowly coming around to the same realization as most of the veteran leaders in Peking: that the peace of the world now depended on normalization of relations between China and the United States and on closer synchronization of their policies regarding the Soviet Union and its expansionist aims. That was in 1971. I was honored and responded immediately when asked by President Nixon to share with him any information that might help him on his forthcoming visit to Peking.

My lecture tour went well. I was invited to return to the United States with my family and become consultant on Chinese studies to the New York State Education Department. We settled down first in Albany and then at Cornell University in Ithaca in the heart of the Finger Lakes country. I lectured, I wrote. I was in a "think tank" as a senior research associate. My wife received her bachelor's degree from New York State University and became a language instructor at Cornell. She was soon ready to publish her first novel. My son, finishing high school, entered Cornell as a freshman with test scores within the top 10 percent in the country. We were living the "American Dream." We had a delightful ranch-style house by a stream and could see twenty miles across open country. We owned our home, had a few rental properties, credit cards, insurance, retirement pensions, social security, Blue Cross, a Volkswagen, and a large garden, which wild deer visited to nibble the grass. We had "made it," and in 1977 I applied for adjustment of my visa from that of "distinguished scholar" to permanent resident.

That showed me that I was indeed an immigrant and no longer a free-floating intellectual. I did not like the word *immigrant* applied to myself. At first it meant to me that I did not belong here, that I was knocking on a door asking to be allowed to come in. Although I have scrupulously observed the legalities of travel, I have long cherished the idea that this world is mine— is everybody's who lives on it—and that we should not be fenced off from our common property. But the immigration officials I met made it very clear from the first that they did not share such utopian ideas.

For the first time in our lives, my wife and I went through the usual hassles of immigration: the innumerable forms to be filled out, in duplicate and triplicate; proofs of qualifications and dates of birth; medical exams; legal advice and interrogations. The process dragged on for months and years. When I later saw a picture of a Chinese boy in 1920 sitting lonely and puzzled before two imposing officials on Angel Island in San Francisco Bay, I could identify immediately with him. I too had been subjected to an interrogation by immigration officers that was designed to test my veracity.

"When were you married?" the investigator asked.

I answered unhesitatingly: "May 1958." I had a picture in my mind of that lovely spring day up in the Western Hills above Peking on my honeymoon with my bride. I had just lost my wallet with all my ready cash in it, and I had no money to pay for the hotel room. No one in China then used checks or credit cards.

I glanced over at the paper in front of the investigator. It was my application form. I stole a look at the box marked "date of marriage." It said April. I was off by three days. I have never been able to remember our wedding anniversary, and my wife is always annoyed about this. I have a memory that sometimes blots out extraneous matter when I am concentrating on something. At the moment, I was writing a chapter in my book on the history of central Asia. Why had he not asked me the date of the crucial Talas River battle? Or the names of the Five Khodjas?

At such a moment, would that young boy in the photograph have been able to remember precisely how many steps right or left he would have had to take to reach the well outside the house where he said he had been living? And yet the immigrants had been asked such questions on Angel Island.

Now I too was an immigrant. I became interested in such things as immigration laws and what other immigrants had experienced. How did they feel about coming to America? Why did they come? And almost before I knew it I was immersed in an exciting search for the truth about us—us immigrants, us Chinese Americans.

It was a difficult task, and it intensified and grew even more enthralling when I was engaged by the Chinese Culture Foundation of San Francisco to coordinate a national exhibition describing the Chinese American experience. I was soon entangled in semantics. I quickly learned that in some circles it was "wrong" to hyphenate *Chinese American* and that *American-Chinese* was doubly out. I could find no single book that told the full story. The last one that tried to do so was more than ten years old. Thus began my search through scores of books and articles, gleaning bits and pieces of a complicated mosaic of history that, according to one's inclination, can stretch for a modest 200 years or to over 2,000 years ago when Chinese travelers journeyed "across the water" to the fabled land of Fusang, now called America.

I found that the immigrants' story is little known even among themselves. Soon the word *immigrant* no longer had a subtly contemptuous ring in my ear. It had the ring of noble metal now, like the words *hero* and *pioneer*. I found that I was one of the majority group of immigrants because, as a native son of Zhongshan County, I came from the same area of Guangdong Province in southern China from which the great majority of Chinese American immigrants come. I had lived in China for a third of my life, but I had never made the effort to go and see the place where my ancestors had lived. But when I heard that a documentary about Zhongshan would be shown at the Chinese Cultural Center in San Francisco, I dropped everything and hurried off to see it.

I found that there were and still are great gaps in our knowledge of the history of the Chinese in America. Some of this is not surprising. It has been hard to get funds for Chinese American research projects. Not many scholars have had the time or means to complete scholarly research projects, which sometimes entail hours, days, and weeks of labor, poring through books and papers and microfilm, sometimes with little to show for it. But I am not speaking only of honest error due to lack of time or material. I am talking about conscious obfuscation, passionate bias pro or con, prejudice, and timidity in the face of vested interests. To read one book, you would never guess that early leaders of the American Federation of Labor staged anti-Chinese racist riots that resulted in people being killed. Another, glossing over the greed and rascality of the Southern Pacific's Big Four, is all too clearly keeping a wary eye over his shoulder at the watchdogs of big business. On the other hand, a well-meaning writer hesitates to describe the appalling economic conditions and terror in old China that drove tens of thousands of Chinese to emigrate. To read another, you would never guess that the Chinese immigrants had among them whorehouse keepers of the utmost brutality or hatchetmen (in the tongs) who were responsible for gangster killings. The author's excuse was that he did not want to revive the Fu Manchu stereotype of the Chinese filmed by Hollywood at its worst. A fifth, for the sake of "ethnic solidarity," fails to mention that American Indians were induced to help tax gatherers track down hiding Chinese miners or that Italian strong-arm methods helped drive the Chinese from the fishing industry in the 1890s. It took a lot of digging to unearth the names of the many white men and women who felt deep sympathy for the persecuted Chinese caught up in the waves of racist violence and who did not hesitate to take up arms to defend them, pioneers like themselves helping to build America. To some, the Chinese of the mid-nineteenth century were "coolies" and nothing more, near-slaves without skills or intelligence to do more than obey their white masters, degenerates who in hordes brought nothing but ill to America.

This kind of bias has to be outgrown if we are to reveal the truth about the Chinese experience in America. What I have tried to do in the following pages is to provide the reader with a coherent picture of the historical record as I have analyzed it, using as much scientific objectivity as I can muster in the search for the truth. This account may annoy and perhaps infuriate the biased. I hope that it will please you who, like myself, want to get at the facts, no matter where they may lead, so that we can use the experiences of the past, good and bad, to make a better future. The record of the Chinese Americans needs no whitewashing or varnishing.

THE
COMING

[The early Chinese immigrant was noted for his] industry, quietness, cheerfulness, and cleanliness and efficiency. [He] did what no one else could do, or what remained undone, adapting himself to the white man's tastes and slipping away, unprotestingly, to other tasks when the white man wanted his job.

MARY ROBERTS COOLIDGE, Chinese Immigration

The Earliest
Arrivals

CHAPTER

1

The quietness and order, cheerfulness and temperance which is observable in their habits, is noticed by everyone. Search the city through and you will not find an idle Chinaman, and their cleanliness exceeds any other people we ever saw.

LOUIS J. STELLMAN of San Francisco, in the 1850s

IT IS not unusual to see the words "swarm" or "flood" of Chinese" or "hordes" in descriptions of the coming of the Chinese to America.* One commentator has even spoken in terms of an American-versus-Chinese "war for the West Coast." The reality was different. Even in 1849, the year of the California Gold Rush, there were just 325 Chinese among the 100,000 men who converged on San Francisco from all parts of the world. In the seventy years before that the number of Chinese emigrating to the United States was very small. When the Chinese Exclusion Act was passed by Congress in 1882 in response to clamorous protests against the entry of "hordes of Chinamen," there were 107,488 Chinese in the country, less than 0.2 percent of the total U.S. population of 62,947,714. When the act was repealed in 1943, Chinese comprised 0.05 percent of the population. In 1970, the 435,062 Chinese made up 0.2 percent of the population of 204,879,000.

The U.S. Immigration Commission recorded the arrival of Chinese for the first time in 1820. In the decade 1820–1830, three arrived. In the next decade, seven more came, but the names of individuals and groups arriving well before 1820 are recorded. A document in the National Archives in Washington gives details of three sailors, Ah Sing, Ah Chuan, and Ah Cun, stranded in Baltimore with several other seamen in 1785 when the captain of their ship, the *Pallas*, took off to get married. They petitioned Congress for funds for their upkeep and lived for almost a year in the care of a merchant in the China trade named Levi Hollingsworth.

---

* During the Korean War, at one of the briefings given by a spokesman of General MacArthur's command, a correspondent asked, "Sir, how many hordes are there in a company?"

On the other side of the continent, in 1788, the English sea captain John Meares, of the British East India Company, thinking to make a profit building ships with the lumber of the well-forested northwest American coast, sailed from Guangdong Province with a crew of shipbuilders, carpenters, metal workers, and sailors. Far more men had volunteered for the work than he could enlist. This indicates the adventurous spirit of the Guangdongese, for these were skilled workers, and the 1780s were still a relatively prosperous time in China—and there was no pressing need for them to seek a living so far away from home. The Meares venture promised to be a great success. The expedition built a fur-trading settlement on Vancouver Island at Nootka Sound, complete with a fort, a wharf, and a slipway. They built a forty-ton schooner, the *Northwest America*, the first ship of that size ever built on these coasts, and it sailed for the Queen Charlotte Islands (off the coast of British Columbia) with a mixed English and Chinese crew. Not all the Chinese shipbuilders left Nootka Sound with her. The Nootka settlement had been augmented by twenty-nine more Chinese settlers brought by Captain Meares and forty-five more brought by the American Captain Metcalf in 1789. Thus, Chinese were working on the West Coast well before the Lewis and Clark expedition arrived in 1804 for the first view of the Pacific Ocean by East Coast explorers.[1]

But the Spanish, who at that time claimed the northwest American coast, feared this attempt by a British subject to establish a foothold there, so they overran the settlement and sent their captives to San Blas. The fate of the Chinese is not known.

The Chinese already had a reputation as skilled workers and shipwrights on the Pacific Coast. The nineteenth-century California historian Hubert Bancroft reports that Chinese were employed by the Spanish as shipbuilders in lower California as early as 1571–1746, and in Los Angeles specifically in 1781.[2]

A German author, Ludwig Louis Salvator, lists at least one Chinese as an inhabitant of Los Angeles when it was founded on September 4, 1781, and it is evident that Chinese accompanied the early Spanish expeditions that traveled north from Mexico to upper California in the late 1700s. It seems that two men from China were baptized into the Catholic faith, one in 1774 and another in 1793 in Monterey. And we know that one Ah Nam was cook to the Spanish governor, Pablo de Sola, in Monterey. He was a Chinshan man from Guangdong Province in South China, who became a Christian on October 27, 1815, two years before he died.[3]

In April 1796, a Dutchman, Van Braam Houckgeest, Canton agent for the Dutch East India Company, arrived to settle in the United States near Philadelphia. He brought five Chinese servants with him.[4]

There were other Chinese visitors. The first five Chinese youngsters arrived to study in an American school. Between 1818 and 1825, they attended the foreign mission school at Cornwall, Connecticut. One of them, Liao Ah-see, became the first Chinese Protestant convert in America. Another, Ah Lum, later became a translator for the famous Commissioner Lin Tse-hsu, who burned the British stocks of opium just before the start of the Opium War.[4] There was said to be a Chinese crew member on the brig *Bolivar* in San Francisco in 1836. The Chinese junk *Keying*, owned by an English sea captain, was sailed to New York by a Chinese crew in 1847. In the New York City Museum, there is a large painting of the *Keying*, riding at anchor in New York Harbor, where she was a nine day's wonder. At least four other Chinese arrived in that same year: Yung Wing,[5] with two more students in New York, and a young merchant, Chum Ming, in San Francisco (*San Francisco Chronicle*, July 21, 1878, p. 5).

In those early days, there seems to have been no specific hindrance to Chinese becoming naturalized American citizens, but only a few availed themselves of the opportunity.* Most, like many immigrants of other nationalities, wanted to return home eventually, although the pull of home was stronger for the Chinese. Of the few who actually became citizens, we hear of a San Francisco Chinese community leader named Norman Asing, although his claim of citizenship remains unsubstantiated by documentation, and the early student Yung Wing, who married an American woman and had a distinguished career in China and the United States. The third appears to have been a Chinese cabin boy named Hong Neok, who arrived in Philadelphia in 1855 and later settled in Lancaster, Pennsylvania. He became a naturalized U.S. citizen and a year later, in 1863, volunteered to serve with the Pennsylvania Militia. However, obeying some inner call, he returned to China in 1864 and became a priest[6] and one of the founders of St. John's University in Shanghai.

In February 1848, two Chinese men and a woman arrived in San Francisco on the brig *Eagle*. The woman was employed in the home of Charles Gillespie, an American missionary who brought the three with him on his return to California from Hong Kong. The men shortly went to work in the mines.[7] It is most likely that they joined the crowd of local people, including a few other Chinese, in the first wave of the Gold Rush. Gold had been discovered northeast of Sacramento a month before.

Like everyone else who reads about them, I was fascinated by the stories of the first Chinese who had come to North America. Chinese records (in the Liang *Shu* and in Volume 231 of the *Great Chinese Encyclopaedia* compiled by Ma Tuan-lin) relate that Hui Shen, one of five Buddhist priests, arrived in a country they called Fusang in A.D. 459, which seems to have been the West Coast of America from British Columbia southward. Although some scholars dispute this story of the early arrival of Chinese on the North American continent, the reported discovery of ancient Chinese artifacts in Victoria, B.C., and in Mexico seems to support it. Hui Shen's party appears to have traveled down the California coast to Mexico. This tallies with the description of Fusang given by Hui Shen and with the Mexican stories of

---

* Not until the early 1870s did a federal court deny Chinese the right to naturalization, although California set the precedent in 1854, when a Chinese applying for naturalization met with refusal.

the legendary arrival of Quetzalcoatl.[8] More recent research by the archaeologist James R. Moriarty of the University of San Diego, California, has unearthed Chinese stone anchors near Palos Verdes Peninsula and off Point Mendocino. In the latter case, the anchor was encrusted with manganese, which showed that it had been lying on the seabed for 2,000–3,000 years (Wang Yung, *"Did the Chinese Beat Columbus?"* San Francisco *Sunday Examiner and Chronicle,* November 25, 1979, quoting a letter from Professor Moriarty to the Chinese archaeologist Jia Lanpo). The Fusang plant that gave the country its name was evidently the century plant, a cactuslike agave commonly used for food and clothing in ancient Mexico.

The persistent story that Asians early visited the area is bolstered by the report of the Spanish traveler Juan Bautista de Anza of sighting the wreck of at least one "oriental vessel" while sailing past Carmelo in 1774.[9] So perhaps neither Columbus nor the Norsemen were the first to "discover" America.

However that may be, it is well authenticated that as far back as the sixteenth century, in 1599, at least 250 years before the California Gold Rush, the Chinese in Canton and Nanking had a map of California drawn for them by the Jesuit priest Father Ricci.[10] As might be expected at that time, it was somewhat inaccurate, but it does show that the Chinese of Guangdong, traditional home of China's seafarers, did know of the West Coast of America well before the Gold Rush of 1849. But in those early opulent days for China there was no urgency about traveling to America. The Chinese went to this new land, as they had gone to many other lands in their long history, in a spirit of adventure. What was it, then, that sparked a fresh and urgent interest in America in the mid-nineteenth century? It was the lure of gold. In 1848, a month after gold was discovered, Chinese were among the first to go into the gold country and send word back to their villages. In the momentous year of 1849, the population of California jumped from 20,000 to 100,000, and scores of thousands converged on the state from eastern and midwestern America, from Latin America and Europe. Although it was easier to get to San Francisco from South China than from New York, just those 325 Chinese arrived. In the next year, only 450 more came. Why was it that in those early days and well into the twentieth century, over 99 percent of the Chinese in America came from just a few districts around Canton (Guangzhou) in South China? Unless one knows the answers to these questions, it is impossible to understand the history of the Chinese of America and the living issues that concern them today.

Why They Left Home

Except for some individual, restless, adventurous souls, one must have a very good reason to leave one's native home and journey 7,000 miles to toil in a foreign land. This was even more so for Chinese in the nineteenth century. Powerful ties of family, religion, and tradition bound them to their native hearths. Furthermore, the legal punishment for emigration from imperial China was death by decapitation. This law was an actual deterrent until 1860 and was only repealed in 1894. Yet tens of thousands of Chinese defied this punishment to seek their fortunes in other lands.

In the mid-nineteenth century, China was a land in turmoil. Unrest and suffering were especially widespread in the southern maritime province of Guangdong, and it was here that the hardy, adventurous, and desperate were best placed to try their luck overseas.

The prime cause of the turmoil was the decaying feudal system, which had dominated China under various dynasties for 2,000 years. The ruling Qing dynasty (1644–1912), established by the rulers of the Manchu people from Northeast China in prolonged warfare, had become one of the great feudal dynasties. Its armies had pushed China's boundaries further outward than in all past history. Farming and handicrafts, the bases of the national economy, had flourished together with trade and culture. Years of peace and a thriving economy more than doubled the population between 1741 and 1800 from 143 million to nearly 300 million. But after Chien Lung (1736–1795), the fourth Qing emperor, died, decay set in.[11]

As is often the case in the twilight of despotic regimes, the glitter turned to empty show and extravagant waste. Corruption spread. The emperor's chief minister and favorite, Ho Shen, amassed a fortune equal to $1.5 billion. The bloated military forces were ineptly trained and led. By the time Chien Lung's heir, Chia-ching (1796–1820), was installed on the throne, the decline was irreversible. Funds for the repair of dykes and dams were embezzled by venal officials, and this undermined the very basis of the country's economic life— irrigation farming, particularly paddy rice culture. Floods became frequent and ever more destructive. An increasing population was forced to live on less land per capita. Inflation was inevitable. The rulers attempted to maintain their income by increasing taxes and levies. As the oppression of the people intensified, secret anti-Qing societies such as the Triads, the Ke-lao Brotherhood, and the White Lotus sect increased their membership and activities. Government repression only intensified the opposition.

It was precisely at this moment when domestic pressures were mounting that the industrialized and imperialist Western powers increased their aggressive pressure to bring China and its vast market into the orbit of world trade.

Wishing to keep their subjects isolated, the Qing autocracy did not want China to engage in extensive contacts and trade with the West. As Emperor Chien Lung declared to King George III in 1790,

Our Celestial Empire possesses all things in abundance and lacks no products within its borders. There is therefore no need to import the manufactures of outside barbarians in exchange for our own produce. But as the tea, silk and porcelain which the Celestial Empire produces, are absolute necessities to European nations and to yourselves, we have permitted, as a signal mark of favor, foreign *hongs* [business establishments] to be established at Canton.[12]

Bertrand Russell once said that unless this special mandate is taken seriously it is impossible to understand China's further relations with the West. But, spearheaded by Britain, the Western powers and later Japan were determined to "open up China." Tensions were building in and around China that shortly came to a head in a series of catastrophes. The Opium War, provoked by Britain (1840–1841), was the prelude. Ignominious defeat shattered the prestige of imperial China. Britain imposed the Treaty of Nanking (1842) on China, the first of many unequal treaties it was forced to sign. China was forced to pay a ransom of $6 million (silver) for Canton and an indemnity totaling $33 million; to open up the five ports of Guangzhou (Canton), Amoy, Fuzhou, Ningbo, and Shanghai to foreign trade (hitherto confined to Canton); and to cede Hong Kong, which became the outpost of British imperialism in China. British nationals were exempt from Chinese law. China could not fix her own tariffs, which were limited by treaty to 5 percent on imported value. This practically deprived her of the right of using tariffs to foster or protect her own industries. Opium, not mentioned in the treaty, was free to flood into China. Other Western powers followed Britain's example in ravaging, humiliating, and exploiting enfeebled China. Each defeat saddled the nation with fresh indemnities that the inept administration in Peking squeezed out of the people.

Although the United States had not participated in the Opium War, it shared in the results. The Treaty of Wangxia (1844) gave it most-favored-nation treatment in trade and other matters, including the right of extraterritoriality for U.S. citizens in China (that is, exemption from Chinese law) and the right to be tried in U.S. consular courts. The French followed suit with the Treaty of Wanbo. China was defeated in the Second Opium War (1856–1860) and signed the Treaty of Tianjin, which resulted in further indemnities totaling 6 million taels* of silver, the right of foreigners to reside in Peking, acceptance of missionary activity, and the opening of additional ports to foreign trade. Cheap mass-produced goods from the industrialized and capitalist West flooded the Chinese market and disrupted China's feudal handicraft economy. China's cottage industries were no match for the power-driven mills of Lancashire and Europe. China had hitherto enjoyed a favorable trade balance by exporting tea and silks. Now the balance turned against her. Unlimited sales of opium siphoned off vast sums in silver. The whole economy was undermined. This was the age of gunboat diplomacy, and verbal protests were useless. China's medieval weaponry of bows, arrows, and antiquated cannon were no match for the modern ships, artillery, and rifles of the West. The Chinese colossus had feet of clay.

Humiliated by the foreigners, the Qing dynasty's prestige and authority plummeted. Burdened by levies and taxation, harassed by invaders, and now contemptuous of their inept rulers, the people revolted. The White Lotus peasant uprising lasted nine years and swept through several provinces before

---

* A tael is a Chinese ounce or 1⅓ oz avoirdupois.

it was bloodily suppressed. The Taiping Revolution of 1851–1864 began in South China, and Taiping armies captured and held Nanjing, the southern capital on the Yangtze River, for several years before they were defeated. This was followed by the Nien and other revolts. Aided by the Western powers, who feared the Chinese people more than they did the Qing emperor, the imperial government succeeded in suppressing these uprisings, but at terrible cost. Millions of people perished—25 million in the Taiping Revolution, for instance—but the Qing dynasty was shaken to its foundations. Hitherto, China had been a feudal but independent state. Now, entering the modern world, capitalist enterprises began to develop, and China for a time was neither wholly capitalist nor wholly feudal. With its sovereignty filched from it bit by bit and at times near complete dismemberment at the hands of foreign invaders, it became a semicolony of the Western world. Statesmen of all the world powers wondered what would become of this "Sick Man of Asia." The masses of China searched desperately for a way out of their sufferings. Patriotic intellectuals looked for a means of national salvation.

South China is a melange of ethnic groups. But the aboriginals, the Miao, and other smaller ethnic groups do not emigrate. The wanderers come from the two main Chinese-speaking groups: the Punti, the older established inhabitants (who were originally from the north and who had intermarried with the aboriginals), speaking the Cantonese dialects, and the Hakka or Kechia (guest people), speaking Hakka, who came later, chiefly at the end of the Sung dynasty (960–1279), from the north. The Hakka had accepted the Qing government's invitation in 1670 to reclaim and settle empty lands on the coast, earlier evacuated by the Punti under a government scheme to remove possible supporters of the previous dynasty. This brought them into close and hostile proximity to the Punti inhabitants. Under pressure of overpopulation, economic crisis, and the breakdown of imperial authority, and given the not unnatural animosity between "old-timers" and "interlopers," a destructive civil war raged between the two groups from 1854 to 1868. Whole villages were razed to the ground and depopulated in this civil strife. Thousands were made homeless, particularly in the Sze Yup or Four Districts area in the Pearl River delta.

Hakka clans, threatened with such a fate and confined to the barrens and hill lands, were naturally attracted by tales of new, free lands overseas. To this day, groups of Hakka live in Hawaii with a few on the Pacific Coast of North America. Other inhabitants of Guangdong Province also searched for a way out of mounting difficulties and sufferings caused by invasion, domestic war, and oppression. There could be no question of trying to emigrate north or west—devastation, war, and dense populations barred the way. The alternative was to move south and overseas. Here at least was a chance of bettering their condition and tiding over the tragic years. Thanks to old maritime contacts, the means of emigration were readily accessible, not only to the South Seas but to the North American continent.

The Junk Trade and the Manila Galleons

Despite the official ban on emigration and trade with the outside world, a considerable number of Chinese traded extensively with the Nanyang, the islands of Southeast Asia, and established settlements there. This emigration was connected with the so-called Junk Trade. Chinese junks of from 150 to 1,000 tons voyaged to Thailand, Indochina, the Malay Peninsula, Java, and the Molucca Islands of Indonesia from China's southern and southeastern ports. Guangzhou and Macao, of course, were centers of the trade with the Western nations for some eighty-five years until 1842, when they became only two of an increasing number of ports forcibly opened up to foreign trade. These included Amoy and Foochow in Fujian Province and Ningbo and Shanghai on the east-central China coast. The Junk Trade thus became the means of an extensive overseas emigration. Coastal Guangdong naturally became the main source of China's seafarers and later, with Fujian, of overseas emigrants. Seafarers and traders from these southern and southeastern regions pioneered the way overseas. In 1603, there were more than 20,000 Chinese traders, artisans, workers and their families in Manila.[13] In 1720, there were 10,000 Chinese in Batavia alone. Rangoon was the western limit of substantial Chinese emigration to Southeast Asia, with Africa and the Near East as trading outposts. The eastern limits of trade, even in the sixteenth century, were far across the Pacific in the Americas. The hardihood of these emigrants was astonishing. This was at a period when they were regarded as tantamount to rebels. An imperial edict of 1712 requested foreign governments to send back expatriates so that they might be executed. In a 1729 edict, Emperor Yung Chung declared that

those who do business abroad are usually undesirable persons, and . . . their numbers are likely to increase in course of time if they are allowed to come and go freely. Those subjects who willingly abandon Fatherland for personal gain deserve no sympathy. We shall set a date for them, and it they fail to return home within the period granted, they will never be allowed to return.[14]

Chinese emigrants had not only the emperor to fear. Local animosities instigated by the colonial rulers frequently sparked attacks on emigrants. In 1603, the Chinese in Manila were attacked.[15] In 1740, Chinese settlers in Batavia were massacred.

The Chinese in the Philippines, merchants, seamen, and their families, played a significant role in the Manila Galleon trade. They manned or chartered Chinese junks that brought silks and other luxury goods from China to Manila for shipment on the Manila Galleons to Mexico. It was a lucrative trade, and it is clear that the Chinese engaged in it visited California long before we have official or even unofficial American reports of Chinese arriving in California. The Chinese who built ships in southern California, and who arrived overland in the early days of the Gold Rush along with groups of Mexicans, had engaged in the Manila Galleon trade.[16]

Tens of thousands of Chinese were therefore emigrating from China, and from Guangdong Province especially, long before they came in any numbers to North America. America was only one of the places they continued to come to, although not in large numbers. In 1894, there were more than 1 million Chinese living and working overseas. The 90,000 Chinese in the United States at the turn of the century were a relatively small number, but they, together with other overseas Chinese,* played a crucial role in the destinies of their homeland. By sending their remittances back home to their families, they were making a considerable contribution to the balance of payments of the mother country in a time of great economic difficulty. But the Emperor Yung Chung was more correct in his assessment of these overseas Chinese than even he suspected. They were indeed "rebels." They transmitted to China revolutionary ideas of democracy; they naturally supported the domestic revolutionaries' efforts to establish a modern government and democratic system in China that would protect their rights and interests both at home and abroad. Their efforts finally helped to topple the dynasty.[17]

The Quest for Gold and Knowledge

What sparked the renewed and increased Chinese interest in America in 1848 was, of course, the news that gold could be picked up in California streams. This news, which electrified adventurous men in many parts of the world, was brought early to China because of the ties already made with California, and that was also why the news first of all came to Canton and its environs.

Among the first of the Chinese argonauts was the enterprising young Chinese merchant named Chum Ming, who arrived in San Francisco in 1847. When Brannan, the Mormon elder, rode into town yelling to all and sundry the news about the discovery of gold northeast of Sacramento, Chum Ming joined the rush.

Placer gold was not hard to find in the streams at that early date and Chum Ming was lucky. He struck it rich.[18] He sent word to a fellow villager of the Sam Yup (Three Districts) area named Chang Yum, who in turn spread the exciting news further before himself setting sail for the Golden Mountain (Gum Shan in Cantonese, or Chiu Jin Shan [Old Gold Mountain] in Mandarin), as San Francisco came to be called. It was not difficult then to evade the imperial edicts against emigration. It required only courage to reach Portuguese Macao or British Hong Kong and there, away from the jurisdiction of the emperor, take ship for California.

The three Chinese who arrived in San Francisco in 1848 were followed by another 323 in 1849 and 450 in 1850. Almost all were from those areas in South China around Hong Kong, Macao, and Canton, that have since

---

* In 1922, there were 6,000,000 overseas Chinese, the majority in non-Chinese territories in Southeast Asia (U.S. Department of Labor bulletin no. 340, 1923).

Map 1. Where the Chinese Emigrants Went

furnished most of China's emigrants and remained the main source of emigration from China to the United States for the next hundred years. In those first two years most of these Chinese were merchants and skilled craftsmen and some who hired out as servants and cooks.

This pattern of goading from behind and attraction from in front continued. It was much the same for other immigrant groups. In Europe as in South China, both of which suffered severe economic and political difficulties in the mid-nineteenth century, America was said to be the land of promise, opportunity, and freedom. The Pilgrims came to escape the intolerance of a tyrannical monarch in Britain, but it was mostly not a quest for freedom of religious belief that brought immigrants. The quest for freedom from hunger and brute oppression was more compelling. Gold could alleviate hunger— but some realized that the knowledge to be found in America was needed even more and in the long run was more potent and lasting. The same year that Chum Ming joined the Gold Rush in distant California, the first typical representative of a unique Chinese student immigration arrived on the East Coast. Yung Wing, one of the first of many Chinese students, came to America seeking not gold but knowledge to modernize his country.

In 1847, New York was a small bustling city of something over 250,000 souls. When the *Huntress* entered her harbor after a voyage of ninety-eight days from the port of Wanbo in South China's Guangdong Province, it brought this young Chinese, Yung Wing, and two other Chinese companions. He was nineteen years old at that time.

Yung Wing, born in 1828, was the son of a poor peasant of a village near the Portuguese colony of Macao. When he was twelve years old, his father died, and he helped the family by peddling candy while his elder brother became a fisherman. He was fortunate in being introduced by a friendly neighbor to a local foreign missionary school; because of this connection and the English he learned there, he was selected to study at the Morrison School in Macao (named after the first missionary to China, sent in 1807 by the London Missionary Society). Here he attracted the notice of another missionary, the Reverend S. R. Brown from Yale, who eventually was instrumental in bringing him and two other young Chinese to America for further education at the Monson Academy, a private school in Massachusetts.

With some help from kind American friends, Yung Wing worked his way through college at Yale and in 1854 was the first Chinese to graduate from an American college. He returned to China that year. Later he married an American woman and was one of the first Chinese to become a naturalized American citizen, a genuine first-generation Chinese American.

Knowledge was harder to get than gold. It was many years before the knowledge Yung Wing acquired was of significant use to China and America, so we will leave him to his studies for a time while we follow the fortunes of the hundreds and thousands of his compatriots who came to America's West Coast in search of gold and happiness.

There were also seekers of freedom. Among the earliest immigrants in 1848 were twenty-five Chinese who, finding themselves tricked into near slavery in Peru, escaped to freedom in America and joined the Gold Rush.

NOTES

1. E. S. Meany, *History of the State of Washington* (New York: Macmillan, 1909), p. 26.
2. Hubert Howe Bancroft, *Selected Works*, Vol. 14 (San Francisco: History Co., 1890), p. 335.

3. James Culleton, *Indians and Pioneers of Old Monterey* (Fresno: California's Academy of California Church History, 1950).
4. Him Mark Lai and Philip P. Choy, *Outlines: History of the Chinese in America* (San Francisco: Chinese-American Studies Planning Group, 1973).
5. Yung Wing, *My Life in China and America* (New York: Holt, 1909).
6. Lai and Choy, *Outlines.*
7. William Speer, *China and California* (San Francisco: Marvin and Hitchcock, 1853).
8. C. G. Leland, *Fusang or the Discovery of America by Buddhist Priests in the Fifth Century* (London: Trubner, 1875).
9. Edward C. Chapman, *A History of California: The Spanish Period* (New York: Macmillan, 1923), pp. 27–29.
10. Arthur Cotterell and David Morgan, *China's Civilization* (New York: Praeger, 1975), p. 216.
11. Immanuel Hsu, *The Rise of Modern China*, 2nd ed. (New York: Oxford Press, 1975).
12. Leon Hellerman and Alan Stein, *China: Readings on the Middle Kingdom* (New York: Simon & Schuster, 1971), p. 145.
13. Wu Ching-Chao, *Chinese Immigration in the Pacific Area* (San Francisco: R and E Research Associates, 1974).
14. Huang-Chiao T'ung-tien, *Comprehensive Institutes of the Ch'ing Dynasty*, quoted by Zo Kil Young, *Chinese Emigration into the United States, 1850–1880* (New York: Arno Press, 1971), p. 89.
15. Edgar Wickburg, *The Chinese in Philippine Life, 1850–1898* (New Haven, Conn.: Yale University Press, 1965), pp. 4–6.
16. Zo Kil Young, *ibid.*
17. Zo Kil Young, *ibid.*
18. Zo Kil Young, *ibid.*

How They Came

CHAPTER

11

These States are the amplest poem,
Here is not merely a nation,
but a teeming nation of nations.

WALT WHITMAN

THE PEOPLING of the United States is one of the
greatest migratory movements in the modern world. In its early days, it was
principally a Europe-based phenomenon. China was the largest source of
migration from the Far East, but of the 500,000 immigrants who arrived in
the 1830s, only a handful were Chinese; of the 1.5 million immigrants of
the 1840s, less than 400 were Chinese. In the 1850s, when immigration from
China was at a peak in the Gold Rush days, Chinese, all told, numbered
only some 35,000 in the States, while 2.5 million immigrants came in from
Europe.

These figures reveal some curious facts: 65,758 Chinese arrived between
1850 and 1859, but even with the 775 Chinese already in California, the
total number of Chinese in America in 1860 was only 34,933. Domestic
conditions in China were in much the same deplorable state as when they
had left. Despite this, nearly 50 percent of the immigrants returned home.
As with the immigrants to the South Seas, some returned to their homes in
China to enjoy the modest fortunes they had made overseas and where 50
percent had left wives. Others chose to remain in America and make it their
home. The proportion between sojourners and settlers was roughly 50:50.
Large numbers of Italian or German immigrants returned to their native
lands after "making their pile" in the United States, and, similarly, conditions
at home had not changed that much. The "sojourner" mentality, though
not unusual among immigrants, was more marked among the Chinese.

Although hunger, poverty and oppression, even terror, were powerful goads,
the Chinese remained reluctant emigrants. In the 1840s and 1850s,
immigrants from Europe mostly came from Ireland and Germany, which

were ravaged by crop failures and disturbed social conditons. Crop failures were disastrous. The 1845–1847 potato blight and famine killed half a million Irish and drove a million and a half to seek succor in America. In Europe, 1848 was the "year of revolutions." Most without skills of greater value than those expected for "common labor," and many of them lacking a knowledge of English, such immigrants lived in Boston and New York in conditions of squalor even a European seaport could hardly parallel. But they stayed and eventually "made it."

The Chinese immigrant too fled civil disorder, poverty, and suffering. The bad situation in China led to the considerable emigration of the 1840s. The urgency of the situation was no less in the 1850s. Yung Wing later described how he returned to his homeland and went to live in Canton near the public execution ground. The people of Guangdong had just staged another abortive revolt against Qing misrule. The newly appointed Viceroy Yeh Ming Shen's estates in central China had been devastated by the Taiping revolutionaries, and he vented his anger on the people of Guangdong. In June, July, and August of 1855, he decapitated 75,000 people, more than half of whom had had no part in the rebellion.

Even so, despite the pressure to escape these horrors, the number of Chinese in the United States in 1860 was only 35,000, a mere 0.1 percent of the total U.S. population of 31,500,000.

The facts dispose of two hoary stereotypes that have long cluttered peoples' thinking about Chinese immigration. Chinese immigrants came in very modest numbers to America in the days before the Chinese Exclusion Acts. Such words as *exodus, swarming,* and *hordes* should immediately alert a reader. So should such words as *coolie* or *coolie trade.* As we shall see, the Chinese who came to America were skilled, mostly yeomen farmers, and they came of their own free will in relatively small numbers.

Although there were similarities with European immigration, in several ways the Chinese immigration was unique. One aspect of that uniqueness is that heavy concentration of immigrants, mentioned earlier, from less than a dozen counties or areas in South China's Guangdong Province.

Where They Came From

These dozen districts are all clustered around Canton, the provincial capital, and in the Pearl River delta south of Canton. A glance at the map shows their nearness to the seacoast and to the ports of Canton, Macao, and Hong Kong and immediately makes clear why they were the source of early emigration. From the 1840s until past the turn of the century, the main sources of emigration were

1. The Sam Yup (three areas): Nanhai, Panyu, and Shunde, including Canton (Guangzhou), capital of Guangdong Province, and its environs.
2. The Sze Yup (four areas): Xinhui, Taishan, Kaiping, and Enping.

Map 2. Places in Guangdong Province from Which the Majority of Chinese Emigrants Came to America Pre-1949

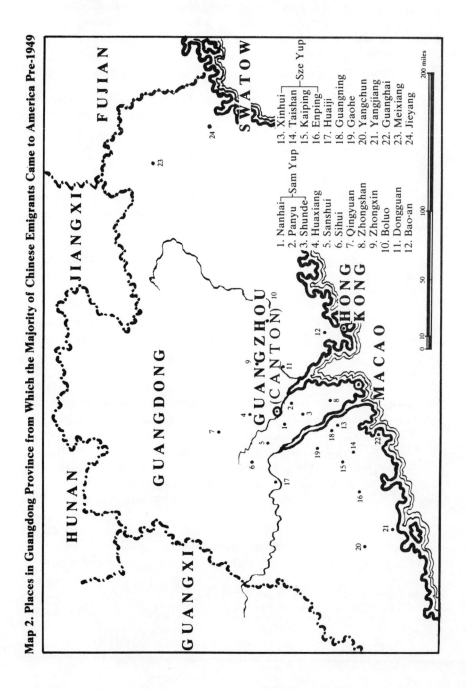

1. Nanhai ⎤
2. Panyu ⎥ Sam Yup
3. Shunde ⎦
4. Huaxiang
5. Sanshui
6. Sihui
7. Qingyuan
8. Zhongshan
9. Zhongxin
10. Boluo
11. Dongguan
12. Bao-an
13. Xinhui ⎤
14. Taishan ⎥ Sze Yup
15. Kaiping ⎥
16. Enping ⎦
17. Huaiji
18. Guangning
19. Gaohe
20. Yangchun
21. Yangjiang
22. Guanghai
23. Meixiang
24. Jieyang

0 10   50   100   200 miles

3. Other areas of Guangdong Province: Hua Xian, Sanshui, Sihui, Qingyuan, Zhongshan, Zhongxin, Boluo, Dongguan, Baoan, Huaiji, Guangning, Gaohe, Yangchun, Yangjiang, Guanghai, Mei Xian, and Jieyang.
4. Hong Kong.

Up until World War I, 60 percent of all Chinese immigrants to America came from the one Guangdong county of Toishan (Taishan or Hoishan), which prior to 1914 was known as Sunning or Hsin-ning.

Taishan is one of ninety-eight counties in Guangdong Province. Its population in 1853 was 680,000, and its area was 3,200 square kilometers. It lives up to its name—Mountain Plateau—rising 800–1,000 feet above sea level. Its rocky, barren farms in those days could feed the population for only four months of the year. They raised rice where they could and also sweet potatoes, peanuts, vegetables, and small livestock. Without enough land to farm successfully, Taishanese of necessity turned their hands to any occupation that promised a livelihood: they traded as pedlers, shopkeepers, or merchants far and wide. They "got around." They did odd jobs, using their skills as carpenters, fish farmers, or basket weavers. They showed great ingenuity in irrigating their fields and building stone levees and landfill dams. They were familiar with life in the big port cities of Canton and Hong Kong. Until 1842, Canton was the only port in which foreigners could trade in China. Even after that it was one of the most important ports for foreign trade in China, losing its premier place only at the turn of the century to Shanghai. The famous American clipper ships in the China trade made Canton a regular port of call. Immigrants from the same district or bearing the same clan name (surname, such as Chen, Wang, Yi, etc.) tended to congregate in certain places and occupations and organize district and family associations, and these early established regular links between San Francisco and the Guangdong villages. This greatly facilitated immigration and maintained the essential contacts between the immigrants and their folks back home. This was and still is a special feature of the Chinese immigration to the United States.*

Like those of the other traditional centers of emigration, Zhongshan people are clannish. The villages there are much alike, each inhabited by people who mostly have the same family names or are related in one way or another. I have never been to Zhongshan, but that is where my ancestors lived and their descendants live now. That is why the district association that includes Zhongshan people was the first to receive me when I arrived in San Francisco to work and settle in 1978.

Han Chinese share some 438 surnames. In English, they may be spelled differently, but the Chinese ideograph in each case is the same. My name,

---

* For further details on the complex question of district and clan associations see Him Mark Lai's and Philip P. Choy's *Outline: History of the Chinese in America* (San Francisco: Chinese American Studies Planning Group, 1973), pp. 114–130. See Chart in Appendix 2, p. 511.

for instance, is Chen, 陳. The Chinese ideograph for Chen is made up of the ideograph for *ear* as the radical and has the character for *east* as the sound indicator (a compound character made up of a tree with the sun shining behind it). In English, I have seen this spelled Ch'en, Tchen, Chun, or Chan, but when I meet people thus named I know we are all related. So close is this surname tie that even today it is regarded as vaguely incestuous for a couple having the same surname to marry, even though they may hale from widely separated parts of the country. My wife and I are both Chens. I am a third-generation Chen born in Trinidad in the West Indies. My wife was born in Shanghai. But when we went to live in a northern Honan village in 1969, I could see eyebrows raised in surprise when we told our names to our village neighbors.

Chinese families are traditionally very close-knit, and the clan or extended family in the nineteenth century was nearly as close as the nuclear family is today. It is only now, under the impact of vast social changes, that the clan unit is finally breaking down not only in China itself but even in those Chinatowns of America where they were strongest.

Another unifying factor among the Chinese emigrant groups—for instance, among Chungshan or Toishan people—is that they have their own dialects. Just as Anglo-Saxons are a majority among the many ethnic groups in the United States, Han Chinese, comprising 94 percent of China's population, are the majority nationality among the fifty-six ethnic groups making up the Chinese nation. Speaking the northern dialect, they moved into southern China, particularly after the tenth century, and Chinese speech developed here in contact with the languages spoken by the local peoples with whom they merged. As a result, while the Chinese written language is understood by all literates, the spoken language is still not uniform. Dialectal variations are numerous and sometimes so sharp that, for instance, a Cantonese cannot understand a Fujianese compatriot. Emigrants therefore have tended to go to those places and engage in those occupations where they can congregate with people speaking their home dialect. Speakers of the Foochow dialect gravitated to Sibu in Sarawak, which became known as New Foochow. Hokien speakers from Amoy went to the Philippines and Malaya. Teochiu speakers from Swatow went to Siam, Sumatra, and Malaya. The Hakka people went in considerable numbers to Borneo. Moreover, people belonging to a particular district or surname group often enter the occupation or trade in which that group specializes. In San Francisco, Sze Yup firms controlled most of the laundries, small retail shops, and restaurants. Sam Yup members dominated the tailoring, repair, mending, and butcher businesses. Zhongshan people monopolized fish retailing, women's garment manufacturing, and horticulture. The Yee and Lee families cook and run restaurants.

District and clan associations, which were powerful cementing factors at home in China, were equally so in the immigrant communities and Chinatowns in America. As I have indicated, the Chinese in the nineteenth century were reluctant emigrants. One thing that helped to overcome their reluctance to "try their luck abroad" was the fact that they were assured of meeting and getting the aid of fellow villagers and clansmen abroad (that and the compelling need to do something to get themselves out of their economic difficulties).

William Lee of Oakland, whose family has been in California for six generations, explaining why his forebears had come to the United States, said, "We were very very much in debt because of the local warfare. We planted each year, but we were robbed. We had to borrow. When news about the Gold Rush in California was spread by the shippers, my father decided to take a big chance."[1] This explanation or something similar crops up in case after case. It generally explains why it was that the people of Chungshan county and other Guangdong areas took the desperate step of emigration as the way out of their difficulties.

Mary Roberts Coolidge, in her *Chinese Immigration*, gave this well-considered explanation of the phenomenon:

In spite of a dense population and great poverty, the united restraints of law, religion and family ties holds them to the land of their birth and only the greatest stress of war and devastation at home, coincident with the lure of gold and marvellous industrial opportunity in California, served to uproot the three hundred thousand who came to the Pacific Coast during the thirty-three years of free immigration [from 1849–1882].[2]

Quite apart from the beheading they risked on return, Chinese emigrants of the 1850–1860s had many things to consider when they thought of emigrating. More than the usual ties of hearth and home bound them to their country. A strong religious belief reinforced them. The spirits of the dead ancestors and their graves demanded constant care by members of the clan in person and not by priestly proxies. Those who abandoned this duty not only were unfilial but also incurred the dire displeasure of the spirits and the condemnation of their neighbors and society at large.

This is why most immigrants, even though going with the blessing of the living clan or family members, left with the expressed intention of returning to the home and resuming their duties to the ancestors. They made arrangements, if they should die abroad, to have their bones returned to be interred on ancestral soil. Thousands returned home from America as bones or ashes. This was one of the duties of the family associations and especially the district associations that maintained the cemeteries. They gathered the remains of their dead members and periodically shipped them back to China. In 1875, the Kong Chow Company shipped 1,002 sets of bones back to China, and records show that cargoes of remains were shipped back regularly.

How They Came

The manner of their coming was itself a test of determination, endurance, and courage. For the emigrants of Guangdong, the emperor's ban on emigration was the least of their difficulties. In the 1850s, imperial authority was at a low ebb. The emigrants made their way to Hong Kong or Macao. Both cities were under foreign rule, and ships could be found there to make the journey. But there was another danger: they had to evade the "pig traders."

The Western imperialist powers needed labor to procure raw materials from their colonies to supply their growing industries. The native populations of some colonies had been almost wiped out.* The slave trade was banned internationally in 1862, and impoverished young peasants in a half-colonized China were recruited to work in Peru, Cuba, and other places. Men were enveigled into signing work contracts that made them little better than slaves. When willing volunteers were not forthcoming, the recruiters resorted to tricks and intimidation. When all else failed, men were simply kidnapped or "shanghaied." Herded into holding stockades or "pig-pens" (barracoons) in Portuguese-ruled Macao (Aomen), they were terrorized and shipped off like cattle to South American or Cuban plantations where they worked under guard. Hakka prisoners captured in the civil war by their Punti enemies were actually sold off to agents of the "pig trade." At the turn of the century, there were 30,000 Hakkas in the Western Hemisphere, partly the residue of this barbarous traffic.[3]

The big ports like Guangzhou (Canton) and Xiamen (Amoy) were centers of this trade. The British consul wrote about Amoy,

When no man could leave his own house [in that city], even in public thoroughfares and open day, without a danger of being hustled, under false pretences of debt or delinquency, and carried off a prisoner in the hands of crimps, to be sold to the purveyors of coolies at so much a head, and carried off to sea, never to be heard of, the whole population of the city and adjoining districts were aroused to a sense of common peril.[4]

The word *shanghaied* went into the English language. Gangsters were employed by foreign traffickers to kidnap unsuspecting peasants coming into the towns to sell vegetables or attend a fair. But one could be shanghaied as well in Swatow, Nanao (Namao, in eastern Guangdong), Canton (Guangzhou), or Macao, from which the victims were shipped out to their destinations.†

The armed vessels engaged in this trade were floating hells. Conditions in the steerage where the victims were confined were overcrowded, poorly ventilated, and little better than the holds of the African slave traders. The hatches were often battened down to prevent escapes. The men were kept

---

* My native Trinidad was once inhabited by Carib Indians. Hardly a single Indian remained in the 1860s when my grandfather arrived from Guangdong as an indentured laborer for a cacao plantation.

† Seamen were also prone to be shanghaied in San Francisco to man short-handed vessels. In the 1860s and 1870s, the best-known crimp there was nicknamed Shanghai Brown. He had inherited the title from Shanghai Kelly, who, along with waterfront harpies Miss Piggot and Mother Brown, were responsible for the shanghaiing of numerous men in the city. In 1896, the red-bearded Irish Kelly was himself shanghaied. One morning, waking from a drunken torpor, as had many of his victims, he found himself enrolled as a seaman on a sailing vessel going around Cape Horn.

on starvation rations to break their spirit. There were murders and riots on almost every trip, and the death rate sometimes ran as high as 45 percent. Of the 140,000 men shipped to Cuba, more than 16,000 died en route. Many more died of their sufferings even after the voyage was over.

This trade in humans was not the work of a gang of depraved and nameless criminals. It had the sanction and connivance of officials and licenced captains. The chief "coolie trader" operating out of Amoy in Fujian Province in 1852 was none other than Tait, the Spanish consul general himself.[5]

The scandals of this trade eventually forced the Qing imperial government to take action. Protests were lodged with the American ambassador John E. Ward (1858–1861), but he claimed that, although the vessels carrying the Chinese were American, the recruiters were foreign nationals over whom he had no jurisdiction. Finally, in 1873, Yung Wing (that young seeker for knowledge) was appointed to deal with the Peruvian commissioner about this traffic and produced damning photographs of Chinese coolies with backs lacerated by whips. The Chinese authorities banned the traffic, and under international pressure the Portuguese rulers of Macao were forced in 1874 to end this trade in humans.

Voyage to the Golden Mountain

Having evaded the pig traders, the next trial was the voyage to the Golden Mountain. In those Gold Rush days, every kind of vessel was being pressed into service to take advantage of the clamorous demand for passages to California. In 1854, seven men attempted the Pacific crossing, each in a 30-foot Chinese junk fitted with cabins. Seven of these craft, built in centuries-old traditional style, set out from Guangdong, and two of them actually made it. One landed at Monterey; the other landed at Caspar Beach above Mendocino. The second one was sailed by Joe Yee's grandfather, who had come looking for gold but found a good living working as a cook for the Kelly family of Mendocino until 1896, when he returned to China. His son, George Yee's father, joined the old man in 1875, arriving in San Francisco at the age of twelve. He worked on the railroad, did laundry work, and finally cooked for the Albion Lumber Company and married a Mendocino-born Chinese girl. In 1923, he too returned to China to die. His wife, who had cared for a family of thirteen, passed away in Tucson, Arizona, in 1948 at the age of seventy-eight. George Yee, who tells the story himself, was born in Mendocino in 1897. He kept up the Joss House which the family had gratefully built there in 1870, and it is still looked after by his granddaughter, Lorraine.[6]

Braving such dangers, over 20,026 Chinese arrived in California in 1852, making the Chinese community there the largest ethnic minority in the state, and there were public murmurs about this.

Until regular passenger vessels were put on the route by the Pacific Mail Steamship Company, immigrants traveled in the holds of cargo vessels, which were sometimes roughly furnished with narrow bunks. Other amenities were minimal or nonexistent. Average annual number of immigrants from China from 1850–1859 was 6,680. At $30 to $50 a ticket, this traffic was worth over $250,000 a year. As competition sharpened, the cost of the tickets went down, and the overcrowding of the ships grew worse. The return passage went as low as $10 a head. Yet a Pacific Mail steamship might carry as many as 1,400 Chinese in steerage as well as other passengers.

As numerous accounts attest, sea travel in those days was hazardous and uncomfortable at best. It was often deadly in the battered hulks pressed into service for the Gold Rush trade. Foreign shipmasters and Chinese entrepreneurs who chartered ships conspired to pack in as many passengers as possible. Travelers in steerage were bundled together shoulder to shoulder and head to toe in poorly ventilated holds. Water was scarce, and the food prepared in the ships' galleys was poor. Fatalities were frequent on voyages that might take from 30 to 60 days or, if adverse winds were encountered, even longer.

There were good captains who did their best for their passengers and crews. When the *Balmoral* docked in San Francisco, it carried a pennant floating from its masthead, a gift from 464 grateful Chinese passengers paying tribute to Captain Robertson. In 1857, the Chinese merchants of San Francisco eulogized a Captain Slate, who brought in 700 emigrants without a single case of sickness or death.

Other captains were not so scrupulous or humane. Conditions were so insupportable that there were riots on some ships. There were nonviolent disasters; 85 of 613 passengers on the *Exchange* out of Macao died en route.[7] Arriving in San Francisco after 80 days at sea, the *Libertad*, in 1854, was a ship of the dead. One hundred and eighty, or a fifth of the Chinese passengers, were dead on arrival, like the captain, killed by scurvy or ship's fever.[8] Steerage on the *Champion* was 7 feet 2 inches high. Three tiers of bunks were 6 feet long and 13½ inches wide, with 17–24 inches headroom. One ship, the *John L. Stevens*, carried 550 immigrants in such conditions. Sometimes standees were carried on this three-months trip and took turns sleeping on the bunks. Competition eventually forced the cost of a ticket down to $13. Huie Kin, who established the first Protestant mission in New York and traveled steerage to America in 1868, writes that there was no water for washing. The passengers collected rainwater when it fell. The voyage took more than 60 days. It is hardly surprising that critics of the Chinese immigration complained of the filth of the Chinese when they traveled by sea.

Huie Kin wrote of travel in 1868,

Finally, the day was set for the ship to sail. We were two full months or more on our way. I do not know what route we took; but it was warm all the time, and we stopped at no intermediate port. When the wind was good and strong, we made much headway. But for days there would be no wind, the sails and ropes would hang lifeless from the masts, and the ship would drift idly on the smooth sea, while the sailors amused themselves by fishing. Occasionally, head winds became so strong as to force us back. Once we thought we were surely lost, for it was whispered around that the officers had lost their bearings. There was plenty of foodstuff on board, but fresh water was scarce and was carefully rationed. Not a drop was allowed to be wasted for washing our faces; and so, when rain came, we eagerly caught the rain water and did our washing.

On a clear, crisp, September morning in 1868, or the seventh year of our Emperor T'ung Chih, the mists lifted, and we sighted land for the first time since we left the shores of Kwangtung [Guangdong] over sixty days before. To be actually at the "Golden Gate" of the land of our dreams! The feeling that welled up in us was indescribable. I wonder whether the ecstasy before the Pearly Gates of the Celestial City above could surpass what we felt at the moment we realized that we had reached our destination. We rolled up our bedding, packed our baskets, straightened our clothes, and waited.

In those days there were no immigration laws or tedious examinations; people came and went freely. Somebody had brought to the pier large wagons for us. Out of the general babble, someone called out in our local dialect, and, like sheep recognizing the voice only, we blindly followed, and soon were piling into one of the waiting wagons. Everything was so strange and so exciting that my memory of the landing is just a big blur. The wagon made its way heavily over the cobblestones, turned some corners, ascended a steep climb, and stopped at a kind of clubhouse, where we spent the night. Later, I learned that people from the various districts had their own benevolent societies, with headquarters in San Francisco's Chinatown. As there were six of them, they were known as the "Six Companies." Newcomers were taken care of until relatives came to claim them and pay the bill. The next day our relatives from Oakland took us across the bay to the little Chinese settlement there, and kept us until we found work.

In the sixties, San Francisco's Chinatown was made up of stores catering to the Chinese only. There was only one store, situated at the corner of Sacramento and Dupont streets, which kept Chinese and Japanese curios for the American trade. Our people were all in their native costume, with queues down their backs, and kept their stores just as they would do in China, with the entire street front open and groceries and vegetables overflowing on the sidewalks. Forty thousand Chinese were then resident in the bay region, and so these stores did a flourishing business. The Oakland Chinatown was a smaller affair, more like a mining camp, with rough board houses on a vacant lot near Broadway and Sixteenth Street. Under the roof of the houses was a shelf built in the rear and reached by a ladder. Here we slept at night, rolled in our blankets much in the manner of Indians.[9]

Conditions on these ships were appalling, but they must be set against the morals and customs prevailing in those days. In 1831, a Rotterdam-based vessel arrived in Rhode Island with only 48 of its 156 passengers alive. In 1850, the ship *Montague* was quarantined in San Francisco Bay. On the way from New Haven, twenty of her crew of 40, including the captain and second mate, as well as six passengers, had died of cholera. In 1855, the *Uncle Sam* left the Nicaraguan coast for San Francisco with 750 passengers aboard; 104 perished en route and 9 more died soon after they arrived.

It was only in the late 1860s that the Pacific Mail Steamship Company put its regular trans-Pacific passenger steam boats into service and only in the 1870s that Congress passed legislation for the establishment of a bimonthly service of screw-driven iron steamers. The first made its maiden voyage in 1874.

They Paid Their Own Way

Contrary to what some writers have alleged, the Chinese who came to America in those early days of the 1850s and 1860s usually paid their own way either out of their own savings or those of their families. Some borrowed money to buy their passage, promising to repay the loan out of future earnings in America. Some brought exotic Chinese goods that were quickly sold on arrival at high prices to defray the cost of their fares. Later the "contract labor system" was introduced. This was no different from the method used by millions of European immigrants to the eastern states. Many early arrivals on the East Coast were indentured workers or servants who paid for their passages by a stated period of labor. "No degradation necessarily attached to an indenture. Many immigrants of high character paid for their passage to America by giving bond service," write Alan Nevins and Henry Steele Commager.[10] The fact that they had little money was no slur. Their wealth as immigrants lay in their sturdy integrity, self-reliance, and energy.

American companies recruited workers through a Chinese or foreign labor contractor. The fare was advanced and later deducted from the wages earned by the worker, who usually contracted to work at a particular employment for a fixed number of years. Railway companies such as the Central Pacific used this method when they urgently needed labor. Such a way of coming to America therefore was no different from the methods used to recruit white labor and can in no way be honestly described as "slave labor." Yet a number of writers have thus tried to label the Chinese workers who came to the United States in those days.

Conditions of work were hard. No legal eight-hour day then existed, and southern plantation owners tried to enforce brutal conditions. Chinese workers on a Louisiana sugar cane plantation put their thumbprints, in lieu of a signature, to a contract stipulating that

1. The worker owed the recruiter $100 for travel fare, to be deducted from future wages
2. The contract was for five years, at a monthly pay of $7
3. Working hours were from sunrise to sunset, with one hour off for breakfast and lunch
4. At cane-pressing time at the height of the season, the worker had to work at night; 50 cents were paid for over six hours of evening overtime
5. The worker also had to do domestic work in the house of the employer[11]

These conditions were harsh even compared with similar agreements of the time. The Chinese, however, soon departed Louisiana, as they did other places in the South. The southern plantation owners believed that the Chinese could be used to replace the black slaves liberated by the Civil War. The Chinese, however, were veterans of the railway construction gangs and already knew something of American ways. They left Louisiana and went northwest into Illinois. In the Appendix, we will follow their story in the Mississippi Delta lands.

As with Huie Kin, young immigrants typically obtained tickets for the voyage either by loan or advance from their families, a group of relatives, and neighbors or by the "credit ticket system." In the latter alternative, a broker (usually a local man) advanced the money for the ticket on the understanding that the advance and accruing interest would be paid for out of the earnings of the immigrant on arriving in America.

Another way was for prospective immigrants to be sponsored by veteran immigrants returning to America from a visit to their home towns in China. The veterans advanced the fares and other expenses of the people they were sponsoring. Repayment of these debts was the first order of business for immigrants. They might evade the consequences of nonrepayment for a time, but eventually word of the wrongdoing would get back to their homes in China. There they were not faceless immigrants but belonged to specific families and clans; what they did was what their families or clans did.

Tickets or sponsors acquired, the immigrants would go off to Canton or Hong Kong to wait for embarkation at one of the *hak-chan* or inns especially established for that purpose. Inns catered usually to a clientele from a special locality and were associated with certain brokers. All the news of shipping and conditions in California filtered through them. If conditions were bad or employment lacking, they usually soon received the news. A special letter service was developed to keep immigrants and their families in touch (a regular Chinese national post office had not yet been established). The service also handled remittances, large or small. In some cases, not money but merchandise was sent back to China, providing additional profit for the family of the immigrant. These organizations, developed to serve the immigrants to the South Seas, became institutionalized between the years 1820–1875. They were readily adapted to the new immigration to America.

What is important in this connection is that bigots and others who did their best to whip up feeling against the Chinese in America habitually used the epithets "coolie" or "slave labor," and all that these words connote, to denigrate the Chinese immigrants. Typical of such propaganda was California Governor Bigler's outburst in 1852 when he charged the Chinese immigrants with being "contract coolies, avaricious, ignorant of moral obligations, incapable of being assimilated and dangerous to the welfare of the state." California Senator Roach was one of the first to use the "coolie labor" argument against the Chinese, a weapon used by similar demagogues for years afterwards and repeated unthinkingly in contemporary books and articles. He warned his hearers that the Chinese had at least 500,000 criminals who would come over as contract laborers and thus expose the American people to a "pestilence as foul as leprosy and the plague."[12] Such rhetoric stirred up violence against Chinese from one end of California to the other. U.S. Senator Morton, however, who originally headed the 1876 Joint Congressional Committee on Chinese immigration, drew the conclusion from the same material, collected by the commission, that Chinese labor in California was absolutely free.[13]

Once in the Land of Gold

In America, the free Chinese immigrant faced many trials. California in the mid-nineteenth century was still part of the Wild West, a frontier land, large areas of which had no representative of law or order. In the mountain settlements, the miners themselves were the law. On two occasions, even in San Francisco, the citizens were so impatient of the established authorities that self-appointed vigilance committees took the law into their own hands.[14] Hollywood has produced hundreds of Westerns but I can remember only one—*McCabe and Mrs. Miller*—that came near the truth. And the truth about the Wild West must be known before one can understand what fueled the anti-Chinese violence that first disgraced the history of California and later spread to other places.

Arriving in San Francisco, immigrants found that, as Huie Kin relates, the institutional network with its threads reaching back home was there to greet them the moment they stepped off the boat. In the very early days, Chinese merchant houses in San Francisco (and later, in other cities) fulfilled many of the functions of welcomers. They provided interpreters, rough housing, community centers, and assistance in finding work. Later, as more immigrants arrived, clan (family) associations were formed to look after immigrants of one surname group and, at about the same time in the 1850s, district associations were formed uniting people from one district or county and speaking one local dialect. Leadership by the merchant group was already established. It was a great relief for immigrants on arrival in a strange land to hear the words of greeting spoken in their own accustomed dialect. This type of organization, the *hui-guan*, was traditional in China: a district mutual-help society in a strange town. The family and district associations by 1854 had formed a federation that later evolved into the Six Companies, representing practically all Chinese from those districts or counties from which the vast majority of immigrants came. The name Six Companies (there have actually been up to nine) was later given by the white community to what in Chinese is the Chinese Consolidated Benevolent Association. This went through several metamorphoses, but in general until the turn of the century it represented the immigrants from the two dozen counties or districts in Guangdong Province from which the overwhelming majority of immigrants came. Although in China the merchant class was not at that time of high social status, under the conditions of the Chinese communities in America in the absence of the gentry and the scholar class, the traditional leadership groups, the merchants assumed the role of leaders. When the Chinese community was invited to take part on August 29, 1850 in the ceremonies marking the funeral of President Taylor or in the ceremonial presentation of religious tracts, it was the merchants who led the procession of Chinese. Their rich and exotic costumes of silk and brocade and their dignified bearing made a distinctly favorable impression on the public and inclined it in favor of the whole Chinese community.

The first hui-guan or merchants guild was organized at the Canton Restaurant on Jackson Street in December 1849, when nearly 800 Chinese had already arrived in San Francisco. Its merchant leadership retained the services of Selim E. Woodworth to advise them. This hui-guan functioned until about 1851, when it divided into two large groupings, one representing all Chinese from the Four Districts (Sze Yup) of Xinhui, Taishan, Kaiping, and Enping and the two additional areas of Gaohe and Zhongshan (Chungshan). Most of the 25,000 Chinese in California in 1851 came from these regions and the less affluent Three Districts (Sam Yup) formed of people from the three districts along the Pearl River Delta—Nanhai, Panyu, and Shunde—who spoke a dialect different from that of the Sze Yup.

The Zhongshan people formed their company in 1852 and named it Yeong Wo. Coming from near Macao, they were a majority of the immigrants to Hawaii. Other companies were the Sue Hing, Hop Wo, and Kong Chow.

The Hakka formed their own small Yan Wo Company in 1852. The largest company was Ning Yung, formed in 1853 as a breakaway from the Sze Yup Association. These Sunning (Taishan) people comprised the majority of immigrants in California, and their company carried corresponding weight. Other associations were formed by splits of these various groupings, and so the organizational structure has changed over the years. Today the board of directors of the Six Companies consists of fifty-five members, drawn from the constituent companies on the basis of one representative per 500 members. By this count, the Ning Yung Company has twenty-seven representatives. Chairmanship of the board rotates among the associations, but the Ning Yung representative serves every other term; that is, six months of every year.

In its heyday, the Six Companies unofficially spoke for the Chinese of San Francisco and took action to promote the interests of the community and its general welfare, arbitrated disputes among individuals or groups, and organized educational courses for Chinese children. Cemetery associations arranged for burials of deceased immigrants and return of their bones to their native villages. In the early years, the Six Companies hired men to police the Chinatown area, fought cases up to the U.S. Supreme Court level in defense of Chinese rights, and ran a hospital. Until the formation of the Chinese Chamber of Commerce in 1910 the Six Companies, together with the Merchants Guild, performed chamber of commerce functions. It also had an arrangement with the shipping companies whereby no Chinese could buy a passage back to China unless he had paid his debts in the United States and got the requisite clearance from the Six Companies.

The clan organizations naturally helped members of their clans when in need, and some maintained hostels for clan members. They formed small power blocs within the district associations. Even within clans there were suborganizations known as *fong*, in which the relations were of a more intimate, individual character.

Thus immigrants soon after arrival in the new land found themselves immersed in the familiar relationships to which they had been accustomed back home: families, clans, districts, dialect groups, guilds, and hui-guan. The familiar physical environment and culture was of enormous importance: the open-fronted shops, the smells and aromas of Chinese cooking, the Guangdong faces and clothes, the Chinese signs and speech—a home away from home: Chinatown in the 1850s. Strangely lacking were women and children. Chinese men, like American men in those days, did not usually bring their wives to the Wild West and it was unthinkable that any proper girl would go off on her own as an immigrant.

Large communities of Chinese in other places usually established similar structures of family and district associations and overarching CCBAs. Later, when the anti-Chinese agitation reached its height in 1882 with passage of the Chinese Exclusion Act, the CCBAs affiliated to form the CCBA of the USA, to coordinate their activities in defence of the Chinese communities.

One further type of organization must be mentioned here, the *tong*. The Triad secret society originated in China as part of the struggle of the Han people loyal to the Ming dynasty (1368–1644) against the Manchu (Qing) dynasty (1644–1911). Many Triad members emigrated overseas, and some who reached San Francisco established a lodge in that city in 1853. Other rival lodges, however, were formed, and there was often conflict over jurisdictions. The name of the overall Triad organization in the United States is the Chee Kung Tong (commonly called the Chinese Free Masons) and it has so been incorporated in San Francisco since 1879.* It aided Dr. Sun Yat-sen in his efforts to overthrow the Qing dynasty and establish a republic. While the Chee Kung Tong was a legitimate entity, some of its members, due to their long frustrated struggle against the established imperial regime in China, became alienated from established society and engaged in illicit activities such as gambling, narcotics, and prostitution.

Numbers of immigrants unable or unwilling to join the normal family and district associations set up their own fraternal organizations or tongs for mutual aid, protection, and socializing. The first San Francisco tong was organized in 1852. Several more were formed in the 1870s, and these too became involved in conflicts over control of various rackets like gambling, prostitution, and drugs. This, as we shall see later, was the source of the notorious "tong wars" or rumbles, the first of which occurred in 1875.

---

* The Chee Kung Tong is a legal political party in the People's Republic of China and has representatives in the National People's Congress and the Chinese People's Political Consultative Conference.

NOTES

1. Shirley Sun, *Three Generations of Chinese: East and West* (Oakland, Calif.: Oakland Museum, 1973).
2. Mary Roberts Coolidge, *Chinese Immigration* (New York: Holt, 1909).
3. Hosea B. Morse, *The International Relations of the Chinese Empire*, Vol. 2 (New York: Paragon Books, 1964), p. 171.
4. H. F. MacNair, *Modern Chinese History: Selected Readings* (Shanghai: Commercial Press, 1927), pp. 409–410.
5. Chen Han-sheng, *The Pig Trade* (Peking: Chinese Academy of Social Science, 1969).
6. George Hee, *Oral History, Mendocino County* (Fort Bragg, Calif.: Mendocino County Historical Society, 1976), Vol. 1, p. 199.
7. Gunther Barth, *Bitter Strength* (Cambridge, Mass.: Harvard University Press, 1964).
8. Chu Shih-chia, *Historical Records on the Oppression of Chinese Labor in America* [*Mei Guo Po Hai Hua Kung Shih Liao*], (Shanghai, 1958), p. 71.
9. Huie Kin, *Reminiscences* (Peking: San Yu Press, 1932).
10. Allan Nevins and Henry Steele Commager, *A Pocket History of the United States* (New York: Pocket Books, 1976).
11. Sun, *ibid.*
12. Coolidge, *ibid.*
13. *Congressional Documents*, No. 20, 1878 (Washington, D.C.).
14. Doris Muscatine, *San Francisco: Biography of a City* (New York: Putnam, 1975).
15. See the accounts of these organizations in Him Mark Lai and Philip P. Choy's *Outlines: History of the Chinese in America* (San Francisco: Chinese-American Studies Planning Group, 1973) and in Victor Nee and Brett de Bary Nee's *Longtime Californ'* (New York: Pantheon, 1973).

The Conquest of
California

CHAPTER

III

That land is my piece of America, and I'll defend it with arms
if need be.

A Lake Tahoe real estate owner commenting in a March
1980 radio interview on a California state plan to buy
several acres of Tahoe lakeside property to maintain open
space there.

CALIFORNIA did not become a state of the Union
until 1850. In 1820, it was still an undeveloped Spanish colonial possession,
its primeval splendor hardly touched by the Catholic missions established at
San Francisco, Santa Barbara, San Diego, and a few other places. Here the
menial work was done by baptized native American Indians settled around
the missions. Nearly all the cattle in the territory belonged to the missions
and were looked after by Indians living under serflike conditions. The main
exports were hides and tallow.

To protect the missions and maintain its sovereignty, the Spanish crown
had established two forts (called *presidios*) at San Diego and Monterey.
Command of the country was divided between them. California under Spanish
rule was a poverty-stricken colonial outpost. The peaceable Indians, robbed
of their way of life and beset with modern diseases brought in by the aliens,
were dying out.

When Mexico in 1821 declared its independence from Spain and extended
its sovereignty over California, the situation grew worse. Although the Indians
were declared to be free *rancheros,* they and the other local inhabitants were
in no way prepared to exercise the democratic rights that were now supposedly
theirs. Their situation actually deteriorated. The mission priests had at least
been more or less permanently associated with the missions and the Indian
serf population and so were personally interested in their upkeep and care.
Now they were restricted to their religious duties and superseded by Mexican-
appointed administrators who were often "men of desperate fortunes," and

down-at-the-heel politicians anxious only to make money as quickly as possible before their tour of duty ended and they could get back to Mexico City from these places of near exile.[1]

Monterey was the principal presidio; San Francisco was a hamlet. Yerba Buena Cove (present-day San Francisco's business center) was an uninhabited inlet, and waves washed the shore where the 48-story Transamerica pyramid now stands. Even twenty-seven years later when the Gold Rush began, San Francisco still only boasted a few adobe huts.

This California was almost unknown to the rest of North America and the world. Only a handful of white trappers and adventurers had gone west of the frontier settlements on the Mississippi River and beyond the Missouri and the Arkansas territories to brave the hazardous 2,800-mile trail over the deserts and the Rocky Mountains and the Sierra Nevada to California and Oregon. But Yankee traders and whalers had made money supplying the Spanish and Mexican settlements in California, and along with their return cargoes of hides and tallow they brought back valuable information to the eastern states.

Thomas Jefferson Farnham, whose *Life and Adventures in California* was widely read in the 1830s and 1840s, gave an enticing picture of this territory:

No country in the world possesses so fine a climate complemented with so productive a soil as the seaboard portion of the Californias, including the territories of the Bay of San Francisco and the rivers San Joaquin and Sacramento, but its miserable people live unconscious of these things. . . . In their gardens, grow the apple, the pear, the olive, fig and orange, the Irish and sweet potato, yam and the plantain most luxuriously, side by side, and yet they sleep and smoke and hum some tune of Castilian laziness, while surrounding nature is thus inviting them to the noblest and richest reward of honorable toil.[2]

The Great Powers Converge

All this was soon to change. The pioneering Americans were settling the Midwest and had crossed the Mississippi. Fur traders and the famous 1803 Lewis and Clark expedition had charted a way across the continent to the West Coast. By 1840, about 400 Americans had settled in California, which was undeniably Mexican territory, and in Oregon, claimed by both Britain and the United States. Trappers from the Hudson Bay Company had wandered down into California from Canada. Even the Russians, pushing forward from their main post at Sitka in Alaska, established a settlement at Fort Ross, just thirty miles north of San Francisco Bay. In 1841, finding themselves overextended, they sold out the settlement's property to John Sutter, the Swiss who had established himself at his fort northeast of present-day Sacramento.

It was clear that, at a time when the world was being divided up into

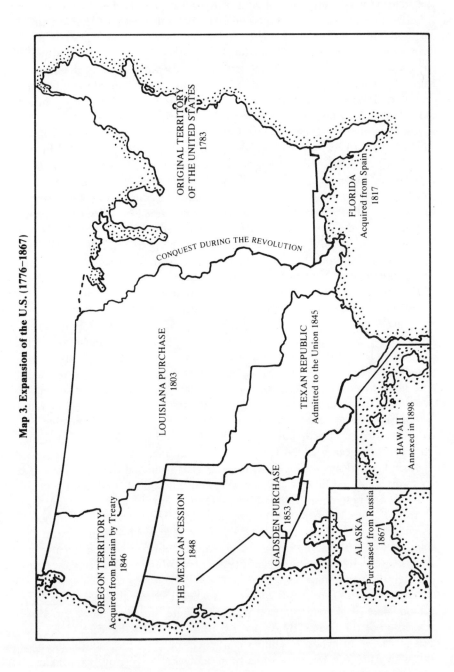

Map 3. Expansion of the U.S. (1776–1867)

ORIGINAL TERRITORY
OF THE UNITED STATES
1783

FLORIDA
Acquired from Spain
1817

CONQUEST DURING THE REVOLUTION

LOUISIANA PURCHASE
1803

TEXAN REPUBLIC
Admitted to the Union 1845

HAWAII
Annexed in 1898

OREGON TERRITORY
Acquired from Britain by Treaty
1846

THE MEXICAN CESSION
1848

GADSDEN PURCHASE
1853

ALASKA
Purchased from Russia
1867

separate national states and empires of the great powers, the West Coast of North America must soon come under the control of either Great Britain or the United States. The hapless Indians had no say in the matter. The Mexicans stood little chance of holding the territory. In fact, they were planning to sell it to Great Britain. There were only a few whites among the 12,000 inhabitants but these spearheaded the powers that stood behind them. Among the 1,200 foreign residents in 1846, most were Americans. Some had married Mexicans or become Mexican citizens—the so-called *Californios*.

Among the first larger groups of Americans to pioneer the settlement of the West Coast was a party of eighty men, women, and children led by John Bidwell, who reached Oregon in 1841 and linked that area firmly to the United States. Some of Bidwell's settlers had crossed the Sierra Nevada further south than the main party and found a welcome with John Sutter in his fort. This was then an armed settlement named New Helvetia at the confluence of the American and Sacramento rivers.

Sutter had established his settlement with the permission of the Spanish governor of California but he actually planned to make it the center for an independent state. He had a dozen cannon bought from the Russians at Fort Ross and was training the nucleus of an army from any recruits he could enlist. His fort was built to quarter 1,000 men.

This was the situation when on March 4, 1845, James K. Polk became president of the United States after being elected on an outspoken expansionist platform. He planned the takeover of both Oregon and California. His original intention was to do this by helping the Californios throw off Mexican rule, and he so informed the U.S. consul at Monterey, Thomas O. Larkin, who was his secret agent. Texas, after gaining its independence from Mexico in 1836, had been annexed and became a state of the Union in December 1845. Mexico protested, and a skirmish on the Rio Grande precipitated the Mexican-American war of 1846–1848. In California, a band of around a thousand Americans—trappers and new settlers—jumped the gun. They rose in revolt, captured the town of Sonoma, and proclaimed the Republic of California. These newer settlers had come to California with a traditional distrust and dislike of the Indians, Spanish, and Mexicans, which had been intensified by the Texan hostilities. The Bear Flag revolt—their flag was adorned with a star and a silhouette of a grizzly bear—forestalled the attempt by Larkin to engineer a more sophisticated revolution in California by acting through the Californios.

However, the issue was finally settled when U.S. naval forces under Commodore Sloat (replaced later by Commodore Stockton) quickly took possession of the region. By August 15, 1846, with little fighting, California was in American hands. Hostilities continued for some few months more, but with American reinforcements from Santa Fe arriving overland under Colonel Stephen W. Kearny, Mexican resistance ended with the Cahuenga Capitulation in 1847. The simultaneous acquisition of Texas, New Mexico,

Nevada, Utah, and all the land between Texas and California expanded the United States by some 918,000 square miles.[3] (In the same year, the Chinese student Yung Wing arrived in New York and the young merchant Chum Ming reached San Francisco.)

Inspired by the same dreams of manifest destiny that motivated their presidents, white American pioneers had fought their way over the plains in almost constant conflict with the American Indians whose hunting grounds they coveted for their farms. Many believed, with President Andrew Jackson (1828–1836), that "progress required the destruction of all Indians." The Indian wars that continued during the following administrations were long drawn out. The Apaches defended their freedom with arms until 1886, when Chief Geronimo was captured.

While reasonable compromises were made with Britain and Mexico in defining borders, the new masters of California—the men on the spot, pioneers, trappers, mountain men, settlers, soldiers, and the merchants supplying their needs—were men of action determined to hold what they had seized with so much difficulty and heavy sacrifice from the British, the American Indians, and the Mexicans.

The Chinese appeared in the western states in the 1850s while these events, and the mental climate they created, were still very much alive. This aspect of California history has to be borne in mind as one considers events in the second half of the nineteenth century. The Chinese were welcomed when they first arrived in small numbers. Principally merchants, urbane and well-bred, "outlandishly" but richly dressed, they took part in the municipal festivities and ceremonies of San Francisco. The skilled artisans, housebuilders, restaurateurs, hotel keepers, and early fishermen who came with them fulfilled urgent needs in San Francisco. But when Chinese began to arrive in the thousands and moved up into the mining areas where placer mining was already yielding diminishing returns, that was another matter, and the first signs of anti-Chinese activity appeared. The "what I have, I hold" attitude of the conquerors of California took over against what was perceived as a new threat to their conquest. The Wild West did not end on the eastern flanks of the Rockies or the Sierra but on the West Coast, and its law was often lynch law, as exemplified by the vigilantes of San Francisco.

The individualistic white miners were mollified when the Chinese miners abandoned attempts to compete with them and contented themselves with taking over abandoned claims and paying most of the taxes. The Chinese were also prepared to work for mining companies that the more individualist white miner disdained.

From the mid- to late-1860s the Chinese work force was concentrated in railway construction (15,000, or nearly 50 percent, were working on the railway; several thousand more were working in the mines). In the 1870s an unfortunate influx of some 20,000 immigrants aggravated anti-Chinese feeling stirred up by grueling economic crisis. The conquerors' war mentality, the Wild West license for violence, exacerbated the situation.

NOTES

1. T. H. Watkins, *California* (New York: Weathervane Books, 1923).
2. Thomas Jefferson Farnham, *Life and Adventures in California* (New York: Nafis and Cornish, 1849).
3. Watkins, *ibid.*

The Manifest Destiny of Gold

When the Depression came in the late 1920s, I used to take a pan, go down to the American River and I could pan out 50 cents a day. It kept me going.

> RICHARD YUE, whose father, Charlie Yue, born in Grass Valley, California, in 1879, supplied foodstuffs to the Auburn gold miners and now has a municipal parking lot named after him in Auburn

See the gray area within the orange of that gash on the mountain there. That is gold-bearing quartz. You could mine that for gold right now. With the present price of gold—$400 an ounce— it's worth mining such outcroppings again. It wasn't worth doing at $18 an ounce. Mines are opening up again.

> JERRY D. MOORMAN, realtor at New Horizon Realtors in Lotus, not far from Sutter's Mill, where the first gold of the Gold Rush was found in 1849

THE SEQUENCE of events was too happily coincidental to be fortuitous. President Polk (1845–1849) was convinced that the manifest destiny of the United States was to extend from the Atlantic ocean to California. On January 24, 1848, just nine days before California was ceded by Mexico to the United States, John Marshall, wheelwright, was examining the tail race of a sawmill he was building for Sutter at Coloma, thirty-five miles northeast of present-day Sacramento. He found gold left there by the rushing waters of the American River. This was the start of the Gold Rush.

Many of California's potentialities were well known by the 1840s: its splendid Pacific littoral with some excellent harbors; its forests and farmlands producing furs, cattle, hides, and tallow. Official Washington certainly knew about its mineral wealth. Following the early American trappers and settlers, the first immigrant wagon train reached California in 1826. In 1841, an American scientific exploration party led by Lieutenant Charles Wilkes reached

California. It included the famous mineralogist James Dwight Dana, and they visited Sutter's fort, where there must have been talk of California riches. Henry Dana, author of *Two Years Before the Mast*, told of gold in California. In 1841, Baptiste Ruelle, a Frenchman, had found gold in Los Angeles County, and in 1842 gold was also found by Francisco Lopez in the San Fernando Valley's Placerito Canyon. A sample of California gold actually arrived in Washington in November 1842. The existence of quicksilver deposits in the form of cinnabar, an ore of mercury, was of course, well known and so were finds of silver, copper, lead, sulfur, coal, and asphalt.

The middle of the century witnessed the triumphant advance of American industrialization, and minerals were its strength. President Polk's interest in California went far beyond the dream of a continent-wide nation. Hard-headed, practical, commonsense business was the stuff of which manifest destiny was made. But the gold find at Coloma and its results far surpassed all expectations. It confirmed the promise of this new American land with its eastern boundary of grand mountains and deserts, its fertile Central Valley, lovely coastline, and vast potential riches.

The Forty-Eighters

John Marshall and Sutter, to whom he had first revealed his find, did their best to keep the discovery secret, but the news leaked out. They had sent their nuggets to San Francisco to be tested. Other workmen had found nuggets and grains of gold and had exchanged them for goods. At that time, California had a mixed population of 800 native American Indians, a peaceable people, and 12,000 easy-going Mexicans and Californios—ranchers and settlers intermarried with Mexicans. In addition, there were 1,200 more foreign settlers, trappers and traders. To all of them finding gold was a wonderful dream, and they were the first to go into the hills in search of it. A few Chinese artisans and traders went with them. There was plenty for everyone.

Most of San Francisco's population left to get themselves some of that gold. A whole Mormon colony, led by their elder, Sam Brannan, took off for the placers, and Brannan collected his tithe from the takings. Even the new American garrison went. Two-thirds of the Oregon population abandoned their farms and businesses and trekked south. By June, 2,000 men were panning for gold, overrunning the fields and crops of Sutter's ranch and killing his cattle. In July, 2,000 more arrived. A good month's work could produce gold worth between $400 and $600, a large sum in those days. Even in 1850 at Rich Bar on the Feather River, a man washed $3,000 out of two panfuls of gravel. In expectation of endless wealth there for the taking, men wasted their money on fancy clothes, horses, and gaming. But they were mostly honest, simple men out to have a good time, panning for free gold with their wives and families up in the hills in the wonderful California weather.

That spring, summer, and fall of 1848 were still the happy heyday of the local gold seekers. Most were men who had ranches, businesses, jobs, and homes on the West Coast, men for whom the finding of gold was just a lucky chance. There was free mining and self-policing. There was plenty of room for everyone. Regulations were simple. You staked and panned a claim of a few square yards on a stream. If you found a lode ("lead") of gold-bearing ore, you had the right to follow it wherever it led.

In August, the *New York Herald* printed the story. The messenger sent from Sacramento to Washington with the official report spread the news all along the way from San Francisco through Peru, Panama, and New Orleans. President Polk in his annual address to the nation in December formally announced the discovery in Congress. "The accounts of the abundance of gold in that territory . . . would scarcely command belief," he said.

The virgin springs of the Sierra yielded placer gold in considerable quantities. At the Rich Dry Diggings, an early comer could pan out several hundred dollars a day in gold dust and nuggets. One man found $15,000 worth in one day. At Moore's Flat, two lucky Chinese found a 240-pound nugget worth over $30,000 at the time. Others found a 40-pound nugget on the middle fork of the Feather River, which they cut into small pieces to avoid attracting attention.

The wealth to be made in California seemed fabulous to ordinary people. In 1849, a mechanic in New England earned $32 a month; a farm laborer, $16. An English industrial worker earned $24; a farm laborer or shepherd, $10; a laborer in China, still less.

As the news spread, more men came from Oregon and southern California, then from Mexico, Chile, and Peru. Tens of thousands streamed in from the Midwest and further afield: New York, New Jersey, the New England states, Europe, and all over the world—and China. By December 1848, the Gold Rush was on.

The Forty-Niners

"Never since the Crusades had such a movement been known," writes the historian J. D. B. Stillman in *Seeking the Golden Fleece*.[1] In 1848, only eight vessels had found it worth while to make the voyage from the East Coast to San Francisco. But in the one year of 1849, a veritable armada converged on the Golden Gate: 777 vessels of all sizes; 242 full-rigged ships, 218 three-masted barks, 170 brigs, 132 schooners, and 15 steamers. Half of them beat their way around Cape Horn braving gales and icebergs on a 13,600-mile journey that might take four to five months.

Two months after President Polk's announcement, 90 vessels were already on their way from various eastern ports to the "New Eldorado." By April 1849, 20,000 men were gathered on the Missouri waiting for the snow to melt and let them complete the 2,800-mile journey to California. In that year, over 80,000 men poured into California to stake claims in the Mother Lode, a 150-mile and more stretch of the western flank of the Sierra Nevada on a north-south line from Mariposa to Downieville.

When the *S. S. California*, the first steamship load of Forty-Niners, arrived in San Francisco in February 1849, everybody on it, including the captain and crew, took off for the mines. By mid-year, argonauts were arriving in large numbers. By July, 15,000 were in the Mother Lode; by December, 53,000 had reached California; by September, close to 100,000.

Chum Ming and the other early Chinese gold seekers had enjoyed the advantage of being with the Forty-Eighters. The 323 Chinese who arrived along with the other gold seekers in 1849, on the first ships they could book passage on, found themselves among a very different kind of men.

The Forty-Niners were fortune hunters, not gold seekers by accident. Many had recklessly abandoned jobs, home, and family in the search for gold and had used their last dollars to make the journey. Undeterred by the dangers of the voyage around Cape Horn, 25,000 men made the passage.

The 5,450-mile journey by ship to Panama, across the pestiferous isthmus, and up the coast to San Francisco was hardly less perilous. The jungle journey across the isthmus was roadless and without proper accommodations. Transport was primitive; many walked. Thievery was rampant, as were mosquitoes, crocodiles, hunger, and disease. Cholera wiped out a quarter of the population of Panama and many travelers. Prices everywhere for the simplest necessities were exorbitant. The time taken for the whole journey might vary from a record 89 days to over 200. There was a terrible loss of life from shipwrecks: the *Golden Gate* burned with a loss of 223 lives, and the *Central America*, making a return voyage in 1857, went down with 423 passengers and crew and the loss of $8 million in gold. The first ship to pick up passengers in Panama took on 400 men. It was built to carry 100.

The overland route might seem at first sight to be easier, but this involved almost 3,000 miles and 180 days of travel from the midwestern roadheads over prairie, desert, and mighty mountains. The trail was marked by the bones of those who never finished it. It lay through territory disputed by the embittered Indians. Previous caravans had exhausted water sources and grazing grounds, necessitating wide detours. Foul weather, sickness, or bad guides could strand a party in impassable mountain snows. In such a pass the Donner group resorted to cannibalism to stave off death by starvation. Yet 55,000 Americans, Irish, Scots, Germans, and others walked, rode, or drove their wagons across. The number of deaths has never been ascertained.

The Gold Rush was a brutal test. Those who survived the journey to California had only begun the test. One of every five died within six months of reaching the West Coast.

Seeing the Elephant and More

A phrase current at that time described the experience of those who made it to the Mother Lode: they had "seen the elephant." It came from the time when the circus became popular in the United States and the elephant was the major attraction. Whoever had "seen the elephant" had seen it all.

The phrase referred to the second wave of prospectors who came to the Mother Lode in 1849.

The camaraderie of the Forty-Eighters was innocent by comparison. In that first wave, everybody who was able had made for the placers. San Francisco and Sacramento had emptied. Local men, they were in their own country, not too far from home. When a man asked for help, he was given it in neighborly fashion. At the gaming tables, loans were made on a man's word without other contract. But the Forty-Niners were another sort of men. Hundreds of ships abandoned by their crews wallowed in the harbor by the Golden Gate. Not even an offer of $100 a month could entice a man to sail a ship when, with a bit of luck, he could make ten times that amount finding gold in the hills. Behind the miners came the merchants, gold buyers, whiskey peddlers, professional gamblers, prostitutes, thieves, robbers, swindlers, and cutthroats.

The pickings were easy. Goods were stacked on the beaches with no place to store them. People lived in tents or flimsy shacks. Almost emptied in 1848, San Francisco filled up again to bursting point with 40,000 people in the fall of 1850. It was the mustering place of parties going to the mines, a rest and recreation center, a refuge for those who found life in the mines too tough. It was the gathering place for the wheeler-dealers, the merchants and those who found catering to the Gold Rush crowds more profitable than joining them. The old, small settlement was surrounded by a new shantytown of wooden hovels and a thousand tents pitched higgledy-piggledy. Drink shops were on every corner. Gambling was a universal pastime, poker and euchre, whist and ninepins, monte, faro and fantan. Prices of everything soared to unbelievable levels. A cheap house rented for $800 a month. An egg cost a dollar. One day, a fire started in this orderless agglomeration of structures, and the whole place went up in flames. Rebuilding started immediately. It was a typical Wild West boom town. Life was rougher and scarcity prices even higher in the isolated mining camps where, by the end of 1850, an army of 150,000 was at work scouring the earth.

Like others, the Chinese newcomers early realized that money could be made not only in the diggings but in business, trade, and services. A third of the arriving Chinese stayed on in San Francisco or Sacramento. They liked to raise and cook their own food even in foreign parts and soon found that others too liked their cooking. The Chinese restaurant business in San Francisco was born.

Many of the Forty-Niners were doctors, lawyers, ministers, farmers, and adventurous gentlemen lured by gold to the diggings, but in general the men of the Gold Rush were a tough lot. They had to be. A writer in *Harpers New Monthly Magazine* described them:

Groups of keen speculators were huddled around the corners in earnest consultation about the rise and fall of stocks; rough customers, with red and blue flannel shirts, were straggling in from the Flowery Diggings, the Desert and other rich points, with specimens of croppings in their hands. . . . Jewish clothing men were setting out their goods and chattels in front of wretched looking tenements: monte-dealers, gamblers, thieves, cut-throats, and murderers were mingling miscellaneously in the dense crowds gathered around the bars of the drinking saloons. Now and then a half-starved Pao-ute or Washoe Indian came tottering along under a heavy press of fagots and whiskey.[2]

The perils and hazards of the journey to California often resulted not in the best getting there but the most ruthless. Arrived in the Mother Lode, they found that panning gravel out in the bush, without proper shelter and with only such food as they could carry with them, was backbreaking toil. Sickness took its toll. Dysentery, fevers, and rheumatism were common.

Up in the Sierra, the streams are icy snowmelt. The winters are freezing; the summers, baking. All this the Chinese endured along with the others. Of necessity, there was rough justice in the placers in those days. One rule set a maximum size to a claim. At Rich Bar, this was 40 square feet. In especially rich diggings like Columbia, it was only 10 square feet. Another rule was that a man could hold a claim only so long as he actually worked it. If he were absent from work, the claim was lost unless he renewed it every ten days or hired a man to work it for him. This might cost him $6 a day.

The lone placer miner shoveled a mass of sand from a likely spot in a stream into his pan or cradle (rocker), let the water clear away the lighter debris, and then carefully washed away the rest until the heavier particles of gold were left at the bottom of the receptacle. By the time the easy pickings had been taken, fifty washings a day might have to be worked over to make a bare living, much less a fortune.

Soon the day of the lone placer miner with his pan or rocker was over. By the 1860s, placer mining was usually no longer profitable. It became necessary to divert whole streams to get at their beds or dig down to bed rock, and this work required large groups of men. Mining companies were organized. A rocker cost $50 to $100 in early 1849. Much more capital was needed to build the Long Tom, a 10- to 20-foot-long troughlike version of the rocker, without the rocking motion to separate the gold from the sand and gravel but with a riddle or sieve of sheet iron allowing the heavier gold and gravel to fall into the trough, or rifle-box, beneath. Four or five men were needed to work the Long Tom. Then came the sluice box, a contraption of several Long Toms put together, and wing dams. These differed from ordinary dams by dividing a river lengthwise, down its center, instead of across, to divert water and get at the riverbed.

Shallow "coyote holes" or deep shafts were sunk vertically into the ground. "Driftings" were shafts dug horizontally, sometimes to a depth of 200 feet into hillsides thought to contain gold sands. These were like regular mine shafts, 5 feet high or so, and, if skillfully planned, paid remarkably well.

Finally, in the drive to wash out more and more gold-bearing gravel, hydraulic mining was introduced in 1852. This demanded larger investments of capital and knowledge of the machines—monitors—that forced powerful jets of water against hillsides to break them down. By the 1860s, the Mother Lode was criss-crossed and scarred with 5,000 miles of man-made waterways. The Sacramento River was so polluted from the gold washings that by the 1880s the salmon had disappeared. The damage done to rivers and crops was so great that hydraulic mining was prohibited in 1884.

The patient Chinese excelled in using the pan. The saying was that once they had combed a digging you wouldn't find enough gold left "to fill the tooth of a bug." In the later stages demanding teamwork, Chinese miners also had an advantage over their more individualistic competitors. They came in groups from their Chinese districts, and in the new land they maintained their groups as working and social units. An average quartz-mining operation needed a capital investment of some $2,000 and a crew of fifteen men. This cooperation alleviated many difficulties of life in the mines. First and foremost, it gave a measure of protection in what was in actuality a lawless land. Although most quartz mines were run by white-owned companies, a number of small Chinese companies operated hydraulic or drift mines.

The hardships of work in the mines should not be romanticized or underrated. While there was the very occasional lucky find, most prospectors faced a steady grind for just a bare living. Work stopped entirely in the winter months. One might dig or pan out $150 or more in gold a month, but the result of several weeks spent building a sluice or dam might be nothing. $100 did not go far. In the mountains potatoes cost $1 a pound and cabbages, when available, $1 each. A slice of bread cost $1, $2 if it was buttered. A shovel cost $50. Initially, the price of gold was $18 an ounce, but local overproduction caused it to drop to $3 an ounce in the early placers. Indians were happy to sell an ounce then for 50¢. Only after 1848 did it rise again to $10 and later to $17 and $18, when regular carriers such as Wells Fargo could get it out to the open market.

There were few normal ways of spending leisure time in the mines. Drinking, gambling, and dancing without women were the usual recreations. It was hard enough to maintain law and order in Sacramento and San Francisco, not to speak of Hangtown (Placerville), Cut Throat Bar, or Murderers' Bar up in the mountains. Brawling, drunkeness, thieving, and violence were rife. Violence warped the nature of many men who now attacked this final frontier. Violence was fuelled, intensified, and channeled by racist prejudice. The single-minded pursuit of wealth led to towns such as Volcano being inundated with mud and sludge as the gold seekers ravaged the hills above them with jets of water. Settlements sank into the earth as men rifled the ground beneath. Of the 546 towns once born in the Mother Lode, 300 have vanished. Of many Chinatowns and China Camps—like that near Sonora with 2,000 Chinese—nothing now remains but a few shacks, a temple or two, and the lacy Trees of Heaven that the Chinese miners planted wherever they lived. At Sutter's Mill, where the Gold Rush started, the only memorial to the Chinese presence is a sign saying: "This is where a Chinese joss house once stood."

Racism in the Mines

White Americans tended to congregate by preempting the lucrative northern claims on the Sierra slopes. They were followed by the Chinese. The claims on the Merced and San Joaquin valleys and highlands were worked mainly by Mexicans, Chileans, Peruvians, and other Latin Americans. At the start, racial groups had tended to mix, but even by the summer of 1849 the largest group of miners were white Americans from the eastern, midwestern, and southern states. Most brought their prejudices with them. The first victims were the native American Indians. Both Northerners and Southerners were at war with the Indians—even with the peaceable Piutes of California.

The Indians were driven out early. Herded onto reservations or killed off by infections against which they had developed no immunity, they were shot and actually hunted for their scalps by some besotted scoundrels. Then came the turn of the blacks and the foreigners. Chileans, banned from using their peons as workers, were forced to either do the work themselves or leave the diggings. Then the "Chilean War" drove out the Chileans and Peruvians in 1849. The "French War" erupted on French Hill near Mokelumne when French miners, elated by an especially rich strike, injudiciously raised their French flag. American miners promptly drove them from their claims. By 1851, almost all these foreign miners were driven out. Mexicans had settled Sonora and named it after the place in Mexico from which they had come. When Americans tried to force them from their rich claims, they retaliated with guns. Every man in Sonora carried a gun. Raids, robberies, and killings were daily occurences. Matters came to a climax when the state legislature passed a law levying a $20-per-month tax on all foreign miners. Enforced at gunpoint, the 2,000 Mexicans departed, but the tax ruined Sonora until it was repealed in 1851.[3]

Then came the turn of the Chinese. In 1850, they numbered about 500 of the 57,787 miners. By 1852, they numbered several thousands in the mines. Their capacity for hard work and frugality, the way they kept to themselves and did not speak "proper" English, their skill in taking over abandoned claims and by diligent toil making them pay did not endear them to the rowdier elements in the mines.

The difference of one race from another is a fertile soil for racial prejudice. It takes more, however, to rear a structure of racial violence, discrimination, and oppression. In any multiracial society, attacks by the dominant group against any one race tends to spread in concentric circles to engulf other ethnic minorities. This is what happened in California.

California was a free state, but slavery was still legal in the United States. A third of the Forty-Niners were southern whites, and a number had even brought their slaves with them. Most brought their racial antipathies with them, too. Northerners wanted no slaves or blacks there. The Southerners wanted blacks but only as slaves. Manifest destiny and "divine providence" ordained that California should be Anglo-Saxon. In the climate of the day, rapacity and violence could be readily excused on grounds of putting blacks and all other "inferior races" in their places. How strong were these racist sentiments is shown by the fact that, although a proposal to ban blacks entirely from the state was defeated in the legislature, the state constitution stipulated that a black could not vote, could not settle on a homestead farm, could not hold public office, serve on a jury, testify in court, or attend school with white children. Until 1864, a black could not ride a San Francisco streetcar. Yet, in the earlier days, free blacks were very much a part of the San Francisco scene. William Leidesdorff, a "man of color" from the Virgin Islands, was a highly respected entrepreneur in trade, transport and builder of one of the first hotels, and a member of the municipal council and of the first school board. A street is named after him. He died in 1848. A few years later under the new constitution, had he lived, he would not have been allowed even to ride a streetcar.

Blacks made courageous efforts to gain equal treatment under law, and white allies helped them gain what victories they did gain. But disappointment led a significant number of them to migrate to British Columbia in 1858 in search of greater freedom and opportunity. It took the Civil War of 1861 before their status really changed, but the struggle is still going on now, more than a hundred years later.

The presence of the southern whites was of crucial import to both blacks and Chinese. The better to keep their human "property" in free California, the southern slave-owners and racists got a law passed in 1849 stipulating that "no black or mulatto person or Indian shall be permitted to give evidence in favor of or against a white person." In a place and time where the law was too often what the man on the spot could make it, this exclusion was a stunning weapon to put into the hands of a racist evil-doer. Because the Chinese were, of course, "men of color," they were also prohibited from testifying under oath against whites. This court judgment was only reversed in 1870.

In the case of *People* v. *George W. Hall* (October 1854), the California Supreme Court (Chief Justice Hugh C. Murray) ruled that the laws of the state prohibited Indians from giving evidence in court against whites, that Asiatics were Indians and that, anyway, he would decide against admitting the testimony of Chinese "on the grounds of public policy."

There was no question that George Hall had killed a man, but the only actual witness was a Chinese. Hall was therefore acquitted. This ruling was affirmed by the same court in *People* v. *James Brady*, in the same year. The opinion of the court was based on the assumption that the Chinese were a people "whose mendacity is proverbial, a race of people whom nature has marked as inferior, . . . incapable of progress or intellectual development beyond a certain point, as their history has shown; differing in language, opinion, color and physical conformation; between whom and ourselves nature has placed an impassable difference." Not until 1861 could a Chinese appear as a witness in court.

White treatment of native American Indians and blacks set a precedent and a standard for racist treatment of minorities in general. There were no Chinese or blacks on the Upper Feather River in Louise Clappe's time, but there were Spaniards, and she reported that "it is very common to hear vulgar Yankees say of the Spaniards, 'Oh, they are half-civilized black men! . . . And when they commit the most glaring injustice against the Spaniards, it is generally passed unnoticed." After a knifing of a Spaniard who merely asked a Yankee to repay a debt, "nothing was done and very little was said about this atrocious affair."[4] In fact, shortly thereafter the Rich Bar white miners passed a resolution forbidding all foreigners to work the mines there. That effectively drove out the Spanish. Racism against any one ethnic group opens the gate to indiscriminate racism.

The Real Wild West

In 1850, California's population had grown to 300,000. By 1860, it was 380,000. The great Gold Rush influx of people had tapered off but it left a most diverse population in its wake. In 1850, 25 percent of the population was foreign born. In 1860, this figure had risen to 40 percent. There were 33,000 Irish, 22,000 Germans, and 16,000 English. Blacks numbered 4,000. The 35,000 Chinese were the largest nonwhite minority, and they became a prime target of racism. The sorry story that followed must be set against the general background of the Wild West.

Violence in the mines was endemic. "In the short space of twenty-four days, we have had murders, fearful accidents, bloody deaths, a mob, whippings, a hanging, an attempt at suicide, and a duel," wrote Louise Clappe.[5] The popular refrain of the 1880s in California, "Good-bye, God, I'm going to Bodie," typified the situation in the mining towns. Hellfire preachers called it a "sea of sin, lashed by the tempests of lust and passion." This town of 10,000 miners was famous at one time for its Chinatown, the second largest in California after San Francisco, and for its average of a murder a day. Surrounded by sagebrush desert, the climate tried tempers. Drink and prostitution were the main leisure activities.

When "law and order" was established, its results were often very much like what they were supposed to do away with.

The state of society here has never been so bad as since the appointment of a Committee of Vigilance. The rowdies have formed themselves into a company called the Moguls, and they parade the streets all night, howling, shouting, breaking into houses, taking wearied miners out of their beds and throwing them into the river. . . . It is said that some of that very Committee were the ringleaders among the Moguls.[6]

Drumhead trials replaced personal vendettas, but a miners' "court" could hang a man for robbery and cut off his ears for petty thievery. Lashes with a lariat and a shaven head branded a man a thief so that he was forced to flee for his life from any inhabited place. Writing from Rich Bar in December 1851, Louise Clappe commented, "At that time, the law did not even pretend to wave its scepter over the place." A thief was sentenced to death by a makeshift court and within three hours was hanged by the jury that had just sentenced him. No one paid any attention to the appointed judge. The early Forty-Eighters "could not have foreseen that in El Dorado they would come face to face with desperadoes for whom slitting a throat and pushing a body over a cliff were all in a day's or a night's work."[7]

The concept of manifest destiny might be couched in the lofty terms of national statesmanship by the president in Washington, but to the average white miner in the Mother Lode it was transmuted into a simple belief that this land and its treasures were not for sharing with "Greasers," "Keskedees" (from the French "Qu'est qu'il dit?"), "Chinks,"and other lesser "breeds" outside the law. A present-day historian of San Francisco, Doris Muscatine, quotes an opinion from the *Annals of San Francisco* in the early 1850s:

Indians, Spaniards of many provinces, Hawaiians, Japanese, Chinese, Malays, Tartars, and Russians, must all give place to the resistless flood of Anglo-Saxons or American progress. These peoples need not, and most of them probably cannot, be swept from the face of the earth; but undoubtedly their national characteristics and opposing qualities and customs must be materially modified, and closely assimilated to those of the civilizing and dominant race.[8]

Legalized Harassment

In such an environment of violence, when racist elements were in a majority or in positions of leadership, their "democracy" made short work of the rights of "inferior races."

The first anti-Chinese riot took place as early as the autumn of 1849 in Tuolumne County, near the southern limit of the Mother Lode. Sixty Chinese working for a British mining company were driven out of their camp by a band of rampaging white miners. This was the first violent manifestation of a contagion that finally affected the highest levels of U.S. government. In August of that year, it is estimated that only one man in a thousand was making a real living in the mines. The miners were finding out that a man might earn $140 a month in the placers but this could only buy him goods worth $25 in New York. Many men became bitter.

The image of "hordes" of Chinese rushing into the gold country during the Gold Rush needs to be refocused. Indeed, most Chinese found that "fortunes," or at least a living, could better be made outside of the Gold Rush than in it, mining for gold. But in the next few years the number of Chinese in California increased rapidly, too rapidly perhaps for their own good. In 1851, there were over 10,000 and in 1852 about 25,000 Chinese working in California in a total population of around 380,000. In 1852, 20,000 Chinese immigrants arrived—the largest number ever in any one year. They came because of widespread misery caused by war, flood, and famine in Guangdong Province and because of the tempting offers made by ships' brokers and shipping companies to entice paying passengers on trans-Pacific voyages.

This influx of Chinese was the occasion of increased anti-Chinese agitation. In 1850, responding to new pressure by white miners (irked chiefly by the presence of Mexicans), politicians of the racist majority in the California legislature levied a tax of $20 a month on foreign miners. But the scheme misfired. The tax was so punitive that it drove men from the mines. Thousands of Mexican miners went back south of the border; Chinese also left and returned to San Francisco and Sacramento, there to work at hotel jobs, carpentry, washing clothes, and running restaurants.

Business in the mining towns suffered. In 1851, the tax law was repealed. The more level-headed members of the white commercial lobby and representatives of the Chinese associations suggested a more reasonable tax of $3 a month, which would go to county treasuries. The Chinese calculated that this would incline local feeling in their favor, and to some extent they were right. After a year, in 1853, this tax was increased to $4 a month. Although the Chinese now outnumbered the Germans but were fewer than the Irish, the tax in practice was collected mainly from the Chinese because it was levied on those who did not desire to become permanent citizens. It was the largest single source (25–50 percent) of state revenue. Because the tax was in effect farmed out to tax collectors who were authorized to keep part of the proceeds, the post of tax collector attracted numerous scoundrels. These sometimes collected the tax several times over and resorted to terror and murder to collect it. "I was sorry to stab the poor creature, but the law makes it necessary to collect the tax, and that's where I get my profit," reads the diary of a tax collector.[9] When Chinese miners fled their claims as these collectors approached, the latter enticed Maidu Indians to help track down the hidden men. It was a typical case of "divide and rule."

The tax, however, provided a considerable share of the counties' incomes. Shasta County used it to defray 25 percent of the cost of its county hospital and most of its other expenses. The tax made up one-third of Calaveras County's income. Other counties would have had to close their schools or even gone bankrupt without the tax income. It was not until 1870, after the tax had been paid for sixteen years, that the U.S. Supreme Court belatedly struck it down as unconstitutional. By then, the Chinese had paid $5 million, eighty-five percent of the total tax collected. Not a cent was ever refunded.

Such violence and injustice forced the Chinese to reconsider their situation. In 1858–1859, some 2,000 left California for newly discovered gold mines in British Columbia. Others, instead of competing with the white miners for fresh claims and risking confrontations, took over abandoned and supposedly worked-out claims. Over 15,000 of them (two-thirds of all Chinese in the state) worked this way in the gold fields of the Sierra and the Trinity Alps. Chinese Camp, known also as Chinese Diggings, south of Sonora, which they settled and where they found rich gold deposits after being driven from nearby claims by intolerant Americans, became the main labor distribution center for the southern mines. Most of its 5,000 inhabitants in 1856 were Chinese.

When there was a mass exodus of white miners in the 1859–1860 season because yields of surface mines were declining, Chinese took over many claims, diligently wringing out the last ounce of gold, which would otherwise have been wastefully abandoned. In this way, they sustained the industry for several more years. In fact, some rated 1863 as one of their best years.[7]

To work abandoned claims, the Chinese introduced new methods.[10] To lay bare the riverbeds, they used wing dams with channels as long as 600–900 feet, made of pine timbers. From their experience with irrigation in their South China homeland, they introduced ancient tools such as the treadle pump. This pump was usually operated by two men working synchronized treadmills having four spokes or vanes on the same axis. They swiftly cleared water out of holes, to the surprise of tenderfoot miners, with a bailing bucket attached to two ropes manipulated by two men. These traditional Chinese methods were new in California, until American ingenuity, spurred in part by the Gold Rush, developed machine technologies such as enormous steam dredges, which in turn astonished the Chinese.

As long as there were gold or minerals, mining was the preferred trade for the Chinese in the West. Between 1864 and 1867, even when an estimated 10,000 Chinese had left the gold mines, 45–50 percent of the Chinese in the United States were still working in mining. They worked in placer, drift and hydraulic mining. In 1868 in the western states, their number was estimated at 15,000 and in 1870 at 17,000. There were still some lonely placer miners, but most men were working for wages for foreign- or Chinese-owned mining companies employing fifteen to twenty men and using mining equipment worth several thousand dollars. Chinese worked in the quartz mines, tunneling and digging canals. Hydraulic mining was monopolized by white businessmen who employed Chinese as workers.

In the 1860s and 1870s, when silver and other minerals were discovered in the Rocky Mountain states of Utah, Nevada, Colorado, Montana, Wyoming, and Idaho, Chinese miners went there looking for jobs, and little Chinatowns were dotted over these mining areas.[11] They worked in the Comstock silver lode. They helped dig a canal for mining in Nevada in 1856, and their worksite there was called Chinatown until it was officially changed to Dayton. Virginia City, too, had a large Chinese quarter. Chinese were also early on the scene when news came of the gold strikes in South Dakota. And they mined coal in northern California, Oregon, and Wyoming. David D. Colton, who employed Chinese in his Wyoming coalmines, stated to the 1876 Congressional commission that "there are no better coalminers in the world now than these Chinamen."[12]

We have a good account of the 200–250 Chinese who worked at the Mt. St. Helena quicksilver mine in Lake County, near Calistoga, California, from 1872–1900, written by the daughter of the mine superintendent.

Map 4. Western U.S. with Early Chinese American Communities

Working, in her words, under "horrible conditions," they produced millions of dollars worth of mineral wealth.[13]

Creating Capital for Western Development

The massive impact of the Chinese miners on the development of the western United States has not yet been adequately recognized. They made an enormous contribution in getting out the minerals needed to industrialize America and open the West. Statistics are hard to come by, but it appears that at the peak periods of their employment they comprised twenty-five percent of the total mining population of California and more than that in the state of Oregon. Table 1 shows the number of Chinese miners in the West according to the U.S. census of 1870, the near peak of their activity in the region.

Table 1. Chinese in Western Mining Areas (1870)

State or Territory	Total Mining Work Force	Chinese Miners	Percentage
Oregon	3,965	2,428	61.2%
Idaho	6,579	3,853	58.5
Washington	173	44	25.4
California	36,339	9,087	25.0
Montana	6,720	1,415	21.0
Nevada	8,241	240	2.9

SOURCE: Thomas Chinn, ed, *The History of the Chinese in California* (San Francisco: Chinese Historical Society of America, 1973), p. 33.

In 1860, there were some 83,000 men in the California mines and 24,000 of these were Chinese, about two-thirds of the Chinese population on the West Coast at that time. In 1870, some 30,000 men were mining and 17,000 were Chinese (27 percent of the Chinese in the country).

These mostly nameless people have written an indelible page in U.S. history. The results of their work were momentous. At a crucial time in the nation's growth, they worked in one of its most important capital-producing industries and helped lay a basis for California's and the nation's future growth and prosperity.

I have found no way of estimating exactly the contribution of the Chinese to the gold-mining industry of the nation. Exact records do not exist; if they once did, they were probably lost in the San Francisco fire of 1906. But, directly or indirectly, the Chinese mined a large part of the colossal amount extracted from the Mother Lode. They also helped the mining effort as cooks, storekeepers, and peddlers and in other auxiliary roles. And their merchants and family and district associations sustained the miners' efforts and morale, bringing in accustomed foods, giving them the important assurance that if they died on alien soil their bones would be carried back for proper burial to their native villages and homes.

In all the years previous to 1848 that California was known to the Western world, its gold mines produced about $8,000 worth of gold. In the following ten years, 1848–1857, with Nevada it produced $400 million, and in the 5 years between 1861–1866, $150 million. In 1852 alone, California produced $80 million worth. Put another way, in the five years before 1848, U.S. average yearly gold production was 52,000 ounces. In 1849, this figure leaped to 1.9 million ounces and in 1850 to 2.4 million ounces, with practically all of this increase coming from California and its boozing, brawling, hard-working miners, to whom no adequate monument has yet been raised.[14]

Other strikes came later in Nevada, where Chinese miners worked in the 1860s and 1870s. In the 1870s, Tuscarora Chinatown was the biggest in the state and Chinese, it is said, extracted $500,000 worth of gold there in 1871 alone. Chinese miners continued working in northern Nevada up to the 1900s. Chinese miners also worked in Oregon and Montana (1852), in Arizona and Colorado (1858), and still later in Washington (1862), where they worked claims for the next 40 years. They worked sparser mines in Idaho, Utah, New Mexico, and Alaska (until the great Klondike strike in 1898), but California alone contributed over one-third of all America's gold output. In the twenty-eight-year span of 1848–1876, the Pacific Slope of the Sierras produced $1,812.5 million in gold and silver. During the period 1848–1883, $1,200 million worth, or two-thirds of the entire U.S. gold production, came from California mines, and a considerable part of that was mined by the Chinese of the mining work force.

California's gold and financial power opened up the mineral and other riches of the Western states from Canada to the Mexican border. It went into commerce, buildings, railways, harbor facilities, transport, industry, irrigation, and reclaiming huge areas of farmland. It created the infrastructure of a modern agricultural and industrial state that is today the first in the nation in agricultural wealth and population and second only to New York in industry. California thus became a modern state within a few years of being settled as part of the United States. This was a tremendous boost to the development that would transform America within the next fifty years into the richest and most powerful nation in the world.

The contribution of the Chinese of California, of course, went much beyond mining. Although most of them at that time had no wish to remain in the United States permanently, they paid taxes, brought business to the state, and performed all sorts of other services. Customs dues paid by them, freight, rents, licenses, insurance, and similar payments accruing to the state amounted to about $14 million in 1861 alone.[15] Seward, in his *Chinese Immigration*[16], estimates that 20,000 or so Chinese miners in California in 1862 would have paid close to a million dollars a year to the state as a result of the $4-a-month mining tax. He quotes a committee of the California legislature stating that 20,000 Chinese miners bought water at 30 cents a man a day, which would make another $2,190,000 a year, and that 15,000 claims were paid for at 25 cents a day, or $1,370,000 a year (1862). In addition to all this, they sent back sizable sums to their home towns (an estimated $11 million in 1876) that helped support their families and modernize Guangdong Province so that it became a seedbed of the nationalist and democratic revolution in China.

Mining was a school of technology for many Chinese, and when the railways began to be built across the country the miners were a main source of labor recruitment. By 1865, the first phase of the transcontinental railway had reached Amador and El Dorado counties, where quite a number of Chinese were working in the mines. By then, they knew some English and were familiar with American ways of work, and some knew how to handle explosives and drilling tools. The railway builders later found them invaluable—indeed, indispensable. The healthy respect they had for dynamite, at which other miners had laughed, served them in good stead when it came to handling the new explosive, nitroglycerin.

By the 1870s, the gold-mining history of California and the Chinese in the West was ending. History moved on. A few made fortunes—these were the owners and stockholders of the big gold-mining companies. Some made it in the mines, but most made it by serving the Gold Rush with equipment, accommodation, transport, food, and entertainment. A typical success story is that of Wells Fargo Company, which made a success of transportation with their famous stagecoach lines, as well as in banking, assaying, and remittance facilities. In less than ten years, the Wells Fargo office in Murphys alone—a town with 5,000 inhabitants—shipped out over $15 million in gold. By the 1880s, it had 573 western offices doing a thriving business with thousands of Chinese clients. To this day, Wells Fargo still has a well-patronized Chinese department. Less long-lasting or notable but no less typical was the bartender who made a profit of $7,000 on every barrel of whisky he sold in the Mother Lode.[17]

There were no Chinese of comparable note in these categories, but many Chinese made modest "fortunes" serving the Gold Rush. And many, including the Chinese, made a hard-earned living, but most found only back-breaking toil, poverty, and, too often, death in the great Gold Rush.

Finally, when the inevitable happened and yields began to sag even for the diligent Chinese, more and more of the miners began to look elsewhere for work to fulfill their dream of making their pile and returning to their homes and families in triumph. Many went to work on the first transcontinental and other railways then being built. Others went into various trades and occupations in the cities and farms of California.

NOTES

1. J. D. B. Stillman, *Seeking the Golden Fleece.*
2. J. Rose Browne, quoted in Ralph Gabriel, ed., *The Pageant of America*, Vol. 2 (New Haven: Yale University Press, 1925), p. 252.

3. *The Mother Lode* (Los Angeles: Travel Research and Publications Department, Automobile Club of Southern California, 1979).

4. Louise Clappe, *The Shirley Letters from the California Mines, 1851–1852* (Santa Barbara: Smith, 1970). Reprint.

5. Clappe, *ibid.*

6. Clappe, *ibid.*, p. 186.

7. Gordon V. Axon, *The California Gold Rush* (New York: Mason and Charter, 1976).

8. Frank Soule, *Annals of San Francisco* (New York: Appleton, 1855), in Doris Muscatine, *San Francisco: Biography of a City* (New York: Putnam, 1975).

9. Thomas Chinn, Him Mark Lai, and Philip P. Choy, *History of the Chinese in California* (San Francisco: Chinese Historical Society of America, 1973), p. 33.

10. Ping Chiu, *Chinese Labor in California* (Madison: University of Wisconsin Press, 1963), p. 27.

11. William S. Greever, *The Bonanza Story: The Story of the Western Mining Rushes, 1848–1900* (Norman: Oklahoma University Press, 1963).

12. George F. Seward, *Chinese Immigration: Its Social and Economic Aspects* (New York: Arno Press and New York Times, 1970), 1881 reprint p. 50.

13. Helen Rocca Goss, *Life and Death of a Quicksilver Mine* (Los Angeles: Historical Society of Southern California, 1958).

14. T. H. Watkins, *California* (New York: Weathervane Books, 1923), and data from the Gold Information Center, Dept. T84, P.O. Box 1269, FDR Station, New York, NY 10022 and *Encyclopedia Britannica.*

15. B. S. Brooks, *Appendix to the Opening Statement and Brief on the Chinese Question (Referred to the Joint Committee on the Senate and House of Representatives)* (San Francisco: Women's Co-Operative Printing Union, 1877).

16. Seward, *Chinese Immigration*, pp. 45–50.

17. *The Mother Lode, ibid.*

San Francisco:
The Golden Gate

V

In the first few years the Chinese were welcomed, praised, and considered almost indispensable. There was no race antipathy in those days. It was subordinated to industrial necessity and the Chinaman could find room and something more than toleration.

ALEXANDER MCLEOD, *Pigtails and Gold-Dust*

WHEN THE American flag was raised on July 9, 1846, on what is now Portsmouth Square, San Francisco had a population of around one thousand, including the troops. It was still a sleepy little frontier town, but the discovery of gold in 1848 soon changed all that. Within a few years, it was a city. In the summer of 1849, it was a Gold Rush town of 5,000. In the 1880s it rivaled in wealth, numbers, and elegance the older eastern metropolises of New York, Philadelphia, and Boston.

Such rapid growth brought its problems, and these too have left an indelible mark on its character. It attracted all sorts of men, not only the miner and the businessperson but also those out for easy pickings. This Wild West boom town had not yet developed civic leaders and administrators. Law and order were notably lacking. Lack of housing and warehouse space forced people to live in flimsy tents and leave their goods out in the open. The organized criminal element was first the Hounds, remnants of a regiment of New Yorkers disbanded in the West. They stole and burglarized and killed until the exasperated citizenry, who banded together to hound the Hounds, drove them out of town.

Next came the Sydney Ducks, desperadoes from the British penal colony in Australia. These were thugs and murderers who would as soon toss a man off a cliff on Telegraph Hill as look at him.

In 1850–1856, San Francisco witnessed 1,400 murders, seven or eight a week, not to speak of other crimes of robbery and violence. Disgusted with the slow courts and ineffective authorities, in June 1851 and again in 1856, citizens' vigilance committees were formed and used the quick justice devised in the mining towns to round up the criminals. Some were summarily executed; others were driven out.

San Francisco's foreshore was like no other in the world. Building materials were in short supply in 1849, but hundreds of deserted ships lay in the harbor. One of the first official acts of the new San Francisco council was to buy the brig *Euphemia* for use as a prison. The *Apollo*, anchored in a cove, was turned into a storeship. Later it was dragged ashore and converted into a lodging house and saloon.

Portsmouth Square, partly a cow pen, surrounded by tents and adobe huts in 1848, was by the late 1850s surrounded by brick and stone buildings, hotels, business offices, shops, gaming places, and restaurants. Drinking saloons frequently occupied all four corners of intersections. The harbor was crowded with shipping. Building lots in the beach area that sold for $50 to $600 in the late 1840s were divided in half, and by 1853 each half sold for from $8,000 to $16,000.[1]

This sprawling metropolis sent out miners and supplies to the gold fields and helped them spend their money when they came back. There were those who worked the mines and those who helped or exploited those who worked the mines, and it seems that, after those few halcyon months of easy surface gold, the latter were more fortunate than the former. While a few lucky individuals in the mines might indeed strike it rich—a less and less likely prospect as mechanized industrial mining by mining companies took over— the overwhelming majority faced grueling work under hard conditions. The fortunes were made by those who provided goods and services to the gold miners: merchandise, equipment, transport, banking and remittance services, accommodations, and entertainment.[2]

The cattle ranchers of southern California were early gainers. They found a large and ready market for their meat among the miners. Philip Armour was a hog farmer and butcher of Placerville in the gold country. It was there that he founded the business that became one of the world's great meat-packing firms. Two of the Southern Pacific Railway's Big Four, Hopkins and Huntington, were solid merchants in Placerville before moving to Sacramento and beginning to make their millions building their railroad empire. Studebaker laid the basis of his automobile fortune as a Placerville wheelbarrow maker. People that today are household names in San Francisco became well-known at that time: Sutro, Dollar, Zellerbach, Macy, Gump's, Magnin, De Young, and many more. Levi Straus made a name and fortune with his tough work clothes for miners.

The early Chinese immigrants also faced the choice between working in the mines and catering to the mines and miners by working in the towns, serving the Gold Rush and the cities' populations. Of the 30,000 or so Chinese in California in the 1850s—and that means in the United States—over 50 percent chose to work and live in San Francisco. The rest were in the Mother Lode on the flanks of the Sierra.

The few Chinese who lived in the small settlement of San Francisco in 1848 were scattered over its area. The liberal atmosphere of the new land allowed them to live more or less where they pleased. In 1850, there was a camp for fishermen, for instance, out at Rincon or China Point. With twenty-five boats, in 1852, they were bringing 3,000 pounds of fish to market every day.

Chinese merchants were established at several locations in the town. Later, in 1850, when some 700 Chinese were in the city, economics dictated that their restaurants, laundries, and shops should cluster around the hotels that had grown up in the then center of the city, Portsmouth Square. The St. Francis Hotel, Brown's City Hotel, the Parker House Hotel, the Opera House, and some Chinese restaurants were on the square or within a block of it. Business was good, and so was the service. There was also a cluster of Chinese businesses and houses on Clay Street between Stockton and Kearny. As their numbers grew, they branched out into neighboring streets, to present-day Grant, to the north, and along Kearny. Called "Little Canton" in 1850, this area had thirty-three retail stores, some fifteen pharmacies (Chinese herbal cures were much appreciated in a city with few doctors), and five restaurants serving both Chinese and non-Chinese. This was the beginning of San Francisco's "Chinatown," the oldest and largest in the United States. Chinatown was so christened by the press in 1853.

Restaurants

Chinese restaurants marked themselves with triangular flags of yellow silk. They early earned a name for themselves in a city famous for its varied and excellent cuisines—French, Italian, Spanish, and Anglo-American. Connoisseurs were probably the more delighted with them because at that time there was no attempt to conciliate Western tastes. The gold miner William Shaw, writing in *Golden Dreams and Waking Realities* (1851), declared that "the best eating houses in San Francisco are those kept by Celestials and conducted Chinese fashion. The dishes are mostly curries, hashes and fricasee served up in small dishes and as they are exceedingly palatable, I was not curious enough to enquire as to the ingredients."[3]

It was a custom in this easygoing city to offer patrons of saloons and restaurants meals of as much as one could eat for a set price. Chinese restaurants followed this trend. Bayard Taylor, the roving reporter of the *New York Tribune* at that time, wrote that "Chinese meals cost $1 to eat as much as you like at Kong-Sung's near the water, Whang Tong's on Sacramento Street, and Tong Ling's on Jackson Street."

From the very start, as the Chinese population in California grew, merchants began to import Chinese foodstuffs. Chinese farmers were soon growing the fresh vegetables and herbs that a Chinese cook must have, and fishermen in the Bay were bringing in the seafood delicacies the southern Chinese love: shrimp, seaweed, abalone, squid, and fresh fish in great variety.

The result is that, from then until now, the food cooked in most Chinese houses and the best restaurants is the same as that cooked in the mother country. Quite a number of Chinese eating places, however, served Western fare.

The flourishing of Chinese restaurants to this day is proof enough of their excellence and the demand for them in San Francisco, which still has the habit of "dining out," part of the tradition of the early days of a pioneer, bachelor society in which most men had no real home. Like Chinatown itself, restaurants are an essential ingredient of the tourist lure that now brings the city over three million tourists and one billion tourist dollars a year.

Laundries

There is an early print of Sacramento Chinese washing clothes on rafts in the river, but Wah Lee is usually given credit for setting up the first large Chinese hand laundry on the corner of San Francisco's Washington Street and Grant Street (then Dupont Street) in 1851. This was probably the first regular Chinese laundry in the United States. Until 1869, the California population was still 70 percent male and, given their decidedly macho character, many so-called women's jobs such as laundering simply went undone. Early San Francisco dandies sent their shirts as far as Hong Kong to be washed and ironed. They paid $12 a dozen, and it took four months to get them back. Then Honolulu began to wash them for $8 a dozen. Wah Lee in San Francisco did them for $5 a dozen. By 1870, some 2,000 Chinese laundries dominated the trade in the city. By 1876, there was one in every district in the city, and there was scarcely a town on the coast without one. Some worked two shifts around the clock. The Chinese laundryman delivering his bundles in baskets slung from a shoulder pole was a familiar sight. The laundries made possible clean, civilized, and sophisticated living. They did a double service to the communities. In San Francisco alone in 1877, Chinese laundries paid $152,000 in rentals and $68,000 in water taxes which went to the city at large. In 1880, some 7,500 Chinese were in the laundry business. How ubiquitous they were is indicated by the fact that it was a Chinese laundrymark that led to the capture of the notorious bandit "Black Bart."[4] Laundry work led restaurants as the main business of the Chinese during Exclusion days. Shops and groceries ran third.

Shops and Home Deliveries

Merchandising was another field in which the Chinese made their contribution to the California style of living, not only through their shops but also through their services as distributors and peddlers of goods. In the early days, housewives looked forward to the fresh vegetables, fruits, and flowers the Chinese brought from house to house. It was the Chinese peddlers who introduced pampas grass to the home market, and this feathery decoration became a "must" in every Victorian household. The visit of a cloth trader was always a delightful event. The peddler did not use the hard-sell, aggressive techniques one usually associates today with house-to-house sales. He brought his goods neatly wrapped in a square of blue cotton cloth and transformed a living room into a private store of exotic wares from which the housewife could choose at her leisure.

At many towns such as Bodie on the California-Nevada border, right up into the 1880s, when Chinese still formed a part of the town, they were the main providers of firewood to keep the communities warm. Vegetable, fruit, and flower peddlers carrying fresh produce in from the countryside were eagerly welcomed in towns where the horse and cart was still a luxury.

Domestics

The excellence of the Chinese as domestic workers was proverbial. They were widely regarded as splendid cooks, quick to learn Western ways of cooking and scrupulously clean when conditions allowed. They commanded good wages for those days, from $40 to $50 a month, as much as white servants or cooks. To this day on Nob Hill, the elite residential district of the city, you can still see the "Chinaman's room" in old houses, the dark basement room that a Victorian society considered suitable for domestic help to live in. Due to the absence of their own families, the Chinese usually lavished their affection on the children of their employers. This is attested to by innumerable testimonials and memoir after memoir. On Nob Hill, few homes did not boast of a Chinese domestic. In the rural areas, as J. H. Russell writes in Cattle on the Conejo, Chinese were almost always the ranch cooks up to about 1919.[5]

The following exchange took place at the congressional hearing held on Chinese immigration in California in 1876:

Q: Why are [Chinese] employed as domestics?"

A: (By Mr. Francis Avery, a longtime California resident) "Because they make better servants. . . . The wages paid them are the same as the wages paid by persons employing white servants."[6]

In the City's Service

It was soon clear, once the gold mines had been exhausted, that San Francisco's destiny and lasting prosperity would be in trade. Trade needed plenty of land for warehouses, roads, and offices. Yerba Buena Cove was rapidly filled in and turned into dry land. Chinese were widely employed in this work in landfill operations and in manning the scows that brought sand to the landfill sites. They leveled and graded many San Francisco streets from 1855 to about 1870, under the contractor David Hewes. The first street graded was Bush, from Kearny to Mason Streets. Their last job was to level the old Yerba Buena cemetery for the building of a new city hall. In the early stages of his operations, Hewes used Chinese labor exclusively.

Before this work was done, the city had been notorious for its mud and potholes. In 1850, three bodies were found mired in the mud of Montgomery Street. On one occasion, a mule and wagon were lost in quicksand inside the city limits.[7]

Building the City

The rapid population increase set off a building boom. Because of lack of local timber and skilled labor, it was profitable to import ready-made houses from many places, China among them. On one trip, the British ship *Kelso* brought in Chinese-made houses, together with the carpenters to put them up. Some of these houses used mortise joints that needed no nails, a decided saving in those days when all such things had to be imported into California, a developing country. Although men of many kinds hurried to California at the start of the Gold Rush, not many were skilled artisans. Whole stone buildings with their stones cut, shaped, and numbered were imported from China, together with the masons to put them up. The Parrott Building, the first stone building in San Francisco, was thus imported. It was the first commercial building of any importance in California. Its Chinese builders worked from sunrise to sundown according to a contact that paid them a dollar a day, a quarter-pound of fish, and a half-pound of rice.

The Parrott Building was due to be erected at the corner of Montgomery and California Streets, but the Chinese workmen protested that the *feng shui* (wind and water) orientation of the site was not propitious, and they refused to build it on the corner selected, preferring a site on the opposite corner. Despite their prognosis, it was built anyway in 1853 while Well's Fargo's new office was built at the propitious opposite corner. When the panic of 1855 occurred, there was a disastrous run on the two banks housed in the Parrott Building, and they went bankrupt. The Chinese who banked with Wells Fargo, however, were unperturbed. They disdained to withdraw their accounts from this good-luck bank, known to Chinese miners from one end of the Mother Lode to the other, and Wells Fargo weathered the financial storm to go on to become one of the largest financial institutions in the West with a capital today of $17 billion.

Entertainment

San Francisco was a rest and recreation center for the mining population, and the place where men came with their savings to take ship back home. Entertainment and the pleasures of the day—good food and song, dance and music, drink and less innocent vices—were part of San Francisco's reason for being. All tastes were catered to.[8] One of the first Chinese theatrical performances in America was a puppet show staged in the back of a Chinese grocery store in Sacramento. Such shows became a regular feature of San Francisco entertainment and prepared the way for the Hook Took Tong, a Chinese theatrical troupe with 123 performers that opened with a program of Cantonese opera at the American Theater (October 18, 1852). This was so successful that the troupe imported its own theater building from China and erected it in Chinatown by the end of the year.

We also hear of a Chinese "Punch and Judy" show (probably a puppet show) on Portsmouth Plaza in the summer of 1853, of a "Chinese dancing salon where exhibitions were given of dancing by elaborately costumed performers" in 1854, and of jugglers and acrobats that astonished audiences. In 1860, a Chinese play, *The Return of Sit Pin Quai*, a comedy, was performed at the Union Theater. The Chinese Theater, with its performances of Cantonese opera, quickly became one of the attractions of the city and Charles Nordhoff, writing in 1872, made it clear that a visit to the Chinese opera was a must for every tourist to San Francisco.[9]

Gambling

The spirit of gambling was in the very air of California in Gold Rush days. Gold was at first easily obtained, and it was much a matter of chance. "Easy come, easy go" was a prevalent philosophy. And this was the spirit around the gambling tables. American and English gamblers preferred faro; Spanish and Italian liked monte. Stakes were often high. On one occasion, $200,000 was at stake on a monte table. The Chinese games were fantan and paijiu (lotteries). Everyone played dice. And when the Mining Stock Exchange opened in 1864 it had a ready made clientele of eager speculators.

A Home Away from Home

Far from being unassimilable, as the leaders of anti-Chinese campaigns later claimed, Chinese adapted their traditional skills to the service of the new land and integrated themselves into the society of pioneering California. The men who worked in the mines and later on the railways were not essentially different from those who were so eagerly welcomed into the intimacy of households as cooks and domestics.

Those who came as "sojourners," like those from Italy and other lands, did not, of course, usually try to learn more of the language than was needed to do their work; they simply did not try to make the great adjustments needed to become permanent residents because when they returned home they would be like fish out of water.

The record shows that the relatively small number who planned to make the United States their permanent home were no less adaptable than other immigrants when convinced that adjustments in their way of work or life had to be made as a condition of enjoying a prosperous and creative life here. They quickly became part of the California scene. They took part in its community parades and activities. The 1888 champion Chinese hose company of firefighters in Deadwood, South Dakota, was generously eulogized. Many photographs exist of Chinese participants in anniversary parades in San Francisco, Calistoga, and other towns. Their contingents in the San Francisco ceremonies to pay tribute to the memory of President Taylor and the admission of California to statehood moved the daily *Alta California* to eulogize them as "among the most industrious, quiet, patient people among us. . . . They seem to live under our laws as if born and bred under them."

Special mention must be made of the Chinese merchants. Their scrupulous business dealings with their American counterparts, the accepted understanding that their word was their bond, had a great deal to do with creating a positive image of Chinese in America.

Tales of life in America were taken back to China, and despite reports of difficulties and worse, there were always those who thought the chances of betterment made the risks acceptable. The attraction of a voyage to California was enormous. In the 1850s a laborer might earn $3 to $5 a month in South China while a wage of $1 a day was common in California. In the gold fields, a man might strike it lucky in a single day and retire to his Guangdong village a rich man. Working on the railway in the 1860s, he could earn $30 to $35 a month and live on $15–18 a month. With savings of $300–$400, he could return in triumph to his family. At the very least, he could send home $30 a year.

And these were not just stories. Returning immigrants and the hard cash they sent ahead of them were proof positive that an enterprising, hardworking man could succeed in the Golden Mountains of the United States. By the 1850s, it became a regular thing for any young man of spirit and filial piety to make the voyage. Emigration fever was endemic in the twenty-seven Guangdong areas that provided the bulk of Chinese immigrants to America.

Chinatown equally astonished the tourist and delighted the immigrant fresh off the boat. Although the buildings were occidental, the atmosphere was Chinese, bustling and noisy, with brightly colored lanterns, three-cornered pennants of yellow silk denoting restaurants, handsome calligraphy on sign boards and bordered flags, a profusion of balcony and window plants, the smells and atmosphere of a Chinese marketplace, flowing costumes, hair in queues, and, most of all, the babble of familiar Cantonese dialects.

In the hostel run by their family or district community or guild, the immigrants were secure. In Chinatown streets, they were at home, or almost. This background was invaluable in giving them confidence to deal with the very considerable pressures of the larger society, which were often extremely severe. The immigrants needed all the support they could get to withstand them.

It is significant that Sacramento Street was known among the Chinese as Tang Ren Chieh (in Cantonese, Tong Yan Gai), the Street of the Men of Tang, China's greatest classical dynasty, when China was indeed the Middle

Kingdom of the world in population, extent, wealth, and culture. When these temporary exiles in a foreign land met with insults from rowdy, drunken hoodlums, they could mutter to themselves, "No matter—I am a man of Tang." Such consciousness of self-worth is a powerful defense against racist attempts to humiliate and demean oppressed minorities.

AH TOY

Tall and with an ivory complexion, Ah Toy in her youth was so beautiful that when news of her arrival reached the goldfields in that land bereft of women, miners put away their picks and shovels and traveled a hundred miles to San Francisco just to look at her. She had arrived in the city alone with her amah and established her salon in a courtyard on Clay Street between Dupont (now Grant) and Kearny.

She gave no favors to anyone but charged an ounce of gold dust (at $18 an ounce) just for the privilege of looking at her face. Men lined up in a queue that stretched for a block and more. At the height of her fame in the early 1850s, when the boat from Sacramento touched shore men would leap from the gunwhales and race to her courtyard in hopes of catching a glimpse of her. She was as famous in her day as Lola Montez the dancer was in hers.

Legend has embellished the hard facts contained in the city's police and court records. She once had two miners arrested for trying to pass off brass filings as gold. Her appearance in court before Police Judge George Baker in this case was a sensation. She pointed out a number of others among the spectators as having committed a like deception on her. Their confusion was obvious. Yet, notwithstanding a basin full of brass filings that she fetched in for the judge to see, she lost the case.

In a remarkable show of spirit, she soon appeared in court again, this time as an unlicensed advocate, to defend a woman friend accused of beating a gentleman named Jonathan Nissum. Ah Toy eloquently pleaded that the beating had been provoked because Nissum had neglected to pay a certain debt. However, she lost this case too, and the defendant had to pay a fine of $20.

When she appeared again in San Francisco, it was as the first madam of its emerging Chinatown and owner of a flourishing brothel at her Clay Street address. Several nice shanties in the courtyard had been occupied by gentlemen who had been forced to move on account of the goings-on there. But when Ah Toy was served with a complaint for keeping a house of ill fame, she showed that she had learned the law and the case was dismissed by Judge R. H. Waller of the Recorder's Court.

Ah Toy, several times married, lived to a venerable age. Unlike tens of thousands in her line of work, she is now enshrined in the hall of famous memories of this remarkable city, which admires enterprise, courage, and the sort of character that could cope with the hazards of survival in the Wild West. It is a commentary on the times that the business she engaged in was one of the very few that in those days could give her an independent living.

NOTES

1. Oscar Lewis, *San Francisco: Mission to Metropolis* (Berkeley: Howell-North Books, 1966).
2. Doris Muscatine, *San Francisco: Biography of a City* (New York: Putnam, 1975).
3. William Shaw, *Golden Dreams and Waking Reality*, 1851.
4. C. M. Goethe, *What's in a Name? California Gold Belt Place Names* (Sacramento: Keystone Press, 1949).
5. J. H. Russell, *Cattle on the Conejo* (Los Angeles: Ritchie Press, 1957).
6. George F. Seward, *Chinese Immigration* (New York: Arno Press and New York Times, 1970). Reprint of 1881 ed.
7. R. E. Lloyd, *Lights and Shadows of San Francisco* (San Francisco: Bancroft, 1871).
8. William Henry Brewer, *Up and Down California in 1860–64* (New Haven Conn.: Yale University Press, 1930).
9. Charles Nordhoff, *California* (Berkeley: Ten Speed Press, 1973). Reprint of 1873 ed.

Linking a Continent
and a Nation

Without the 'Chinamens' knowledge and respect for explosive
powders, ability to work on the side of near vertical cliffs at
dizzying heights and survive hardships which white men could
not endure the Central Pacific would never have been completed
when it was but much later.

R. W. HOWARD, *The Great Iron Trail*

The Chinese filled swamps, cut into mountains, dug tunnels,
built bridges. As one historian notes, "The work was so obviously
needed and all groups and areas vied with each other to build
a railroad in their area, so that they would have welcomed the
devil himself had he built a road. The lack of white laborers
was too evident to cause even the most ardent anti-Chinese to
resent their employment on such work."

ROBERT E. WYNNE, *Reaction to the Chinese in the Pacific
Northwest and British Columbia*

THE EXPANSION of the railroad system in the United
States was astonishingly swift. England had pioneered the building of railways
and for a time was the acknowledged leader in the field, but from the moment
the first locomotive was imported into the United States in 1829 the farsighted saw railways as the obvious solution for transport across the vast spaces
of the American continent. By 1850, 9,000 miles of rails had been laid in
the eastern states and up to the Mississippi. The California Gold Rush and
the opening of the American West made talk about a transcontinental line
more urgent. As too often happens, war spurred the realization of this project.

The West was won. California was a rich and influential state, but a
wide unsettled belt of desert, plain, and mountains, separated it and Oregon
from the rest of the states. As the economic separation of North and South
showed, this situation was fraught with danger. It could lead to a political
rift. In 1860, it was cheaper and quicker to reach San Francisco from Canton
in China—a sixty-day voyage by sea—than from the Missouri River, six months

away by wagon train. The urgent need was to link California firmly with the industrialized eastern states and their 30,000 miles of railways. A railway would cut the journey to a week. The threat of civil war loomed larger between North and South over the slavery issue. Abraham Lincoln's Republican administration saw a northern transcontinental railway as a means to outflank the South by drawing the western states closer to the North. In 1862, Congress voted funds to build the 2,500-mile-long railway. It required enormous resourcefulness and determination to get this giant project off the drawing boards. Not much imagination was required to see its necessity, but the actual building presented daunting difficulties. It was calculated that its cost would mount to $100 million, double the federal budget of 1861.

It was Theodore Judah, described by his contemporaries as "Pacific Railroad Crazy," who began to give substance to the dream. An eastern engineer who had come west to build the short Sacramento Valley Railroad, he undertook a preliminary survey and reported that he had found a feasible route crossing the Sierra by way of Dutch Flat. But the mainly small investors who supported his efforts could not carry through the whole immense undertaking. With rumors of civil war between North and South, San Francisco capitalists, mostly Southerners, boycotted the scheme as a northern plot, and pressed for a southern route. Then the Big Four, Sacramento merchants, took up the challenge: Leland Stanford as president, C. P. Huntington as vice-president, Mark Hopkins as treasurer, and Charles Crocker, in charge of construction, formed the Central Pacific Railway Company. Judah was elbowed out.

The Big Four came as gold seekers in 1849 or soon after but found that there was more money to be made in storekeeping than in scrabbling in the rocks in the mountains. As Republicans, they held the state for the Union against the secessionists. Leland Stanford, the first president of the Central Pacific, was also the first Republican governor of California.

The beginnings were not auspicious. The Union Pacific was building from Omaha in the East over the plains to the Rockies, but supplies had to come in by water or wagon because the railways had not yet reached Omaha. The Civil War now raged and manpower, materials and funds were hard to get. The Indians were still contesting invasion of their lands. By 1864, however, with the Civil War ending, these problems were solved. The UP hired Civil War veterans, Irish immigrants fleeing famine and even Indian women, and the line began to move westward.

The Central Pacific, building eastward from Sacramento, had broken ground on January 8, 1863, but in 1964, beset by money and labor problems, it had built only thirty-one miles of track. It had an even more intractable manpower problem than the UP. California was sparsely populated, and the gold mines, homesteading, and other lucrative employments offered stiff competition for labor. Brought to the railhead, three out of every five men quit immediately and took off for the better prospects of the new Nevada silver strikes. Even Charles Crocker, boss of construction and raging like a mad bull in the railway camps, could not control them. In the winter of

1864, the company had only 600 men working on the line when it had advertised for 5,000. Up to then, only white labor had been recruited and California white labor was still motivated by the Gold Rush syndrome. They wanted quick wealth, not hard, regimented railway work. After two years only fifty miles of track had been laid.[1]

James Strobridge, superintendant of construction, testified to the 1876 Joint Congressional Committee on Chinese Immigration: "[These] were unsteady men, unreliable. Some would not go to work at all. . . . Some would stay until pay day, get a little money, get drunk and clear out."[2] Something drastic had to be done.

In 1858, fifty Chinese had helped to build the California Central Railroad from Sacramento to Marysville. In 1860, Chinese were working on the San Jose Railway and giving a good account of themselves, so it is surprising that there was so much hesitation about employing them on the Central Pacific's western end of the first transcontinental railway. Faced with a growing crisis of no work done and mounting costs, Crocker suggested hiring Chinese. Strobridge strongly objected: "I will not boss Chinese. I don't think they could build a railroad." Leland Stanford was also reluctant. He had advocated exclusion of the Chinese from California and was embarrassed to reverse himself. Crocker, Huntington, Hopkins, and Stanford, the "Big Four" of the Central Pacific, were all merchants in hardware, dried goods, and groceries in the little town of Sacramento. Originally, they knew nothing about railroad building, but they were astute and hard-headed businessmen. Crocker was insistent. Wasted time was wasted money. The CP's need for labor was critical. The men they already had were threatening a strike. Finally fifty Chinese were hired for a trial.

Building the Transcontinental Railroad

In February 1865, they marched up in self-formed gangs of twelve to twenty men with their own supplies and cooks for each mess. They ate a meal of rice and dried cuttlefish, washed and slept, and early next morning were ready for work filling dump carts. Their discipline and grading—preparing the ground for track laying—delighted Strobridge. Soon fifty more were hired, and finally some 15,000 had been put on the payroll. Crocker was enthusiastic: "They prove nearly equal to white men in the amount of labor they perform, and are much more reliable. No danger of strikes among them. We are training them to all kinds of labor: blasting, driving horses, handling rock as well as pick and shovel." Countering Strobridge's argument that the Chinese were "not masons," Crocker pointed out that the race that built the Great Wall could certainly build a railroad culvert. Up on the Donner Pass today the fine stonework embankments built by the Chinese are serving well after a hundred years.

Charles Nordhoff, an acute observer, reports Strobridge telling him, "[The Chinese] learn all parts of the work easily." Nordhoff says he saw them "employed on every kind of work. . . . They do not drink, fight or strike; they do gamble, if it is not prevented; and it is always said of them that they are very cleanly in their habits. It is the custom, among them, after they have had their suppers every evening, to bathe with the help of small tubs. I doubt if the white laborers do as much."[3] As well he might. Well-run boardinghouses in California in those days proudly advertised that they provided guests with a weekly bath.

Their wages at the start were $28 a month (twenty-six working days), and they furnished all their own food, cooking utensils, and tents. The headman of each gang, or sometimes an American employed as clerk by them received all the wages and handed them out to the members of the work gang according to what had been earned. "Competent and wonderfully effective because tireless and unremitting in their industry," they worked from sun-up to sundown.

All observers remarked on the frugality of the Chinese. This was not surprising in view of the fact that, with a strong sense of filial duty, they came to America in order to save money and return as soon as possible to their homes and families in China. So they usually dressed poorly, and their dwellings were of the simplest. However, they ate well: rice and vermicelli (noodles) garnished with meats and vegetables; fish, dried oysters, cuttlefish, bacon and pork, and chicken on holidays, abalone meat, five kinds of dried vegetables, bamboo shoots, seaweed, salted cabbage, and mushroom, four kinds of dried fruit, and peanut oil and tea. This diet shows a considerable degree of sophistication and balance compared to the beef, beans, potatoes, bread, and butter of the white laborers. Other supplies were purchased from the shop maintained by a Chinese merchant contractor in one of the railway cars that followed them as they carried the railway line forward. Here they could buy pipes, tobacco, bowls, chopsticks, lamps, Chinese-style shoes of cotton with soft cotton soles, and ready-made clothing imported from China.

On Sundays, they rested, did their washing, and gambled. They were prone to argue noisily, but did not become besotted with whiskey and make themselves unfit for work on Monday. Their sobriety was much appreciated by their employers.

Curtis, the engineer in charge, described them as "the best roadbuilders in the world." The once skeptical Strobridge, a smart, pushing Irishman, also now pronounced them "the best in the world." Leland Stanford described them in a report on October 10, 1865, to Andrew Johnson:

As a class, they are quiet, peaceable, patient, industrious, and economical. More prudent and economical [than white laborers] they are contented with less wages. We find them organized for mutual aid and assistance. Without them, it would be impossible to complete the western portion of this great national enterprise within the time required by the Act of Congress.

Crocker testified before the congressional committee that "if we found that we were in a hurry for a job of work, it was better to put on Chinese at once." All these men had originally resisted the employment of Chinese on the railway.

Four-fifths of the grading labor from Sacramento to Ogden was done by Chinese. In a couple of years more, of 13,500 workers on the payroll 12,000 were Chinese. They were nicknamed "Crocker's Pets."

Appreciating Chinese Skills

The Chinese crews won their reputation the hard way. They outperformed Cornish men brought in at extra wages to cut rock. Crocker testified,

They would cut more rock in a week than the Cornish miners, and it was hard work, bone labor. [They] were skilled in using the hammer and drill, and they proved themselves equal to the very best Cornish miners in that work. They were very trusty, they were intelligent, and they lived up to their contracts.[4]

Stanford held the Chinese workers in such high esteem that he provided in his will for the permanent employment of a large number on his estates. In the 1930s, some of their descendants were still living and working lands now owned by Stanford University.

The Chinese saved the day for Crocker and his colleagues. The terms of agreement with the government were that the railway companies would be paid from $16,000 to $48,000 for each mile of track laid. But there were only so many miles between the two terminal points of the projected line. The Union Pacific Company, working with 10,000 mainly Irish immigrants and Civil War veterans, had the advantage of building the line through Nebraska over the plains and made steady progress. The Central Pacific, after the first easy twenty-three miles between Newcastle and Colfax, had to conquer the granite mountains and gorges of the Sierra Nevada and Rockies before it could emerge onto the Nevada-Utah plains and make real speed and money. The line had to rise 7,000 feet in 100 miles over daunting terrain. Crocker and the Chinese proved up to the challenge. After reaching Cisco, there was no easy going. The line had to be literally carved out of the Sierra granite, through tunnels and on rock ledges cut on the sides of precipices.

Using techniques from China, they attacked one of the most difficult parts of the work: carrying the line over Cape Horn, with its sheer granite buttresses and steep shale embankments, 2,000 feet above the American River canyon. There was no foothold on its flanks. The indomitable Chinese, using age-old ways, were lowered from above in rope-held baskets, and there, suspended between earth and sky, they began to chip away with hammer and crowbar to form the narrow ledge that was later laboriously deepened to a shelf wide enough for the railway roadbed, 1,400 feet above the river.[5]

Behind the advancing crews of Chinese builders came the money and supplies to keep the work going. This was an awesome exercise in logistics. The Big Four, unscrupulous, dishonest, and ruthless on a grand scale, were the geniuses of this effort. The marvel of engineering skill being created by

Strobridge and his Chinese and Irish workers up in the Sierra was fed by a stream of iron rails, spikes, tools, blasting powder, locomotives, cars, and machinery. These materials arrived after an expensive and hazardous eight-month, 15,000-mile voyage from East Coast ports around Cape Horn to San Francisco, thence by river boat to Sacramento, and so to the railhead by road.

The weather, as well as the terrain, was harsh. The winter of 1865–1866 was one of the severest on record. Snow fell early, and storm after storm blanketed the Sierra Nevada. The ground froze solid. Sixty-foot drifts of snow had to be shoveled away before the graders could even reach the roadbed. Nearly half the work force of 9,000 men were set to clearing snow.

In these conditions, construction crews tackled the most formidable obstacle in their path: building the ten Summit Tunnels on the twenty-mile stretch between Cisco, ninety-two miles from Sacramento and Lake Ridge just west of Cold Stream Valley on the eastern slope of the summit. Work went on at all the tunnels simultaneously. Three shifts of eight hours each worked day and night.

The builders lived an eerie existence. In *The Big Four*, Oscar Lewis writes,

Tunnels were dug beneath forty-foot drifts and for months, 3,000 workmen lived curious mole-like lives, passing from work to living quarters in dim passages far beneath the snow's surface. . . . [There] was constant danger, for as snows accumulated on the upper ridges, avalanches grew frequent, their approach heralded only by a brief thunderous roar. A second later, a work crew, a bunkhouse, an entire camp would go hurtling at a dizzy speed down miles of frozen canyon. Not until months later were the bodies recovered; sometimes groups were found with shovels or picks still clutched in their frozen hands.[6]

On Christmas Day, 1866, the papers reported that "a gang of Chinamen employed by the railroad were covered up by a snow slide and four or five [note the imprecision] died before they could be exhumed." A whole camp of Chinese railway workers was enveloped during one night and had to be rescued by shovelers the next day.

No one has recorded the names of those who gave their lives in this stupendous undertaking. It is known that the bones of 1,200 men were shipped back to China to be buried in the land of their forefathers, but that was by no means the total score. The engineer John Gills recalled that "at Tunnel No. 10, some 15–20 Chinese [again, note the imprecision] were killed by a slide that winter. The year before, in the winter of 1864–65, two wagon road repairers had been buried and killed by a slide at the same location."[7]

A. P. Partridge, who worked on the line, describes how 3,000 Chinese builders were driven out of the mountains by the early snow. "Most . . . came to Truckee and filled up all the old buildings and sheds. An old barn collapsed and killed four Chinese. A good many were frozen to death."[8] One is astonished at the fortitude, discipline and dedication of the Chinese railroad workers.

Many years later, looking at the Union Pacific section of the line, an old railwayman remarked, "There's an Irishman buried under every tie of that road." Brawling, drink, cholera, and malaria took a heavy toll. The construction crew towns on the Union Pacific part of the track, with their saloons, gambling dens, and bordellos, were nicknamed "hells on wheels." Jack Casement, in charge of construction there, had been a general in the Civil War and prided himself on the discipline of his fighting forces. His work crews worked with military precision, but off the job they let themselves go. One day, after gambling in the streets on payday (instigated by professional gamblers) had gotten too much out of hand, a visitor, finding the street suddenly very quiet, asked him where the gamblers had gone. Casement pointed to a nearby cemetery and replied, "They all died with their boots on." It was still the Wild West.

It is characteristic that only one single case of violent brawling was reported among the Chinese from the time they started work until they completed the job.

The Central Pacific's Chinese became expert at all kinds of work: grading, drilling, masonry, and demolition. Using black powder, they could average 1.18 feet daily through granite so hard that an incautiously placed charge could blow out backward. The Summit Tunnel work force was entirely composed of Chinese, with mainly Irish foremen. Thirty to forty worked on each face, with twelve to fifteen on the heading and the rest on the bottom removing material.

The Donner tunnels, totaling 1,695 feet, had to be bored through solid rock, and 9,000 Chinese worked on them. To speed the work, a new and untried explosive, nitroglycerin, was used. The tunnels were completed in November 1867, after thirteen months. But winter began before the way could be opened and the tracks laid. That winter was worse than the preceding one, but to save time it was necessary to send crews ahead to continue building the line even while the tunnels were being cut. Therefore, 3,000 men were sent with 400 carts and horses to Palisade Canyon, 300 miles in advance of the railhead. "Hay, grain and all supplies for men and horses had to be hauled by teams over the deserts for that great distance," writes Strobridge. "Water for men and animals was hauled at times 40 miles."[9] Trees were felled and the logs laid side by side to form a "corduroy" roadway. On log sleds greased with lard, hundreds of Chinese manhandled three locomotives and forty wagons over the mountains. Strobridge later testified that it "cost nearly three times what it would have cost to have done it in the summertime when it should have been done. But we shortened the time seven years from what Congress expected when the act was passed."[10]

Between 10,000 and 11,000 men were kept working on the line from 1866 to 1869. The Sisson and Wallace Company (in which Crocker's brother was a leading member) and the Dutch merchant Cornelius Koopmanschap of San Fancisco procured these men for the line. Through the summer of 1866, Crocker's Pets—6,000 strong—swarmed over the upper canyons of the Sierra, methodically slicing cuttings and pouring rock and debris to make landfills and strengthen the foundations of trestle bridges. Unlike the Caucasian laborers, who drank unboiled stream water, the Chinese slaked their thirst with weak tea and boiled water kept in old whiskey kegs filled by their mess cooks. They kept themselves clean and healthy by daily sponge baths in tubs of hot water prepared by their cooks, and the work went steadily forward.

Crocker has been described as a "hulking, relentless driver of men." But his Chinese crews responded to his leadership and drive and were caught up in the spirit of the epic work on which they were engaged. They cheered and waved their cartwheel hats as the first through train swept down the eastern slopes of the Sierra to the meeting of the lines. They worked with devotion and self-sacrifice to lay that twenty-odd miles of track for the Central Pacific Company in 1866 over the most difficult terrain. The cost of those miles was enormous—$280,000 a mile—but it brought the builders in sight of the easier terrain beyond the Sierra and the Rockies. Here costs of construction by veteran crews were only half the estimated amount of federal pay.

By summer 1868, an army of 14,000 railway builders was passing over the mountains into the great interior plain. Nine-tenths of that work force was Chinese. More than a quarter of all Chinese in the country were building the railway.

When every available Chinese in California had been recruited for the work, the Central Pacific arranged with Chinese labor contractors in San Francisco to get men direct from China and send them up to the railhead. It was evidently some of these newcomers who fell for the Piute Indian's tall tales of snakes in the desert "big enough to swallow a man easily." Thereupon "four or five hundred Chinese took their belongings and struck out to return directly to Sacramento," reports the *Alta California.* "Crocker and Company had spent quite a little money to secure them and they sent men on horseback after them. Most of them came back again kind of quieted down, and after nothing happened and they never saw any of the snakes, they forgot about them." At least one Chinese quit the job for a similar reason. His daughter, married to a professor of Chinese art, told me that her father had worked on the railway but quit because "he was scared of the bears." He later went into domestic service.

By September 1868, the track was completed for 307 miles from Sacramento, and the crews were laying rails across the plain east of the Sierra. Parallel with the track layers went the telegraph installers, stringing their wires on the poles and keeping the planners back at headquarters precisely apprised of where the end of the track was.

The Great Railway Competition

On the plains, the Chinese worked in tandem with all the Indians Crocker could entice to work on the iron rails. They began to hear of the exploits of the Union Pacific's "Irish terriers" building from the east. One day, the Irish laid six miles of track. The Chinese topped this with seven. "No Chinaman is going to beat us," growled the Irish, and the next day, they laid seven and half miles of track. They swore that they would outperform the competition no matter what it did.

Crocker taunted the Union Pacific that his men could lay ten miles of track a day. Durant, president of the rival line, laid a $10,000 wager that it could not be done. Crocker took no chances. He waited until the day before the last sixteen miles of track had to be laid and brought up all needed supplies for instant use. Then he unleashed his crews. On April 28, 1869, while Union Pacific checkers and newspaper reporters looked on, a combined gang of Chinese and eight picked Irish rail handlers laid ten miles and 1,800 feet more of track in twelve hours. This record was never surpassed until the advent of mechanized track laying. Each Irishman that day walked a total distance of ten miles, and their combined muscle handled sixty tons of rail.

So keen was the competition that when the two lines approached each other, instead of changing direction to link up, their builders careered on and on for 100 miles, building lines that would never meet. Finally, the government prescribed that the linkage point should be Promontory, Utah.

Competition was keen, but there seems to be no truth in the story that the Chinese and Irish in this phase of work were trying to blow each other up with explosives. It is a fact, however, that when the two lines were very near each other, the Union Pacific blasters did not give the Central Pacific men timely warning when setting off a charge, and several Chinese were hurt. Then a Central Pacific charge went off unannounced and several Irishmen found themselves buried in dirt. This forced the foremen to take up the matter and an amicable settlement was arranged. There was no further trouble.

On May 10, 1869, the two lines were officially joined at Promontory, north of Ogden in Utah. A great crowd gathered. A band played. An Irish crew and a Chinese crew were chosen to lay the last two rails side by side. The last tie was made of polished California laurel with a silver plate in its center proclaiming it "The last tie laid on the completion of the Pacific Railroad, May 10, 1869." But when the time came it was nowhere to be found. As consternation mounted, four Chinese approached with it on their shoulders and they laid it beneath the rails. A photographer stepped up and someone shouted to him "Shoot!" The Chinese only knew one meaning for that word. They fled. But order was restored and the famous ceremony began; Stanford drove a golden spike into the last tie with a silver hammer. The news flashed by telegraph to a waiting nation. But no Chinese appears in that famous picture of the toast celebrating the joining of the rails.

Crocker was one of the few who paid tribute to the Chinese that day: "I wish to call to your minds that the early completion of this railroad we have built has been in large measure due to that poor, despised class of laborers called the Chinese, to the fidelity and industry they have shown."[11] No one even mentioned the name of Judah.

The building of the first transcontinental railway stands as a monument to the union of Yankee and Chinese-Irish drive and know-how. This was a formidable combination. They all complemented each other. Together they did in seven years what was expected to take at least fourteen.

In his book on the building of the railway, John Galloway, the noted transportation engineer, described this as "without doubt the greatest engineering feat of the nineteenth century," and that has never been disputed.[12] David D. Colton, then vice-president of the Southern Pacific, was similarly generous in his praise of the Chinese contribution. He was asked, while giving evidence before the 1876 congressional committee, "Could you have constructed that road without Chinese labor?" He replied, "I do not think it could have been constructed so quickly, and with anything like the same amount of certainty as to what we were going to accomplish in the same length of time."[13]

And, in answer to the question, "Do you think the Chinese have been a benefit to the State?" West Evans, a railway contractor, testified, "I do not see how we could do the work we have done, here, without them; at least I have done work that would not have been done if it had not been for the Chinamen, work that could not have been done without them."[14]

It was heroic work. The Central Pacific crews had carried their railway 1,800 miles through the Sierra and Rocky mountains, over sagebrush desert and plain. The Union Pacific built only 689 miles, over much easier terrain. It had 500 miles in which to carry its part of the line to a height of 5,000 feet, with another fifty more miles in which to reach the high passes of the Black Hills. With newly recruited crews, the Central Pacific had to gain an altitude of 7,000 feet from the plain in just over 100 miles and make a climb of 2,000 feet in just 20 miles.

All this monumental work was done before the age of mechanization. It was pick and shovel, hammer and crowbar work, with baskets for earth carried slung from shoulder poles and put on one-horse carts.

For their heroic work, the Chinese workmen began with a wage of $26 a month, providing their own food and shelter. This was gradually raised to $30 to $35 a month. Caucasians were paid the same amount of money, but their food and shelter were provided. Because it cost $0.75 to $1.00 a day to feed a white unskilled worker, each Chinese saved the Central Pacific, at a minimum, two-thirds the price of a white laborer (1865 rates). Chinese worked as masons, dynamiters, and blacksmiths and at other skilled jobs that paid white workers from $3 to $5 a day. So, at a minimum, the company saved about $5 million by hiring Chinese workers.

Did this really "deprive white workers of jobs" as anti-Chinese agitators claimed. Certainly not. In the first place, experience had proved that white workers simply did not want the jobs the Chinese took on the railroad. In fact, the Chinese created jobs for white workers as straw bosses, foremen, railhandlers, teamsters, and supervisors.

The wages paid to the Chinese were, in fact, comparable to those paid unskilled or semiskilled labor in the East (where labor was relatively plentiful), and the Chinese were at first satisfied. Charles Nordhoff estimated that the frugal Chinese could save about $13 a month out of those wages.[15] The *Alta California* estimated their savings at $20 a month and later, perhaps, as wages increased, they could lay aside even more. With a bit of luck, a year and a half to two years of work would enable them to return to China with $400 to buy a bit of land and be well-to-do farmers.

But the Chinese began to learn the American way of life. On one occasion in June 1867, 2,000 tunnelers went on strike, asking for $40 a month, an eight-hour day in the tunnels, and an end to beating by foremen. "Eight hours a day good for white man, all same good for Chinese," said their spokesman in the pidgin English common in the construction camps. But solidarity with the other workers was lacking, and after a week the strike was called off when the Chinese heard that Crocker was recruiting strikebreakers from the eastern states.

When the task was done, most of the Chinese railwaymen were paid off. Some returned to China with their hard-earned savings, and the epic story of building the Iron Horse's pathway across the continent must have regaled many a family gathering there. Some returned with souvenirs of the great work, chips of one of the last ties, which had been dug up and split up among them. Some settled in the little towns that had grown up along the line of the railway. Others took the railway to seek adventure further east and south. Most made their way back to California and took what jobs they could find in that state's growing industries, trades, and other occupations. Many used their traditional and newly acquired skills on the other transcontinental lines and railways that were being swiftly built in the West and Midwest. This was the start of the diaspora of the Chinese immigrants in America.

The Union and Central Pacific tycoons had done well out of the building of the line. Congressional investigation committees later calculated that, of $73 million poured into the Union Pacific coffers, no more than $50 million could be justified as true costs. The Big Four and their associates in the Central Pacific had done even better. They had made at least $63 million and owned most of the CP stock worth around $100 million and 9 million acres of land grants to boot.

Ironically, the great railway soon had disastrous results for the Chinese themselves. It now cost only $40 for an immigrant to cross the continent by rail and a flood of immigrants took advantage of the ease and cheapness of travel on the line the Chinese had helped to build. The labor shortage (and resulting high wages) in California turned into a glut. When the tangled affairs of the Northern Pacific line led to the stock market crash of Black

Friday, September 19, 1873, and to financial panic, California experienced its first real economic depression. There was devastating unemployment, and the Chinese were made the scapegoats.[16]

Building Other Lines

The expansion of the railroads was even faster in the following decade. In 1850, the United States had 9,000 miles of track. In 1860, it had 30,000. In 1890, it had over 70,000 miles. Three years later, it had five transcontinental lines.

The first transcontinental railway was soon followed by four more links: (1) the Southern Pacific-Texas and Pacific, completed in 1883 from San Francisco to Texas by way of Yuma, Tucson, and El Paso; (2) the Atcheson, Topeka, and Santa Fe, completed in 1885 from Kansas City to Los Angeles via Santa Fe and Albuquerque; (3) the Northern Pacific completed in 1883 from Duluth, Minnesota, to Portland, Oregon, and the Great Northern (1893). The skill of the Chinese as railroad builders was much sought after, and Chinese worked on all these lines. Some 15,000 worked on the Northern Pacific, laying tracks in Washington, Idaho, and Montana; 250 on the Houston and Texas line; 600 on the Alabama and Chattanooga line; 70 on the New Orleans line. Nearly 500 Chinese were recruited for the Union Pacific even after the lines were joined. Many worked in the Wyoming coal mines and during the summer months doubled as track laborers. They carried the Southern Pacific lines over the burning Mojave Desert. They helped link San Francisco with Portland in 1887.

The Canadian Pacific seized the chance to enlist veteran Chinese railwaymen from the Southern Pacific and Northern Pacific railroads and also brought Chinese workers direct from China. In 1880, some 1,500 were working on that line, increasing to 6,500 two years later. Casualties were heavy on this line. Hundreds lost their lives while working on it.

Chinese railwaymen helped on the Central and Southern Pacific's main line down the San Joaquin Valley in 1870 and 1871. They worked on the hookup to Los Angeles and the loop with seventeen tunnels over the Tehachapi Pass completed in 1876. On this line, 1,000 Chinese worked on the 6,975-foot San Fernando Tunnel, the longest in the West. This rail link between San Francisco and Los Angeles, tapping the rich Central Valley, played a major role in the development of California's agriculture, later its biggest industry. They worked on the line north from Sacramento along the Shasta route to Portland, which was reached in 1887. In 1869, the Virginia and Truckee line employed 450 Chinese, veterans of the Central Pacific, to grade its track. When the Virginia and Truckee's Carson and Colorado branch line was planned from Mound House to Benton, its tough manager Yerington arranged with the unions for the grading to be done by white labor to Dayton and by Chinese from Dayton on south. "If the entire line had to be graded by white labor, I would not think of driving a pick into the ground, but would abandon the undertaking entirely," he said.[17]

Chinese laborers worked on the trans-Panamanian railway, which linked the Pacific and the Atlantic before the Panama Canal was completed. This railway played a major role in speeding up the economic development of the United States, but it was not built without sacrifice: hundreds of the Chinese builders died of fever and other causes during its construction.

This by no means completes the list of contributions of the Chinese railway workers. The transcontinental lines on which they worked "more than any other factor helped make the United States a united nation," writes the *Encyclopedia Britannica* ["Railways"]. They played a major role in building the communications network of iron roads that was the transport base of American industrial might in the twentieth century.

Speaking eloquently in favor of the Chinese immigrants, Oswald Garrison Villard said,

I want to remind you of the things that Chinese labor did in opening up the Western portion of this country. . . . [They] stormed the forest fastnesses, endured cold and heat and the risk of death at hands of hostile Indians to aid in the opening up of our northwestern empire. I have a dispatch from the chief engineer of the Northwestern Pacific telling how Chinese laborers went out into eight feet of snow with the temperature far below zero to carry on the work when no American dared face the conditions.[18]

And these men were from China's sun-drenched south, where it never snows.

In certain circles, there has been a conspiracy of silence about the Chinese railroadmen and what they did. When U.S. Secretary of Transportation John Volpe spoke at the "Golden Spike" centenary, not a single Chinese American was invited, and he made no mention in his speech of the Chinese railroad builders.

NOTES

1. Wesley S. Griswold, *A Work of Giants: Building the First Trans-Continental Railroad* (New York: McGraw-Hill, 1962).
2. Oscar Lewis, *The Big Four* (New York: Knopf, 1938).
3. Charles Nordhoff, *California* (Berkeley: Ten Speed Press, 1973). Reprint of 1873 ed.
4. George F. Seward, *Chinese Immigration* (New York: Arno Press and New York Times, 1970), pp. 22–23. Reprint of 1888 ed.
5. Lewis, *The Big Four*, pp. 74–75.
6. Lewis, *ibid.*, p. 74.
7. Quoted in *The Chinese Laborer and the Central Pacific* (San Francisco: The Southern Pacific Railway Co., 1978).
8. *Ibid.*

9. Lewis, *The Big Four.*

10. *Ibid.*

11. Alexander Saxton, "The Army of Canton in the High Sierra, *Pacific Historical Review* 35 (1966), 141–152.

12. John Galloway, *The First Trans-Continental Railroad, Central Pacific and Union Pacific* (New York: Simmons, Boardman, 1950).

13. *Chinese Immigration*, p. 25.

14. *Ibid.* p. 29.

15. Nordhoff, *California.*

16. *The Old West: The Railroaders* (New York: Time-Life Books, 1973).

17. Lucius Beebe and Charles Clegg, *Virginia and Truckee* (Berkeley, Calif.: Howell-North, 1963), pp. 15, 38.

18. Oswald Garrison Villard, "Justice for the Chinese," *Christian Century*, Vol. 6 (May 26, 1943), pp. 633–634.

Strength and
Skills for Hire (I):
On the Land

"Their value as farm laborers has been generally recognized and but for their ready and cheaper labor the farmer would often have been at a loss to clear his field and gather his crop. For the cultivation of sandy and less productive soil, and for the hot and marshy valley of San Joaquin, they prove more efficient than white men. . . . [They are] scarcely excelled [as vegetable growers].

HUBERT BANCROFT, California historian

The Chinese, being a despised minority fighting for the very right to exist in a hostile territory, could be employed at sub-subsistence wages. In other respects, moreover, they were ideal farm laborers. . . .
The Chinese actually taught their overlords how to plant, cultivate and harvest orchard and garden crops.

CAREY MCWILLIAMS, *Factories in the Fields: Story of Migratory Farm Labor in California*

THE CHINESE who came to America came to work. Where the work was, there they went. In 1870, there were 63,199 Chinese in the United States. Some had taken the railroad they themselves had helped to build and gone east or south, venturing into areas where few or no Chinese had ever been before, forming the nuclei of future Chinatowns in St. Louis, Chicago, Boston, New York, Philadelphia, and smaller communities scattered from the Canadian border to the Mississippi Delta. Others took jobs on new railways that were being built. A little Chinatown even grew up where the Texas-Pacific Railway passed through the dusty town of El Paso at the southern end of the Rockies.

They Went Where They Were Needed

We will speak of these ventures later; now we will follow the fortunes of those Chinese railway builders—the majority—who returned to the more familiar terrain of California. They made up over 12,000 of the 50,000 Chinese in the state. Some made their own way back to California. Others were gathered together by the Central Pacific, transported back to Sacramento or San Francisco, and there left to their own devices. The job completed and money saved, some returned to their ancestral villages in China. Most stayed on, because these were boom days in California. The placer mines had been exhausted, but, with the varied skills they had acquired in farming, land reclamation, building, and construction in China, and new skills mastered in America, these men could and did enter many occupations in the developing West.

Completion of the transcontinental railway brought a steady stream of white immigrants to California from the eastern and midwestern states, and California's population increased almost eighty percent between 1860 and 1870. The newcomers were not the footloose argonauts of the Gold Rush but settlers, artisans, farmers, and young men looking for careers. This burgeoning population needed food, clothing, and consumer goods of all kinds. The rancheros of California, turning into farmers, urgently needed hands for clearing fields, draining and irrigating, ditching and damming, planting and harvesting—skilled hands of all kinds. Adaptable labor was also in big demand for manufacturing in San Francisco and other towns. Before 1860, almost all industrial goods in California were imported from the East. Chinese labor, a fifth of the California labor force, switched from mining to the railways and to the farms and urban industries. Precisely because of their sojourner status, unencumberd by families, the Chinese could move readily from area to area, from occupation to occupation as needed.

Between 1860 and 1870, the Chinese populations in the mines were halved as the Chinese increasingly engaged in urban occupations and industry and in all kinds of farm work. Sacramento's Chinese population tripled. San Francisco in 1860 had only eight percent of the state's Chinese population; by the 1870s this figure was nearing thirty percent. In 1877, the *Alta California* reported 18,000 Chinese in the city's factories and several thousand more in the laundries and domestic service.[1] Farming became California's newest frontier and the state's biggest money maker. Between 1860 and 1880, the number of Chinese increased from 139 to nearly 2,000 in the San Joaquin Valley and from 22 to 2695 in Santa Clara.

Most of the existing literature fails to do justice to the variety and importance of the work that the Chinese did in nineteenth-century America. Their work was not a sometime thing. Besides producing millions of dollars in gold, silver, and coal and providing the major work force on the western end of the first transcontinental railway and several other lines, they also pioneered the California fisheries and worked the West Coast and Alaskan canneries; sailed American ships, fought in America's naval battles, cut lumber and firewood, and fed the lumber camps. They built houses of wood and stone. They worked in California's tin shops, fledgling paper and powder mills, and lead works; in the cigar, woolen, boot, shoe, and slipper industries; in tanneries, rope walks, and oakum shops. They made clothes, bags, brooms, cordage, matches, blacking, candles, soap, bottles, pottery, sacks, and leather goods. They drained the Sacramento and San Joaquin delta marshes. They helped put California's agriculture on the world market. They built roads, laid out vineyards, dug wine cellars, and established the raisin and fruit-growing industries. They washed clothes and provided the Wild West and, later, cities in the rest of the country with the delights of Chinese cuisine. In those early days, when there were few women in the West, the Chinese cooked, washed, and served in countless households needing domestic help. They provided essential urban services. They created capital and built major capital construction projects for the development of the West. Multi-million-dollar industries are now operating on the basis of the foundations they laid.

San Francisco Landfill

San Francisco's valleys and hills and its waterfront delight and astonish visitors today, but a massive job of excavation and landfill had to be done to fill in the marshes and tidelands, move the sand dunes and the haphazard hillocks, and lay down the streets and terrace the hillsides so that houses could be built on them. At a time when no machines existed for doing such work, it early attracted Chinese labor. On Market Street today, at the Bush Street intersection, a bronze plaque embedded in the pavement shows the original coastline and the new Embarcadero waterfront along the six-mile-long sea wall from Third Street, at the China Basin anchorage, to Aquatic Park. This indicates how extensive was the area of tideflats that had to be filled in behind the seawall. Landfill operations continued here for years as the Chinese with their carts and shovels poured in debris from the surrounding hills. Today, this area is the heart of the business and financial district—the highest-priced land in the Bay Area, selling at over $300 a square foot. One wonders what the Chinese who worked on this treasure with their carrying poles and baskets would have thought of it.

Finally, in the early 1870s, the Chinese were edged out of landfill work by white laborers and mechanization. They lost out to the "steam paddy."*

Farming the Central Valley

Strange as it may seem, land was a scarce commodity in California by the 1870s. The Pacific West was the American farmers' last frontier. Farmer settlers continued to arrive after the Gold Rush by wagon train in

---

* Paddy was the nickname given at the time to Irishmen, like Hans for Dutchmen and John for Chinese.

response to enticing advertisements. Many more came to the Golden State along the new transcontinental railway, but they found the best and most conveniently located farmlands near towns, roads, and railways already taken up by earlier arrivals, gold seekers turned settlers, speculators, and the big railway corporations who seemed to be grabbing everything within reach, both the old Mexican land grants and new government lands.

For building the first transcontinental railway, the Central (Southern) Pacific and Union Pacific Railway companies had received from Congress not only payment per mile but an extra 10 square miles of land for each mile of track they laid. Two years after that line was completed, another line was built, for a payoff of 40 square miles of land for each mile of track. From 1850 to 1880, the railway corporations acquired as land grants 180 million acres of land alongside their tracks, or almost one-tenth the area of the United States. In California alone they held 20,000,000 acres.[2] (In 1860, they had been given approximately 16 percent of all government-owned land.) The even sections of land between the alternate sections of land granted to the railroads were held reserved by Congress. Under the Homestead Act of 1862, this land was set aside for settlers. Citizens had the right to claim 80 acres free as a homestead or 160 acres by preemption at $2.50 an acre; however, they were under obligation to actually engage in farming and develop the land. But soon these lands were all taken up, and real estate brokers, land speculators, and railroad companies had a field day. In 1871, some 516 men owned 8,685,439 acres of land, and large-scale farms are still a feature of California agriculture. Newcomers either had to buy land from them at their prices or push out into the wilderness and reclaim land. It thus became economical to reclaim swamp and arid land that before would have been considered worthless.

The first attempts to raise crops in California were not promising. It took time and experience for farmers from the eastern states to realize that farming had to adjust to the peculiarities of the California climate. Even in 1872, Nordhoff commented that, while mining was played out, agriculture had not yet taken its place as the great money maker of the state. But this soon changed. In 1870, farm workers already made up thirty percent of the California labor force.

The valleys and deltas of the Sacramento and San Joaquin rivers comprise some of the finest farmlands in the state and nation. Forty miles wide from the Coast Range to the Sierra Nevada in the east, the Sacramento Valley contains 5 million acres of fertile, well-irrigated land. The San Joaquin Valley stretching to the south, with an average width of 40 to 50 miles between the Diablo Range and the Sierra, contains about 7 million acres from Stockton to the Tejon Pass, a distance of 300 miles. With contiguous valleys and low foothills, it provides some 18 million acres of farmland suitable for corn, wheat, flax, barley, vegetables, cotton, and subtropical fruits.

PART One THE COMING

Chinese immigrants on the *Alaska* on their way to the Golden Mountain
(San Francisco) from their South China villages. An 1876 print from *Harper's Weekly*.
Credit: The Bancroft Library.

A Chinese forty-niner with his rocker on his shoulder pole heads for the Mother Lode.
One in five of all forty-niners died within six months of reaching the West Coast.
Credit: The Bancroft Library.

Crack Chinese tracklayers of the Central Pacific place the last tie of the first transcontinental railway on May 10, 1869. *Credit: The Southern Pacific Co.*

A Chinese fishing junk on San Francisco Bay was nothing unusual in the nineteenth century. They were prohibited in 1894. *Credit: Stanford University Library.*

Chinese farmers helped lay out the first California vineyards in the Napa and Sonoma valleys. In 1886 Chinese made up 87.5 percent of California's farm labor. Hazing regulations drove them out of the vineyards. *Credit: California Historical Society.*

In 1888 labor in the salmon canneries of California and the Northwest Coast was 86 percent Chinese. This fell to 30 percent in 1935. No Chinese work in the industry now. *Credit: Oregon Historical Society.*

Chinese cooks were a familiar sight in West Coast lumber camps until well into the present century. *Credit: The Bancroft Library.*

A Chinese fishing village at Point San Pedro in San Francisco Bay. Chinese pioneered the West Coast fisheries from Oregon to Baja California. Only one fishing village remains today, that in Marin County. *Credit: The National Archives.*

When Wheat Was King

In 1872, Nordhoff described the San Joaquin valley: "Wheat, wheat, wheat, and nothing but wheat is what you see . . . as far as the eye can reach over the plain in every direction."[3] Huge acreages were sown to wheat. Two or four thousand acres was rated a "small farm." Twenty or forty thousand acres or more under wheat was an astonishing sight to farmers accustomed to the acreages more usual back East or in Europe. This valley alone sent 180,000 tons of wheat to San Francisco in 1872. California as a whole exported an estimated 700,000 tons. By that time, the railway ran the length of the valley as far as Merced and by the next year reached San Bernadino. Seven hundred 1,000-ton ships would be needed to transport the 18,000 wagonloads of wheat that were trundled to Stockton and then shipped in huge barges to San Francisco. In the 1870s, California farming employed more people than mining and produced a greater annual value of goods. Soon the state began exporting grain in ever larger amounts.

In 1881, San Francisco harbor was filled with 559 sailing ships come to load a single season's harvest. Rail freight was still uneconomically high, so it was well worth shipping this grain out by bulk over the 15,000 miles around Cape Horn to the eastern ports. Railways had idled much shipping in the eastern states and Europe, so vessels came from New England, from Britain's Liverpool and Glasgow, and from Norway, Germany, and France. Between 1881 and 1885, some 1,180 ships were carrying California grain. Industrialization in the urbanizing Western nations opened up new markets for California grain.

In 1856, California was producing just enough grain to feed its population of around 300,000. In 1860, it was growing 6 million bushels, more than all the other western states combined. By 1868, it was growing 20 million bushels and exporting 6 million bushels to Australia and England. In 1870, it grew 16 million bushels. By 1873, it was the largest wheat-growing state in the United States. In 1889 it produced 40 million bushels, valued at around $30 million.

By the mid-1870s, grain had replaced mining as the state's biggest employer and money maker. In those days and on into 1890, the Sacramento and San Joaquin Valleys, leading California's six main agricultural regions, were "the bread basket of Northern Europe." Grain took the place of gold as the main source of capital accumulation in the new state. The largest wheat farm in the world at that time was in the San Joaquin Valley. Chinese had gone into the fields in the 1870s and even before, and their numbers increased there steadily until by 1886 some 30,000 Chinese made up 87.5 percent of the agricultural labor force in California[4] and California's diversified, specialized farming in fruit, vegetables, and hops was growing up. This gives some inkling of the very considerable contribution of the Chinese in building the agricultural and financial power of the state.

This was the time when Yankee ingenuity was constantly astonishing the Old World. The gang-plow had been invented; four to eight plows mounted on a sturdy wooden frame and drawn by teams of up to eight horses could plow and sow 8–10 acres a day. The seed sower mounted in front of the plow scattered the seed, and the plow turned it under. Sowing was done in December to March, with the harvest in July, in the long, dry summer. A good farmer could raise five bushels of wheat an acre and make $3.50 an acre clear of all costs. Large landowners who preferred to rent out their land could expect to get nearly 100 percent annual return on their original investment. But Nordhoff noted that "the only care of owner and tenant is to get as much wheat out of the land each year as they can at the least expense."[5] In those days, the land was being ruthlessly exploited for a quick return. Nemesis was being sown.

Indians had been used as laborers on the early farms, but they were few in number, and the Chinese became the preferred labor. Nordhoff reported,

> The Chinese also make useful farm laborers, and are every year more used for this purpose. They learn very quickly, are accurate, painstaking, and trustworthy, and especially as gardeners and for all hand-labor, they are excellent. White laborers are—as in every thinly settled country—unsteady and hard to keep.[6]

In 1869, the Reverend A. W. Loomis reported in the California *Overland Monthly* (Vol. 2) that "on many ranches, all the laborers are Chinese." By the 1870s, the lion's share of work in the fields of California was done by Chinese.

The Chinese at first imported the sort of food they were accustomed to (they still do, to a considerable extent), but soon they were growing and fishing for a great deal of it in the valleys, rivers, and coastal waters of California, not only for themselves but also for the general public. In 1872, Nordhoff calculated, they produced two-thirds of all the vegetables in California. Carey McWilliams estimates that in 1870 one-tenth, in 1880 one-third, and in 1884 one-half of California's farm workers and market gardeners were Chinese. As late as 1902, says McWilliams, the *Los Angeles Times* reported that "the Chinese are the only people who will do ranch work faithfully."[7] The white labor going out to the fields and available for transient work at that time tended to be tramps and were unreliable workers.[8]

Some have questioned Carey McWilliams' estimate of the numbers of Chinese in the California farm labor force, but Harry Krade, assistant director of California's Department of Food and Agriculture in 1979, supports McWilliam's estimate.

Because Chinese constituted the majority of the field hands, their contribution was decisive in the emergence of wheat, fruit and vegetables as the prime element at that time in accumulating capital for the further growth of California. George F. Seward, former U.S. ambassador to China, who took a deep interest in the Chinese immigrants, states flatly that the California farmer "received a great deal of assistance from the Chinese both directly and because of the average cheapening of labor marked by their competition. Whether it would have been possible at higher wages to cultivate wheat for exportation may be doubted."[9] It was this grain produced so abundantly by Chinese labor and American technology that enabled aggressive entrepreneurs such as Isaac Friedlander to develop the export market and so create more jobs in trade, transport, and industry.

This cheap labor should not be cursorily dismissed. Too many scholarly writers tend to sneer at these "cheap" laborers. Their labor may have been relatively cheap, or more correctly "less expensive," but it was good, honest, and skilled. Actually, it was not cheap. It was competitive. At $20 a month, it was comparable to the going rate in the eastern states but below that demanded by the white labor available in California, where labor was scarce and wages demanded by white labor high. Unable to get Chinese labor, California farmers would have had to employ white labor (hard to get anyway) at a cost of least $30 a month with board. At that rate, they simply could not have made their farms competitive on the export market, and all California would have suffered. As it was, paid $2 a day with food, in the three harvest months of frenzied work, many Chinese and others could with luck make their "fortunes" in a few years. The Chinese also quickly learned the ways of the free enterprise system and, as soon as feasible, demanded the going rate for the job.[10] Even in 1867, they were getting $1.50 a day and board.

As for taking jobs away from white labor, this was nonsense. White farm labor was simply not available in sufficient numbers. As might be expected at the start, Chinese used to working with slow-footed water buffalo or oxen, were not good at managing teams of horses or running machinery. So, on the farms, as on the railway, Chinese labor was often complementary to white labor rather than competitive. The Chinese farm worker riding the header wagon, discharging the load, sacking the grain and binding the sheaves, gave the competitive edge to the California farmer.

As regards the general character of Chinese farmworkers, the descriptions offered by reliable observers stand in marked contrast to the recurrent racial slurs. Witnesses at the 1876 congressional committee hearings on Chinese immigration enthusiastically praised the Chinese farm workers. Colonel Hollister, when asked, "Could you raise wheat here and export it without Chinese labor?" answered, "I think not." George D. Roberts, a farmer, testified that Chinese farmhands were "better than the Swede, and the Swede is the best worker we have had. There is no doubt that the Chinaman is the best laborer we have had for certain classes of work."[11] Forbidden by the 1870 Alien Land Law to purchase land, quite a few Chinese rented plots to work on or worked others' plots and shared the profits with them. They brought with them their traditional farming skills.

In the 1870s and 1880s, most of the peanuts grown in California were raised by Chinese farmers in Napa and Tahama. The *Red Bluff Beacon* in its November 15, 1865, and September 1, 1870, issues described the Tehama County peanuts as "the sweetest we ever tasted."

In the 1870s Chinese farmers worked strawberry patches on leased land in Santa Clara valley, and they were the first to raise celery as a commercial crop in California. It was as late as 1891 when a group of them were contracted by a Mr. D. E. Smeltzer in Orange County to reclaim marshland and raise celery on it.

A firm at St. Gabriel started a mulberry plantation and took on forty Chinese on four-year contracts that provided them a house and garden if they stayed on permanently. This was the first such inducement to Chinese to bring in a family. But this project to raise silk in California failed; the climate was unsuitable.

Some Chinese farmers rented fruit trees from their neighbors, tended the crop, then harvested, packed, and sold it.

Reclaiming the Tule Lands

Monopolization of huge areas of land by the railways and land speculators and the consequent shortage of cheap farm land now made it well worth the effort to reclaim California's swamps and fertile, although arid, deserts, and especially the tule reed lands in the Sacramento and San Joaquin river deltas and bordering floodlands.

The tule lands are simply floodland deposits of silt and decayed vegetable matter composed of swamp grasses, tule (which grows ten feet high in a season and decays every year), and other reeds. Such swamplands had been given by Congress to the state, and the state had given them almost free to individuals. They were sold for a dollar an acre, with only 20¢ down, this being refunded to the owners who reclaimed the land within three years. The early farmers here, jumping from one soggy patch to another, were nicknamed "tule hoppers."

In winter and spring, the deltas were vast spreads of water. In the early days, even in 1861 or 1862, river pilots at flood time could take their paddle-wheelers clear across country in a straight line from Stockton to Sacramento over wheatfields and Chinese potato patches covered with twelve feet of water.

As noted earlier, the Chinese who came to this area were predominantly from the Pearl River delta in China's Guangdong Province. They knew the techniques of draining, reclamation, and flood prevention in this type of country better than any others from China—and perhaps in the world, except for the Dutch. They brought these techniques with them from their native villages, and they applied that knowledge with magnificent results in far-off California.

When one of the tule hoppers learned of the prowess of the Chinese, he hired a gang of them to raise a levee 12 miles long around his island. Soon all the fifty-five tule islands in the delta were protected by "China levees" such as the 29-mile one around Grand Island and the 49-mile one around Sherman Island.

The smaller islands could be reclaimed piecemeal but the land bordering the main channel could only be reclaimed on a massive scale. Farmers banded together to form reclamation districts. Taxes on the benefited land were used to pay for the levees and drainage channels. Chinese disillusioned with seeking gold found steady and usually more familiar work here, although it held no promise of quick wealth. It was hard work. They often labored waist deep in water. Pay was a dollar a day—and they supplied their own food—or 13½ cents per cubic yard of earth moved. Most white laborers in those days, more interested in gold mining, would not take such work and, when they did, asked for a dollar a day and board. When Charles Nordhoff passed this way in 1872, 600 miles of levees had been completed among the islands alone. By that time, thousands of Chinese workers had returned to California from building the transcontinental railway, and reclamation work was going ahead on a big scale. Nordhoff reports that "Chinese labor is used almost entirely in making the levees."[11]

After an engineer had planned the work, groups of Chinese under their foremen contracted for the jobs. They worked as teams, as they had on the railway, providing their own food and living in their movable tent towns, taking care of the whole job of building the levee and burning off the tule reeds to prepare for the first planting on this potentially rich soil. If the dry tules had not been washed away, a man was sent to dig holes through the upper sod. He was followed by another, carrying a load of straw wisps, who stuck a wisp into each hole, lit it with a match, and went on. At this rate, 1,500 acres could be burned for $100. Floods often undid months of work, but slowly the Courtland River, as the Chinese called the Sacramento, after the once thriving Chinatown at Courtlands, or the "Big Ravine" (Daihang), was harnessed.

By the end of 1877, they had reclaimed over 5 million acres of tule land. These produced 75 bushels of grain per acre and were also excellent for fruit and vegetable growing. Values rose from $1 to $100 an acre.[12]

California vegetable and fruit farming expanded rapidly to satisfy the demands of eastern markets. The surveyor general of California, in testimony before the congressional investigating committee at its San Francisco hearings preparing to introduce the Chinese Exclusion Act, stated that by 1876 Chinese labor on the railways and the tule lands reclamation projects alone was worth over $289 million to the economy of the state of California.[13]

In the late 1880s, the character of the work on the levees changed. Mechanization was introduced. "Fresno scrapers" were brought in, and Swedes and Irish drovers were hired to handle the teams of horses or mules that powered them. When the first teams ran into difficulties, a Chinese devised the "tule shoe" that prevented their hooves from sinking into the boggy soil. But the day of skilled Chinese hand labor was over.

This work of building the levees and preparing the land for cropping went on for nearly half a century. Today, a great system of levees has been built up by steam-powered dredges and bulldozers. They are as broad as two-lane highways and are eight times as massive as the Chinese-made levees that form their cores. It is a stupendous sight to drive along these levees for mile after mile. Several feet below them are the tops of pear and peach orchards, spreading as far as the eye can reach in every direction. The Sacramento Delta supports a $400 million agricultural industry. The total length of the levees is over 2,000 miles, holding within their banks 1,000 miles of scenic waterways used by freight vessels and a thriving tourist boat industry.

Grain, Fruit, and Flowers

As the land was reclaimed, many Chinese stayed on as farm hands and harvested its crops of grain, vegetables, and fruit. Because of the Alien Land Act of 1870, forbidding ownership of land by aliens, not many farmed independently. Some who did rented land and turned sandy patches and wasteland in the open spaces and suburbs of San Francisco into flourishing truck gardens. Others worked plots on a profit-sharing basis with owners of land. They collected the wild mustard of Monterey. In Santa Clara county the Chew, Wong, Yee, and Chow families raised most of San Francisco's chrysanthemums and sweet peas. (They still raise fifty percent of the mums. Their total crop is worth some $5 million a year.) The Chinese peddler of flowers and fruit was a familiar figure. Today just a few Chinese are farming, producing fine crops of vegetables, including Chinese cabbage, *bai cai*, for the restaurants and greengrocers of Chinatown, delivered fresh each day.

Wheat's uncontested reign in California was soon to end. Canadian, Australian, and Argentinian competition reduced prices and California growers realized that this monoculture was impoverishing their soil. In the crisis-ridden "terrible seventies," 100 percent profits had dropped to 4 percent, and furious debates switched farmer's interest to fruit and vegetables and sugar beet.

Pear trees had been planted in the Mother Lode country during the Gold Rush as far north as Shasta County, and by 1860 there were 350,000 still growing. In 1872, nearly two million apple trees were growing in the state. On this basis the California farmers used Chinese farm labor to create a flourishing new industry of such cash crops as pears and apples, plums, walnuts, almonds, hops, and other fruit and vegetables. They worked the first fields of asparagus. They did most of the squat work in the valleys. Between 1871 and 1884, fruit shipments from California increased from 1.8 to 12 million pounds.

It is generally agreed that much of the development of the present multimillion-dollar fruit industry of California could not have been done without the traditional lore that the Chinese farmers brought with them to the West and introduced to the farmers there between the 1860s and 1890s. Without them, California's growth would have been long delayed. For over four decades, the Chinese were the "mainstay of the orchardist" in California, tending, picking, and packing these crops. Over 2,500 of them worked each season in the Sacramento valley orchards. In raising root crops, they planted, hoed, weeded and harvested. They cut firewood and made charcoal. They played a big role in bringing irrigation to a million acres of California farmland by 1890. This was a vital contribution to fruit and vegetable farming. They worked on the Pilarcilos Creek reservoir.

When railway freight charges finally dropped, when refrigerated cars were introduced in 1888, and when Luther Burbank introduced new well-traveling fruit strains, wheat was finally dethroned by the new California-style specialized (diversified) agriculture. Carey McWilliams contends that the introduction of large-scale fruit farming, with its demands of intensive labor (and that at a time when wheat farming too was developing), would have been delayed perhaps a quarter century if a large and capable Chinese labor force had not been available.[14] Chinese were also early workers in the sugar beet industry in Isleton, near the mouth of the Sacramento River. The first sugar beet factory in California opened in Alvarado, Alameda County, in 1870.

Expulsion from the Fields

Although in the mid-1870s economic crisis and its resulting unemployment, riotous mobs had attacked Chinese orchardists and farm workers in northern California's Chico, Oroville, Grass Valley, Colusa, and Lava Beds, most of the big farmers in the county farm associations vigorously opposed the expulsion campaigns and violence. They wanted Chinese labor for its availability and skill. This was so also in the anti-Chinese riots that rocked many small towns in the mid-1880s. Colonel Bee, an American and consul for the Chinese in San Francisco, testified that at that time, there were few white farm workers in California. The only exception to this was in the northern counties of the Central Valley. Here lumbering and mining operations had concentrated a white labor force that, in the 1873–1878 depression years, drifted into farm work and became the nucleus of California's future army of migrant and often vagrant farm workers.

The number of Chinese farm workers employed in the lower San Joaquin Valley and the new fruit-growing districts around Los Angeles actually increased in the 1880s. As in the gold fields and on the railway, they were accustomed to migratory work in well-organized and disciplined collectives, were uncomplaining (even under hard conditions) as long as they were reasonably well-paid, fed themselves, and in the off-seasons were out of the way, hibernating in the larger Chinatowns.

Large-scale, national-market-oriented, diversified California farming on its seasonal north-south axis early developed the need for an army of cheap labor willing to follow the crops. And it was preferable that this army should be able to move itself, not bothering its employers with demands for proper accommodation or expecting to be looked after when there was no work to be done. The Chinese fit the bill. They were available in large numbers after the end of gold mining and work on the transcontinental railway, they had no families to bring with them to the fields, they were adaptable, and their numbers were regularly replenished from Guangdong.

But in the 1890s Australia, Canada, and Argentina were dumping their grain crops on the world market, and the price of wheat fell from $1.48 per hundredweight to $0.90. Wheat farming was also on the decline in the Great Plains, and when at the same time the silver crisis shut down hard-rock mining in the mountain states, more and more unemployed white workers from the East drifted down into California's central valleys. By June 1893, twenty-seven banks in California had failed. Another of the ten-year cyclical economic crises hit the economy as the sudden massive increase in the numbers of white unemployed caused radical change. There was renewed and violent agitation against the Chinese, who had jobs others wanted.

As in every anti-Chinese campaign, economics had a great deal to do with the way various groups reacted. The San Joaquin Valley was becoming the center of the fruit growing industry, and the local fruit growers at that time were largely dependent on Chinese labor for tending, harvesting, and packing their crops. They protested the forcible expulsion of the Chinese because they were simply unwilling to trust their delicate crops to the tender mercies of "sandlot hoodlums and agitators." "The Chinese have become the only considerable body of people who understand how to pack fruit for Eastern shipment," wrote the *Pacific Rural Press* on June 10, 1893.

But in August that year, the rumblings grew louder. In Fresno, where there was much white unemployment, worried businessmen called on local growers to dismiss Chinese help and take on white labor. The growers, however, had found the Chinese perfectly filled their need for cheap, skilled, mobile and temporary labor and were by no means eager to take on untrained white labor as a welfare measure.

In those days, there was no welfare system, no unemployment insurance to sustain the victims of an economic crisis. The 1893 crisis was especially severe. Sacramento physically drove its unemployed out of the city. Although rioters were accused of being out for plunder and gratification of their taste for violence, most were simply desperate men whose families had no means of succor except inadequate charitable institutions. On August 18, 1893, Fresno, center of the raisin industry, erupted in an anti-Chinese riot and 500 Chinese were driven from their jobs in nurseries and vineyards. The *Los Angeles Times* reported similar attacks in Tulare, Visalia, and other points in the San Joaquin Valley, in Riverside, Selma, Madera, Stockton, Bakersfield, Compton, Huron, San Bernardino, and in Calistoga, Vacaville, Ukiah, and other places. Chinese were driven out at gunpoint and loaded on trains for San Francisco. In Southern California's citrus country, Chinese in Redlands were attacked and robbed and their homes set on fire and looted. The National Guard was called out and martial law enforced for several days.

What made matters worse for the Chinese was that passage of the Exclusion Act in 1882 and other subsequent acts (like the draconian Geary Act) gave a stamp of Congressional approval to anti-Chinese violence. Faced with an alliance of unemployed and small farmers who were hard put to compete

with the big growers—the main employers of Chinese labor—the big growers
had also decided that it was more prudent to go along with the rioters than
with the voteless Chinese. The mass exodus of Chinese from the fields resulted,
according to one estimate, in half a million acres of land temporarily going
out of production.[15]

When fruit farming faltered in the wake of the expulsion of the Chinese
from the fields, and the California growers needed a quick profit crop, they
found it in the sugar beet. Chinese had been the first workers back in the
1870s when the first sugar beet factory had been set up in Alvarado, Alameda
county, and the Chinese had worked in the early sugar beet fields in Isleton
in the Sacramento delta. But the real expansion of that crop and of the
strawberries that were raised with it took place in the later 1890s, when Japanese
labor had replaced Chinese.

So it was that the Chinese were the first of that strange army of migrant
farm workers in California, which has been successively replenished by the
Japanese, Koreans, Hindus, Filipinos, and Mexicans (Chicanos). As Carey
McWilliams pointed out: "From 1860–1930, a majority of the migratory army
has been made up of foreign workers, most of them ineligible to citizenship."[16]

Although most of the Chinese farm workers had packed up and left or
retreated to the relative safety of San Francisco, even late in the 1920s and
after numbers of Chinese remained in such communities as Locke, which
had steadfastly resisted racist agitation, or gradually returned to such places
as San Mateo and Santa Clara to resume their flower growing.

The economy began to pick up in 1896 and boomed in the McKinley
era of successful war against Spain, and the Alaska Gold rush. As usual in a
period of economic prosperity, the Chinese issue tended to be relegated to
the storeroom. The Japanese had taken their place as scapegoats for such
discontent as there was. And Samuel Gompers of the AFL was already
preparing the ideological ground for attacks on other immigrant groups such
as the Southern Italians, Southern French, and Slavs. In the 1940s, there
were practically no Chinese among the 243,000 farm workers in California.

Chinese continued to farm and harvest asparagus in small communities
in Courtland, Isleton, Walnut Grove, and Lockport up until the 1950s. By
that time, many of the old-timers had died, and the increasingly urbanized,
educated younger generation (with a few notable exceptions) showed no
inclination to go into agriculture.

The Chinese of America had toiled well in the California fields and in
Hawaii too. (See Appendix 1.) Both of these states today have flourishing
agricultural economies. In 1979, California was the nation's leading farm state
and the sixth greatest agricultural state in the world. Its farms produced $11
billion a year in income and 10 percent of the value of the nation's exports.
The San Joaquin Valley alone, on 8.5 million acres of farmland, produced
half of that amount in tomatoes, sugar beets, grapes, hay, cotton, and other
crops.

In the Vineyards

When you savor some delightful California wine, give a thought to the Chinese pioneers who helped lay out these flourishing vineyards. They did yeoman work in building up the California wine industry. John Sutter began cultivating the native California wild grape in the early 1840s, but that, unaided, would not have sufficed to create a viable national wine industry. It was Agonston Haraszthy, who became the Father of California viniculture. In 1860–1861, with the help of Chinese workers recruited for him by the San Francisco labor contractor Ho Po, he planted 195,000 selected European vines in his Buena Vista vineyard in Sonoma County, and when these were well set he was producing 6,500 gallons of wine a year, in addition to the fresh grapes he sent to market in San Francisco.

He paid his Chinese work force the eastern states' wage for laborers' work: $8 a month with board. White labor in labor-short California was demanding $30 a month with board, a wage that would have made it impossible for California winemakers to get a foothold and compete successfully in the industry. As the industry prospered, however, the Chinese demanded and received the same wages, but that lessened their competitive appeal, and white political agitation drove them from the vineyards.

Haraszthy's work force comprised part of the thousands of men who had been left unemployed by completion of the transcontinental railway. Soon other vineyard owners were following his example, and Chinese were not only preparing the land for sowing, but planting the vines, doing the field work, and building in the Napa and Sonoma valleys. Haraszthy had them cut his first wine storage tunnel through solid limestone rock in 1864. It was 170 feet long and 12½ feet high. They cut two other cellars for him later, and 100 worked for him permanently in the vineyards on improvements. They cut other cellar caves at the Beringer winery in 1877, and at the Schramsberg winery in the late 1860s and 1870s. These are documented.[17] Locals say that everybody knows they dug the Cresta Blanca caves as well, three cave tunnels cut in 1884 in Livermore, totaling a fifth of a mile underground. When Richard Nixon made his historic visit to China in 1972, he served Schramsberg champagne at his state banquet to his Chinese guests. (Henry M. Rubin, "Chinese Heritage," *San Francisco Chronicle*, November 12, 1969). They also cut tunnels 150 feet into the limestone hills in 1884 at the Jacob Grin winery in the Napa valley and built the Greystone winery, managed by William B. Bourne and Everett Wise, which was then the world's largest such winery built of dressed natural stone.[18]

When the Chinese were not cutting tunnels, they did all the vineyard work, from clearing and tilling the soil to harvesting. In 1887, torrential rains threatened to ruin the crop in the Napa Valley, so they waded out in mud impassable to carts and brought the grapes out by hand. They did all the work of making raisins, too, from picking the grapes to drying and packing them, for $1 a day. As late as 1871, making raisins was still considered an iffy business—just a few tons were produced. But when Charles Nordhoff visited the central valleys a year later, he found the industry established and considered one of the most promising in the state. The biggest merchant in the trade told him that there was a market for all the raisins that could be produced and that the best were preferred to foreign imports, even to the Malaga. The Chinese were doing all the work of raisin making.

Raisins are made out of fully ripe grapes. The bunches were cut and laid out on a hard clay floor in the open air or on brown paper laid between the vine rows. After being turned from time to time and cured in the sun for 18 to 24 days, the bunches were then put in layers about a foot thick on shelves in a raisin house and allowed to "sweat" a little for five or six weeks until dry enough to box.

The Chinese were in the raisin country from the 1870s to the 1880s–1890s, when around 20,000 tons were produced. Fifty-three percent of the grape crop was made into wine and brandy; the rest was sold as table grapes or made into raisins. The raisin industry, based in Fresno County and growing some 250,000 tons of raisins, is now worth over $258 million a year to California.

By 1880, California was producing $600,000 worth of wines, rising to $1 million in 1890 and $4 million in 1900, when its 40 million gallons of wine constituted 80 percent of all wine made in the United States. "Without the Chinese who worked so diligently . . . there would not be the great wineries, beautiful cellars . . . and green fields which made the Napa Valley one of the most inviting places in the world in which to live," writes Charlotte T. Miller.[19]

William Heintz of Glen Ellen, who probably knows more than any man about the Chinese in the wine country, estimates that in the 1880s Chinese made up 80–85 percent of the vineyard workers. Their efforts in setting up the industry enabled it to grow into the $2 billion-per-year enterprise it is today, with an annual output of some 500 million gallons of wine. But in 1885–1890 they were gradually driven out of the industry and its fields, and others took over. A punitive discriminatory tax of $2.50 a month was levied on them, and California labor leaders introduced a "Made with White Labor" label that winemakers were forced to put on their bottles, true or not. When investigators came to the vineyards, owners gave their Chinese hands the day off to keep them out of sight. But this subterfuge wore thin. With completion of the transcontinental railways, more of the settler type of immigrant came to California from the eastern states. A labor shortage turned into a labor glut, and the Chinese were edged or driven out. Anti-Chinese outbreaks were sporadic until the mid-1870s. Then they became coordinated into an anti-Chinese movement.

Santa Rosa is one example. The *Santa Rosa Democrat* of Sonoma County wrote in 1886; "We all want to get rid of the Chinamen. They can be starved out by non-patronage." Nonpatronage resolutions were passed by racist groups and, having witnessed in other places what that meant, the Chinese fled the vineyards. That very year, 500 of 600 Chinese left the county. T. J. Geary, author of the notorious Geary Chinese Exclusion Bill, was Congressman from Sonoma. But the Chinese of America have their monument in the fact that in all these three industries in which they played so large a role in founding—grapes, wine, and raisins—California still stands first among all the United States.

This chapter on the Chinese immigrants' contributions to American farming would not be complete without a mention of three men: Guey Jones, a former laundryman who helped to pioneer the superior strains of rice in Glenn County California that became staples of the California rice economy. When outside supplies of rice were cut off in World War I, he was one of the Chinese farmers in Glenn and Colusa Counties who rapidly expanded rice production. His descendants are still carrying on his work today, cultivating as much as 1,000 acres. Ah Bing, a gold miner and a cook, who finally went to work as a nurseryman with Seth Lewelling in Milwaukie, Oregon, where he was largely responsible for developing the Bing cherry. And, finally, Luey Gim Gong.

LUEY GIM GONG

They called Luey Gim Gong the "Chinese Burbank." In 1872, at the age of twelve, he came to America from South China's Guangdong Province without formal education or money. He bred the orange bearing his name and helped to lay the foundation for Florida's multimillion-dollar citrus industry.

He sailed from Hong Kong in a small schooner and after two months at sea sailed through San Francisco's Golden Gate. Met at the dock by the greeters of the Six Companies, he was whisked away to the hostel for newcomers and was glad to get a job at a wage of just over a dollar a day in a shoe factory. The state was booming. He, like everyone else, was sure that he was going to get rich. All one had to do was work hard and save. Up to that point, his experiences had been the same as those of tens of thousands of other Chinese immigrants from the impoverished South China villages. But within the year, the dream was shattered. The crisis of the Terrible Seventies had begun. Factory owners, pleading hardship, cut wages to levels on which only famine-inured Chinese farm boys could survive. A prison superintendent complained that wages in the free world outside were undercutting wages paid to jail inmates. The anti-Chinese agitation ignited, and working Chinese were vilified.

A peaceable soul, Luey Gim Gong was glad to volunteer to work in a shoe factory owned by one Calvin Sampson on the other side of the continent in North Adams, Massachusetts, but when he arrived there he found that he and the other Chinese with him had been brought in as strike breakers. But the plight of the Chinese who did not know a word of English, moved the New Englanders, and hostility turned to understanding. They set up courses to teach the immigrants English, and eventually cordial relations were established.

This was how Luey was befriended by Miss Fanny Burlingame, a cousin of the former U.S. ambassador to China who, as the Chinese representative, had negotiated the Burlingame Treaty. That friendship saved Luey's life. In the close atmosphere of the factory and the harsh New England weather, he contracted tuberculosis and was glad to leave the mill at her invitation and become her gardener. Using the skills of artificial pollination he had learned from his mother in their garden plot in China, he began to breed new strains of fruit, particularly the tomato. But his health continued to deteriorate, and when he was told by the doctor that he had only one more year to live, he returned to China to die. He was fourteen years old.

Back home in subtropical Guangdong, he recovered and when Miss Fanny offered him work as gardener in her new Florida home, he eagerly accepted and sailed again for America. In the congenial atmosphere of De Land in a quiet garden and adjacent orchard, he resumed his experiments in breeding cherries, apples, and citrus fruit. He had a special interest in oranges. They had been brought from China to the United States by the Spaniards in the eighteenth century, but had not taken well in Florida and often mottled and rotted on the branches when the season was wet. Luey pollinated the late-ripening Hart orange with pollen from the Mediterranean sweet orange and got one orange with fifteen seeds from this crossing. Twelve trees matured from these seeds, and one was the first of the famed Luey Gim Gong orange strain.

But the final prize was the result of a further mating of the flowers of this tree with the Hart Late, Tardiff orange. This produced five trees with remarkable fruit. The new oranges were juicy, sweet and good keepers. They could hang for months on the bough and keep fresh. The trees, too, were cold resistant, hardy, and stood up well to rainy weather. Because the fruit could hang for so long on the tree, ripening from June to September, it could be shipped when other oranges were scarce and thus command the highest price. The first test shipment was to North Adams. There was no spoilage en route, and they sold for $2 a box more than other oranges.

The American Pomological Society awarded the new orange its Wilder Medal in 1911. The next year, the well-known Glen Saint Mary Nurseries of Florida signed a contract with Luey to market the new variety, and it was launched with great fanfare in its catalogue. Growers gave it lavish praise. "A marvel in the citrus family," wrote the manager of the Florida Citrus Exchange. The Glen Saint Mary Nurseries correctly prophesied that it would "far surpass in value and in reputation any other variety of any kind of fruit we have ever introduced." It gave Florida what California already had: an all-year-round orange. It became so advantageous to raise that California itself turned to it.

Fanny Burlingame died in 1903, leaving her protegee the Florida grove and $12,000. Luey did well with his plant breeding, but he was not a good businessman and unscrupulous people stole the results of his labors. In the end, lame and unable to get around, he lived in deep poverty, helped only by a few friends until his death in 1925. He became a naturalized American citizen, a unique exception to the exclusion laws.

NOTES

1. Alexander Saxton, *The Indispensable Enemy: A Study of the Anti-Chinese Movement in California* (Los Angeles: University of California Press, 1971).
2. Carey McWilliams, *Factories in the Fields: The Story of Migratory Farm Labor in California* (Santa Barbara; Pereguine, 1971).
3. Charles Nordhoff, *California.* (Berkeley: Ten Speed Press, 1974). Reprint of 1873 ed.
4. Report of the State Bureau of Labor (Washington, D.C., 1886).
5. Nordhoff, *California.*
6. *Ibid.*
7. Carey McWilliams, *California, the Great Exception* (New York: Current Books, 1949), p. 152.
8. Stan Steiner, *Fusang* (New York: Harper & Row, 1978), pp. 144–145.
9. George Seward, *Chinese Immigration.* (New York: Arno Press and New York Times, 1970). Reprint of 1888 ed.
10. Nordhoff, *California.*
11. Seward, *Chinese Immigration.* p. 59.
12. McWilliams, *California.*
13. Ho Yow, quoted by Tien-lu Li, *Congressional Policy on Chinese Immigration* (New York: Arno Press, 1979). Reprint. See also How Yow, "The Attitude of the United States Towards the Chinese," *Forum* 29, p. 388.
14. McWilliams, *Factories.* Ibid.
15. M. B. Schrieke, *Alien Americans* (New York: Viking Press, 1936).
16. McWilliams, *ibid.*
17. Idwal Jones, *Vines in the Sun* (New York: Morrow, 1949).
18. *Ibid.*
19. Charlotte T. Miller, *Grapes, Queues and Quicksilver.* Unpublished manuscript, 1966. Quoted in St. Helena *Star*, July 17, 1883.

Strength and Skills for Hire (2): In the Fisheries

VIII

The Chinese pioneered much of the early days of fishing in California and deserve more credit than they have received.

WILLIAM L. SCOFIELD, *Marine Fisheries Dates*

WHEN YOU enjoy San Francisco's succulent seafood these days, remember the men and women who pioneered the West Coast fisheries and laid the basis for what is today a $140 million-dollar fishing industry.

Pioneering the California Fisheries

The Chinese first began to fish West Coast waters in a small way in 1849, and in 1852 one group was fishing on a commercial scale off San Francisco's Rincon Point (near Mission Creek) while another group was based in Monterey. A year later, the Monterey group had a whole fleet of Chinese-style craft. In 1854, the Rincon Point village had 150 men with twenty-five boats, landing a daily catch of 3,000 pounds of sturgeon, shark, and herring. Soon other Chinese fishermen were catching salmon on the Sacramento and San Joaquin rivers, and other villages were set up at Point San Bruno. Scouting out the best fishing grounds, they started the fishing industry in smelt in San Diego, and by the 1880s they were fishing from Oregon to Baja California. They caught general market fish in San Francisco Bay outside the Golden Gate, Monterey, and San Diego. Their small sampans brought in smelt, sole, rock cod, and other rock fish. Fishermen using large junks caught barracuda. Importing bag nets from China, they caught shrimp from camps at Hunter's Point, China Point, and other places on the Bay. They caught clams, crabs, and lobsters. They gathered abalone as far south as Bahia de Tortugas and began to harvest seaweed from Humboldt Bay before 1857. And they introduced seaweed, abalone, and squid (in 1863) to the early California diet, which was severely limited.[1]

At a time when California had not yet developed its rich agricultural resources, gold miners up in the hills in the early 1850s subsisted on a basic diet of salt pork and hardtack biscuits. But when the Chinese developed the fisheries, fish were sold fresh and often alive in San Francisco, as is the custom to this day in Chinatown. Part of the catch was dried for the use of Chinese miners up in the hills.

By the late 1860s, when work on the first transcontinental railway was ending, more Chinese entered the trade. By 1870, about 100 shrimpers were bringing in regular catches of succulent blacktail shrimp. Ten years later, their number had increased over eight times. The 1880s and 1890s were boom times for the trade. Chinese fishing camps were dotted up and down the coast from Humboldt Bay in Oregon to Baja California in Mexico, at Rio Vista, on the Sacramento River; San Pablo Bay, Point San Pedro (Marin County); Bay View (South San Francisco); Oakland; Pescadero (San Mateo); Soquel (Santa Cruz); Carmel; Point Mugu; Santa Barbara and off San Diego. They were bringing in salmon, sturgeon, smelt, flounder, sculpin, shrimp, crab, abalone, clams, oysters, and other seafood.

By 1888, there were over twenty villages in San Francisco and San Pablo bays, one at Tomales Bay, four in the Monterey-Pacific Grove area, two near San Diego, one on the island of San Clemente and others on the Sacramento River, with over 2,000 fishermen all told.

In 1892, California held sixth place among the United States in value of seafood. But by that time the numbers of Chinese in the trade had begun to drop sharply. While they still made up 50 percent of the fishing crews in the 1880s, by 1890 Italians made up 30 percent of the work force. A smaller number of Portuguese and whites made up the rest, fishing whales and barracuda outside the bays. Anti-Chinese agitation and harassing legislation spurred on by the 1882 Exclusion Act was making it more difficult for Chinese

Graph 1. Duration of Chinese Fishing Operations on the West Coast

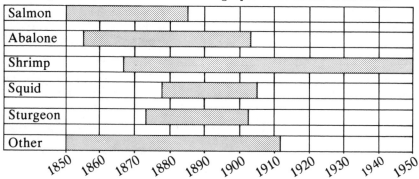

Source: Robert Nash, *"Chinese Shrimp Industry in California"* (Ph.D. diss., UCLA, 1973). Maritime Museum, San Francisco.

to fish. The attacks were sporadic and sometimes strictly localized. For example, Chinese abalone junks were not allowed to leave for lower California. Even in the 1860s feeling against the Chinese in the Sacramento River area was so intense that a Chinese found fishing there for salmon stood a good chance of being lynched on the spot. Taking advantage of the situation, other fisherman used strong-arm harassment to push the Chinese out of fishing. By 1890, Chinese made up only 20 percent of the work force; Italians, Portuguese, Anglo-Saxons, Scandinavians, and Slavs comprised the majority. Between 1895 and 1898, the San Diego, Sacramento, and San Joaquin villages disappeared. The Monterey village was set afire by an arsonist in 1906, and the inhabitants were prevented from rebuilding.

Some fishing camps represented considerable investments. The one set up by the Sah Wong Ty Company in 1895 for thirty men on a marshland site was a $15,000 investment. Decline in numbers of Chinese in the industry was swift. In 1900, there were 1,000 fishermen in thirty camps and villages. By 1910, there were fewer than ten settlements. In 1913 and 1914, still more men left for homes in China or took up other occupations. No fishery used by the Chinese was ever destroyed by them. They were edged out of the trade sector by sector. By 1905, less than a hundred were left in shrimping, their last foothold. Jenny Lynd's Hunter's Point Shrimp Company, the last Chinese shrimp enterprise, went out of business in 1956. Today, one last Chinese fisherman, Frank Quan, still fishes out of China Point in the North Bay. There is talk of making the remains of the Chinese fishing village there an historic site, and it is said that the shrimp driven out by water pollution are now coming back.

Shrimping

For a decade or more, Chinese fishermen and shrimping in California were almost synonymous. Shrimp fishing beginning in the 1860s was the largest and longest-lasting Chinese fishing enterprise in the state, and its story is instructive. The Chinese made it a productive industry. The bag nets they imported cost only $12 apiece. A net was 25–40 feet long with a mouth 20–30 feet wide. A 60-foot junk could handle up to sixty nets and take in 8,000 pounds of shrimp per tide. Shrimp then sold at 1½ cents a pound. In 1871, Chinese did most of the shrimping. In 1879, some 5 million pounds of shrimp were sold in San Francisco, in the railway and mining camps where Chinese still worked, and also exported to China, Hawaii, and Australia. Chinese merchants developed these steady export markets, and the income both from dried shrimp and squid was a substantial addition to California's economy. The Chinese by that time made up 50 percent of the work force, and in 1880 California led the nation in shrimp production, exporting $100,000 worth of dried shrimp and shells.

Then more of the other ethnic groups entered the lucrative trade, and twenty-five years later only a handful of Chinese remained in it. This was only partly due to competition by others using more advanced methods of fishing. Italians in the 1870s introduced the lampara net, which could catch 5–20 tons of shrimp at one haul. The Chinese boats could not compete with this, although Chinese merchants managed to retain control of marketing operations, at which they were adept. The main cause of the Chinese exodus was legal or illegal harassment, as shown by the following list:

1860   A fishing license costing $4 a month was required of Chinese fishermen. This was abolished in 1864 because it produced little revenue due to the difficulty of collecting.

1876   Italians, Greeks, and Yugoslavians entering the industry got a law passed regulating the size of Chinese net meshes and so reducing their catches.
Chinese were at one time forbidden to use any but bag nets. Thirty years later, they were forbidden by law to use these same nets.
At one time, they were required to throw back small fish. At another time, they were required to keep the small fish and throw back the large ones.

1879   The California legislature refused fishing licenses to aliens ineligible for naturalization (that is, the Chinese). When challenged in the courts, this regulation was declared unconstitutional, but while such cases were pending the results were devastating to the complainants.

1880   A fishing tax of $2.50 per month was imposed on Chinese fishermen. That same year, David Starr Jordan and his successor, Norman E. Schofield of the California Fish and Game Department, who devoted strenuous efforts to harass the Chinese fishermen and shrimpers, declared, after a study of less than two weeks, that the fishing in the Bay was "being constantly and rapidly diminished by the Chinamen with their fine-meshed nets" (*San Diego Union*, April 2, 1880). This statement alone scared quite a number of Chinese out of the trade. Also, aliens ineligible for naturalization were prohibited from fishing for sale. This was at the height of the anti-Chinese agitation that led to passage of the Exclusion Act in 1882.

1887   All fishermen were required to obtain licenses to fish. Chinese immigrants, however, knew that this would not be just a routine procedure for them.

1889   A new law was passed prohibiting the use of nets commonly used by Chinese fishermen, such as bag nets.

1894   California-based junks were prohibited in Pacific coastal waters. This ended Chinese abalone fishing.

1895   The use of gill nets by Chinese fishermen was prohibited.

1897   On Schofield's advice, the State Board of Fish Commissioners ordered a closed season in shrimp fishing from May to October. This included the best fishing period, from June to August. Chinese fishermen challenged this ruling but lost the case. There were twenty-six Chinese shrimping camps. (A campaign was on to drive all Chinese out of the country.)

1905   The regulation ordering a closed season for shrimp was repealed, but the export of dried shrimp was prohibited. This reduced the number of Chinese shrimp boats by 50 percent.

1910   Use of the Chinese shrimping bag net was prohibited, and pressure by white seafront hoodlums instigated by other fishing groups forced many Chinese out of general market fishing. San Pablo Bay was declared a sport fishery. Net fishing was banned.

1912   The closed season for shrimp was reinstated. Chinese began trawling for shrimp, but this gave only temporary relief.

1915   The Chinese bag net was again permitted, and the shrimping industry revived over the next decade.

1917   Sturgeon fishing was entirely prohibited.

1930   Export of dried shrimp was prohibited again. Only fourteen Chinese shrimping camps remained.

1935   The San Francisco Bay Area fisheries declined noticeably due to pollution, and most of the Chinese left the industry.

By 1945, Chinese shrimping operations had all but ended in San Francisco Bay.

The shrimp camp in the cove south of Rat Rock in San Pablo Bay was typical of the Chinese fishing villages that once dotted the California coast. This was home for a few hundred shrimpers and their families, mostly from Guangdong, who had a background of fishing back home in China. It had a few shops for general and marine supplies, a barbershop run by a spare-time barber, and a small school. School fees were $2 a month for general instruction and English and $.50 a month extra for religious instruction. There were sheds for storing fishing gear, sails, spare parts, and cordage. There were open-work wooden racks for drying fish hauled in along with the shrimp. There were no large junks here but sampans, traditional, rather flat-bottomed craft up to 20 feet long. At the end of the jetties were vats in which to cook the shrimp for ten to fifteen minutes as soon as the catch was landed. A shallow brail (a large, open-work ladle) of brass or copper was used to remove the shrimp from the vat. In a nearby shed, the shrimp were drained off and then graded in boxes with riddled bottoms or in mechanical shakers. Behind the houses on the hillside was a cleared floor of tamped earth or wood where the shrimp were dried for four or five days. Some companies used ovens for quickly drying small lots of shrimps. After drying, the shells were crushed by men wearing wooden clogs and dragging corrugated, square-ridged stone rollers over them. Sometimes tampers or wooden pestles were used. Crushed shrimp were winnowed in flat baskets or in a rotary fan mill. The shells were sold as fertilizer. Shrimp picking—taking the head and shell from the meat—was usually done by the women and youngsters of the camps sitting around the picking tables. This was a time for singing folksongs and hearing the older people tell folktales.

Life in these very self-contained villages was in some respects bucolic, lived well apart from the sometimes daily harassment that Chinese were subjected to in the cities during the exclusion years. Most of the fishermen were "sojourners" intending to return to China once they had saved a few hundred dollars, but a larger proportion of fishermen than other Chinese workers were able to bring in their wives to America because of their merchant standing, and this gave a family air of sobriety and good living to the villages. Many sojourners did indeed return to China with their modest savings.

A number of specious arguments were advanced to explain the attacks on Chinese fishermen. One was that they exported most of the catch, as if this were some underhand and reprehensible method of robbing the people of California. But even today 90 percent of the California catch is exported, and no Chinese is taking part in that trade.

Chinese merchants pioneered the export market in fish for California, and the lines of trade they opened to Hawaii and other points around the Pacific rim are still being used today. Even the humble Chinese fish peddler with yoke or carrying pole and two baskets of fresh fish helped develop the California fisheries by popularizing fish food throughout the Bay Area towns.

The Chinese were also accused of overfishing and destroying the San Francisco Bay Area fisheries. But there is no evidence that overfishing had anything to do with it. Human activity of another kind was the cause. When San Francisco Bay was discovered by white colonists, it was twice the size it is now. In 1850, some 42 percent of its area was marsh and tideland flats. Much of this has been filled in over the years for industrial, residential, and leisure use. Dumping and industrial and harbor pollution upset the delicate balance of this ecosystem and drove the fish and shrimp away. Finally, San Francisco had to import shrimp. Between 1886 and 1908, imports ranged from $1,778 to $39,631 annually.

Modern science makes one aware of the havoc that early unwise exploitation of the environment has caused. A 1976–1977 study by the State Water Control Board, following up earlier studies by the State Fish and Game Department, showed that fish caught today contained significant and in certain cases dangerously high levels of mercury content traceable to gold-mining operations in the last century. The Environmental Protection Agency standard is 0.5 parts per million. A squaw fish taken at Green's Landing on the Sacramento River in 1976 yielded 0.18 parts per million. A carp from the Yuba River yielded 1.98 parts per million. It would seem that those who so busily harassed the Chinese immigrants for degrading the Bay fisheries would have been better advised to look elsewhere if they really wanted to preserve this valuable California resource.

Squid Fishing

In the mid-nineteenth century, as the Chinese fishermen from Guangdong soon discovered, the waters off Monterey teamed with sturgeon and squid. Chinese sampans put out onto the bay on dark nights. One boat carried a lighted torch in a wire basket suspended from a pole over the water to attract the shoals of squid. Two other sampans then gradually encircled the squid with a giant purse seine 180 feet long and 18 feet deep and quietly closed its mouth. At the last moment, the torch boat would row out of the encirclement, and the squid were caught. This catch found a ready market. Fresh or dried, it is a traditional food of the Cantonese immigrants. San Franciscan gourmets soon learned to prize it as a delicacy, and thereafter it was in constant demand in Chinese restaurants in the United States and around the Pacific basin.

Seaweed Gatherers

The Chinese fishing camps added seaweed to the California table in the 1880s. At first in northern California, American Indians gathered and sold the seaweed to the Chinese, who made it into a nutritious iodine-rich soup. Later, when regular Chinese fishing villages were established, the women and children there did the gathering. In southern California, there was a Chinese operation based on Moss Beach. Kelp farming by the Chinese only became an important activity near the 1890s. Most of the seaweed was exported to China, but some, apart from eating, was used locally as fertilizer.

Abalone

The native American Indians had gathered abalone shells occasionally to make shell ornaments and for barter trade, but the Indians were accustomed to a simple natural economy in which trade played but a small part. It was the Chinese fishermen who first realized the potential commercial importance of these shells with their tasty meat and pearly, irridescent inner surface. By the mid-1850s, abalone were being gathered both for their shells and their meat, and by the 1870s a million-dollar export trade had been built up based on the abalone fisheries on the Channel Islands and in Monterey and San Diego. Abalone shell ornaments and inlays became one of those crazes that, like pampas grass or hula hoops, have periodically caught the American fancy; this lasted well through the turn of the century and has recently made a strong comeback. The wholesaling end was mainly handled by American merchants.

Just at the time that motor-powered boats were being widely introduced into the trade, opening a whole new field of technology, the Chinese fishermen were being edged out. Thus in the nineteenth century few of them ever really entered through the magic portals of the age of mechanization. They remained for the most part locked into the age-old handicraft technology.

NOTES

1. Rich materials on the Chinese in the California fishing industry can be found in the library of the Maritime Museum in San Francisco; in Thomas Chinn, Him Mark Lai, and Philip P. Choy, *History of the Chinese in California* (San Francisco: Chinese Historical Society in America, 1973); Him Mark Lai and Philip P. Choy, *Outlines: History of the Chinese in America* (San Francisco: Chinese-American Studies Planning Group, 1973); L. Eve Armentrout-Ma, *Sampans, Junks and Chinese Fishermen in the Golden State* (San Francisco Maritime Museum, 1979); *The Life, Influence and Role of the Chinese in the United States 1776–1960* (San Francisco: Chinese Historical Society of America, 1975); and Robert Alan Nash, "Chinese Shrimp Fishing in California" (Ph.D. diss.r, U.C.L.A., 1973).

Strength and
Skills for Hire (3):
North to the Canneries

CHAPTER

IX

One of the major resources of North America [salmon fishing and canning] and one that spurred its development would undoubtedly not have progressed at the rate it did without Chinese participation.

ROBERT A. NASH, *The China Gang*, from *The Life, Influence and Role of the Chinese in the United States, 1776–1960*

IN THE salmon fishing and canning industry of the northwestern United States, the Chinese applied their considerable skills at a very early date and up until the mid-1930s. Their participation in the canneries is not surprising. Most of the early immigrants from coastal Guangdong Province were farmers and/or fishermen. Their way to the Mother Lode naturally led them along the broad Sacramento River, where the native American Indians had long been accustomed to fish. Chinese began to fish salmon commercially in that river as early as 1849, and they were among the first to work in the cannery started by George Hume in 1864 in Washington, opposite Sacramento. They fished and canned salmon on the San Joaquin River, too. Later, when they were edged out of fishing by Italians and Portuguese, they still continued to work in the canneries. They comprised most of the work force in the twenty Sacramento canneries in 1881. But hydraulic mining on the upper reaches of the river polluted the water so badly that the salmon disappeared. By 1919, all the canneries had closed.

In 1872, Chinese were manning the Columbia River canneries in Oregon, and five-sixths of the $600,000 annual payroll went to them. In 1881, some 3,000 were in the canneries there. From 1884 onward, they were hired in San Francisco in increasing numbers to work the canneries of the Alaska Packers' Association (APA) in southern Alaska, the Gulf of Alaska, and Bristol

Bay. By 1888, they made up 86 percent of the cannery workers in California, Oregon, and Washington states. By 1892, their numbers had increased to 2,460 working in thirty-six canneries along with 1,900 white workers and 1,500 Alaskan natives. In 1900, there were 3,570 cannery workers there. From 1892 to 1935, they averaged 52 percent of the work force but totaled less than 30 percent in the later thirty-two of those years. This steady decline in the numbers of Chinese employed was due to the Chinese Exclusion Acts in 1882 and later. These reduced the number of young, tough Chinese able and willing to endure the hard work and conditions of these northern cannery rows. The veterans were getting too old for the job, and no new replacements were coming in.

Moored to a dock near Fisherman's Wharf in San Francisco is the sailing ship *Balclutha*, which once took Chinese north to the canneries in Alaska and which is now a maritime museum for tourists. It is a fine ship that made the 2,500-mile voyage in the usual twenty-five to thirty days (but at least one vessel took fifty-seven days to reach its destination). When steamships began to make the run in 1925, it took about ten days. It was always an uncomfortable voyage. As in the *Balclutha*, the ships' "Chinatown" was up forward and was usually infested with fleas and lice. No fresh water was supplied to that area for washing. It was not usually a dangerous voyage, but in 1908 the *Star of Bengal* ran aground in a storm, and 110 Chinese were drowned. Their families received no compensation. In thirty-six years, the APA lost nine ships on the Alaska run. This was not a bad record, considering that this was a voyage beset with fogs, gales, and the rocky hazards of the Redwood Coast. There is no full record of lives lost, only ships. Many of the APA vessels signed on Chinese seamen.

After 1871, there was a ready market for the catch in Britain. King salmon, the pride of the fisheries, sometimes weighed twenty pounds. The packers arrived six to eight weeks before the salmon run commenced. There was plenty to do in that time. The Chinese hands made the cans from sheet metal (until 1901); cleaned, gutted, and cut the fish; packed and cooked them in the cans; and then did the sealing, lacquering, labeling, and packing. Work went on nonstop until the job was done.

Working and living conditions in the nineteenth-century Alaska canneries were deplorable and sometimes scandalous. Workers were recruited through seventy-four Chinese labor contractors and the ships' captains and cannery superintendants. The boss foreman handled their wages from the cannery owners and, excluding advances, paid them off on their return to San Francisco in the fall. On board ship, he was in charge of them and had his office and slop chest with its opium and tobacco and other small goods next to their "Chinatown." Ships usually returned to San Francisco only at the end of the season, so a worker who quit work in Alaska was stranded there without possibility of other work until the fall.

The labor contractors supplied the packing workers with food and equipment. The cannery owners provided transportation, fuel, salt, water, and a place to sleep. Rated "good, reliable workers," the Chinese packers nevertheless received $0.40 a case in 1980–1900 compared to an Indian's wage of $0.60 a case. In Bristol Bay, their rate was $0.45 per case machine filled and $0.60 hand filled; $0.80–.85 per case was paid for making cans. Wages ranged from $30 to $90 a month, depending on the job.[1] Many factors determined what wage a worker could demand, such as the state of the market and the bargaining clout the packers could muster. In 1934, Chinese packers were paid $70 a month; Mexicans were paid $50. An average packer might save $125 to take home for the six or seven months away from San Francisco. Cooks and foremen's wages were considerably higher: $450 to $1,000 a season.

Over the turn of the century, the canneries were increasingly mechanized. The "Iron Chink" was invented in 1890 to clean and gut the fish. Developed and introduced in APA operations in 1901, it could handle 30,000 fish in ten hours, replacing fifty men. But the market for Alaskan salmon was so good that both it and the Chinese packers worked together.

Conditions of work in the canneries were such that rascally contractors could and did exploit the packers, greatly increasing the hardships they faced under "normal" contracts that set low wages, minimal amenities in living, and long hours of hard work. A packer had to agree to an eleven-hour work day, on demand until the canning of the hauls of fish was done. Contractors sold the packers shoddy outfits at high prices, demanded "kickbacks," and doctored accounts. Seventy-seven percent of a gang of packers might be illiterate, so it was easy to take advantage of them. Even in 1890, of 1,284 packers only 977 knew some English. The firm of contractors called Miers and Young was indicted for peonage and its principals jailed in St. Quentin when a San Francisco reporter shipped under them to the Alaska canneries and published an account of his experiences there. Conditions then improved. The monotonous diet of rice and fish became more varied when the Chinese packers learned to grow vegetables in the north. But, by the time the canneries were unionized in the mid-1930s and wages and hours improved, the Chinese packers had dwindled to a few hundreds. At this time, quite a few ambitious Chinese financed part of their college education with summer work in the canneries. But by the end of the 1930s the Chinese role in this industry had ended: the old-timers had died or retired; the young men could find better ways of making a living.

NOTE

1. Oral history in Andrew B. Lee MSS in San Francisco Maritime Museum Library.

Strength and
Skills for Hire (4):
In Light Industry

CHAPTER

X

The Chinese in California have contributed as much as, if not more than, any other single race to the State's early economic development and played a strong, vital role in the formative stages of many of California's major industries.

WILLIAM HEINTZ, Introduction to *The Chinese in California: A Brief Bibliographic History*

THE CHINESE had shown their worth in mining, railway building, land reclamation, farming, and fishing. But even from 1864 to 1869, when most able-bodied Chinese workers were concentrated on the railroads, there was always a core of Chinese working in the cities of San Francisco and Sacramento and in smaller towns. They had early made their mark there as merchants and in the restaurants, laundry, and general service trades. They could be found working in quite a number of other urban occupations at a surprisingly early date. They had appeared in modern manufacturing industries for the first time making cigars and woolens in 1859, but it was some years later that they entered industry in fairly large numbers. This was particularly so when the first transcontinental railroad was completed in 1869 and the Chinese in that labor force began to scatter into a large number of occupations and also emigrated to other parts of the country. They reached Texas in 1870, Boston soon after, and New York about the same time.

The performance of the Chinese workers in the industries they entered shows conclusively that, given normal conditions, they would quickly have emerged as a valuable part of the industrial working class of America. There are numerous testimonials to their skills, diligence, and discipline. But the American Federation of Labor unions refused to bring the Chinese workers into their organization. On the contrary, Samuel Gompers and his colleagues (with some notable exceptions) led the anti-Chinese chorus. Years of tragedy and sorrow would have been avoided had they remained true to their declared principles of labor solidarity and brotherhood. As it was, Chinese workers hopefully entered a number of industries in the developing West and made good only to be driven out by senseless prejudice.

Cigar Making

The first few Chinese entered the cigar industry in the 1850s, primarily in the San Francisco establishment of Engelbricht and Levy. They helped get the industry going. Yet the Cigar Makers' Association almost immediately sounded the alarm against the employment of Chinese as "tending to destroy the true basis of our country's prosperity" and likely to prove "destructive to the general welfare and retard the advance of civilization and the manifest destiny of our country." They argued that it would "bring want and suffering to the homes of our people."[1]

History, however, shows that it was not Chinese labor that overwhelmed the western cigar makers' manifest destiny, but eastern competition and the cigarette. The cigar industry, like most other western industries at that time, was short of skilled labor. Gold mining was still the main attraction, and the men attracted to the gold fields were not likely to accept jobs in a cigar factory. However, the "advance of civilization" decreed the need for more cigars. The big expansion of the San Francisco cigar industry took place after 1864.

Digesting the rich results of the Gold Rush and the later Comstock silver bonanza, an increasingly affluent San Francisco encouraged an expansive style of living. The cigar was one of its status symbols. The output of cigars jumped from $2,000 in 1864 to $1 million two years later. Within another two years, brash California had overtaken Massachusetts as the fourth largest maker of cigars in America. Chinese adaptability and initiative was a key part of this successful drive. The number of Chinese workers in the San Francisco factories rose from 450 out of a total work force of 500 in 1867 to a peak of 5,500 out of a total of 6,500 in 1877.* By this time, large numbers of Chinese who had worked on the railroads were available. Even in 1866 half of the cigar factories in the city were Chinese owned, and along Battery, Front, and Market Streets where they clustered it was an open secret in 1874 that they adopted such trade names as Cabanes and Ramirez for their Chinese-made "Havanas." These cigars were of good-quality Cuban tobacco but were much cheaper than the real thing. Anti-Chinese agitators forced shopkeepers to boycott Chinese-made cigars and put up placards stating that their goods were "Made with White Labor Only." Samuel Gompers, inveterate foe of

---

* *Alta California*, November 2, 1867. But Ira B. Cross in his *History of the Labor Movement in California* (Berkeley: University of California Press, 1935) states that in 1866 about 2,000 Chinese were making cigars, while Alexander McLeod in *Pigtails and Gold Dust* (Caldwell, Idaho: Caxton Printers, 1947) states that over 4,000 Chinese were in the industry in 1862.

Chinese labor, was president of the Cigarmakers International Union.

The Chinese West Coast cigar makers were certainly competitive. Cigar making demands no very complicated machinery but considerable manual skill, and this the Chinese workers had in a marked degree. Meanwhile, the Chinese merchant entrepreneurs were showing considerable skill in modern business.

Chinese worked in white-owned or Chinese-owned factories or at piece rates for Chinese contractors, who received tobacco from white-owned firms and delivered the finished product to them to be sold under their labels. Fifty Chinese might labor for 50 to 70¢ per hundred in a 15- by 20-foot room, each making up to 200 cigars a day. Chinese on the West Coast were willing to work for relatively low wages in order to get a foothold on the ladder of American opportunity, but there was a steady flow of Irish, Germans, and southern and eastern European immigrants ready to compete with them on the East Coast. Although white cigar workers in the eastern states demanded higher wages, Eastern cigar factories finally got the competitive edge by introducing more efficient techniques such as the molder and by streamlining production with more specialized divisions of labor. Such methods demanded larger premises and more workers, requiring larger capital outlays than the Chinese entrepreneurs could usually afford.

The Chinese workers had their own labor guild named the "Hall of Common Virtue" (Tung De Tang), which aimed to get a union shop where possible and use strike action when necessary to achieve it. The experience of this Chinese worker's guild proved that, far from being nonunion men, as some union leader detractors claimed, the Chinese could quickly adapt their traditional guilds to modern union practices.

Chinese also worked in and operated the related cigarbox-making industry. Here too, they worked in both white- and Chinese-owned establishments, and in 1881 they accounted for one-sixth of the California production of boxes.

For reasons not entirely clear, Chinese labor played a major role in the cigar-making industry even during the years of the most virulent anti-Chinese agitation. The white cigar-makers' union only succeeded in driving the Chinese out in the mid-1880s, when the industry itself declined in California. In 1878, the work force in the cigar industry had declined to 6,000, and by 1892 it totaled 1,200, with only 700 Chinese workers. In 1881, the California cigar industry was making $5,600,000 but soon cigar smoking was giving way to the less expensive cigarette, which the British even at that time appropriately termed the "gasper." Yet even in 1905 there were still five factories in San Francisco with 80 Chinese workers out of 140 employed.[2]

In the Woolen Industry

In some parts of California and Nevada, Chinese were hired as shepherds and sheep shearers on the developing ranches, and as the output of wool and the demand for woolens increased Heyneman, Pick and Company opened the first woolen mill in San Francisco in 1859 and hired Chinese as well as other workers. The number of Chinese workers in the woolen and knitting mills increased rapidly when the men who had been working on the railway lines began to drift back to San Francisco. By 1869, some 500 were employed. One writer testifies that "scarce anything would induce the proprietors to exchange them for other labor."[3] In 1865, Chinese made up 70–80 percent of the workers in the industry. At that time, it was almost impossible to get white labor for such work in the West at an economic wage.

The labor market in California had two peculiarities that had a long-lasting effect on the Chinese in the state. I have already described the general character of the Forty-Niners. Men of that character, gold seekers, were not likely to take to the humdrum tasks of factory or field work and, still less, work as domestics or in the service trades without some extra financial inducement. Due to its relative scarcity, wages for white labor in California were unusually high compared to the national average. This made Chinese labor relatively cheap even though it might cost the same as labor in the Eastern states.

In addition, in the 1860s California's population of 380,000 people was three- quarters male. Even this was an improvement on the situation in the 1850s, when women were only 8 percent of the population and only 2 percent in the mining camps. This gave a strange twist to the character of the state and created jobs for men that back East would normally have been filled by women. Chinese were willing to do these jobs, such as laundry, cooking, domestic service, or work in a woolen mill, which white males considered fit only for women. The presence of a pool of skilled and willing Chinese labor was therefore a godsend to the western entrepreneur.

The president of the San Jose Woolen Mill testified in 1876 before the Joint Congressional Commission to Investigate Chinese Immigration:

We employ Chinese because it is necessary to compete in our business. To our white help, we have to pay wages far in advance of what is paid in similar institutions in the eastern states, with which we come directly into competition. To Chinamen, on an average, we pay less. If the Chinamen were taken from us we should close up tomorrow.[4]

The representative of the Pioneer Mills of San Francisco stated, "It would be an absolute impossibility to have run our factory on white labor, simply because we could not get white operatives."[5] On this point, H. G. Kuhl, secretary of the Golden Gate Mills in San Francisco, said in 1882, "It is difficult to make the [white] boys and girls pay sufficient attention to their work. . . . they are not steady and industrious enough and think that after working a few weeks their wages ought to be doubled."[6] It was no surprise that Western capitalists opposed the anti-Chinese agitators' demand that they dismiss their Chinese workers, who were helping them maintain their manufacturing positions against eastern competition.

San Francisco was not the only center for the woolen industry in California.

Mills were set up in several other cities and towns: Stockton, Sacramento, Marysville, San Jose, Merced, San Bernardino, and Los Angeles. All employed Chinese workers, to a total of 800 out of 1,600 workers in the industry in 1882.

But finally the competition was too severe. The President of the San Jose Woolen Mill stated that eastern mills were paying their hands 20 percent less than the Chinese workers were being paid in Western mills, which was $.90 to $1.12 per day in 1876. With lower wages and better technology, they could undersell the western mills, and by the 1880s the value of San Francisco woolen production dropped from $1,700,000 to $350,000 in 1890.[7] In 1905, only twenty Chinese remained in the woolen industry in San Francisco.

Garment Makers

Among several industries that Chinese entered in the 1860s and 1870s was the garment industry. The Reverend A. W. Loomis, writing in the *Overland Monthly* in 1869, reports them working "very extensively" in the sewing trades in San Francisco. In 1873, they were working in twenty-eight Chinese-owned factories making shirts, drawers, overalls, pants, and other garments. Each factory hired from 50 to 100 men, to a total of around 2,000. A number were doing piecework in their own homes, so the total in the industry was between 2,000–3,000 workers.

The number of Chinese in the garment industry seems to have been maintained for some time despite the anti-Chinese agitation and the Exclusion Act of 1882. The 1880 census lists 1,178 Chinese workers in the trade including 114 sewing machine operators. With tailors and seamstresses, the total would be somewhere around 2,000. They made the bulk of the ready-made clothing and nearly all the underclothing bought in San Francisco. Eighty percent of the San Francisco shirt makers were Chinese.[8]

Wages were $1.26 a day in the mid-1870s but competition from the eastern states forced these down to $1.10 or lower in the 1880s. Finally, the eastern states' newer and more efficient technology and more modern organization of work captured the market. The San Francisco factories were crowded out.

The garment industry in San Francisco's Chinatown had characteristically Chinese (or, rather, Guangdongese Pearl River delta) features. In those early days, people from the Sai-chu area of Nanhai District virtually monopolized work in male clothing and tailoring. Factory owners making shirts, ladies' garments, and underwear were mostly from the Zhongshan District, and overalls and working clothes were manufactured by men from the Shunde area.[9]

The workers had three guilds:

1. The Tung Yeh Tang (Tung Yip Tong, in Cantonese), or Hall of Common Occupation, formed by workers in ready-made clothing and tailors

2. The Chung Yi Hang (Gwing Yi Hong), or Guild of Bright Clothing, formed by shirt makers and ladies garment and undergarment makers
3. The Chin Yi Hang (Gum Yi Hong), or Guild of Brocaded Clothing, formed by those making overalls and other work clothes in 1880. In their heyday, they were able to some extent to regulate hours of labor and bargain on wages, but as women entered the trades, the guilds, which had no provision for such an unlooked-for development, gradually collapsed. The first guild disappeared some time after 1900 and the second by the 1920s. The third went completely out of existence in 1967.

The garment industry, the only considerable industry existing in Chinatown today, is now almost entirely staffed by women. We will deal with it in its modern form in a later chapter.

Boots, Shoes, and Slippers

Most of the boot and shoe factories in California were set up in San Francisco in the 1860s after the Civil War. Chinese workers helped get the industry started but they were only hired in any numbers in the later 1960s when the railway building was done. It is regrettable and boded ill for the future that they were first hired by Buckingham and Hecht when their white operators went on strike in 1869, but as usual the Chinese were found to be productive and disciplined, and by 1870 they were 19 percent of the work force. By 1873, half the boots and shoes in San Francisco were being made by Chinese labor. Under these conditions, a struggle was inevitable between the Chinese and the white workers organized in the Knights of St. Crispin. The terms of that struggle were complicated by the rapid introduction of machinery in the industry. This made it possible for factory owners to dispense with adult male workers, white as well as Chinese, and to hire women and young people at lower wages.

In 1875, there were only eight Chinese-owned firms in San Francisco in this trade. By 1880, there were forty-eight, and they had taken over numbers of skilled Chinese operatives dismissed from white-owned factories. Concentrating on cheap shoes, by the mid-1870s they were employing 2,000 of the 2,300 Chinese in the industry, and Chinese workers were making half of California's output of boots and shoes. Eleven of the twelve slipper-making workshops in San Francisco were Chinese-owned.

As in the garment and other trades, competition with eastern imported footwear forced down prices in California by 15 to 20 percent and the whole industry there was in trouble. The driving out of Chinese labor due to anti-Chinese agitation and superior technology gave eastern competition the edge over the West. The whole California boot and shoe industry declined from fourth place nationwide to no mention at all in 1900.

Experience in the boot and shoe industry shows that the Chinese workers were quite amenable to labor union organization and would have made good

union members if given the chance. They had their own labor guild, the
Lei Xing Tang (Li Sheng T'ang, or Hall for Treading the New) to protect
their rights. They learned how to organize strikes to back up their demands.
But lack of solidarity between white and Chinese workers led to them being
used and pitted against each other by white employers. In San Francisco,
for instance, two of the large white-owned factories brought in white youngsters
to replace Chinese workers. In 1870, the Chinese themselves were used as
strikebreakers when seventy-five were contracted to work in the shoe factory
run by Calvin Sampson in North Adams, Massachusetts. This case has often
been cited and made much of, but it was an isolated case. The seventy-five
Chinese from San Francisco were hired under a three-year contract that they
signed and were bound to, and, while the contractor who hired them knew
what was up, the men themselves only became aware of the actual situation
when they arrived in North Adams and were kept in virtual seclusion in the
factory barracks. Only one of them knew any English. Later they built up a
warm relationship with the North Adams people. Luey Gim Gong, the famed
Chinese pomologist, was, as I have related, one of their number.

Other Industries

Chinese worked in the Pacific Jute Company of Oakland, established in
1868, making burlap from jute. The company could not keep its white
employees at the wages it paid ($1 a day for manual labor), and by 1876
the 120 Chinese employed did most of the work.

Chinese began work in the broom-making industry in the 1870s and some
were soon running their own small businesses. In its heyday, the industry
had fifty factories on the West Coast, twenty of these being in San Francisco.
Half of the 300 workers were Chinese. But gradually they all succumbed to
anti-Chinese agitation and advancing technology.

In the 1870s and 1880s, Chinese made up a fourth or more of the workers
making the following products: cordage, matches, candles and soap, bottles,
pottery, whips and bricks (44 percent). Although in 1877 the total number
of Chinese working in San Francisco's factories was around 18,000, with some
thousands more in the wash houses, restaurants, service trades, and domestic
service, the number in each of these industries was relatively small. They
were in significant numbers of from 1,000 to 3,000 only in the woolen (32
percent) cigar (84.4 percent), garment (over 50 percent), and boot and shoe
trades (52 percent).

Toehold in Industry

The growth of San Francisco industry was extremely rapid, financed and
spurred by the gold, silver, railroads, and agriculture. While the first industries
were severely practical, oriented to the basic necessities of the miners, by
1852 they had expanded greatly in scope and scale. Out of the 19 banks,

160 hotels and restaurants, 63 bakeries, and a dozen mills of the early 1850s, a solid industrial structure developed by the 1870s: there were tanneries; woolen and lumber mills; foundries making industrial wagons, carriages, farm implements, and machines; and factories producing glass, chemicals, and paper. By the early 1870s, a well-rounded economy had developed. California was no longer a developing country, economically dependent on the eastern states. After a run of only twenty years, its plants were making locomotives, cable cars, and large-scale farm machines such as steam-powered combine harvesters.

It is in this context that Chinese participation in California's industry must be considered. The Chinese were only able to join some of the light industries, either as owners or workers. These were little more than handicraft industries using some machines, such as sewing machines, presses, and saws. Chinese were not found in the big, well-unionized industries such as industrial construction, steel, shipbuilding, engineering, and assembly-line production. The toehold that the Chinese immigrants had, although large in a few industries, was still marginal in relation to industry as a whole, and when the trade unions in such powerful key industries as the metal trades (which were strongly unionized) and the craft unions launched the anti-Chinese agitation, the Chinese toehold in industry was quickly dislodged. Chinese were driven out or squeezed out of even those industries in which at one time or another they were in the lead. Thus, while other immigrants were able to be retrained and to graduate from handicraft traditions similar to those of the Chinese, to become modern industrial workers in the mainstream of American life, during the exclusion years more and more Chinese crowded into such traditionally urban Chinese occupations as the service trades, laundries, restaurants, and small-scale merchandising.

Only in World War II, with the urgent national demand for more labor power, were young Chinese men and women able to get out of the Chinatown ghettoes and begin to join the industrial working class of America in hitherto segregated factories and unions.

The industrial activities of the few Chinese entrepreneurs were also crippled. A Chinese industrial middle class had only just begun to form in the 1870s when its white competitors squeezed it out of business. Chinese Chinatown business to this day is typically small-scale. Chinese big business has been mainly generated outside Chinatown among the new immigrants who came in the 1940s and later from Shanghai and Tianjin, Hong Kong and Taiwan.

NOTES

1. Thomas Chinn, Him Mark Lai, and Philip P. Choy, *History of the Chinese in California* (San Francisco: Chinese Historical Society of America, 1969).
2. *San Francisco Municipal Report* (1905), p. 122.

3. A. W. Loomis, "How Our Chinese Are Employed," *Overland Monthly*, 2 (1869), 231–240.
4. George Seward, *Chinese Immigration* (New York: Arno Press and New York Times, 1970). Reprint of 1888 ed.
5. Report of the Special Committee to Investigate Chinese Immigration, 44th Congress, 2nd Session, 1876–77.
6. *Ibid.*
7. Mary Roberts Coolidge, *Chinese Immigration*, (New York: Holt, 1909), p. 374.
8. Ping Chiu, *Chinese Labor in California* (Madison: University of Wisconsin Press, 1963).
9. Chinn, Lai, and Choy, *History of the Chinese.*
10. Seward, *Chinese Immigration.*

The Cultural
Contribution

CHAPTER

XI

[The Chinese] panned gold, opened up mines, brought in timber
to build houses on land they reclaimed. They opened up the
vineyards and rich farmlands.

They added dignity and discipline, order and wealth to a
frontier land that when they came was not yet a state, not yet
a community of law and order. They helped to link it with
the rest of the continent and so make possible its greater
settlement. . . . The cleanliness, politeness and good behavior
of the Chinese was on everybody's mouth and what they
contributed saved several counties from bankruptcy.

FRANKLIN TUTHILL, *History of California*

IN THE second half of the nineteenth century, racist
demagogues succeeded in clouding the judgment of the western states by
spreading two stereotypes of the Chinese immigrant. One was that of cheap,
unskilled Chinese "coolie" labor. The second was the stereotyped image of
the dark-minded, "inscrutable," unlettered "coolie" as the archetypal Chinese.
Both were palpably false. The emphasis in these pages has up to now been
on the technical skills and organized labor that the Chinese brought with
them, but these were enhanced by their spiritual values, which, although
they cannot be expressed in dollars, were an invaluable part of what they
contributed to America.

Chinese immigrants from Guangdong came with treasures in their heads.
There was trash there too, but although their traditional culture had, as a
whole, grown out of date compared to the advanced thought of the West—
this was part of the reason for the decline of the feudal imperial empire of
China—it had enduring positive values that are far from being out of date
even now, over a century later.

The cultural values the Chinese immigrants brought were many-faceted.
They shared with the best of Americans the work ethic, an ingrained respect
for work, the ideas that work is noble and elevating and that a job worth

doing is worth doing well. Regard for skilled craftsmanship is traditional in China and, in fact, institutionalized. As James A. Whitney reports in a description of traditional China:

> When a man made anything that probably no one else could be able to do, he carried it to the governor demanding a recompense for the progress he had made in the art . . . and if he passed the tests set up for his work, he was rewarded with a government position.[1]

As a continuation of this old tradition, cities such as Peking or Shanghai to this day hold regular demonstrations of craftsmanship. Butchers display their skill in carving up a chicken; cooks serve up their most delicious dishes on table displays; counter clerks in department stores show how well, quickly, and artistically they can tie up packages. Without knowing this, it is impossible to understand the devotion that the Chinese lavished on the building of the first transcontinental railway, the stone embankments on the Donner Summit, and the stone walls on the Silverado trail in the Napa Valley wine country. This was the spirit that animated Luey Gim Gong through the years he spent breeding his prize-winning orange.

Western America—and the early history of Chinese Americans up to the 1870s unfolds almost entirely in the West and mainly in California—was primarily interested in the Chinese as workers, and it was this devotion to their work that first attracted attention and made them "Crocker's Pets." Newspaper reporters investigating their work, historians going over the records, and ordinary people who knew them intimately as cooks and servants have penned many eulogies of the Chinese American worker. Even their detractors never complained about shoddy work done by the Chinese. On the contrary, they were vilified *because* they worked well and economically and were too competitive on the labor market.

Another aspect of their way of life that excited comment was their sense of family. In the early days, the ratio between males and females in the Chinese communities was hundreds to one or, even as late as 1890, dozens to one. The vast majority of Chinese in America were therefore here without their families, but the ties of family were no less strong. They had families back home in China; parents, brothers, sisters, and in 50 percent of cases, wives. They were here in the United States precisely because they had families, and Chinese society expected them to earn money to send to those families for their upkeep. They worked steadfastly and self-sacrificingly for those families. Some of the merchants and a very few of the working men had families with them. They toiled to bring up those families, often under extraordinarily adverse conditions. Their prime ambition when possible was to "give the children an education." It was the expression of the age-old aspiration of the Chinese family to "have a scholar in the family." The traditional obedience of the children to their parents made it easier to maintain the strict discipline needed to excel academically. Some children carried on normal American school studies and, in addition, after school mastered Chinese reading and writing and acquainted themselves with the traditional learning. This made for a heavy study load. But the children knew how much their family expected from them, and this made it a rewarding effort to excel at school. At a time when juvenile delinquency was making headlines in the 1950s and 1960s, the stability and discipline of the Chinese families in America also made headlines. The cohesion of the Chinese family has markedly limited the number of Chinese on welfare. Chinese families are traditionally expected to look after their own.

Like the work ethic and frugality, this esteem for the family was in line with the traditional outlook of American society, the outlook that made the yeoman farmers and artisans the pioneers and grass-roots builders of the new American nation. The Chinese could fit in comfortably with early American society. But it was the destiny of America to produce a new capitalist industrial society, a new nation, out of the peoples who settled it. This demanded radical changes in traditional Chinese outlooks.

Other cultural attributes that the Chinese brought with them were respect for the seniors, for the established authority, a high regard not so much for "law and order" but for stable tradition and social stability, and a concept of the individual primarily as a member of a collective with a supreme duty to the collective. This partial list indicates how much they brought with them that did not tally with the common ideas of the society into which they came. Such ideas would inevitably have to be resolved, reconciled, or transformed to meet the pressures of the newly emerging, highly individualistic, democratic and capitalist American society and its new cultural attitudes. But such adjustments were no more than those required of other immigrant groups with other cultural backgrounds. Given normal conditions, Chinese, like other immigrants, in time shed those customs and folkways that caused too much discomfort and adopted new ways. The first article of American dress that the Chinese miner adopted was the miners' leather boot. He soon learned that the soft-soled Chinese slipper was no footwear to be worn in the rugged, stony, and muddy placer mines. Later he cut off his queue to show his emancipation from the Qing emperor and wore instead a crew cut. He doffed his cartwheel sunhat or black skullcap and crowned himself with a cap or hat. He exchanged his loose-cut, comfortable jacket and trousers for the blue or red shirt of the miner and the trousers or frock coat of the gentleman just as he adapted his thinking to the new society.

The Chinese brought with them a living folklore that sustained them under difficult conditions. Louise Clappe describes the fiddlers she met in the mining camps, the singers and dancers, the tattered books that went from hand to hand, folk arts, and the cooking and whittling that made for civilized life in long periods when men were half-starved in isolated communities, snowed in or held in by torrential rains that made hardly existent paths impassable.[2] Without these things, men resorted to drink and gambling and became brutes. The Chinese, too, were sustained by their fiddlers and flautists, by their singers and storytellers relating tales of the Guangdong villages or the great national epics, such as *Monkey Sun Wu Kung*, the *Three Kingdoms*, and the *Stories of the Marshes* ("Shui Hu Chuan," or "All Men Are Brothers"). Young Chinese male performers from San Francisco (in those days women did not go on the stage) used to tour the mining communities, including Butte and Marysville, and give concerts of traditional dances and excerpts of operas. Chinese goods, carvings, silks, and brocades brought a taste for Chinese beauty to San Francisco, and to this day old families there display Chinese works of art as treasured heirlooms.

Among the more valuable Chinese cultural imports were the traditional herbal pharmacopia and acupuncture. For several years, Chinese herbs were popular cures in San Francisco until more modern Western doctors and medicaments arrived. A Dr. Li Po-tai was one of the most popular physicians in the state and grew wealthy with fees from a large white clientele. Chinese pharmacies did a profitable business, as they still do, on Washington Street.

As for literacy, Charles Nordhoff states emphatically, not once but twice, in his book *California*, that most of the Chinese there in 1872 could read in Chinese—at least, I suppose, to the extent of what is now called "functional" literacy. There were scholarly merchants, and later the district associations brought in scholars to help them with their activities, but there is no evidence that these scholars did much to carry their lore outside of the Chinese community. Inside the community, they helped maintain the scholarly tradition in knowledge and the arts. They helped give the young the traditional education they would have received in China. One fishing camp, on San Pablo Bay, had a resident teacher for its children.

Religion, organized and unorganized, was part of the life of the Chinese communities. The "consolations of religion" is an apt phrase, as we have seen, to use here. Confucianism, with its quasi-religious aspects associated mainly with belief in the duties of the living to the dead ancestors, permeated the life of all immigrants. Most immigrants were either Buddhist or Taoist, except for those very few who joined one or other of the Christian sects, such as the Methodists, Presbyterians, or Catholics. In the forms practiced here, Buddhist and Taoist beliefs are inextricably intertwined, and so are the pantheons of the two religions. Guanyin, goddess of mercy, or Amitabha in Buddhist terminology, is the favorite protector and confidante of women.

Cai Shen, the god of wealth, and Guan Gong, the protector, the god of war, were the images one saw most frequently in the shrines, temples, or joss* houses that every self-respecting community would try to set up as soon as it felt itself more or less permanently anchored in a place. These things bound a community together. So too did observances of the great traditional festivals: the Dragon Boat Festival on June 1, the Ching Ming Festival or day of remembering the ancestors, the Mid-Autumn Festival, and, preeminently, the Lunar New Year Festival, the Spring Festival, when every house was swept clean, the icons were renewed, debts were paid, and Cao

---

* From the Spanish *Dios*, "god."

Shen, the kitchen god, was sent on his way to Heaven to report on the households' deeds, good and bad, for the past year. To this day, joss houses are dotted around the San Francisco area and the Mother Lode region. Some are elaborate structures with some pretensions to architectural beauty. Some are simple buildings of wood. Some have carved wood interior decorations of great intricacy, vermillion and gilt, with richly caparisoned images; embroidered banners, curtains, and votive hangings; tables for offerings of fruit and meat; and cast bronze altar utensils and incense bowls. Some are just tiny shrines.

Elaborate funeral ceremonies were held whenever the means were there, but for the early sojourners, burial in a cemetery was regarded as a temporary affair until the remains or the bones at least, of the deceased could be transported back for proper internment in his or her native village. As mentioned earlier, the special agencies of the district or family associations saw to these arrangements and shipped the remains back in groups. When the French ship *Asia* returned to China in 1858, it took back 321 sets of bones. When the *Flying Cloud* sailed from San Francisco, part of its cargo were the bones of 200 Chinese who had died in the United States. Chinese would not travel on ships that insisted on giving sea burials to the bodies of people who died at sea.

Of exotic interest were the pseudo-sciences indulged in by some members of the Chinese communities—just as they are today by seemingly sophisticated members of the larger society—the arts of divination by means of palmistry, phrenology, astrology, or other means. Worshippers at temples burned incense and then picked out a sliver of bamboo from a small bundle kept in a holder. Then the temple attendant, for a small fee, read the corresponding prognostication incised on the bamboo stick. Sometimes the temple attendant was a member of a recognized Chinese monastery or temple in the homeland come to administer to the needs of the faithful; sometimes he was simply a self-appointed lay priest for whom care of the joss house or temple was a way of making a living. Joss houses either in use or preserved as cultural monuments can be found today on Grant Avenue in San Francisco's Chinatown, in Weaverville, and in Auburn. While there are devout religious devotees and even fanatics among the Chinese, I think it is true to say that, for most Chinese, religion is a somewhat pragmatic activity. Maybe the gods, like the ancestors, will answer one's prayers or supplications, but it is better to accept the rituals as a perhaps necessary insurance in this life and in the life to come. In the nineteenth century, it was almost unheard of for immigrants to declare themselves agnostic and without faith in religion of some form or other.

But the general public in California in those days did not have the time, opportunity, or inclination to study and consider the fine points of Confucian, Buddhist, or Taoist lore. What impressed them was the demeanor of the Chinese, their life as seen in public. What they saw in actuality were "outlandishly" dressed people (that is, dressed unlike the general public), clean in their personal habits (miners and railway workers who washed themselves regularly each evening after the work was done—regular bathing was not customary in those times), who lived frugally, were highly disciplined in their work, regular on the job, not given to drunkeness and carousing over the weekend, and displayed to a remarkable degree that characteristic of the true Christian: forbearance.

The generally admirable character of the early Chinese immigrants was attested to by numerous writers of the time. Lucia Norman, writing in 1867, described the Chinese as "unobtrusive, honest and industrious, content to work when white men would starve, they were at first welcomed with pleasure."[3]

With rather heavy-handed irony, Samuel Williams wrote in 1875, "He [the Chinese] is free from most of the grosser Christian vices . . . he does not drink . . . [or go about] insulting peaceable citizens, garroting unwary pedestrians or pistolling policemen."[4]

The Chinese exhibited these traits under conditions of the utmost provocation. Because of the character of the heterogeneous multitude that entered the state with the Gold Rush, California in those times also urgently needed the spiritual and cultural capital of the work ethic and social sobriety and discipline. This the Chinese immigrants contributed in abundant measure.

The Contribution of the Sojourners

The Indians had been all but decimated and herded out of sight on to reservations. The blacks were held down on the post-Reconstruction plantations and, later, in the urban ghettos of the North. The Chinese immigrants retreated into Chinatowns, but they soon made it clear that they had not been done away with. In law suits and by ingenious stratagems, they parried harassment by bigots and overzealous immigration authorities. Their friends in the outside white society sought them out in Chinatown for their friendship, and services.

Up to a point, cultural oppression of these ethnic minorities, the attack on their identities and self-esteem, succeeded for a time. Years were needed for the American Indian to recover from the trauma of conquest, loss of ancestral lands, and cultural heritage. Blacks suffered from deprivation of their cultural identity and heritage lost in the brutal uprooting from Africa. The Chinese were fortunate in having a rich and living culture to sustain them and give them confidence and a sense of self-worth that buoyed them up even in the most adverse circumstances.

Over half of the 300,000 Chinese who reached America before the 1880s returned to China. Some of these were immigrants who might have stayed had conditions favored them; some were sojourners intending all along to return to China. But, whether the one or the other, as numerous sources of the time show, they made a good impression on the people they met and worked with as bearers of the folk culture that was as much a part of the national culture and civilization of China as its more renowned productions. They were in general clean living and hardworking, cheerfully seeking the fortune they hoped to bring back to their families in the old country. They were mainly the free peasantry of China, yeomen farmers, the firm foundation of Chinese society. They shared the frailties of all men, and these were accented by the abnormal conditions of California of those days: the lack of women and normal family life fostered gambling, prostitution, and opium smoking.

This process of conflict and resolution, of mutual adaptation, was going on among other ethnic groups—Irish, Germans, Anglo-Saxons, Italians, French, Jews, and others—as they rubbed shoulders and borrowed from each other, learning to live together. Because of its very nature, America had to produce a new nation of nations, a unique amalgam of the many peoples flocking to its shores. Within half a century of its founding by the thirteen former British colonies on the East Coast, the new America was pushing forward a constantly expanding frontier westward to the opposite Pacific shore, opening up enormous riches on the way for farming and industry. This generated a driving initiative to develop technology to unlock those riches. This was vividly exemplified by the advance of technology in the Mother Lode. Within a few months and years, it advanced from the simple pan to the rocker, to the Long Tom and the wing dam, to the house-sized dredgers, quartz mines and the powerful monitors of hydraulic mining disemboweling the earth in the search for gold. Villages such as San Francisco were transformed in months into busy, brawling towns and then into fabulous cities importing wholesale all the technologies and luxuries of the old Western world.

Former peasants, yeomen farmers, and artisans from mainly agricultural and artisan societies were forced to adapt their lifestyles and thought just as rapidly to the needs of this new capitalist society, with its enlarging nuclei of urban, machine-industrial economies. America was now spearheading the industrial revolution initiated in England, and in less than another half-century would surpass its mentor. A profound revolution was taking place in America, and all who were in it were being swept along. All the various ethnic groups were experiencing this change, some joyously, with typically American exuberance; some with deep misgivings, like the Amish of Pennsylvania, secluding themselves in almost unchanging rural enclaves. Some adapted more readily and rapidly, more or less successfully. The Chinese too were carried along by this universal process of change and, as we have seen, were at first very much a part of it. They were being very successfully acclimatized to capitalist industrialism (this had far-reaching effects when these immigrants returned to China). Until the tragedy of exclusion, they suffered little more than the hardships suffered by other groups with the exception of the American Indians and blacks.

But then technological advance outdistanced them. The early immigrants had brought with them certain skills from China with its relatively advanced farming and artisan technology. These were of great use in the western states of America, which even in the mid-nineteenth century lagged behind the eastern states, separated from them by a still roadless continent. But by the 1870s the transcontinental railroads were built, and the very latest technology was coming into the West from the East. Much that the Chinese had for hire in the way of technology was now obsolete, uneconomical, and unneeded. In building the railway, they outmoded themselves.

It was now more than ever necessary for them to adapt themselves to the modern industrial technology of America by going into new trades, learning to run, tend, and make machines. That they had the capacity for this is obvious, but the opportunity was long denied them.

The new industrial system in its spread to the West brought with it the workers needed to run it and organized labor and its leaders. In the fight to unionize labor in the western states and in San Francisco in particular—the premier industrial and transport center—labor leaders such as Frank Roney and Samuel Gompers consciously used the goad of racial prejudice. By using this unworthy weapon to mobilize large numbers of people under their unions' leadership, they hoped to boost their unions' political and economic clout. Some union leaders, like Sigismund Danielewicz, inspired by the internationalist ideas of socialism and by the democratic ideals of America, advocated that Chinese and other ethnic workers should be brought into the unions and aided in their struggles against exploitation and oppression by the employers, but in the climate of America at that stage these men were voted down. The seamens', builders', and engineers' unions were all exclusionist, and with the spurious outcry against the Chinese and "slave" and "coolie" labor they set the tone for the policy followed by organized labor.[5] The Chinese immigrants and workers had been moving ahead steadily in concert with other immigrants as part of the great American advance to modern technology and thought, but now, deserted and attacked by their natural ally, organized labor, their progress was tragically interrupted and made infinitely more painful by exclusion.[6]

NOTES

1. James A. Whitney, *The Chinese and the Chinese Question* (New York: Thomson and Moreau, 1888).
2. Louise Clappe, *The Shirley Letters from the California Mines, 1851–1852* (Santa Barbara: Smith, 1970). Reprint.
3. Lucia Norman, *A Youth's History of California* (San Francisco: Roman, 1867).
4. Samuel Williams, *The City of the Golden Gate: San Francisco in 1875* (San Francisco: Book Club of California, 1921).
5. Alexander Saxton, *The Indispensable Enemy: A Study of the Anti-Chinese Movement in California* (Berkeley: University of California Press, 1971).
6. Stanford Lyman, *Asian in the West* (Reno: University of Nevada, 1970) and *Chinese Americans* (New York: Random House, 1974).

EXCLUSION

Two

1882–1943

There is a destiny which makes us brothers;
   None goes his way alone.
All that we send into the lives of others,
   Comes back into our own.

> EDWIN MARKHAM, poet of Placerville
> in the Gold Country of California

We hold these truths to be self-evident, that all men are created
equal, that they are endowed by their Creator with certain
unalienable Rights, that among these are Life, Liberty and the
pursuit of Happiness.

Declaration of Independence, 1776

How It Happened

XII

Hundreds of Chinamen have been slaughtered in cold blood
in the last five years by the desperadoes that infest our state.
The murder of Chinamen was of almost daily occurrence.

The Shasta Republican (California), December 18, 1856

NO APPRECIATION of the Chinese experience in the
United States is possible without an understanding of the traumas caused
when the first American Indian was shot in cold blood and the first African
slave was brought into the country. However, there have always been opponents
of such racism and violence. Supporters of democracy, equality, and
brotherhood defy the attack of the racists, which continues today.

Violent racism was early made a part of the California scene. T. T.
Waterman, in *Ishi, The Last Yahi*, tells of a pioneer who, in no military
capacity but simply for pleasure, had unprosecuted killed Indians for their
scalps as trophies.[1] And in 1849, San Francisco was plagued by the gang of
toughs known as the Hounds. These were former New York Bowery Boys
who had come to California under the command of Colonel J. D. Stevenson
to help "liberate" California from the Mexicans. When peace was declared,
they formed their own gang of hoodlums, tracking down at $25 a head seamen
who had jumped ship. Later, still making war, they had taken to terrorizing
and shaking down the Mexicans, Chileans, and Peruvians who lived in the
North Beach area, apparently solely on the ground that, as Doris Muscatine,
the San Francisco historian, tells it, "they were not proper Americans."[2] On
July 15, 1849, they raided the district known as Little Chile, ripping down
tents and shacks, raping women and beating up men. One woman was
murdered.

This sort of racist violence was endemic in the gold mines. The West
was "wild" because social conditions created a climate of violence. After the
Latins and the Mexicans, the Chinese were attacked.

This was an unexpected problem. Existing treaty relations between China and the United States made no provision for such occurrences. The imperial Chinese government had no interest in protecting its overseas citizens. It regarded them as felons and self-exiles. And the United States had been confident of its citizens' good behavior. Substantial citizens in the West had no unfriendly feelings toward the Chinese in the early days. They found them good employees. It was chic to have a Chinese cook or gardener, and in these capacities the Chinese were much appreciated by their employers. It was expected by the entrepreneurial class that Chinese labor would help develop the western states—development which was then regarded as a matter of urgency. And they were not disappointed. They were also hoping for a substantial growth of trade with China. Here, too, they were not disappointed until anti-Chinese policies went out of control not only in California but also in Washington, D.C. Anti-Chinese sentiment, which later found expression in the 1852 punitive tax on Chinese miners, was not yet widespread.

The Burlingame Treaty, 1868

The first treaties between the United States and China, the Treaty of Wangxia in 1844 and the Treaty of Tianjin in 1858, although imposed on China under threat of armed force, spoke of mutual respect and friendship but made no mention of Chinese in the United States. The Burlingame Treaty of 1868 dealt specifically with the question of Chinese immigration to America as part of American policy looking to the development of trade and economic relations between the United States and China in a cooperative spirit.

The Burlingame Treaty was a remarkable document. Anson Burlingame had so recommended himself to the Chinese in his six years as U.S. ambassador to Peking that they asked him to represent their interests in negotiations with the United States and other powers. He agreed, resigned his U.S. post, and received his diplomatic appointment from the emperor on November 22, 1867. With his Chinese colleagues, he then negotiated the 1868 treaty with William H. Seward, then secretary of state, who thought along much the same lines as Burlingame himself. The Burlingame Treaty thus expressed ideas that sound astoundingly progressive if they are taken to represent the thought of the emperor of China, the Son of Heaven.

After establishing the right of the emperor to appoint consuls in U.S. ports to look after the interests of Chinese trade and immigrants (whom he had previously only wanted to decapitate), Article IV prescribed reciprocal rights of freedom of worship and conscience of each country's citizens while in the other's country. Article V reads,

The United States of America and the Emperor of China cordially recognize the inherent and inalienable right of man to change his home and allegiance and also the mutual advantage of the free migration and emigration of their citizens and subjects, respectively from the one country to the other, for the purpose of curiosity or trade or as permanent residents.[3]

Article VI granted reciprocal most-favored-nation treatment to such immigrants or travelers, although "nothing herein contained shall be held to confer naturalization upon citizens of the United States in China or upon the subjects of China in the United States" (but this article in no way prohibited naturalization). And Burlingame farsightedly had Article VII inserted, giving the Chinese the right to enjoy "all the privileges of the public educational institutions under the control of the government of the United States."

The treaty at first received a good press. It was approved by the establishment of the time but did not still the opposition of the reactionary Know-Nothings and the racists. In 1860, those who wanted to keep the Chinese down and out had persuaded the California legislature to pass an act to prohibit "Mongolians" from attending U.S. public schools. Sporadic anti-Chinese activities continued. By 1870, anti-Chinese animosity was well established in California.

As the months went by the extravagant American hopes for rapid expansion of trade with China faded. With anti-Chinese racist sentiment on the increase, the racists saw the Burlingame Treaty as a major obstacle in their path. Law after law passed against the Chinese was struck down by U.S. courts as unconstitutional because they contravened the solemn treaty obligations of the U.S. government. The treaty thus became a prime target of anti-Chinese groups. Events played into their hands. Completion of the transcontinental railway in 1869 had unforeseen results for California and for the Chinese who had worked so devotedly to build it—an influx of labor, sharp competition for jobs, mass unemployment, and an economic crisis that had begun in the eastern states.

Racism

Anti-Chinese agitation, which culminated in the Chinese Exclusion Act of 1882 and resulted in decades of anti-Chinese violence, segregation, and discrimination, was a complex phenomenon. It fundamentally contradicted the principles of human rights and democracy on which the polity of the United States is based. The Exclusion Act and other legislation that supported violence against the founding principles of the United States had to be foisted on the American people by devious means.

Xenophobic, racist attitudes brought from the Old World to the New made slavery possible in the South, and one-third of the forty-niners were from the Deep South. They brought with them their slaves and prejudices and had to resort to all sorts of subterfuge to maintain their hold over their slaves in the free state of California. One important means was the court-upheld judgment that blacks could not testify against whites in court. This also applied to the native American Indians, with whom Chinese were then classified. This racism poisoned the wellsprings of political life in the new nation and outraged the sensibilities and good sense of decent men and women. Slavery in the South was incompatible with the free market in goods and labor of the industrializing, modernizing North. The Civil War of 1861–1865 decided that issue. The black slaves were emancipated, but more than one hundred years later the struggle is still going on to make emancipation a complete reality.

Interethnic hostility was, of course, not limited to blacks and Chinese. New England Puritan settlers were suspicious of non-English immigrants; ancient animosities even between the Irish and English passed with them to America. British Pennsylvanians objected strongly to the German "Palatine Boors" who "swarmed into our settlements and by herding together established their language and manners to the exclusion of ours." The writer of those lines feared that these aliens "would Germanize us rather than being Anglicized and would never adopt our language or customs any more than they would acquire our complexion." The same sort of prejudice was shown by San Francisco "sandlot politicians" against the Chinese. It seemed to matter little that these racist allegations lacked logic. While Irish mobs raided Chinese laundries in San Francisco, Irish hamlets were being burned by anti-Irish bigots in Pennsylvania. Anti-Chinese sentiment, like all racism, was compounded of this same sort of xenophobia, shortsighted economic greed, and rabid hatred feeding on fear. In 1873, this witches' brew was brought to the boil by sudden economic crisis, financial panic, and mass unemployment. Unprincipled political expediency did the rest.

Racist exploitation of one ethnic group by another is based on a twin foundation of psychosocial and economic factors. The "strangeness" felt by one ethnic group when confronted by the different color or speech or customs of another becomes an attitude of contempt when the more powerful group manages to subjugate or economically exploit the weaker. Given time to develop, racist antipathy and superiority become institutionalized. The dominant group arrogates special rights; it establishes segregated and inferior areas for the dominated group. It ensures itself better facilities in housing, transportation, eating, and entertainment and leisure suited to its higher social and economic status. These are familiar and well-documented aspects of racism. The dominant group also reinforces these institutionalized forms of segregation by a system of etiquette that becomes obligatory and almost instinctive for both the dominant and dominated groups. Both learn to use certain habitual and complementary gestures, body language, demeanor, and forms of address. The ruling race calls, "Boy!" The exploited race answers "Yessir!" The one stands forbiddingly upright. The other obsequiously bows his head. These forms of etiquette presume an ingrained sense of self-worth or lack of worth.

In the pre–Civil War South, whites and blacks each had their places and their obligatory ways of speech in relation to each other. Whites, unless they were "white trash," were always "Massa" or "Mister" or "Mistress"; blacks were plain "boy" or "girl" or called by their first names. The customary attitude of the black before whites was "cap in hand." As long as traditional circumstances continued, the brainwashed, conditioned adult of the dominant group and the oppressed group both knew almost instinctively how they must react in a particular situation. In the pre-civil rights era, a black person on entering a bus stepped to the back; a white, to the front. The threat of violent enforcement was always there.

Violations of these etiquette norms, whether conscious or unconscious, shock both sides. Both find it confusing when the opposite side does not conform to the stereotype, the imposed pattern. When the "inferior" acts "uppity," the "superior" feels bound to react. At sight of a black civil rights demonstration, the white chief of police in an Alabama town called on his troops to open fire. When new, unusual circumstances evolve, both groups can find themselves at a loss how to speak and act. When the "superior" approaches the "inferior" as an equal, the "inferior" mutters "slumming!" They may try to adapt traditional etiquette patterns to the new situation. If that fails, more drastic adjustments have to be made.

After the emancipation of the slaves in 1863, postbellum conditions in the South demanded traumatic changes in both white and black outlooks and attitudes. Gradually, these were evolved and continued until new changes due to the civil rights struggles of the 1960s and 1970s forced even more dramatic changes.

When two dominant racist etiquettes come into conflict, the results can be devastating. The collision between Aztec overlords and Spanish conquistadors in Mexico was such a collision. The Aztecs went to the wall, compelled to acknowledge the military superiority of the conquistadors. The 1870s confrontation between southern whites and Chinese immigrants in Mississippi led to surprising results. At first, the southern white equated the Chinese laborers with the former black slaves, whom they were meant to replace. But the Chinese refused to accept that equation. They turned into Christian grocers and businesspeople and, after being for a time neither black nor white, found a new niche as a "white." There was no other category in southern experience in which they could be put. As Doris Muscatine writes,

Ethnic groups tended to band together, then as now, and to guard their own prejudices. The largest group of migrants, from the summer of 1849 on, were Americans from the East. Intolerant of all Indians and all foreign born, emboldened by greed, and encouraged by the impermanence of their society, many of these men expressed their attitudes through actions that ranged from verbal bigotry to actual violence. Native Americans suffered the most severely at their hands, but the Chinese, Mexicans, and Spanish-Americans were not far behind. Racial or ethnic prejudice was often the source of injustice in the mining community.[4]

Events were taking place so fast and in an atmosphere so far removed from normal experience that people's reactions were not governed by normal tradition or custom. People did things that in the normal environment of their home towns, under the scrutiny of their neighbors and family, would have been unthinkable.

The Anti-Chinese Movement

When there were few or relatively few Chinese in a community, each one could be judged on his or her own merits by the larger community. Later, as the number of Chinese increased or were concentrated more heavily in one area, individuality disappeared. The unthinking spoke not of Ah Chen or Lee Sung but of "the Chinese." The conscious racists quickly evolved the handy stereotype: "those inscrutable (or "cunning" or "wily") Chinese" and when to that was added a hankering after that "wily Chinaman's" job, or mining claim, anti-Chinese fever took hold.

Indulgence in viciousness must always be paid for, always demands retribution. Slavery, the "peculiar institution" of the southern states, was paid for in the very costly Civil War—and is still being paid for. The anti-Chinese atrocities of the 1870s and 1880s were paid for and are still being paid for in the social distress of other ethnic minorities, in the social disturbances of the civil rights movement of the 1960s and 1970s, and in the catastrophic results of unwise foreign policy decisions inspired by racist attitudes rather than by prudent assessments of the nation's best interests. Who knows if the bill has yet been paid in full? America is a nation of nations. Shackling the creative activities of any of its constituent peoples is a loss to all the others.

In the West, the Chinese were only one target of bigoted racism. The Mexicans had been expelled. The Indian wars were barely over. The Indians were crowded into tribal reservations. The French were suspect because they tended to fraternize with the Hispanics and were therefore also undesirable aliens. Although blacks comprised only 1 or 2 percent of the population of California during the 1850s, they were still considered "a problem." California was free and loyal to the Union, but blacks (like Asians and Indians), were denied the most basic civil and political rights.

The Chinese immigrants had their defenders among those who knew them and those who were true to their American heritage, but the white racists grew more vocal and persuasive. Such racists were by no means confined to the beery sand lot politicians or the "pike," described by Charles Nordhoff as a "wandering gypsy-like southern poor white' who wanted to 'Drive the Chinese out of the State.' " In his notorious pamphlet *Some Reasons for Chinese Exclusion,* Samuel Gompers, the president of the American Federation of Labor, explained that the "racial differences between American whites and Asiatics would never be overcome. The superior whites had to exclude the inferior Asiatics, by law, or if necessary by force of arms." Stan Steiner quotes a statement by the Workingmen's Party of California: "We declare that white men and women, boys and girls, cannot live as people in this great republic . . . with[a] single Chinese coolie." He also quotes a spokesman for the white farmers of California: "This State should be a State for the white man. We want no other race here."[5] The writer William Thayer, in his *Marvels of the New West*, stated flatly that "the Anglo-Saxon race has laid the foundations of our Western empire" and that "Anglo-Saxons control the destiny of the human family"[6] The first constitution of California, reflecting these sentiments, stipulated that only white male citizens should have the right to vote.

At this time, a California legislative committee reported: "To develop . . . [the state's] latent resources and vitalize all her powers, we need sound, liberal, farseeing legislators; men who can mould and harness *all* inferior races to work out and realize her grand and glorious destiny."[7]

Powerful racist forces were thus arrayed against the Chinese. But, as we have seen, in the early 1850s and particularly while the first transcontinental railway was being built, the Chinese did so much useful work that the voices of prejudice were at first drowned out by praise for the Chinese contribution to the building of the West. Mary Coolidge, in her classic study of Chinese immigration, wrote, "In the first few years, the Chinaman was welcomed, praised, and considered almost indispensable; for in those days, race antipathy was subordinated to industrial necessity."[8] The daily *Alta California* on May 12, 1852, wrote chirpily, "The China boys will yet vote at the same polls, study at the same schools and bow at the same altar as our own countrymen."

In the first thirty-three years of free immigration, some 300,000 Chinese had come to the United States. Many died here. But in all, nearly two-thirds returned to China. That left 105,465 Chinese in America at the time of the 1880 census, or 0.21 percent of the population. Were the Chinese therefore really such a threat to America? They were "different," that is true. But so were the looks and mores of all other groups. None came here as Americans. What made latent anti-Chinese sentiment erupt into the violence that disgraced the West and claimed the attention of national statesmen so that they, in Washington, finally forced through the Exclusion Act against the real conscience of America, the stated ideals of America?

The United States in 1876

The general situation in the United States when the Exclusion Act was passed favored the anti-Chinese demagogues. In 1876, at the end of its first century, the U.S. population had grown from 2.5 million to 46 million. The nation was becoming a major industrial world power. It had 35,000 miles of railroad track from California to New York. This was the time that the great Philadelphia Centennial Exposition unveiled its wonders to the visiting world, among them the enormous 1,500-horsepower Corliss engine. People were speaking over Alexander Graham Bell's miraculous telephone.

Industrialism was an ascendant giant, confident of the future. Such changes do not occur without attendant social upheavals. Power and authority pass from older social groupings to new, and this process is often painful and sometimes traumatic. Washington, D.C., was already the stately capital of the democracy. Impatient financial and industrial tycoons were creating great fortunes and demanding a share of power from the old elite. After months of political maneuvers and fraud, Rutherford B. Hayes (Republican, 1877–1881) had become president in a closely contested election. This was the age of trusts and monopolies. In a drive for unbridled freedom to amass wealth, corruption had invaded the highest levels of government. President Grant's (1869–1877) own secretary had been operating with the Whiskey Ring in St. Louis, which defrauded the government of millions in excise taxes. President Theodore Roosevelt (1901–1909) wrote of the "riot of individualistic materialism, under which complete freedom for the individual . . . turned out in practice to mean perfect freedom for the strong to wrong the weak." It was one of those times when the American people in their tumultuous growth have had to deal with forces among them challenging the very spirit of their democracy and in a prolonged struggle have for a time been hard pressed until they have eventually reaffirmed their faith in the democratic principles on which the new nation was founded.

It was a rough time in the still Wild West. Gone were the days of simple trapper and homesteader. The population of California had grown from 93,000 in 1850 to close to 600,000 in 1870. San Francisco, its largest city, was a sprawling metropolis of 150,000. Land was hard to acquire. San Francisco had a restless mass of transient citizens anxious only to "get rich quick." The railway had brought into California a steady stream of working-class immigrants from the eastern states and settlers lured by colorful railway advertisements of opportunities in the West. "Go West, young man, go West!" became a familiar exhortation. Tens of thousands bought tickets and arrived to find their hopes dashed. The railway also brought to the West Coast the economic crisis already born in the East, with its relative overproduction and consequent unemployment. The United States had indeed created a single continental market. Moreover, California was generating its own economic crisis. The frontier was substantially disappearing. The Wild West with its wide-open spaces was no more. No one knew for certain, but it appeared that some half a dozen men controlled over half the readily arable land. Goods, instead of going around Cape Horn to and through San Francisco, now went straight to the inland towns by rail, and San Francisco was losing its favored middleman position garnering entrepôt profits.

The 1870s Crisis

Gambling had been the bane of the state ever since the easy money days of the Gold Rush. To make matters worse, besides saloon gambling at cards, everyone was gambling on the stock market. The gambling spirit reached its peak in the 1870s.

Between January and May 1872, the market value of stocks traded on the San Francisco Exchange rose from $17 million to $81 million. Speculation fever raged, with stocks as the thermometer. In their heyday, in 1874, the aggregate value of Comstock silver shares had risen at the rate of $1 million a day for nearly two months. Then came the crash. Yields began to drop.

When news spread that the Comstock Lode's richest mines, the Consolidated Virginia and the California, were nearing exhaustion, the market value of their stocks plummeted $140 million in a matter of days, a loss of "an average of $1,000 for every white adult in the city," according to the historian Theodore Hittell.[9] The Bank of California was forced to close in August 1875. This triggered a series of bankruptcies, and hardly a person in San Francisco escaped the resulting crisis.

The result of unbridled and unbalanced growth, the financial and economic crisis of the "terrible seventies" compounded the crash of Comstock stock. A million tramps roamed the nation. From 50,000 to 100,000 were unemployed in California. Of San Francisco's labor force of 150,000, some 15,000 were searching for work. And that labor force had been swelled by many thousands of the 12,000 Chinese paid off after working on the transcontinental railway and thousands of workers and their families fleeing from the eastern states. Its first real depression hit the West Coast.

Drought in the winter of 1876 had ruined the wheat harvest. Fruit and cattle farms suffered heavy losses. Thousands of Chinese and other farm laborers drifted into San Francisco to swell the ranks of unemployed. Small investors, clerks, shop assistants, workers who had invested in stocks and lost their savings, unemployed, and city speculators suffered a shock that had to find a scapegoat. The most visible one was the Chinese.

Some 30 percent of the state's work force was unemployed. Between 1873 and 1875, the railway brought in 262,000 people from the eastern states. Up to 66,000 were workers looking for jobs. Chinese immigration reached its highest level precisely at the time when unemployment and economic distress was at its peak in the bitter 1970s. Over 80,000 Chinese reached California from China in 1870–1875. In 1873 alone, 20,000 arrived, and more continued to arrive, despite the warnings of the Six Companies. And these immigrants were no longer only the yeomen farmers of the 1850s and 1860s. They included many urban lumpen-proletarians, unskilled labor taking advantage of the labor contractors' offers to advance wages to pay for the sea journey made cheaper by the introduction of steamships. The situation grew tense. With their long, black queues and loose, black suits, the Chinese were a highly visible minority of 10 percent of California's population, the largest minority in the state. The *New York Times* warned that the western states were being turned into "Chinese colonies." Anti-Chinese propaganda was a staple of the daily press.

Labor, just beginning to organize, was wracked by a split between those who pressed the demand for labor's rights and the solidarity of labor and those who wanted to sound a retreat and sacrifice principles to expediency. New immigrants formed a cheap labor pool that could be used to pressure American workers into accepting lower wages. Wages in some trades were, in fact, cut back 50 percent. Wherever a large and visible group of immigrants gathered, they inevitably became a target of animosity of those who felt themselves threatened. The new immigrants became convenient scapegoats for all the distress of the time, and racism became a major ingredient of the hostility against them. The economic soul of racism is reflected in the fact that, while the Irish were the backbone of the anti-Chinese agitation on the West Coast, in the anthracite coalfields of Pennsylvania they themselves were the embattled victims of economic oppression and political strife. As they were driven to desperation, violence flared. Twenty of the riotous rebels, the Molly Maguires, were arrested, tried, and sentenced to death.

Unfortunately, public leadership and administration in the West was not of the best. Capable political leaders and civic administrators found ample and rewarding opportunities in the eastern states. One writer, John Caughey, described the California legislature of the 1860s as "an infamous, ignorant, drunken, rowdy, prejudiced and traitorous body of men."[10] Even making allowances for political rhetoric, it was a damning assessment. With a large constituency of tough, adventurous, violent, and often lawless men roaming the streets and wharves, and saloons and gambling dens to back the demagogues up, the stage was set for tragedy.

"The Chinese Must Go!"

The Chinese issue was forced into state and national politics. All through the 1850s, the Democratic Party controlled California politics and government. It had elected six of California's seven governors up to that time and seven of the state's eight senators. From 1849 to 1862, it had controlled all but one of the state legislatures. By the 1860s, however, the newly formed Republican Party (launched in 1854) split the Democratic Party ranks and gained votes by supporting the Union against the proslavery Confederate Democrats and by advocating the building of the northern transcontinental railway.

The Republicans were backed by the *Sacramento Union*, "the most powerful newspaper in the state," which advocated trade with China and, as a supposedly necessary corollary and by-product, Chinese immigration. Business and industrial interests in the Republican Party were quite candid about wanting to employ "cheap Chinese labor" to help the new industries of California compete with their well-established eastern competitors. Until 1875, the *Union* opposed total exclusion of the Chinese, not only for business reasons, but also because it would be "contrary to the spirit of Republican institutions." However, the Republicans were badly defeated in the 1875 elections. The Democrats, seeking to erase the negative image of their proslavery stand in the Civil War, had espoused the anti-Chinese cause and now proclaimed their opposition to "servile" Chinese labor. Although spurious, this issue gained them support not only among genuinely antislavery groups but also among disgruntled labor and all the riotous urban riff-raff that had a vote. It was soon clear that an easy way to political success lay in exploiting the Chinese issue. The Democrats had passed their first official anti-Chinese resolution at their convention in Benicia in 1852. Now, in 1876, they staged a special anti-Chinese rally that attracted a crowd of 25,000. Together with the question of the land and railroad monopolies, the Chinese issue had become a key political issue in California.

More potent anti-"coolie" societies were now formed: the United Brothers of California and the Anti-Chinese Union of San Francisco in 1876 and the California Workingmen's Party in 1877.

Reading the signs, the new Republican presidential candidate, Rutherford Hayes, himself seeking an issue that would exorcise the financial scandals of the preceding Republican (President Grant's) administration, put an anti-Chinese plank in his platform and upstaged the Democrats. He narrowly lost the popular vote in the 1876 election but won by one hard-to-come-by vote in the electoral college.

Violence marked anti-Chinese agitation at every stage. It began in the mining areas, always a hotbed of violence, with the 1849 Tuolumne riot. It continued with the May 1852 county resolution banning Chinese from mining there, an example followed in Marysville with the expulsion of 400 Chinese from Horseshoe Bar and another 300 from the North Fork of the American River. Then in 1858 150 white miners in Folsom attempted to drive 200 Chinese from their homes and to take over the claims they worked for the Natoma Ditch Company. Violence spread further to the California lowlands. The first big anti-Chinese riot in San Francisco erupted in the summer of 1866, when Chinese were given jobs filling in a tideland area. White workers, dismissed because they demanded $1.25 a day (a higher wage than the Chinese demanded), attacked the Chinese, leaving one dead and fifteen injured. But up to 1870 this violence was sporadic. In 1870, it became a co-ordinated, sustained campaign.

The 1870 census showed that 42 percent of the white population on the West Coast was foreign born: Irish, British, German, Spanish American, French, and Italian. That year, many of these became naturalized, and then the racists among them could vent their anti-Chinese sentiments not only with their cudgels but also with their ballots, as citizens. The Chinese were not eligible for naturalization. Their children born in the United States (and there were few at that date, anyway) had only just acquired the right to U.S. citizenship by virtue of the Fourteenth Amendment, effective on July 28, 1868. Unable to testify against whites (1854 California Supreme Court decision), they had no recourse either to the courts or the ballot box, so they suffered blow after blow.

Special interests in many cases had succeeded in getting county and state legislatures to pass a number of local anti-Chinese hazing ordinances, some of which are listed as follows:

LOCAL ANTI-CHINESE LEGISLATION

1852   Miners in Foster, Atchinson's Bar, Columbia, and other camps exclude Chinese from mining. Foreign Miners Tax of $3 a month raised to $4.

1855   A $50 head tax is levied on "aliens not eligible for naturalization."

1860   Chinese children are denied admission to general public schools. After 1866, they were allowed to attend if white parents did not object. Chinese are denied admission to San Francisco City Hospital.

1870   San Francisco prohibits hiring of Chinese on municipal works. City ordinance bans use of Chinese carrying pole for peddling vegetables.

1873   San Francisco taxes laundries $15 per quarter of a year for using poles to carry laundry, while the tax on horse-drawn vehicles is $2 a quarter.

1873–1875   San Francisco passes various ordinances against use of firecrackers and Chinese ceremonial gongs.

1875   San Francisco Anti-Queue Law orders shaving off queues of all Chinese arrested. San Francisco ordinance requires 500 cubic feet of air within rooming houses (a health regulation aimed at clearing out Chinese ghettoes).

1880   San Francisco Anti-Ironing Ordinance passes, aimed at shutting down Chinese nighttime laundries.

1882   San Francisco New Laundry Licensing Act requires licensing of mostly Chinese facilities.

STATE ANTI-CHINESE LEGISLATION AND JUDICIAL DECISIONS

1850   Foreign Miners Tax (1850,1852,1853, and 1855) is aimed at forcing Chinese out of the mines. The tax levied varies from $3 to $20 a head per month.

1852   Bond Act requires all arriving Chinese to post a $500 bond.

1854   California Supreme Court decision makes Chinese ineligible to testify in court against whites.

1855   Head tax requires shippers to pay $50 for every Chinese passenger they bring to America. California legislature extends to Chinese an existing law barring the testimony of Indians and blacks in court in cases involving whites.

1858   Act to Prevent Further Immigration of Chinese and Mongols prohibits Chinese entry.

1860   A Fishing tax is levied on Chinese activities in fishing.

1870   Act to Prevent Kidnapping and Importing of Mongolian, Chinese, and Japanese Females for Criminal Purposes prevents entry of Chinese women without special certificates. Act to Prevent Importing of Chinese Criminals prohibits Chinese males' entry unless person is proved of good character. Chinese are prohibited from owning land in the state.

1875   Law to regulate the size of Chinese shrimping nets reduces catches. [See Chapter 8, on Chinese in the fishing industry.]

1879   California state constitution prohibits corporations and municipal works from hiring Chinese and authorizes cities to remove Chinese residents from their boundaries to specified areas.

1880   Fishing Act prohibits Chinese from engaging in any fishing business. Act to Prevent the Issuance of Licenses to Aliens deprives Chinese of licenses for businesses or occupations.

1882   California legislature declares legal holiday to facilitate public anti-Chinese demonstrations.

1885   Political Codes Amendment prohibits Chinese from attending general public schools, forcing attendance at segregated schools.

1887   Penal code institutes fishing license tax aimed against Chinese fishermen.

1891   Act Prohibiting Immigration of Chinese Persons into the State prohibits Chinese entry.

1893   Fish and Games Act prohibits use of Chinese nets in fishing.

A number of these taxes and levies and prohibitions were later contested in the courts and declared null and void, but in the meantime, they did considerable damage to the interests of the Chinese involved. I can find no evidence that taxes paid or losses incurred under unconstitutional laws were ever refunded. This is by no means a complete list but it is enough to illustrate the situation that was being created by the late 1870s. Such laws proclaimed an officially backed open field day against the Chinese. The results soon made themselves felt.

In 1871, in the wake of protests against the "pro-Chinese" Burlingame Treaty, a massacre of Chinese took place in Los Angeles. Twenty-two Chinese were killed, and hundreds were driven from their homes. $35,000 worth of property was stolen. Brave Americans tried to save them. Judge Widney, a lawyer, had the courage to go out pistol in hand among the lynch mob and save the life of a Chinese who already had a rope fixed around his neck.[11] White cigar makers called for a boycott of Chinese-made cigars. Racist labor groups led by men like Samuel Gompers, instead of unionizing the Chinese workers, declared that the Chinese worked for depressed wages and were beyond the pale of labor. The International Workingmen's Association and the Knights of Labor advocated an end to Chinese immigration. The craft unions especially wanted to fight off any influx of labor into their trades.

The Anti-Chinese Issue in Labor Politics

One of the most blatant examples of exclusion as a weapon in trade union in-fighting was the case of the Cornish miners. In 1869, they had been brought over especially to do rock tunneling on the transcontinental railway, but they had been bested by the Chinese and publicly told about this by no less an authority than Crocker himself. In 1869–1870, they formed the California Workingmen's Society so that "all those of Mongolian origin should be prohibited from entering California."[12]

The Chinese imperial government, which had paid no attention to the plight of the Chinese in America, now took belated action at the urging of such Americans as former Secretary of State William Seward, and appointed Ch'en Lan-pin and Yung Wing (that first of Chinese students to come to America) as imperial commissioners to look after their interests in the United States, Peru, and Spain. This territory was so extensive that their efforts were, of course, too dissipated to be very effective, but they did succeed in ending the "pig trade."

Agitation against the Chinese grew to a peak in the depression of the mid-1870s. Chinese were driven out of many small towns in California. Their houses and business premises were set on fire and gutted. The violence spread from California to Oregon and Washington. In 1877, employers of Chinese labor began to receive threatening letters.

Sandlot Agitators

On July 23, 1877—"Riot Night," in San Francisco history—a crowd of some 10,000 gathered on a vacant lot near City Hall to hear speeches on the eight-hour day and the nationalization of the railroads. Suddenly two shots were fired, wounding two workers, and a riot erupted. Bands of men sped off on a rampage through the streets, assaulting Chinese with cudgels and setting fire to twenty-five Chinese laundries. The next night, the riot resumed. There were more burnings and clashes with the police. Chinese laundries and homes were ransacked. The Six Companies, speaking for the Chinese, appealed to the city authorities for protection. Chinese dared not go out on the streets. On the third day, an attack was launched on the docks of the Pacific Mail Steamship Company, said to be the largest carrier of Chinese into the country and hirer of Chinese for its crews. The dock was defended by the police, but nearby lumber yards were set on fire. Then another attack was launched against the Chinese settlement on Rincon Hill, with more casualties. Finally, army troops, the navy, and a contingent of some 5,000 citizen vigilantes and their "Pickhandle Brigade" quelled the rioters. Half a million dollars worth of damage had been done.

But the end of the riot was clearly just a lull in the storm. In the summer and fall of 1877, the vacant lots of the city became rallying grounds for the anti-Chinese elements. They were inflamed by the oratory of such men as Denis Kearney, a former sailor and owner of a small drayage business, who was backed by the Anti-Chinese Union (formed the year before) and the United Brothers of California. Kearney attacked big corporations such as the Southern Pacific Railroad for exploiting the situation in the state and making millions by hoarding and speculating with the land grants, and for battening on the people's misery. He pledged to fight against corrupt government, the capitalists and monopolists, but mostly he attacked the Chinese immigrants for working for starvation wages and robbing American workers of jobs.

Kearny did not need to look far for proof of the attitude of Big Business toward Chinese labor. The wealthy California landowner Leland Stanford, one of the Big Four of the Central Pacific Railway and one-time Governor of California, said: "I think the wealth of the country will be due to the advent of cheap labor. . . . I would open the door and let everybody come who wants to come . . . until you get enough here to reduce the price of labor to such a point that its cheapness will stop their coming."

So Kearny began and ended his tirades with the cry, "The Chinese must go! They are stealing our jobs!"

The popular press, looking for an issue to boost sales, avidly reported his activities and took up his cry. Scurrilous anti-Chinese cartoons appeared in newspapers and magazines. To get more clout in the legislature, the leaders of the movement formed the Workingmen's Party of California, with some thirty-five clubs functioning in the city.

The rabble-rousing became more strident. Economic conditions in the city grew steadily worse as the depression entered its fourth year; 50,000–100,000 were unemployed in the state. Thousands were homeless and hungry. Private sources of relief were exhausted. Hungry men looked for a way out. The cry went up to drive the Chinese from their homes and jobs. Kearney was jailed when he proposed to solve the problem by erecting gallows on the vacant lots, but his place was quickly taken by one Mr. Gannon who proclaimed that if the public would take action "the city will be levelled to ashes and the ruins filled with roasted bodies within twenty-four hours." To head off the Kearneyite anticapitalist extremists, the Southern Pacific Railway tycoons hurriedly put together a Republican-Democratic bloc guaranteeing that the full force of popular discontent would be diverted against the Chinese.

The Workingmen's Party showed surprising strength in the elections to the California State Constitutional Convention in 1878, called to modernize the 1849 constitution. With 51 of the 152 delegates, it was able to introduce a whole series of anti-Chinese articles. The constitution prohibited further immigration of Chinese laborers and prescribed their removal outside the limits of certain cities and towns. Chinese were deprived of employment in any state, county, municipal, or other public works. Provision of special police officers in parts of cities and counties known as the "Chinese Quarter" or Chinatown was prohibited. That constitution was amended more than 300 times after its adoption and has been described as "one of the most detailed and confusing ever contrived . . . anywhere, anytime."[13] Special police in San Francisco Chinatown were prohibited because the marching and drill societies of the Workingmen's Party were planning to raid Chinatown. All that stopped them was the presence of the special non-Chinese police, who were paid by the Chinese community organizations, and the tongs with their fighting men and the arms that it was suspected had been brought into Chinatown for its defense. Alexander Saxton declares that "Chinatown itself had become a fortress."[14] But densely populated Chinatown, which seemed at first sight to be so vulnerable to fire, was so tightly knit against the outside danger that all attempts to set it ablaze failed, and the threatened catastrophe was averted.

The League of Deliverance persuaded forty San Francisco labor unions to urge a general boycott of Chinese-made goods and to oust Chinese from their jobs whatever they might be. A new California law stipulated that any individual or corporation employing any Chinese was guilty of a misdemeanor and subject to a fine of not less than $100 nor more than $1,000 or by imprisonment for from 50 to 500 days or both fine and imprisonment.

The Workingmen's Party then went en masse to various factories and mills to demand the dismissal of Chinese workers. Several mills complied: the Pacific Jute Mills dismissed 700 Chinese, and the Pioneer Woolen Mills and the Golden Gate Mills in Potrero pledged not to hire Chinese any more. Their doors closed, a welcome saving to them in a depression winter. They then took their case to court and won invalidation of the state laws and those articles of the constitution that supported the Workingmen's Party demands.

The Chinese, too, fought back in the courts, backed by their family and district associations. A number of anti-Chinese ordinances were struck down under the Civil Rights Act of 1870 and the Fourteenth Amendment (originally passed to protect blacks) and also, most importantly, under the Burlingame Treaty. The presidents of the Six Companies and the San Francisco Chinese Y.M.C.A. in 1876 addressed a memorial to President Grant:

Our people in this country, for the most part, have been peaceable, law-abiding, and industrious. . . . They have found useful employment in all the manufacturing establishments of this coast, in agricultural pursuits, and in family service. While benefiting themselves with the honest reward of their daily toil, they have . . . left all the results of their industry to enrich the state.

By that time, the frustrated Workingmen's Party was being phased out. It was now clear that Kearney's cry of "The Chinese must go!" must remain only a cry unless it could be transformed into the law of the land, and that transformation was blocked by the Burlingame Treaty. The situation of the Chinese was not helped by the fact that in these years their immigration continued at a relatively high level. It had averaged 13,710 from 1859 to 1872 but suddenly increased to over 22,292 in 1873 and to 22,781 in 1876. Steamship companies were offering bargain fares to would-be immigrants.

In August 1877, therefore, a convention was held in Sacramento to demand abrogation of the Burlingame Treaty. Denis Kearney called for repudiation of the Treaty in a speech on Thanksgiving Day, 1877. Oakland workers sent a petition to President Hayes in December, and the California legislature sent a delegation to Washington to demand modification of the treaty. The

44th Congress, for the first time, answered these and numerous other appeals with a joint resolution calling on the president to have the treaty modified.

NOTES

1. T. T. Waterman, *Ishi, The Last Yahi* (Berkeley: University of California Press, 1918).
2. Doris Muscatine, *San Francisco: Biography of a City* (New York: Putnam, 1975), p. 264.
3. Li Tien-lu, *Congressional Policy on Chinese Immigration* (New York: Arno Press and New York Times, 1978), p. 120. Reprint of 1916 edition.
4. Muscatine, *San Francisco*, p. 99.
5. Stan Steiner, *Fusang* (New York: Harper & Row, 1979).
6. William Thayer, *Marvels of the Old West*, quoted in Steiner, *Fusang.*
7. Maisie Conrat and Richard Conrat, *The American Farm* (Boston/San Francisco: Houghton Mifflin/California Historical Society, 1977).
8. Mary Roberts Coolidge, *Chinese Immigration* (New York: Holt, 1909).
9. Theodore H. Hittell, *History of California* (San Francisco: Stone, 1886–1897).
10. John Walton Caughey, *Gold is the Cornerstone* (Berkeley: University of California Press, 1948).
11. C. P. Dorland, *Chinese Massacre at Los Angeles in 1871* (Los Angeles: Annual of Historical Society of Southern California, 1894), vol. 3, pp. 22–26.
12. Arthur Cecil Todd, *The Cornish Miner in America* (Truro, England: Barton, Glendale Clarke, 1976).
13. T. H. Watkins, *California* (New York: Weathervane Books, 1923).
14. Alexander Saxton, *The Indispensable Enemy:* A Study of the Anti-Chinese Movement in California (Berkeley: University of California Press, 1971).

Exclusion Goes to Washington (1)

CHAPTER

XIII

It is a well-known fact that there has been a wholesale system of wrong and outrage practiced upon the Chinese population of this State, which would disgrace the most barbarous nation upon earth.

Report of the Two Houses of the California Legislature, March 11, 1862

THE WORKINGMEN'S PARTY was the noisy, extreme, and conspicuous spearhead of the drive against the Chinese; it was the street contingent. When six Chinese tenant farmers were attacked and five of them killed, the murderer confessed to being under orders from the Workingmen's Party. Behind it, exploiting and bridling it, were much more powerful forces that finally ensured that the outcries against corrupt politicians, capitalists and land monopolists became more and more muted and the anti-Chinese demagogy more strident. Chief of these forces were the leading groups in the Republican and Democratic parties and organized labor led by the American Federation of Labor. This coalition did not arise all at once. It formed by degrees and was never even acknowledged. The Republican Party took over the driver's seat on the anti-Chinese bandwagon. The *Sacramento Union*, now under new ownership, deserted its former liberal stand and followed the party's lead, although they disdained the crude methods of the Kearneyites.

It is important to recognize what was really in the minds of the participants in this vast charade that was being played. The Kearneys represented the rabble-rousing racist storm troopers. Organized labor—or, rather, leaders such as Gompers or Frank Roney trying to organize labor—had a generous dose of the same motivation, but while Kearney was swayed by the intoxication of the cause he sponsored Gompers and Roney would have invented the Chinese issue if they had not encountered it ready made. Once that issue was no longer effective as a tool for marshaling their wayward followers, they readily switched from it to the Japanese issue and then the eastern European issue. "The Caucasians," Gompers declared in 1905, "are not going to let their standard of living be destroyed by negroes, Chinese, Japs, or any others."[1]

The still more powerful personages who directed the two great political parties were some more, some less, influenced by racist considerations. Almost all were of the Anglo-Saxon establishment or aspired to be, but while some were calculatedly opportunistic quite a number sincerely believed in their rationalizations, however erroneous these might be or might have been seen to be on closer examination. Typical of these latter was Frederick Low, California's ninth governor (1867), who, literate and articulate, left in his *Reflections* a reasoned summary of his views on the Chinese.[2] Low was an intelligent man who had come to California in the Gold Rush days and later became a banker, state representative in Congress, and U.S. ambassador to China. He defended the Chinese from the violent attacks of their persecutors and actively promoted trade with China, but he opposed Chinese immigration because he considered the Chinese not capable of

Assimilating with our people and able to take part of the responsibility and burden of the country . . . an alien mass we cannot give the ballot to and to whom it would be unsafe to give the ballot. . . . No Chinaman who would emigrate here in the ordinary life of the Chinese would ever be able to understand that he should vote intelligently or honestly, and it would create a great mass of votes for sale and increase— if such a thing were possible—the corruption in our politics.[3]

The 45th Congress tested the situation again when, in 1879, it passed a bill prohibiting vessels from bringing more than fifteen Chinese at one time to the United States. Similar bills had been declared unconstitutional by the U.S. Supreme Court because they violated the Burlingame Treaty, so this bill was vetoed by President Hayes. However, he added, "I regard the very grave discontent of the people of the Pacific States . . . as deserving the most serious attention by the people of the whole country and a solicitous interest on the part of Congress and the Executive."[4] He recalled that, while Congress had authority to terminate a treaty, the power of making new treaties or modifying existing treaties was not lodged by the Constitution in Congress but in the president, by and with the advice and consent of the Senate.

The Treaty of 1880

With abrogation of the Burlingame Treaty now a primary aim of anti-Chinese agitation, the federal administration, with the concurrence of Congress, initiated negotiations with China to modify the treaty and so remove this diplomatic obstacle to exclusion. Ambassador G. F. Seward in Peking, aware of the political realities both in China and in the United States, wished to prepare the way gradually in friendly fashion for a wide-ranging discussion with China on the immigration question and to avoid an abrupt, precipitate tone of ultimatum. In 1879, he therefore limited his negotiations to the reasonable issue of preventing emigration of four classes of people—namely, criminals, "lewd" women, diseased people, and contract laborers. There was naturally no difficulty in getting Chinese concurrence.

But this request was the thin edge of the wedge. When U.S. commissioners John Swift (California) and William Trescot (South Carolina), with James Angell, who now replaced Seward as ambassador to Peking, arrived in the Chinese capital, they immediately got down to what they really wanted. The subsequent negotiations were a shabby performance on both sides. The words *chicanery* and *hypocrisy* immediately come to mind. The American negotiators demanded the right to "regulate, limit, suspend, or prohibit" the coming of Chinese laborers, the words "Chinese laborers" signifying all immigration other than that for "teaching, trade, travel, study, and curiosity."

With the exception of the word *prohibit*, the pliant imperial government negotiators gave them what they wanted. They knew they faced the threat of wholesale abrogation of the Burlingame Treaty. When they asked for clarification about the laws or measures that would be taken by the Americans to regulate, limit, or suspend immigration of Chinese laborers, they were told that these could not be revealed, that "two great nations discussing such a subject must always assume that they will both act in good faith and with due consideration for the interest and friendship of each other."[5] The Chinese government knew quite well that at that very moment Chinese were being killed, beaten, and humiliated in America, but they supinely accepted these patently hypocritical and deceptive statements and promises. While before it had had no interest in protecting its nationals abroad, now, thirty years before its total collapse, the Qing government had brought the nation to such a pass that it could not protect them even if it wanted to.[6]

In the new treaty signed on November 17, 1880, China agreed to regulation, limitation, or suspension, but not absolute prohibition, of immigration of Chinese laborers into the United States as long as the entry of other classes was not affected. In return, the U.S. government undertook to protect against personal maltreatment or abuse all Chinese already in the country and secure them the same rights and privileges as nationals of other countries enjoying most-favored-nation treatment.

The new Republican tactics paid off with victory in the 1880 elections. Ratification of the 1880 treaty opened the way for what was really in the minds of its congressional backers: total exclusion of the Chinese. The Republican Party at its convention stated that they would regard unrestricted immigration of Chinese as an evil of great magnitude and would invoke measures to restrain it. The Democratic Party Convention, not to be outdone, declared that "their influence being corrupt and corrupting, Chinese should not have lot or part among the American people."[7] The difference in wording was minimal. Both great parties were committed to exclusion and, despite a number of courageous voices opposed to it, were locked in a partisan struggle to make maximum use of this vote-catching policy.

Learning that exclusion legislation would soon be introduced, Chinese in considerable numbers hastened to beat the deadline. Through their district and family associations, the main centers of Guangdong emigration were probably better informed than most people in Peking about American matters. But even they underestimated the results of exclusion.

In 1880, some 9,604 entered the United States, and 11,890 in 1881. In 1882, more than ever arrived—39,579. Thousands, apprehensive of the future, left, but the net gain was 29,213. That was still only 105,465 Chinese in a total population of 50,155,783 or 0.2 percent of the total.*

The 1882 Exclusion Act

Debates in the Congress on the proposed Chinese exclusion bill were highly charged. Anti-Chinese rhetoric was often inflammatory. Those demanding exclusion spoke of the Chinese' vicious habits and degrading influence; they were unassimilable, took low wages, competed with white labor, sent their money home, and introduced loathesome diseases. They were slaves and heathens and did not bring their wives and families. At least Denis Kearny was no hypocrite. It would be a bold woman to leave China for the United States in those days. One would have thought that only the Chinese frequented San Francisco brothels, gambled, and smoked opium. All these vices were common in Western society at that time.

Senator Farley of California averred that "we are not oppressing these people in any way by this proposed legislation, we are simply doing that which the treaty itself provides that we should do." He further proposed that Chinese should not be eligible for naturalization.[8]

The opponents of exclusion were eloquent but in a minority. Senator Brown of Georgia asked, "Is there a Senator here who can say that this bill is within the spirit of the treaty?"[9] Dawes of Massachusetts was sarcastic and prophetic: "In this bill we do not absolutely prohibit for twenty years any Chinese laborer from coming; we only declare that if he does come, he will go to the penitentiary."[10] Nevertheless, the bill passed by twenty-nine votes to fifteen; 32 were absent.

In the House of Representatives debate, Orth objected to the Chinese because "they do not wear our kind of clothes . . . and when they die, their bones are taken back to their native country."[11] Senator Sherman of Ohio, said about the bill, "It is unnecessary . . . it is against the policy of our Constitution and laws . . . it goes beyond the power conferred by the treaty and . . . will injure us commercially."[12] Nevertheless, the bill was passed in the House by 201 votes to 37 with 51 not voting. When the bill was sent to President Arthur for his signature, he vetoed it on the grounds that it was "unreasonable" and "unjustified," that a twenty-year suspension of Chinese

---

* Some apologists for the California racists have argued that since there were an "excessive" number of Chinese on the West Coast—10 percent of its population in 1870—it is juggling with figures to point out that the total number of Chinese in the United States was only 0.16 percent of the population. But the Exclusion Act was not passed simply to reduce the percentage of Chinese in California but throughout the country.

immigration was tantamount to prohibition, and that the personal registration and passport requirements were repugnant to the democratic spirit of American institutions.

The U.S. Senate and House of Representatives therefore amended the bill, reducing suspension of immigration to ten years, and it was signed by the president just over a month later on May 6, 1882. The exclusion of Chinese from the United States had become the law of the land.

In its final form, the act prohibited the immigration of Chinese laborers, skilled and unskilled, for ten years; required the registration of Chinese and the carrying of valid passports; made Chinese ineligible for naturalization and forbade entry to wives of Chinese laborers then in the United States. The so-called "exempt classes"—teachers, students, merchants, tourists, and diplomatic personnel—were not banned from entering the United States, but such "discretionary" powers were given to the immigration authorities that a number of exempt Chinese found the humiliations heaped on them too much to endure.

This was, in effect, an exclusion act based on race, the first such law to be passed in the United States. Honest voices were not lacking. Congressman Joyce declared that

> I would not vote for it if the time were reduced to one year or even one hour, because I believe that the total prohibition of these people from our shores for any length of time, however short, is not only unnecessary and uncalled for, but it is a cowardly repudiation, in our dealing with a weak nation, of a just and long established principle in our government as well as a bold and open violation of the letter and spirit of our solemn treaty obligations with the people of China.[13]

Discussing the Exclusion Act, the California historian Walter Bean comments, "Very few nations had ever withheld the privilege of naturalization on racial grounds, in doing so the United States had been in the company of Nazi Germany and the Union of South Africa."[5]

Even granted that the 1880 treaty gave the United States the right to limit or suspend Chinese immigration for a reasonable period, this right was conditional on need: "when the coming of Chinese laborers . . . endangers the good order of certain localities." At the time of the passage of the bill, it was clear that this condition did not in fact exist. The passage of the 1882 bill, however, created that condition over wide areas.

It had just been decided by the State Department (in 1881) that Chinese students would not be admitted to American military and naval academies. This was a terrible disappointment to that first of Chinese students in the United States, Yung Wing, who had been working hard precisely to get such training for his compatriots. Because of this rebuff and other discriminatory U.S. legislation, the Chinese government ordered all government-sponsored students to return to China. Fears on the part of conservative Chinese elements that Chinese students in America were picking up "dangerous" modern ideas also had a lot to do with this decision.

NOTES

1. Samuel Gompers, *American Federationist*, 12 (1905), 636–637.
2. F. F. Low, *Some Reflections of an Early California Governor* (Sacramento: California Book Collectors Club, 1959).
3. *Ibid.*
4. *House Journal*, 45th Congress, Third Session, 1878–79, p. 606.
5. Li Tien-lu, *Congressional Policy on Chinese Immigration* (New York: Arno Press and New York Times, 1979). Reprint of 1916 ed.
6. Li, *Congressional Policy*, p. 32.
7. *Congressional Record*, 47th Congress (1882), Vol. 13, Part 3, p. 2130.
8. *Ibid.*
9. *Ibid.*, p. 1642.
10. *Ibid.*, p. 1670.
11. Li, *Congressional Policy*, p. 38.
12. *Congressional Record, ibid.*, p. 2206.
13. *Congressional Record, ibid.*, p. 2185.
14. Walton Bean, *California, An Interpretive History* (New York: McGraw-Hill, 1968), p. 512.

Exclusion Goes to Washington (2)

XIV

The work was so obviously needed and all groups and areas vied with each other to build a railroad in their area, so that they would have welcomed the devil himself had he built a road. The lack of white laborers was too evident to cause even the most ardent anti-Chinese to resent their employment on such work.

ROBERT E. WYNNE, "Reaction to the Chinese in the Pacific Northwest and British Columbia"

How DID a local California partisan issue become the politics of the national Congress?

Exclusion Becomes a National Issue

By the late 1870s, it was clear that the road to political power in California required an anti-Chinese platform, and both the Democratic and Republican parties took this path. Because the strength of the two major parties was so nearly equal nationally in these years (see Table 2) and because the Pacific Coast states held the balance of power, this single issue of Chinese immigration largely determined how the national elections would go. In a series of elections, the parties finished neck to neck. The 1876 election hinged on one electoral college vote. Everything depended on the few voters in the western states who could be persuaded to cross over party lines, and these swing votes were tied to the Chinese Exclusion issue. California political issues became the fulcrum of national politics.

It must also be recalled that by the 1870s the attitude of the eastern states on immigration in general had changed radically. Six million immigrants entered the country between 1840 and 1870, bringing the U.S. population in 1870 to 40 million. This led to grave industrial and social problems for

Table 2. Party Balance (1876–1892)

Presidential Candidates	Political Party	Popular Vote	Electoral College Vote
1876 Election			
Rutherford B. Hayes	Rep.	4,033,768	185
Samuel J. Tilden	Dem.	4,284,125	184
1880 Election			
James A. Garfield	Rep.	4,449,053	214
Winfield S. Hancock	Dem.	4,442,035	155
1884 Election			
Grover Cleveland	Dem.	4,911,017	219
James G. Blaine	Rep.	4,848,033	182
1888 Election			
Benjamin Harrison	Rep.	5,440,216	233
Grover Cleveland	Dem.	5,538,233	168
1892 Election			
Grover Cleveland	Dem.	5,556,918	277
Benjamin Harrison	Rep.	5,176,108	145

the eastern entry cities like New York and Boston, and public demand for restriction of all immigration had intensified. Although Chinese immigration did not affect the eastern states, in these circumstances eastern politicians had become more sympathetic to California demands for restriction of Chinese immigration. Cases of the use of Chinese as strikebreakers in North Adams (Mass.), Belleville (N.J.), and Beaver Falls (Pa.) were widely publicized.

Thus Chinese exclusion became a national issue and the policy of a great democratic nation in its relations with one of the oldest civilizations and cultures on earth. The results, although difficult to assess at the time, were enormous.

Anti-Chinese agitation and acts in California and elsewhere did not cease with the passage of the Exclusion Act. Violence increased as if given license, and segregation and discrimination against the Chinese became institutionalized for over sixty years. Chinese settlements were burned, and Chinese were shot in gold-mining towns in Oregon and Idaho.

In September 1885 occurred one of the most atrocious incidents in this whole campaign. Twenty-eight Chinese were massacred in the Wyoming mining town of Rock Springs. Eleven were burned alive in their cabins. Many were wounded and driven from their homes. That same month, a band of white men and two Indians attacked a camp of thirty-five Chinese in Issaquah, east of Seattle, killing three and wounding two. The rest fled. In November, a Tacoma mob herded 700 Chinese there into wagons and, after a night of exposure in the open country in which two died, put them on a Portland-bound train. Fearful after the Tacoma incident, 150 Chinese fled Seattle for San Francisco; 350 others were driven out soon after. Anti-Chinese violence spread like an epidemic north along the West Coast and the valleys from Santa Barbara to Port Townsend. Pasadena, Hollister, Redding, Los Angeles,

Sacramento, Sonoma, Chico, Merced, Anderson, San Buenaventura, Vallejo, Wheatland, Santa Cruz, Yuba City, Truckee, Napa, Placerville, Carson, Dixon, San Jose, Petaluma, Lincoln, Gold Run, Eureka, Santa Rosa, Auburn, Nevada City, and San Francisco were all affected. In 1886, the concerted movement to "clear the Chinese out" continued. Thirty-five California communities reported expulsions between January and April 1886. In three months, 20,000 Chinese poured into San Francisco's Chinatown. In 1887, thirty-one Chinese miners were massacred on the Snake River in eastern Washington. From the 1870s to the 1890s, Chinese were terrorized up and down the West Coast. The scale and viciousness of these outbreaks has never been fully described. In 1887, Tacoma again gathered 3,000 more Chinese who had fled outlying areas and gave them twenty-four hours notice to leave. For decades after, no Chinese were allowed to live in that city. At the Treadwell Mines in Alaska in August 1886, despite the efforts of the governor, all the Chinese miners but one, the too-well-liked China Joe, were forced aboard small boats and cast adrift. Luckily, they succeeded in making it to Wrangel Island.

Driven out of the small towns, many Chinese left for China, others were forced to take refuge in the larger Chinatowns such as those in San Francisco, Seattle, and Los Angeles, as in beleaguered fortresses. Exclusion transformed the Chinatowns into a "phenomenon peculiar to this nation and no other," in the words of Stan Steiner.[1] Chinatowns were many things to the Chinese of the exclusion days. One was a refuge. In San Francisco, middle-aged Chinese can remember the time when they did not dare venture beyond Chinatown limits because they feared being abused.

The anti-Chinese agitation produced an ugly and voluminous record of crimes against a long-suffering people. It also produced a massive literature that purported to substantiate its demands. For example, Horace F. Page, California Representative in Congress, said, "They have no children to support or educate. . . . They contribute nothing to the support of the government."[3] But Page neglected to mention that conditions had been created such as to make any Chinese hesitate to bring wife and children with him to the West and that, far from contributing nothing to the support of the government, whole counties in California had survived and prospered on the illegal miner's tax levied on the Chinese miners, while Chinese-paid taxes at one time made up one quarter of California's income. He was also forgetting a stupendous railway, vast reclamation projects and landfills, and valuable agricultural undertakings that were now the heritage of America.

In those days it was calculated that a male immigrant represented, in addition to the cash he brought with him, a capital value of $1500. That means the 300,000 Chinese who came to California during 1849–1880 enriched the country by over $400,000,000. And this was a constantly renewing source of wealth and labor. Half of the Chinese were sojourners who left after putting in a period of work, to return home and be replaced by fresh work hands.

"[The Chinese are] by the unalterable structure of their being voluntary slaves," stated the California Senate in a memorandum to the U.S. Congress in 1878.[3] But the memorandum omitted to mention that none of the Chinese workers were slaves, but had paid their own way or had come on contract to such major enterprises as the Southern Pacific Railway Company. The only slaves were the women kidnapped and brought to America to be prostitutes, often with the connivance of the courts and the immigration authorities.

How far from being servile these Chinese immigrants were is exemplified by the case of the American ship *Robert Browne*. It sailed from Amoy (in Fujian Province) in 1852 carrying 450 Chinese who thought they were on their way to the United States as laborers. When they discovered that they were actually being transported by force to Peru to be used as contract "coolies," they mutinied and forced the ship aground on the Liuchu Islands east of Taiwan. In the ensuing melee, scores were thrown into the sea and the captain killed.[4]

Chinese hard work in the American tradition did not make them universally popular. Senator George Hearst wrote, "One of my greatest objections to them is that they can do more work than our people and live on less, and for that reason . . . they could drive our laborers to the wall." But he omitted to state that this was in the tradition of American free enterprise and the open market for labor as well as goods. As a matter of fact, the Chinese made great efforts, often successfully, to improve their wage rates and, wherever they could, forced their wages by means of the competitive market into line with wages for other workers.

Some politicians took their arguments against the Chinese into the realms of theology.

A witness named Pixley said, before the Joint Congressional Committee to Investigate Chinese Immigration in 1876, "[The Chinese are] as inferior to any race God ever made . . . There are none so low. I believe that the Chinese have no souls to save, and if they have, they are not worth the saving."[5] If this was the rhetoric used by responsible members of the legislature and their witnesses, one can imagine what the language of the "sandlot politicans" was like.

It was also said that the Chinese were overrunning the United States. But Chinese at the time numbered less than .25 percent of the population. And the Chinese were accused of sending money out of America to China. This they did, if they were frugal, out of a wage of around a dollar a day for a twelve-hour and more workday. But American merchants made $9 million out of the opium trade in China alone, which they promptly sent back to America, and not one of these bigots objected to that.

Spokesmen for American labor issued such statements as "Chinese brought with them nothing but filth, vice and disease. . . . All efforts to elevate them to a higher standard have proven futile" *(AFL Convention Report)*, and "Every incoming coolie means . . . so much more vice and immorality injected into our social life" (Samuel Gompers, then AFL President). Even in 1908, Gompers and Herman Guttstadt of the AFL were still uttering such misinformation and racial slanders as "The offspring of miscegenation between Americans and Asiatics are invariably degenerate."[6]

It was thinking and propaganda such as this that caused miscegenation laws to be passed in a number of states. California banned marriages between whites and Chinese in 1906. Similar laws were passed in Arizona, Georgia, Idaho, Louisiana, Mississippi, Missouri, Nebraska, Nevada, South Dakota, Utah, Virginia, and Wyoming. California repealed its law in 1948, and the Supreme Court in 1967 ruled the other miscegenation laws unconstitutional.

Additional Restrictions, 1884

The 1882 Exclusion Act was so threatening in its import and results that many Chinese fled the country. Others, taking over American ways, carried the fight against it to the courts. The gross injustice of its provisions invited evasion. Matters were made worse when in the following years a series of amendments were made to the act intended to plug loopholes in its operation, make the prohibition of entry more inclusive and circumvent Chinese attempts to evade it. It was a cat and mouse game played out with human lives, with some immigration officers trying to ingratiate themselves with their superiors by catching more and more Chinese in their nets. As in many such cases, small bureaucratic heads delighted in exercising power, and so the game took on a life of its own.

The introducers of new anti-Chinese legislation in 1884 contended that there were real problems: Chinese seamen were jumping ship in U.S. ports; Chinese in transit were disappearing en route; Chinese were smuggling themselves over the Canadian and Mexican borders; coming from countries other than China, they were pretending to be merchants when they were only peddlers. Additional difficulties were made for Chinese already in the country, while demagogic politicians got welcome publicity for protecting the country from invading alien hordes.

The courts were indeed burdened with 300 Chinese immigration cases, but, as one California politician pointed out, these cases were mostly caused by the immigration authorities refusing to recognize the valid passports of Chinese and arbitrarily arresting them. Seaman Chae Chan Ping had to go all the way up to the U.S. Supreme Court to prove his right to be in the United States with a valid reentry certificate after paying a visit to China. Another Chinese, taking a train to the East Coast, was unfortunate enough to book his passage on one that went from Detroit through Canada to Niagara. He was stopped there and sent back, only to be detained again in Detroit. Scared of violating American laws, a British sea captain put his Chinese crew members in irons below decks to prevent them going ashore while in New York harbor.

A new bill was prepared, passed by both House and Senate, and signed into law by Republican President Arthur on July 4, 1884. It extended the Exclusion Act to include Chinese coming from "any and every port"; it imposed a fine of $1000 or one year imprisonment for infractions of the act, and prescribed a more stringent definition of the term "merchant." This legislation was supposedly needed because the 1882 Exclusion Act was inadequate. But Collector of Customs Sullivan of San Francisco, who was surely in a good position to know, testified that "while a few Chinese may have gained admission who were not legally entitled to it, the main object of the law has been accomplished and the influx of Chinese laborers stopped." The special agent of the U.S. Treasury Department who administered the law in Port Townsend, Oregon, testified that there was no truth in the rumors of wholesale violations of the act. In fact, while there had been a rush of 39,579 Chinese to enter the United States in 1882 before the Exclusion Act became law, the total number of Chinese in the United States dropped by 12,159 in 1883. After peaking to a high of 107,488 in 1890, the number of Chinese in the United States declined steadily, to a low of 61,639 in 1920.

These much-publicized congressional attacks on the Chinese encouraged the terror against them on the West Coast and further east. There is no doubt that the Exclusion Act was understood in the street as an invitation to "Go, get the Chinamen!"

The Scott Act, 1888

The same anti-Chinese sentiment and demagogic politicking for votes characterized the Scott Act of 1888, even though the speeches and maneuvering made it difficult to discern the reality behind the posturings. Twenty thousand Chinese with valid reentry permits were either in China or on their way back to the United States, and the authors and instigators of the Scott Act were determined to prevent their return. They also wanted to force out the Chinese remaining in the country. But they did not want this brought out into the open.

The Exclusion Act had baneful results all round. By 1884, exclusion and discrimination were facts of life that the Chinese communities regarded as something unlawful to be handled as best one could. A number of officials in charge of immigration, while not believing in the real validity of the law, saw it as a chance to make some money on the side by soliciting bribes. A number of them were found out and transferred following charges of corruption. Anxious to beat the deadline of exclusion, immigrants crowded onto the trans-Pacific ships, resulting in that unfortunate all-time high of 39,579 in 1882. One result of this influx was a wave of anti-Chinese pogroms sweeping up the West Coast and beyond. Appeals for help relayed by the Chinese ambassador to the U.S. State Department went unanswered for months. When Secretary of State Bayard did answer in February 1886, he put the blame on foreign troublemakers and disclaimed responsibility, but a month later, Democratic President Cleveland recommended that Congress, solely from the sentiment of generosity and pity for the innocent and unfortunate stranger (as he said), give some aid to the victims of violence.

Congress responded to these events by increasing pressure against the Chinese. Bills were introduced to extend the ban on the entry of Chinese laborers, to have those who went away carry a photographic likeness for identification, to limit the numbers who came on any single ship to one per 50 tons deadweight, to abrogate all treaties made with China, and "absolutely prohibit the coming of Chinese to the United States, except for diplomatic, consular and other officers."[7]

In August 1886, the supine imperial Chinese government itself proposed of its own accord to ban the immigration of Chinese laborers into the United States but asked that those who were already there be accorded the right to come and go of their own free will and be treated according to treaty obligations. The U.S. State Department immediately presented a draft of a treaty to prohibit the immigration of Chinese laborers for thirty years. However, the Chinese ambassador replied that he was under instructions not to negotiate a treaty until indemnification had been settled for the Chinese victims of earlier attacks. A little later, he protested that no justice had yet been achieved for the Chinese who had been outraged, beaten, and burned to death. The guilty had been released almost as soon as they had been arrested, and this hardly had the deterring effect of justice.

The diplomatic sparring over, the two sides got down to the business of drafting a treaty. It absolutely prohibited the coming of Chinese laborers for twenty years, unless they already had lawful wives, children, or parents here or property amounting to $1000. This ban did not affect the rights of the "exempted classes." The United States, without reference to the question of liability, agreed to pay the sum of $276,619.75 as full indemnity for all losses and injuries sustained by the Chinese in the recent rioting. The treaty, to remain in force for twenty years, was signed by representatives of the two sides on March 12, 1888. However, in discussing the treaty the Senate appended two amendments that Secretary of State Bayard assured the trusting Chinese ambassador, Chang Yen Hoon, "did not alter the terms of the treaty in any degree."[8] In fact, the first amendment was "This prohibition [absolutely banning the coming of Chinese laborers] shall extend to the return of Chinese laborers who are not now in the United States." In other words, the target of the amendments were the 20,000 Chinese workers preparing to return to or already on their way back to the United States.

Nevertheless, anti-Chinese sentiment particularly on the West Coast was not mollified and the Democratic Cleveland Administration on the eve of a national election faced the possibility of a crucial loss of votes. The Republican San Francisco Bulletin editorialized on July 12, 1888,

The treaty . . . is the most outrageous sell-out of the administration. It may be regarded as a treaty to facilitate Chinese immigration. Under it this country will be flooded with Chinese. Every coolie now ashore can be duplicated as often as he departs, while new hordes can be introduced by the transit privilege.

In 1888, just twenty-six Chinese entered the country so it was not clear just how many made a horde then. But it was clear that the Republicans were stealing the Democrats anti-Chinese thunder.

Rumors were then circulated that the Chinese government would reject the treaty. Although such men as Senator Morgan of Alabama thought the treaty so harsh that he doubted if "any government in the world which had much self-respect would ratify it," Senator Dolph of Oregon on July 11 introduced legislation that would in fact enact as law the provisions of the treaty, pending its ratification. This bill was passed by both Senate and House on August 8 and signed into law by President Cleveland on September 13, 1888. On Sunday, September 2, a London dispatch had reported that China had rejected the treaty and the very next day, Senator Scott (Democrat) of Pennsylvania, stressing the need to keep Chinese laborers out of the country and urgency because of "rejection" of the treaty by China, introduced a bill that would supplement the 1882 Exclusion Act and specifically deny reentry of all Chinese laborers.

China almost immediately informed the United States that, in fact, it had not rejected the treaty but was only considering it. But this made no difference. President Cleveland signed the Scott Act into law on October 1, 1888. In his message to Congress, he blamed the inadequacy of the 1880 treaty and the Exclusion Law of 1882 for producing discontent among the people, especially on the West Coast. He stated that the Chinese government had itself appreciated the situation and need for a remedy by offering to ban the emigration of Chinese laborers; he cited the reduction of the period of the ban from thirty years to twenty as an example of the readiness of his administration to meet the requests of the Chinese government. He characterized the refusal (sic) of the Chinese government to ratify the treaty as "denying the United States the cooperation she had been led to rely on." He urged that some provision should be made for those Chinese laborers already on their way back before passage of the bill and that an indemnity be allocated for the Chinese victims of mob violence.

The harsh provisions of the Scott Act turned into scraps of worthless paper the certificates of return held by some 20,000 Chinese. It cruelly disrupted whole families and shattered the legitimate hopes and plans of these thousands of immigrants. The *New York Globe* (September 8, 1888) exposed the unsavory partisan maneuvering:

> Both Democrats and Republicans have manifested a keen anxiety to take advantage of the rejection [sic] of the treaty and to use the opportunity in such a way as to win the anti-Chinese vote. . . . The Democrats have been too quick for their adversaries by proposing the most vigorous laws for the exclusion of the Chinese.

Both great parties had been led into an unworthy competition to outdo each other at the polls at the expense of the hapless Chinese immigrants. The New York *World* (September 6, 1888) revealed that the Scott Act really originated in the White House Kitchen Cabinet. "Mr. Scott brought that bill from the White House . . . it was written on administration paper."[9] Scott was indeed the president's most intimate friend and a member of the Democratic National Committee. The spirit of Denis Kearney was haunting the White House of the United States.

Friends of the Chinese People

Throughout these troubled times, the Chinese in America had staunch friends. Erskine Ross, who at the height of the Los Angeles anti-Chinese riot single-handedly stopped a raging mob in its tracks, saving many Chinese and their property. The Reverend Johnson of the Reformed Presbyterian Church in San Francisco, indefatigable in opposing the exclusion laws. Donaldina Cameron of the Presbyterian Mission in San Francisco, who for forty years (from age eighteen) worked with the Chinese community to end the prostitution of its young women. William Lloyd Garrison, son of the abolitionist. Senators Charles Sumner of Massachusetts and Lyman Trumbull of Illinois, who worked hard in Congress to remove discriminatory legislation against the Chinese: in 1870 they introduced legislation proposing that Chinese be granted citizenship and voting rights; both bills were defeated by large majorities. They did this at a time when championing the Chinese was regarded by pragmatists as tantamount to ending one's political career.

Senator Oliver P. Morton of Indiana, who served as chairman of the Joint Special Committee to Investigate Chinese immigration in 1877 and wrote a minority report, declared that if the Chinese had been white no such outcry would have been raised against them. Concerned citizens in San Francisco formed a Chinese Protection Society to curb mob violence. This is only a very partial list. Cynics may say that these men and women were either out to get cheap labor for American capitalism, or to gain their gratitude in order to convert them, yet it is a fact that one way or another they supported the American democratic tradition. But democracy is vulnerable to ignorance and fear, especially in economic crises. Anti-Chinese discrimination could not be stopped immediately by these friendly interventions.

NOTES

1. Stan Steiner, *Fusang* (New York: Harper & Row, 1979).
2. Horace F. Page, speech in *Report of the Committee on Education and Labor* (Washington, D.C.: Congressional Reports, 1882).
3. California Senate, *Memorial to Congress* (1878).
4. Mary Roberts Coolidge, *Chinese Immigration* (New York: Holt, 1909).
5. Seward, *Chinese Immigration* (New York: Arno Press, 1970), p. 225.

6. Samuel Gompers and Herman Guttstadt, Asiatic Exclusion League pamphlet, 1908.
7. Li Tien-lu. *Congressional Policy on Chinese Immigration* (New York: Arno Press and New York Times, 1979). Reprint of 1916 ed.
8. Li, *Congressional Policy*, p. 59.
9. *Ibid.*

Exclusion in Washington

XV

He doesn't stand a Chinaman's chance.
A saying from the 1880s

As EXPECTED, eight days after the Scott Act was passed, the first of the 600 Chinese caught by its passage in mid-ocean arrived in San Francisco. Those holding return certificates naturally expected to be admitted. They were not. Chinese in transit to Cuba were likewise refused a landing unless they had a through ticket and posted a $200 bond. A hubbub had been raised about "hordes" of Chinese arriving ostensibly in transit but actually remaining in the country. But the U.S. Treasury Department (which was charged with immigration matters) declared in April 1890 in answer to a Senate inquiry, that "No Chinese who have entered the United States under these regulations have failed to depart." However, Chinese continued to arrive in the country although in small numbers:

        26   in 1888
       118   in 1889
     1,716   in 1890
     2,836   in 1891
      none   in 1892

This immigration produced a small net increase to 107,488 in 1890 or 0.17 percent of the 63 million population of the United States—hardly a horde.

In view of this "threat" to the racial homogeneity of the American population, a number of bills were introduced to plug up the last loopholes left to Chinese immigration and ensure that exclusion would be continued when the 1882 act lapsed in 1892. The following list summarizes the legislative context of these bills:

IMPORTANT FEDERAL ACTS AND DECISIONS
AFFECTING CHINESE IMMIGRATION

1798   Alien Act gives the president authority to expel aliens whom he perceives to be dangerous to the peace and security of the nation. Repealed in 1800.

1808   U.S. Constitution bans importation of slaves (Article I, Section 9).

1875   Communists, prostitutes, and mental and physical incompetents are prohibited by act of Congress from entering the United States.

1876   U.S. Supreme Court (in *Henderson* v. *Mayor of New York*, 92 US 259, 1875) makes admission of immigrants sole responsibility of the federal government. All state statutes restricting immigration declared unconstitutional.

1878   Burlingame Treaty assures reciprocal right of voluntary immigration.

1879   Congressional act limits to fifteen the number of Chinese that may enter the United States from one ship at a time.

1880   Burlingame Treaty Amendment prohibits entry of Chinese laborers.

1882   Chinese Exclusion Act bans immigration of Chinese laborers into the United States for ten years and prohibits naturalization of Chinese.

1888   Scott Act prohibits Chinese reentry after temporary departure.

1892   Geary Act extends ban on immigration of Chinese laborers for ten years; Chinese must carry residence certificates on penalty of deportation with no right of habeas corpus bail procedure.

1893   McCreary amendment to Geary Act increases restrictions on Chinese businessmen.

1894   New U.S.-China treaty absolutely prohibits immigration of Chinese laborers to the United States for ten years.

1898   Chinese Exclusion Act extended to Hawaiian Islands.

1902   Act of April 29 continues and extends Exclusion Acts to Philippines.

1904   General Deficiency Appropriations Account Act (April 29) extends Chinese Exclusion Act indefinitely (not linked to any treaty), allocates $100,000 to introduce Bertillon system of criminal identification for Chinese arrivals.

1907   Immigration Act extends existing restrictions on immigration and prohibits entry of aliens over sixteen years of age who cannot read; further restricts immigration of Asians to the United States for permanent residence.

1921   Congress sets limit of 350,000 immigrants annually. Number of aliens of each nationality set at 3 percent of foreign-born people of that nationality living in America in 1910.

1924   National Origins Law: (also known as the "Second Exclusion Act") Congress establishes a permanent numerical restriction on immigration to the United States from all parts of the world except the Western Hemisphere. Under a ceiling of 150,000 per year, national quotas are based on ethnic composition of the United States in 1920.

Prospective immigrants required to have a sponsor in the United States and a visa from an American consulate abroad. Immigration of all aliens ineligible for U.S. citizenship (Chinese) prohibited. Entry of Chinese students restricted. Chinese wives of U.S. citizens not entitled to enter the United States.

1940   Alien Registration Act requires all aliens in the United States to register and be fingerprinted. Exclusion and deportation of criminal and subversive groups is expanded.

1943   Magnuson Act repeals Chinese Exclusion Acts.*

The Geary Act, 1892

The tone was set by Thomas Geary (Democrat) of California, who had already succeeded in driving the Chinese out of Sonoma County. His bill and amendments appalled a number of legislators with their unabashed racism. His original bill sought to prohibit all Chinese (except diplomats and merchants) from coming to the United States even in transit. The penalty for perjury in submitting immigration or visa applications would be a fine of $1000 and hard labor for not less than one year. No Chinese would be admitted to citizenship, and it was left to the customs collectors to decide who was or was not a Chinese. A Chinese arrested under the bill was denied the right to bail during habeas corpus proceedings. All Chinese in the country within one year would be obliged to carry a certificate of residence with an identifying photograph. The Chinese in America would, in other words, be in the same position as blacks in apartheid South Africa, compelled to carry a passbook at all times or face summary arrest.

Senator Butler of South Carolina described these provisions as "a disgrace to the country." Representative Hitt of Illinois correctly forecast that the bill violated the nation's word and that many losses would follow this proposed measure of no intercourse. He pointed out that the pass system reversed the whole legal system that presumed a person innocent until proven guilty. By this act, Chinese, *per se*, were considered guilty unless they could prove themselves innocent. "Never before was this system applied to a free people, to a human being with the exception of the sad days of slavery," he said.[2]

The Geary bill in all its severity was passed by the House by a vote of 178 to 43, with 108 abstentions. In consultation with the Senate, it was amended somewhat, but the final bill as passed by the Senate and House stipulated that no bail would be allowed on application for a writ of habeas corpus by a Chinese; that within one year after passage of the bill, all Chinese laborers in the United States would have to apply for a certificate of residence; and that failure to have such a certificate would make one liable to arrest

---

* The survey of congressional legislation on Chinese immigration is continued on pp. 211–212.

and deportation. Anyone found falsifying a certificate would be fined $1,000 or imprisoned for not more than five years.

Meanwhile, the Chinese ambassador Tsui had been sending protest after protest to the U.S. State Department (six in all between March and November 1892). This followed several previous protests delivered by his predecessor. Finally, after cooling their heels for three years since sending their first protest in January 1889, the Chinese legation received a reply. Rejecting the Chinese protest, the State Department contended that identification and certification of Chinese laborers was aimed at protecting their persons and the rights of Chinese entitled to residential privileges and at preventing their fraudulent enjoyment by those not entitled thereto. Acting Secretary of State Wharton also saw fit to compare the democratic United States with the decrepit feudal empire of China under the Manchu Qing dynasty. He wrote,

> The provisions of this legislation are practically designed to accord such Chinamen lawfully resident in the United States privileges and a measure of individual freedom far beyond those accorded to American citizens in China.[3]

He contended that from the very start the position of the foreigner in China had been one of exclusion, so presumably this justified like treatment of Chinese in America.

The McCreary Amendment, 1893

While the Geary Bill was being debated, some of the most eminent lawyers of the day expressed the opinion that the proposed law was "repugnant to the Constitution of the United States" and would be declared unconstitutional. The Chinese therefore followed the advice of their clan and district associations, and 80 percent of them did not register for certificates of identification. The U.S. Supreme Court, however, in the test case *Fong Yue Ting* v. *the United States* surprisingly ruled that the registration requirement was constitutional. This decision came ten days after the 12-month period allowed for registration had ended. As a result, some 85,000 of the 106,688 Chinese in the country had not registered and were now liable to immediate arrest and deportation.

The Chinese associations (CCBA) followed the advice of counsel in advising noncompliance with the registration requirements. They had argued cogently that the law made no distinction between Chinese who were aliens and Chinese who were U.S. citizens and therefore entitled to the same rights and privileges as any other citizens. Congress had no power to provide for the deportation of a citizen as a penalty for any crime.

> The fifth amendment of the Constitution provides that no person shall be deprived of life, liberty, or property without due process of law, and the eighth amendment provides that cruel and unusual punishment shall not be inflicted. Fourthly, the treaty between the United States and China, provides that Chinese subjects visiting or residing in the United States shall enjoy the same privileges, immunities and exemptions as subjects of the most favored nation.[4]

But now 85,000 Chinese faced arrest and deportation because of this advice. Luckily, it would cost some $7,000,000 to deport all these men and women—a minimum of $35–$50 a head for transport alone—and the 53rd Congress was reluctant to spend millions on this act of vengeance. It was certain that test cases would be brought to court, and litigation would increase the cost astronomically. The Chinese Consolidated Benevolent Associations raised $200,000 to fight test cases in the courts.

The Chinese ambassador in Washington was fearful that an outburst of anti-Chinese violence would erupt as a result of the Geary Act and that wholesale deportation would trigger a crisis in Sino-U.S. relations. He addressed a new message to the U.S. State Department. A special session of Congress was being convened in August 1892 to discuss the financial crisis, so he asked the department whether it would not be possible to get the Geary Act repealed and so give time and opportunity to deal with the matter diplomatically. The secretary of state replied that it was not expedient to bring up the question of the Geary Act at the special session, that the act would probably be modified at the next regular session of Congress, and that, anyway, measures to implement the act would necessarily be delayed. This lulled the Chinese into a false sense of security. On May 5, 1892, the U.S. Treasury issued instructions to all those charged with immigration matters not to make any immediate arrests of Chinese under the Geary Act when it went into full force the next day. Less than three weeks later, however, another instruction told them to take vigorous action to arrest and prosecute Chinese laborers who could not show they were lawfully admitted to the United States.

A wave of arrests of Chinese took place. Twenty were arrested in San Francisco, twenty-three in Oakland, and twenty-four in Los Angeles for not registering under the Geary Act. These men were held without right of bail unless they could carry their cases to the U.S. Supreme Court and get a reversal of the no-bail rule, a lengthy procedure.

Fear and dismay spread through the Chinese communities. This was no village pogrom of riotous men. It was the Congress of the United States, seemingly backed by the Harrison administration (Republican), flying in the face of the Constitution to strike at one of the smallest ethnic groups in the nation, citizens as well as aliens. In these days the phrase "Not a Chinaman's chance" was born.

Public opinion reacted sharply. The 52nd Congress received twenty-three petitions, resolutions, and memorials from public, commercial, and religious organizations calling for repeal of the Exclusion Act; fifty more such petitions were received by the 53rd Congress for repeal of the Geary Act, and several bills were introduced to do this. The Committee on Foreign Relations introduced the McCreary bill to amend the Geary Act. This extended for six months the one-year grace period to comply with the registration order. But Geary was relentless. He proposed successfully an amendment that

Upon complaint under oath made by any citizen of the United States before a United States judge stating that any Chinese person is unlawfully within the United

States, a warrant of arrest shall be issued by the judge and the said person shall be subjected to all of the provisions of this Act and the Act to which this is an amendment.[5]

This amendment was passed. It more precisely defined "laborer" as both skilled and unskilled, and "merchant" was also defined more strictly—a person applying to enter the United States on the ground of having been a merchant in this country had to "establish this fact by two credible witnesses *other than Chinese*" (my emphasis). Pending an order of deportation, the Chinese person should remain in custody and not be admitted to bail. The bill and amendments were passed by the House by 178 votes to 1. Geary was calling for a mobilization of public informers.

Senator Hoar of Massachusetts publicly deplored the provision that a person arrested and held for deportation should not be admitted to bail on habeas corpus. This clause clearly opened the way to abuses. Senator Palmer of Illinois refused to vote for the bill because it required the testimony of "at least one credible witness other than Chinese," thereby discriminating against a whole race as unworthy of credit. Davis of Minnesota opposed the Geary Act and amendments and wished this "flagititious and ferocious legislation" wiped off the statute books. The bill was passed by the Senate and approved by President Cleveland the next day (November 3, 1893).

Senator Hitt of Illinois (Republican) noted that this bill was the only one on the issue of Chinese immigration that had not been tabled on the eve of an election. It averted an ugly situation by stopping the threatened deportation of tens of thousands of Chinese and giving them another extension of six months in which to register. Otherwise, it did little to ameliorate the rigors of the Geary Act. The failure of judgment by the leaders of the Chinese Consolidated Benevolent Associations in advising Chinese not to register led to a catastrophic drop in the associations' prestige. This led to serious consequences, especially in San Francisco and New York Chinatowns. Gangster tongs moved in to fill the vacuum of authority.

The 1894 Treaty

Chinese in the United States were painfully aware of the implications of the 1893 McCreary Bill. In fact, it meant that, on the statement of any U.S. citizen to a judge that a certain Chinese was unlawfully in the United States, that Chinese could have a warrant of arrest issued against him or her and be held in custody without bail pending deportation. Under these conditions of incarceration, he would have to prove himself innocent of guilt and that proof would require the evidence of at least one witness who was not Chinese. There is also no doubt that conditions would have been made tougher for the Chinese but for the fact that wholesale deportation would have required very considerable sums, and this at a time of economic stringency. Between 1901 and 1905, for example, 3,093 Chinese were deported at a cost of $324,682. To deport 85,000 would have cost around $9 million.

Relations with China, even a weak China, were deteriorating. Trade decreased markedly. Negotiations were therefore begun to readjust treaty relations between the two countries to provide a basis for the restoration and continuance of friendly relations between the two countries in "honor, dignity, and friendship."

This was the rhetoric. In fact, the resulting treaty was concluded specifically for the purpose of regulating and limiting Chinese immigration. Chinese laborers were absolutely prohibited from coming for a period of ten years. Those with valid reentry certificates were allowed to return. Chinese were also permitted transit. It was reaffirmed that Chinese should enjoy protection of their persons and property and all rights given by U.S. law to citizens or subjects of the most favored nation. However, they would not have the right of naturalization.

The Chinese imperial government agreed to the registration requirement of the Geary Act, but this bitter pill was sweetened somewhat by U.S. recognition of the Chinese government's right to enact and enforce similar laws for registration of laboring U.S. citizens in China. This seems like a reciprocal right until it is remembered that there were few if any American laborers in China. Otherwise, this treaty was very similar to the 1888 treaty. It did supersede the punitive Scott Act in permitting the return to the United States of Chinese laborers with valid certificates of reentry. It also permitted the return of Chinese laborers with spouses, children, or parents in this country or assets valued at $1,000 or more.

The treaty was signed by the two parties on March 17, 1894. It was debated behind closed doors by the Senate on May 6 and again in August. Ratifications were exchanged in December and promulgated by President Cleveland the next day.

A clue to the reason for the closed-door sessions of Congress and the relatively conciliatory tone of the negotiations is suggested by the international situation at the time. China was to some small extent modernizing itself and building up its army and navy. Thinly veiled retaliatory measures had also been taken against Americans in China. In December 1893, Americans traveling in China were informed through the American ambassador that they should report their movements to subprefects and magistrates en route. This was represented as a measure "to give protection to foreigners while traveling." Fifty American missionaries and their families were not permitted to go up to the hill resorts and had to endure the sweltering summer heat in the cities. This too was for "their protection," although everyone knew that there was not the slightest danger to them in the usual summer resorts.

Unfortunately for China, its new defense forces suffered a crushing defeat at the hands of the Japanese in the 1898 Sino-Japanese War, and again it was in no position to give real support to its overseas nationals, at least fifty of whom served with the U.S. fleet under Admiral George Dewey at the Battle of Manila Bay against the Spanish fleet on May 1, 1898 (*New York Times*, February 23, 1899, p. 5). "They served faithfully, were efficient, obedient in service, active and brave in battle and freely risked their lives in our cause," wrote California historian Hubert Bancroft.[6] Admiral Dewey unsuccessfully urged Washington to admit these men to the United States. Also excluded were 100,000 Chinese seamen who served in the U.S. merchant marine during the period 1876–1906.

Restrictive Legislation, 1902

By the turn of the century, the diplomats of both countries were increasingly reacting to pressure from a force that in time completely transformed relations between them—the mounting force of nationalism in China. Nationalism in the modern sense had not been a part of the Chinese political scene before the second part of the nineteenth century. Like the ideas of democracy and internationalism, it was a product of the modern era, a product of the growth of a middle class, a bourgeoisie, in China. Until the late nineteenth century, the diplomatic representatives of China had been officials of the old regime, trained only in the Confucian classics and Confucian ideas of the imperial state and its relations with other countries. Strictly speaking, other sovereign, equal states did not exist for them. There were only China (the one Middle Kingdom) and "other countries." Such a concept might have had some relevance when the Chinese empire was at the height of its power and glory. It had no real relevance in the modern era of nation states and still less when China itself was the "Sick Man of Asia," threatened by dismemberment at the hands of the great powers and misruled by inept and ignorant mandarins. But, by the turn of the century, China was stirred by immense new forces of revolutionary change, nationalist and democratic. It would take many more years before these forces produced the socialist People's Republic of China, with a great, progressive industrial working class, but at the start of this process in the late 1800s its spearhead was the emerging commercial and industrial middle class. These were increasingly modern-educated men and women, not feudal mandarins. Led by such men as Dr. Sun Yat-sen, they were determined that China, with her enormous potential in manpower and natural resources, should take her proper place in the concert of nations. They were not prepared to allow themselves to be kicked around by anyone. The ties between the Chinese merchants in the United States and overseas and their homeland compatriots and colleagues were naturally close. News of the anti-Chinese agitation and the humiliations suffered by Chinese in America were reported back home and aroused natural anger. Modern-trained diplomats such as Wu Ting-fang, ambassador of China to the United States in 1897–1902 and 1908–1909, representing these new political groups in China, forcefully expressed their ideas. American foreign policy makers responsive to the pressures of their exclusionist, vote-conscious, political leaders were slow, however, to realize what was happening. One might even argue that it took the appalling losses of post–World War II intervention in China in 1945–1949 and the Korean War and the Vietnam War to get them to realize what was happening in China. Exclusionist policies meanwhile continued and were even intensified.

A number of measures were taken by the U.S. Treasury Department to make existing exclusion legislation more effective. For instance, Chinese crewmen on ships arriving in American ports were obliged to post $300 bonds with customs collectors to guarantee their departure when they landed even for a day in port. Two other major acts extended the exclusion laws to Hawaii (in 1898) and the Philippines (in 1902) when these two territories were incorporated into the United States. These acts were protested by the Chinese ambassador Wu Ting-fang on the grounds that they were departures from the announced policies of the President that normal conditions on these islands would not be changed and that this would damage friendly relations between the two countries. But because of the then weak state of China these protests, like most previous ones, went unheeded. Nevertheless, Wu did what he could. In this, he was aided by the change in the character of Chinese immigration to the United States and in the social profile of its Chinese communities. Where before farmers and laborers had predominated, now the proportion of students and merchants had increased, and they were able to mobilize a more effective protest against the humiliating exclusion regulations—a boycott of American trade with China.

"Not a Chinaman's Chance"

Harassment of one kind or another had become a feature of life for Chinese in America. In 1900, a regular blockade of San Francisco Chinatown was staged on the suspicion that it was a source of plague. Honolulu's Chinatown was totally destroyed by a "sanitary fire." The numbers of Chinese who fled or passed away and were not replaced reduced the Chinese community in the United States from 107,488 at its peak in 1890 to 88,863 in 1900; that is, from 0.17 to 0.11 percent of the population of 76 million.

But the racist elements were not satisfied. Expressing "alarm" at the arrival of a few thousand Chinese youngsters under the subterfuge of "paper sons"and daughters" in what became known as the "slot racket" (see p. 189), the American Federation of Labor in its Kentucky convention asked Congress to strengthen the Chinese exclusion laws and extend them to all "Mongolian labor," with the Japanese especially in mind. It was even thought necessary to call a Chinese Exclusion Convention in San Francisco (November 22, 1901). Twenty bills were introduced to the 57th Congress calling for more stringent exclusion of Chinese. Sixteen bills called for the exclusion of all Asians. To "protect American institutions," Senator Mitchell of Oregon introduced a bill containing all the old, onerous provisions of the previous exclusion legislation and in addition prohibiting entry of Chinese laborers indefinitely. This indicates the temper of the more rabid exclusionists. Finally, the 1902 bill was passed by Congress, reenacting and extending the previous laws to American insular possessions, where regulations had been more liberal. Extension of Chinese exclusion to Hawaii, in fact, was opposed by leading local administrators. The governor, speaking of Chinese on the sugar plantations, so important to the islands' economy, said that Chinese labor "never has, does not now and never will interfere with either American skilled or unskilled labor," and therefore Hawaii was entitled to legislation favorable to its greater prosperity.[7]

In 1899, there were 20,000 Chinese in Hawaii and 100,000 in the Philippines. All were affected by extension of the exclusion laws to these territories, whose economies suffered noticeable damage.

The fact that Chinese labor and enterprise benefited Hawaii and the Philippines was not seriously disputed. The issue was that, as in the continental United States, the heirs of the doctrine of manifest destiny and the myth of the "yellow peril" were determined on racial grounds to exclude Chinese and Chinese culture from all these lands annexed by expanding American imperialism.

New harrassing regulations were issued by the immigration department. One provided for certificates of identification to be made in a "convenient size" for carrying on the person; in other words, a racial "pass." Another, in 1903, instituted the notorious Bertillon system of registering criminals to be used for workers, but members of the "exempt classes"—students, merchants, and visitors—also found themselves being stripped, measured, and photographed.[8]

In response to growing nationalist feeling in China and the urging of the overseas Chinese, the Chinese government, weak though it was, on January 24, 1904, notified the U.S. government that it would terminate the 1894 treaty at the end of its ten-year period and proposed the opening of negotiations for a new treaty dealing with immigration. Although willing to accept class exclusion of Chinese laborers, it was under pressure to remove racist exclusion and improve treatment of the "exempt classes."

The U.S. Congress thereupon hurriedly attached to a routine appropriation bill—the General Deficiency Appropriation Act of April 29, 1904—an amendment that was, in fact, a new bill to regulate Chinese immigration on expiration of the 1894 treaty. This new bill in effect separated domestic legislation on Chinese immigration from treaty obligations with China. It plugged leaks in the Exclusion laws, made restrictions even more stringent, and extended exclusion indefinitely. Administration of the exclusion laws was transferred from the secretary of the treasury to a new department under the secretary of commerce and labor. The bill was passed by the House and Senate and approved by President Theodore Roosevelt on April 29, 1904.

Not Exclusion but Extermination

At the turn of the century, a nationalist, imperialist wave was sweeping through America. This nation of immigrants' whole attitude to immigration was changing. The idea of closing the gates to immigrants was gaining ground, and Chinese immigration was the whetstone on which this idea was being honed. The extremist, chauvinist wing of this antiimmigration movement considered exclusion inadequate. They were demanding expulsion of the Chinese and, by extension, all Asiatics. Theodore Roosevelt himself in 1894 believed that "to admit Chinese would be ruinous to the white race."[9] Even after landing procedures had been complied with, Chinese—and Chinese-American citizens too—were harassed. Many found life in the United States so intolerable that they fled.

This new situation was legitimatized not by act of Congress directly, although Congress' acts were harsh enough, but by bureaucratic regulations initiated by the new commissioner general of immigration, Terence V. Powderly, who had actually been in charge of immigration matters since 1897. Powderly was a former leader of the anti-Chinese Knights of Labor, who shared the ideas of Gompers of the AFL on this question. The AFL (formed in 1886), speaking for the craft unions and determined to retain their privileged position in the labor ranks, was becoming increasingly influential. Supported by the Knights of Labor, the Western Labor Union, and the Railroad Brotherhood, it was influential enough to be consulted by the president.

It was Powderly and his successor (1902–1908), Frank Sargent, another labor leader and friend of Gompers, who passed and implemented the draconian regulations charting the new course of exclusion. It was Powderly who in 1899 appointed one of the most notorious Chinese-baiters, James Dunn, another former union man, to be inspector of Chinese in San Francisco, principal port of entry for Chinese travelers. But it was President Theodore Roosevelt who, in 1904, to reinforce his West Coast political base, chose Victor Metcalf, a racist California politician, as his secretary of commerce and labor in charge of immigration. This put anti-Chinese racists firmly in charge of supervising Chinese immigration, and their aim was not only to prevent new Chinese immigration but to get rid of the ethnic Chinese already here, whether aliens or American citizens.[10]

With such leaders, immigration officers now interpreted the law to mean that all Chinese were excluded except those specifically exempted by treaty or domestic law or regulation—that is, teachers, students, merchants, and travelers—and even then very narrow definitions of these categories were prescribed. Merchants did not include salesmen, buyers or clerks, bookkeepers, or traders. A student had to be enrolled in a college and have proof of means to carry on studies not available in China.

No Chinese could expect to be immune from harassment. They might be penned up for weeks in detention sheds while their cases were being considered. Although the exempt classes were supposed to enjoy the same rights as those of the most favored nation, in fact they were often brutally mistreated. A Methodist Chinese minister was arrested while visiting Texas, tried, and deported as a laborer because the immigration officers decided that a preacher was a laborer. The court upheld that judgment. A wealthy merchant arrested in Spokane, Washington, was jailed for nearly three months on a charge of engaging in manual work without a laborer's certificate. It was cases like these in 1904 that made a whole generation of Chinese tight-lipped and anxious to avoid even the least contact with immigration officers or indeed officials of any kind.[11] "The United States Immigration Service held unbelievable powers over immigrants and fear of it by Chinese is not surprising, especially at a time when it had practically carte-blanche to deport as they wished," wrote J. Campbell Bruce.[12]

William Howard Taft, then U.S. secretary of war, declared in a June 15, 1905, speech at Ohio State University that the exclusion policy was "not only wrong in principle, unjust in operation but most inexpedient and unwise in policy."[13] Merchants were unable to do business under threat of constant harassment. Besides suffering individual acts of hoodlums, they found themselves under government and police surveillance, not for what they had done but for what they might have done, and they had to prove that they had not done it. A merchant doing thousands of dollars of business who invested a dollar in a hotel or restaurant could lose his status as a merchant and be summarily deported. Found without a registration card, he could be jailed without bail. In Denver and Boston in 1903, the Chinese quarters were surrounded by police, and Chinese of any class found without certificates were arrested and jailed, their status arbitrarily decided on by the local immigration authorities until court proceedings could decide otherwise—sometimes a lengthy process.

As Dr. Ng Poon Chew, editor of *Chung Sai Yat Pao*, San Francisco, wrote in 1908:

> The Chinese Exclusion Law as now enacted and enforced was in violation of the letter and spirit of the Treaty between the United States and China and also in opposition to the original intention of Congress on the subject. . . . The exclusion law has been carried out with such vigor that it has almost become an extermination law.[14]

It had to be officially decided by Powderly himself that a merchant could wash his own clothes without losing his merchant status. It took quite some time to decide that a banker was a "merchant" and therefore exempt. It was under Powderly's successor Sargent that the October 11, 1903, Boston roundup of Chinese took place. Police without warrants raided restaurants and homes, arrested 250 Chinese, and kept them in two rooms packed so tightly that they had to stand from eight at night to the late afternoon of the next day. Ultimately fifty were deported. In another incident, the diplomat Tom Kim Yung, an attaché, was so humiliated by his treatment at the hands of San Francisco immigration officials that he committed suicide.

A Presbyterian missionary, Miss Luella Miner, gave wide publicity to the case of the two Chinese students she had brought to America to study in Oberlin College. One of them was H. H. Kung, a descendant of Confucius and later finance minister of China. They had risked their lives to save the lives of foreign missionaries during the Boxer Uprising; their certificates had been issued by Viceroy Li Hung-chang himself and approved by the U.S. consul, but it took thirteen months to get them out of detention in San

Francisco, a week of that spent in the dockside detention shed. Sargent took a personal part in this case.

Exclusion had been tolerated at first because it excluded laborers with little influence among the mandarin bureaucrats in Peking, but under the Powderly-Sargent regulations it was hitting hard at all Chinese, including the upper classes who were sending sons and daughters to study in America, and the increasingly influential middle classes.

John Hay, U.S. secretary of state in 1905, wrote of the "barbarous methods of the Immigration Bureau" in this period.[15] In the latter half of 1901, for instance, 200 of 1,000 transit passengers were stopped. Until then, 37,000 Chinese had passed through America without incident.

Special efforts had been made to encourage China to participate in the St. Louis Exposition of 1904 commemorating the Louisiana Purchase, and China built a beautiful and much-admired exhibition hall there. But James Dunn had been transferred to St. Louis from San Francisco, and he orchestrated a series of incidents involving Chinese exhibitors and visitors. Yu Kit Men, a Chinese commissioner at the exposition, was roused from sleep in his railway state room en route to St. Louis, asked for his pass, and kept under detention in Buffalo until he could prove he was not a laborer.

Those who dared protest such treatment were at risk. When Dr. Sun Yat-sen, the father of the Chinese Revolution and later the first president of the Chinese Republic, testified before a congressional committee about the personal indignities he had suffered at the hands of the Immigration Bureau, he was denounced as an "anarchist."

Chinese in America were living in a state of constant apprehension. In the twelve months after June 1904, 1,402 were arrested and 647 deported on suspicion of unlawful residence. Exasperated and alarmed, San Francisco Chinese and other communities sent out urgent appeals for help to Washington and China. The Chinese Empire Reform Association among others petitioned the government to take action. Students and merchants in China responded with a boycott of American goods that spread from Shanghai, the most important industrial center of the growing middle class of China, up and down the coast and then inland. When this movement began in May 1905, it was strongest in Guangdong and Fujian, the main centers of emigration to America, and in the ports of Canton, Shantou (Swatow), Fuzhou, and Xiamen (Amoy), but this was a nationalist movement, and it won the support of Chinese in Tianjin, Nanjing, and Hankou and in the overseas Chinese communities in Havana, Hawaii, Victoria (British Columbia), the Philippines, and Sumatra.

In a belated effort to head off trouble, Commissioner General Sargent issued instructions to immigration officers on May 19, 1905, that "in performance of their duties, every possible endeavor shall be exercised to prevent the occurrence of any just cause of complaint concerning the treatment accorded Chinese either in word or deed." But it was too late for purely cosmetic reforms. U.S. trade with China declined by 50 percent in two years, from $57 million in U.S. exports in 1905 to $44 million in 1906 and to $26 million in 1907.

The boycott, the first use of this economic weapon in China, was not very well organized, but it lasted until well into 1906 and continued for some time, even after the San Francisco Chinese were financially as well as physically struck by the earthquake of that year and had to concentrate on sheer survival.

The boycott has sometimes been described as a failure. It was not. It did not achieve the aims of its most radical supporters to end the racist exclusion of Chinese, laborers or not, but it did achieve some crucial successes. Southern racists had usually voted with California politicians on the Chinese issue but a drop of two-thirds in U.S. cotton exports to China (May 1905 to May 1906) certainly had an effect on them. Nationwide attention was drawn to the wanton racism, insensitivity, and brutality of the exclusionist elements in official positions. American liberal opinion was incensed. President Roosevelt was forced to reconsider the policies adopted by his subordinates, and he took pragmatic steps to ameliorate interpretation of the laws and avert a threatened catastrophe in Chinese-American relations. Oscar Straus, the first Jew to hold a cabinet post, replaced the racist Metcalf as secretary of commerce and labor in 1906. A Roosevelt-appointed commission of inquiry exposed cases of bribery and fraud, and some venal immigration officers were removed. The U.S. consular service was overhauled and made a regular part of the civil service under the State Department, and Peking, prodded by Washington, adopted the modern practice of issuing national passports from a central office and doing away with the locally issued certificates that had so often been challenged by the U.S. immigration authorities. These measures alone did a great deal to lessen official corruption and bureaucracy on both sides. In 1905, some 29 percent of all certificates were rejected; only 6 percent were rejected in 1906.

The humiliating Bertillon system of registration was abandoned. In San Francisco, Angel Island Detention Center, although bad, replaced the even worse "detention sheds." Special food was provided for wealthier detainees. Periods of detention were reduced. Visitors and transit passengers were accorded more courteous treatment.

The more liberal regulations for students were especially important. In 1905 in China 77 percent of the foreign teachers were American, and 20,000 students were enrolled in American-run and supported schools. Chinese students appreciated the generosity of the American people in supporting this educational effort, but they grew cynical when they contrasted the Christian teachings of their American teachers with the actions of the American government. The number of Chinese students in America declined. More began going to Japan: some 5,000 were there, 2,000 of them on Chinese government scholarships. This trend of the younger generation of Chinese, moving away from America and turning to hostility, worried farsighted Americans. Straus ended the worst abuses and liberalized the definition of "student" to permit youths to attend not only colleges but schools. Roosevelt gained credit by getting part of the Boxer indemnity allocated to fund Chinese students in American colleges. However, his administration passed the 1904 act extending the exclusion laws indefinitely and the 1907 act further restricting Asian immigration.

Incomplete as it was, the boycott forced the racists to abate their attempt to eliminate the Chinese community in America. It showed that the policy of racist exclusion of Chinese, and, by extrapolation, all Asians, could lead to an international explosion (at one stage during the boycott Roosevelt was moving naval forces to the China seas) that would be against the interests of both America and China. Exclusion flouted the basic principles of American democracy. It was producing dangerous strains in the social fabric of America and threatening to bring on war. Fortunately, the healthy forces of the United States averted these dangers.

For several years after this, no new exclusion laws were passed. An increasing Japanese immigration diverted the focus of racial animosity from the Chinese to the Japanese. But the number of Chinese in the United States continued to decline. There were only 71,531 in 1910, with a great disproportion of 26 to 1 between males and females. This made natural increase a very slow process. But the increasing number of Chinese American citizens born in the United States—over 10 percent of the Chinese community in that year—signaled a notable change.

From Reform to Revolution in China

More and more Chinese in America became convinced that, however admirable might be their joint efforts with their American friends, there could be no real end to exclusion until China itself commanded international respect by modernizing itself. They looked with increasing interest at the advance of the forces of nationalism and democracy in China and themselves made notable contributions to that advance.

The Chinese imperial government at first tried to strengthen its armed forces with Western arms without changing either the government structure or political and social system, but the inadequacy of this one-sided attempt at reform was fully exposed by China's disastrous defeat at the hands of the Japanese in the Sino-Japanese War of 1894–1895. Chinese ships fighting Japanese ironclads were armed with dud shells supplied by a corrupt bureaucracy. The empress dowager herself wasted naval appropriations on building a summer palace. Unless radical efforts were made to revive China, much more than Taiwan Island and parts of Northeast China would be lost. The reform movement, led by the Cantonese scholars Kang Yu-wei and Liang Chi-chao, failed after the hundred days of success it had enjoyed in 1898 with the support of the young Emperor Kuang Hsu. The old empress dowager outwitted the reformers with the aid of the treacherous viceroy of Chihli Province, Yuan Shih-kai. Kang Yu-wei and other reformers were lucky to escape abroad, while the emperor himself was incarcerated in his palace and later murdered by his mother. With the die-hard conservatives returned to power, new disasters were inevitable. Following the turmoil attendant on the Boxer (Yi Ho Tuan) Uprising of 1900 when eight invading foreign powers occupied Peking, the empress dowager reluctantly instituted limited but long-overdue reforms in 1901–1905. But the sickness from which imperial China suffered was not to be cured so easily, and the more responsible and farsighted of the governing classes began to demand constitutional changes on the model of western Europe and Japan. Even these moderate demands were frustrated by the empress dowager right up until her death in 1908.

Despite these setbacks, the progressive and nationalist forces in China grew, and they would continue to grow. Consciousness of these historic facts prompted the disquietude of the more farsighted leaders of America. Secretary Straus had made some headway against the worse racists, but even in 1907 he complained to President Roosevelt that

> As the present laws are framed, however, it would appear that the purpose was rigidly to exclude persons of the Chinese race in general and to admit only such persons of the race as fall within certain expressedly stated exemptions, as if, in other words, exclusion was the rule and admission the exception. I regard this feature of the present law, as unnecessary and fraught with irritating consequences.[16]

Straus was expressing the new attitude toward these momentous questions, which the more farsighted were bringing into the conduct of U.S.–China relations. Previous presidents were tempted to play short-term politics with the issue of Chinese immigration. The pressure was most urgent during the 1870s and 1880s elections when the national vote hinged on the ballots cast in the swing states of the West Coast and when California especially was crucial in deciding whether Democrats or Republicans would rule and distribute the "spoils of office." The Chinese issue still had political potential in the 1890s. It was not really a live, political, vote-deciding issue in the early twentieth century, but, as so often with such issues, it continued to generate a life of its own as the hobby-horse of special interests such as the AFL's craft unions, and it took on fresh spirit as it became linked with the chauvinistic imperialism of the time.

Roosevelt was an imperialist but he was also a considerable statesman. He was careful not to base exclusion on race alone but openly on class and economic considerations and so mollify the increasingly influential American trade unions, while admitting the Chinese traders, the middle and upper classes less likely to remain permanently in the country and clearly able to organize effective retaliatory action. He realized that the politics of Western demagogues might not be suitable politics for the nation in the twentieth century. The issue of Japanese immigration was emerging and would have to be dealt with. He realized that, in view of the changes going on inside China, especially the growth of nationalist sentiment and the prospect that a weak China might soon be transformed into a strong China under some form of republican and democratic system, it was already important not to indulge in brutal and provocative behavior, especially toward influential Chinese. As Straus noted, there were still all too many instances of harassment of the "exempt classes."

While deep changes were taking place inside the Chinese communities in the United States in the second decade of the twentieth century, their relations with the larger society were little changed. However, feeling that their situation in America could only be improved by a strong China, they played a considerable role in Chinese affairs, where they helped to bring about radical changes. They gave crucial support in money and manpower to the revolutionary forces led by Sun Yat-sen, which finally overthrew the inept Qing dynasty and established the republic in 1912.[17]

Unfortunately, the republic in turn was subverted by Yuan Shih-kai and various other foreign-backed warlords, and it was not until the 1920s that new hope dawned with the establishment of Sun Yat-sen's new government in Canton and, despite his death in 1925, the start of the Northern Expedition in 1926 to free the country from warlord and foreign rule. In 1927, this effort too was subverted by the treachery of Chiang Kai-shek, commander-in-chief of the revolutionary forces who usurped the leadership of the Kuomintang Party, split the revolutionary forces, and unleashed yet another civil war between the forces led by the Chinese Communist Party (formed in 1921) and his own Nanjing government. China remained divided and weak.

Thus the end of the 1914–1918 World War, the war "to make the world safe for democracy," found China being dismembered at the Versailles peace conference and the Chinese in America still suffering from exclusion. Worse than that: the 1921 Congress enacted further restrictions against Chinese immigration and extended them to include all Asians.

The last major act of Congress aimed to "plug the loopholes" of the exclusion laws was that of 1924. This act was directed chiefly against Japanese immigration, but it also hit the Chinese hard. They lost the right, even as native-born American citizens, to bring in their wives and children if these were born in China.

Chinese who remember that time speak of the shattering effect that "Second Exclusion Act," as they call it, had on them. They had been working, sometimes for decades, to save enough to bring over wives and families, looking forward to having a home, a real home in the United States, and now there was no hope. The doors were barred again. In the next five years, not a single Chinese woman arrived in California from China. The aim of the 1924 law was in part achieved. In the next ten years, more Chinese left the United States permanently than entered it.

I have hitherto concentrated attention on the negative tendencies in this tragic period. These were pushing America further and further away from the democratic principles on which it had been founded. But this period was also a period of struggle for the reaffirmation of those founding principles.

Although at times it must have seemed a disheartening struggle, powerful voices were at every stage raised against the violation of democratic principles by those who sought to subvert the U.S. Constitution. We have quoted some of those voices in public life and in the Congress and administration. Many more could be quoted.

Throughout this tragic period, Chinese in the United States had been fighting for their human and civil rights with whatever means they had at their disposal—in the press and, with their friends, in the legislatures and courts. In *Look Tin Sing*, a habeas corpus case (1884), the circuit court ruled that a U.S. native-born of Chinese descent was a citizen. The Supreme Court in *U.S.* v *Wong Kim Ark* (1893) reaffirmed this. In *Quan Hing Sung* v *White* (1918), the circuit court ruled that sons of citizens of Chinese descent were also citizens. California's Alien Land Laws (1913, 1921, 1923, 1927) forbade aliens ineligible to citizenship the right to buy or own land. This and similar laws in Arizona, Idaho, and Oregon were declared unconstitutional by the Supreme Court in 1947. A ruling in *Mamie Tape* v *Jennie M. S. Hurley* affirmed the Chinese right to public education. (The ruling led, regrettably, to segregated schools.) In addition to these and many similar court battles, Chinese Americans also fought for their rights in the trade unions until in the 1930s the doors of some Pacific unions were opened to them; some craft unions followed suit in the 1950s.

Changing conditions in the world, in America at large, in China and in the Chinese communities and Chinatowns of the nation finally brought success to their efforts.

YUNG WING

Yung Wing was fortunate in being born in 1828 just four miles southwest of the Portuguese colony of Macao in South China. An English mission school was opened there in 1834, and, thanks to an introduction by the school janitor, a friend of the Yung family, seven-year-old Yung Wing was admitted. A bright boy, he learned to speak and write English, but when his father died, leaving the mother to raise the family of four children, Yung Wing had to return home and hawk candy for 25 cents a day to help feed the family. Thanks to his English, he got a job as a folder in a Macao printery at $4.50 a month ($1.50 for board and lodging) and then, again fortunate, was admitted to the new Morrison School in Macao. Here the missionaries were instrumental in sending him and two companions to study in the United States. They arrived in New York on April 12, 1847, and soon after were enrolled in the Monson Academy, in Massachusetts. Here Yung Wing stayed with a friendly family and paid $5 a month for board and lodging.

He could have returned to China on completion of his school courses but, as he himself writes in his autobiography, "The lamentable condition of China was before my mind constantly. . . . I was determined that through Western education, China might be regenerated, become enlightened and powerful." This ambition guided him throughout his life. He therefore decided that he would complete his studies in America and with a little help from his missionary and merchant friends, he worked his way through college and graduated from Yale in 1854, the first Chinese to graduate from a major American college. He then returned to China and had a joyful reunion with his mother, for whom he cared until she died.

Yung Wing's hope of creating a modern educational system in China was a vast revolutionary undertaking that would require the complete transformation of the traditional society. This was eventually accomplished, by many hands and with many sacrifices, over the next century. Being a practical man, he concentrated on a plan of getting a modern American education to as many young people as he could. This too was no easy task.

He had to make a living, so he worked as private secretary to an American acquaintance at $15 a month, then as a court interpreter in Hong Kong for $75 a month, a position from which he was forced to resign by a combination of bureaucratic and professional infighting. He then joined the Imperial Customs Administration in Shanghai but resigned his $200-a-month post there because he could not stomach the graft that riddled the service or the way the foreign officers relegated their Chinese colleagues to subordinate positions. Seeking freedom of action, he then went briefly into the tea business. This took him into the area controlled by the Taiping revolutionaries and, on the invitation of an old friend from Guangdong, now a high official in the Taiping regime, he was invited to visit their capital at Nanjing. Here he was offered a high position, but he declined this because he doubted their leaders' ability to govern. Yung Wing has described the imperial system in China at the time as "founded on a gigantic system of fraud and falsehood" but he found the Taiping state to be little better. However, he gave them some good advice about the need for a modern educational system, advice that of course went unheeded.

His tea business was prospering, but he gave this up when he saw a chance to realize his educational schemes with the help of the powerful imperial viceroy Tseng Kuo-fan who succeeded in crushing the Taiping insurrection. Yung Wing helped the viceroy establish the famous Kiangnan machine works near Shanghai (later the Kiangnan Arsenal), which was conceived as the seed bed for a vast scheme to mechanize China. The viceroy was pleased and in return appointed Yung Wing to organize the Chinese Educational Mission in 1870. This enabled Yung Wing to bring 120 young Chinese boys to the United States for a modern education at imperial expense. For a crucial eleven years, all went well. In that time, Yung Wing was additionally successful as official Chinese representative in helping to end the notorious "pig trade"—the kidnapping of Chinese to work as virtual slaves in Peru. Then the enemies of this worthy endeavor, both in America and China, succeeded in scuttling the Educational Mission.

PART Two EXCLUSION

Twenty-eight Chinese coal miners were killed in the Rock Springs, Wyoming, Massacre of 1885. This was one of many tragic results of the 1882 Chinese Exclusion Act, the first racist law passed in United States history. *Credit: The Bancroft Library.*

The cartoonist Thomas Nast's comment on the way the Republican and Democratic parties seized on the issue of Chinese immigration for partisan ends. *Credit: San Francisco Public Library.*

" '(Dis) Honors are Easy.' Now Both Parties Have Something To Hang On." Thomas Nast's cynical comment on the Chinese question.

Typified by the gentleman pictured here in ceremonial attire, a merchant elite controlled the district and family associations in which the bulk of Chinese immigrants, working class people, farmers, and craftsmen were organized. *Credit: Nevada Historical Society.*

Immigration officials interrogate a young immigrant on Angel Island, the detention center in San Francisco Bay where an immigrant might be held for as long as two years. *Credit: The National Archives.*

The traditional leadership of the Chinatown communities broke down under the stress of urban ghetto conditions in the exclusion era and the ghettos spawned a crime wave. Above is Doyers Street in New York Chinatown, scene of many gangster rumbles, the so-called tong wars at the turn of the century. *Credit: The Library of Congress.*

Early Chinatown stores in San Francisco were modeled on the shops in the area around Canton, South China, from which the overwhelming majority of Chinese immigrants have come. *Credit: The Bancroft Library.*

A Chinese American aviator of the USAF in World War II. Forty percent of the 78,000 Chinese American community joined the nation's war effort on the home front and in the armed forces in the battle against fascism and its racist ideology. They celebrated the repeal of the Exclusion Acts in 1943. *Credit: The National Archives.*

Anti-Chinese agitation forced the abandonment of many small Chinatowns in the West, such as this one in Prescott, Arizona. *Credit: Sharlot Hall Historical Society, Prescott, Arizona.*

The Japanese invasion of China in 1937 spurred the first mass demonstrations of Chinese Americans calling for a ban on U.S. war supplies to Japan. *Credit: The Oregon Historical Society.*

PART Three INTEGRATION

Bustling San Francisco Chinatown today. *Credit: San Francisco Visitors and Convention Center.*

One-third of the housing is substandard in overcrowded New York and San Francisco Chinatowns. This is especially hard on senior citizens. *Credit: James Motlow.*

Street youth in New York Chinatown. An influx of new immigrants following the liberalized entry laws of 1965 led to severe strains on Chinatown social services. Juvenile delinquency and crime soared. *Credit: Corky Lee.*

Garment making is one of the few industries in the big San Francisco and New York Chinatowns, but it is plagued with poor working conditions and low wages, especially for women workers. *Credit: Corky Lee.*

Political activism in the civil rights movement of the sixties and seventies and the continuing struggle between pro-Peking and pro-Taiwan factions often led to sharp conflicts. *Credit: Corky Lee.*

Confucius Plaza in New York reflects the drive to build a new Chinatown with proper housing as a prime goal. *Credit: Corky Lee.*

The Dragon of Happiness and Prosperity revels through the streets of San Francisco Chinatown at the traditional Spring Festival celebrations. *Credit: San Francisco Visitors and Convention Center.*

Anti-Chinese sentiment was rampant in Washington. The U.S. State Department refused Yung Wing's request to permit Chinese students to enter the Military Academy at West Point or the Naval Academy at Annapolis. This rebuff gave the Chinese conservatives, who had all along opposed the Educational Mission, the chance to demand the recall of all the students to prevent them from being "contaminated" by American ideas. Yung Wing was forced to end the mission in 1881.

The rest was epilogue. Yung Wing suffered another devastating blow when his American wife Mary died in 1886. In the midst of the 1894 war between China and Japan, he again offered his services to China, but all efforts to assist the corrupt imperial government were futile, and he threw in his lot with the Reform Party that gathered around the young emperor Kuang Hsu. When the emperor's Hundred Days of Reform in 1898 were ended by the Empress Dowager's coup d'etat and the emperor was deposed, Yung Wing's life was endangered, and he was obliged to flee China and return to America, where he died in 1912.

No account of the role of Chinese Americans is complete without consideration of the role of Yung Wing, who was both a Chinese and an American citizen. His lasting memorial was the good work that many of the students of his Educational Mission did in helping to modernize China and bring her into the modern concert of nations.

NOTES

1. Senate Executive Document No. 106, 1889–1890, quoted by Tien-lu Li, *Congressional Policy on Chinese Immigration* (New York: Arno Press and New York Times, 1979). Reprint of 1916 ed.
2. Quoted by Li, *Congressional Policy.*
3. Senate Executive Document No. 54, 52nd Congress, 2nd Session, 1892–1893, Vol. 2, pp. 41–43.
4. *Congressional Record,* 58th Congress (1893), Vol. 25, Part 2, p. 2443.
5. Li, *Congressional Policy.*
6. Hubert Bancroft, *Selected Works* (San Francisco: History Co., 1890).
7. Li, *Congressional Policy,* pp. 102–103.
8. *Laws, Treaties and Regulations Relating to the Exclusion of Chinese* (Washington, D.C.: Government Printing Office, 1905).
9. Howard K. Beale, *Theodore Roosevelt and the Rise of America to World Power* (Baltimore: 1956), p. 28.
10. Delber McKee, *Chinese Exclusion v. the Open Door, 1900–1906* (Detroit: Wayne State University Press, 1923) is an excellent source for information on these events.
11. Ng Poon Chew, *The Treatment of the Exempt Classes* (San Francisco: self-published, 1908).
12. J. Campbell Bruce, *The Golden Door: The Irony of Our Immigration Policy* (New York: Random House, 1954).
13. McKee, *Chinese Exclusion versus the Open Door Policy,* p. 127.

14. Ng, *The Treatment of Exempt Classes.*
15. McKee, *Chinese Exclusion versus the Open Door Policy,* p. 128.
16. *Annual of the American Academy of Political and Social Science,* 34 (1909), No. 2. Articles by J. P. Young, MacArthur, Yoell, and others. Philadelphia, 1909.
17. Harold Z. Schiffrin, *Sun Yat-Sen and the Origins of the Chinese Revolution* (Berkeley: University of California Press, 1970), and Lyon Sharman, *Sun Yat-sen: His Life and Meaning* (New York: 1934).

Exclusion
—Chinatowns

CHAPTER

XVI

New York Chinatown is located in the oldest section of the
city, where old-law tenements are still in use and living quarters
crowded. . . . The majority of the workers who have no family
here in the States sleep in their family "fongs" [rooms], places
where people bearing the same surname have their headquarters.
Those who pay a couple of dollars per month can occupy a
cot there. These fongs are the most congested places in
Chinatown. In New York's Chinatown, the highest single cause
of death among the residents is tuberculosis. Undoubtedly the
combined forces of unwholesome air, long and strenuous working
hours, improper sleeping quarters, malnutrition, and lack of
outdoor exercise are responsible for this condition. The ratio
of females to males in the population is very unequal. In 1920,
there were about eighteen males to one female, at present the
ratio is approximately ten to one.

> JULIA I HSUAN CHEN, *The Chinese Community in New
> York, 1920–1940*

EXCLUSION transformed the old Chinatowns into
exclusion Chinatowns—part fortress, part haven and refuge, part ghetto-
preserver, which physically decayed and festered until the movement for the
1943 repeal of the Exclusion Act began the slow process of regeneration.

The squalor of exclusion Chinatown starkly contrasted with the opulence
of San Francisco, which by the 1870s had become the metropolis of the
West. Its banks and commercial houses crowded the downtown area east of
Chinatown; its hundreds of factories and other business establishments rivaled
the eastern cities. Leland Stanford, the railway tycoon, was a millionaire ten
times over, with his partners, Huntington, Crocker, and Hopkins, not far
behind. They were soon being rivaled by the Silver Kings: McKay, Fair, Flood,
and O'Brien, Irishmen all, who dominated the Comstock Lode of Nevada
silver and gold, pouring around $500 million of capital into the economy.

As these and other aggressive entrepreneurs put together their financial empires, they built mansions, hotels, libraries, parks, an opera house, other cultural embellishments and steel-framed banks to make their city a worthy monument to themselves and their time. The Palace Hotel, built by the ill-fated Ralston for $7 million, occupied a whole city block and was in its time the most opulent hostelry in the world. San Francisco was the financial, industrial, and cultural hub of the whole of western America. In the 1890s, with 300,000 people, it was second only to New York in value of foreign and domestic trade.

Within a stone's throw of this opulence were the twelve blocks of exclusion Chinatown, a warren of cobbled streets and crowded wooden and brick houses, with restaurants and steaming laundries, curio shops and business houses, temples and family and district associations, huddled, crowded homes, fetid rooming houses for the bachelor majority, cribs for prostitutes, opium dens, headquarters of the fighting and criminal gangs and the gambling halls they controlled, guarded by iron-plated doors and by the police who were supposed to put them out of business. Some 22,000 or more people lived in the quarter, ever watchful for arsonists, looking after their own, venturing at their risk across their boundaries into the territory of other, hostile ethnic groups.

These conditions were not unusual for their time. Irish immigrants in Boston and New York not many years before were described as living in conditions of "squalor even a European seaport could hardly present a parallel to." If exclusion Chinatowns were "filthy," that is not surprising. Force peasant farmers accustomed to open-air village life into overcrowded urban slums, and those slums will inevitably be filthy. What was remarkable was the great personal cleanliness of the Chinese there.

San Francisco's Chinatown was festering under the blight of exclusion. The authority of the traditional leaders of the Six Companies was seriously undermined as a result of their failure to fend off the anti-Chinese Exclusion Act and imposition of the Geary Act and its passbook requirement. The vacuum of authority was filled by those gangster tongs, which imposed their influence through violence and threat of violence.

The tongs had innocent-sounding names. Some *were* in fact innocent enough,* but for a time the most powerful were those engaged in criminal activities and vice. The Hip Sing Tong or "Hall of Victorious Union" was originally organized to protect the gambling tables. The On Leong Tong or "Chamber of Tranquil Conscientiousness" and the Kwong Duk Tong protected the cribs and brothels and trafficked in sing-song slave girls. But, greedy for wealth and power, they began to "shake down" other businesses as well, forcing merchants to pay them protection money. Howard Ah-Tye of Oakland, writes that his grandfather Yee Lo Dy, who came to San Francisco in the 1840s, donated a parcel of land on Pine Street to house the Kong Chow Temple, but this so riled his Yee clan association, which had felt itself entitled to

---

* Some were simple mutual aid associations. The Chee Kung Tong aided Dr. Sun Yat-sen in his revolutionary activities.

the land, that an attempt was made on his life. He thereupon organized the Suey Sing Tong for self-protection. Later, its control passed into other hands.[1]

The Suey Sing Tong was involved with the Kwong Duk Tong in the first of the infamous tong "wars" in Chinatown in 1875. There had been a quarrel and a murder over a sing-song girl, and war between the two tongs was declared by the Suey Sing posting a red paper *chun hung* on a bulletin board on Clay Street. Two hours later, the challenge was accepted by the posting of a Kwong Duk *chun hung*. The following night was designated as the time and Waverly Place the battlefield. Hatchets, knives, and daggers were readied for twenty-five men on each side, and when the clash occurred at the stroke of midnight. The Suey Sing was victorious. The dead and dying were picked up by the police, but no charges were filed, because no witnesses could be found to testify and the victims refused to talk. The Suey Sing accepted a settlement offered by the defeated tong. The Chinatown populace lived in terror of tong secrecy and violence for over forty years. Normal law enforcement agencies could not or would not deal with this problem, and the merchant leaders of the Six Companies were themselves terrorized.

The tongs thrived because of the Six Companies' loss of prestige and because of the unreasonable dominance exercised within the Six Companies by the family associations with the most members and therefore the most votes: the Wongs, Chins, Lees, Yees, and the "Four Brothers" group of the Lau, Kwan, Chang, and Chew families.* Failing to get satisfaction either in Six Companies' councils or through the U.S. courts, which tended to back the established leadership, the smaller family groups and those individuals without family resorted to their own organizations—the tongs, of which the Kwong Duk Tong was one of the earliest organized.

Tong gangsterism gave a bad name to Chinatown because the "wars" spilled over into communities across the nation where tong members carried their feuds. According the Him Mark Lai and Philip Choy in their *Outlines: History of the Chinese in America,* the Bing Kung Tong, Hop Sing Tong, Suey Sing Tong and Jan Ying Tong operated mainly on the West Coast; the Hip Sing Tong, Chee Kung Tong were coast-to-coast organizations; the Ying On Tong was established in California and Arizona and the On Leong Tong in the East, Midwest, South and Texas.

It was a difficult and dangerous task to curb them. Gold Rush conditions left San Francisco 70 percent male even in 1870. The ratio of Chinese males to females in the United States was twenty to one in 1880. This, coupled with the Exclusion Acts that prohibited the entry of Chinese wives of workmen, practically institutionalized prostitution and the brothel. In 1870, of 1,769 Chinese females over fifteen years of age in San Francisco, 1,452 were prostitutes. Most were kept in virtual slavery. The situation grew worse in the exclusion 1880s. Under the conditions of exclusion in the predominantly

---

* Named after four warriors in ancient times who banded together against their common enemy.

bachelor society of San Francisco Chinatown, prostitution, gambling, and opium smoking among the largely illiterate male population was inevitable. All three vices were, of course, widely indulged in by the larger society as well (although opium was there replaced by other drugs and alcohol).

Gangsterism, like vice in Chinatown, was linked up with gangsterism in San Francisco as a whole. Corruption was routine, a legacy from Wild West days. The Reverand Otis Gibson, who, because of his social work in Chinatown and knowledge of Chinese knew a great deal about conditions there, declared before the 1876 Congressional Commission that a portion of the profits of the Hip Yee Tong went to men "not Chinese." Mr. Gibson stated that $5 a week was given certain policemen for the privilege of keeping a brothel open. Lottery houses paid $8 a week. Representatives of the Six Companies told the commission that payoffs were made to City Hall by the gambling and prostitution rackets. These payments must have amounted to considerable sums. There were then 200–300 lotteries and over 80 gambling joints.

Payoffs to police and the immigration authorities were common, but the scale and closeness of ties between organized crime and the authorities reached its peak under Mayor Eugene E. Schmitz, elected in 1901, 1903, and 1905 and backed by the Union Labor Party and its political boss Abraham Ruef.[2] As a student, Ruef's thesis was "Purity in Politics," but he ended his career faced with multiple charges of bribe taking and payoffs running into six digits. In 1905, the Ruef machine succeeded in electing the mayor and the full board of supervisors (councilmen) and was soon taking shakedowns and kickbacks from every business that needed a city license or favor: restaurants, brothels, gambling halls, saloons, and shops. Ruef's henchman in Chinatown was Fong Ching, known as Little Pete, a former shoemaker become shoe manufacturer and gangster who collected payoffs from Chinatown vice and made huge sums by fixing horse races. Little Pete died in typical gangster fashion, shot down in his barber's chair while his bodyguard was absent for a moment getting a betting sheet.[3] All this happened while the Six Companies was torn by a feud between two of its largest associations, the Sam Yup, controlled by the more affluent merchants, and the less affluent Sze Yup.

The battle against the San Francisco tongs took a decisive turn when the 1906 earthquake destroyed Chinatown and their accustomed hideouts and handouts, and the city as a whole carried forward the campaign started by an exasperated citizenry to smash the Ruef machine and its sources of graft. Chinatown itself was roused to action against the tongs. The Presbyterian Mission in Chinatown had begun a drive in the 1870s to help Chinese women enslaved by the tongs in their brothels, and this went into high gear through the efforts of Donaldina Cameron (1869–1968),[4] a redoubtable Scotswoman who in 1895 spurred Chinese efforts and goaded the police into action. She had an effective aide in Inspector Manion, who for twenty-five years (1921–1936) headed the Chinatown squad.

The decline in tong influence was due to a combination of these and other causes. Attrition by death and exclusion reduced membership and the supply of "highbinders," as tong hitmen were called. Tong wars had become so dangerous to all Chinese, and so scandalous, that the consular representatives of the Chinese imperial government itself intervened and threatened drastic action against the relatives in China of particularly obnoxious tong members. Under such pressure the power of the tongs waned. A peace council organized through intermediaries in the Chinese Consolidated Benevolent Associations forced the tongs to agree to settle their conflicts by arbitration rather than violence. Thus an accomodation was reached between the tongs and the CCBAs which has continued until the present time. The last old-style tong killing was in 1927.

These events must be seen as part of a national phenomenon. As they have done periodically, the American people were on the march again in a great crusade for social justice. That movement produced such figures as Jane Addams of Hull House in Chicago, who, like Donaldina Cameron in San Francisco, was waging a dedicated struggle against the blight of the slums and the vice of the gangsters.

All this did not by any means signify the end of the tongs. Tongs are excluded from overt membership of the CCBAs in San Francisco, but not in New York. On one occasion there a leading tong member was actually also chairman of the CCBA. In the 1960–70s, there was a recrudescence of tong criminal activity connected with growing juvenile delinquency and an epidemic of youth gangs.

Vice and crime were only two of the problems fostered by exclusion in both San Francisco and New York Chinatowns and that still trouble them more than thirty-seven years after repeal of the Exclusion Act. Neglect of housing, sanitation, health services, and education still remain issues.

San Francisco Chinatown during exclusion days was a slowly decaying ghetto slum. The beautification of the city was passing it by. Housing typically was crowded, and sanitary facilities, baths, and lavatories woefully inadequate. Most of it was owned by outside slumlords. Chinese children, few in number, were in effect barred from the public schools in 1870. The gap was filled by schools run by Christian missions and several private schools zealously supported by a people with a traditional respect for learning. A public school for Chinese children was established in 1885 when the California State Supreme Court in *Tape* v. *Hurley* decided that they could not be refused admission to public schools. Such segregation lasted until 1946, and in some cases longer. Chinese were not admitted to most public hospitals. Only in 1925 was a Chinese hospital built. In view of these conditions, it was not surprising that people tried to get out of exclusion Chinatowns as soon as possible.

The Diaspora

In Gold Rush days, there were several Chinatowns in the California gold country, but most of them gradually disappeared as the gold-mining industry declined. Chinese were in Hawaii in 1794 and in Los Angeles and San Diego either at the same time as they reached San Francisco or soon after. By the 1850s, some 10,000 Chinese passed on into Washington and Oregon following the mining discoveries there (there were 1,200 in Jackson and Josephine counties in 1857) and then into the western mountain states such as Colorado, Montana, Nevada, and Arizona in the 1860s and 1870s. In these states, new Chinatowns were gradually established, such as in Portland (1851) or Seattle (1860). After completion of the first transcontinental railway eased their way, the Chinese immigrants in 1869–1870 passed on into Chicago and St. Louis (1870); Mississippi (1869); New York and Philadelphia (1869); Boston (1870); Augusta, Georgia (1873); and Minnesota (1870s). They reached, and some of them settled in, El Paso when 1,200 of them, working on the Southern Pacific's most southerly transcontinental line, passed that point.

The real diaspora, however, took place later. In the 1880s, at the height of the anti-Chinese movement in the West, San Francisco Chinatown was bursting at the seams with over 30,000 people, mostly men fleeing the anti-Chinese riots that rocked the smaller West Coast centers. But as the crisis blew over, more and more Chinese fled the unfriendly climate of the West. They began to move out to the other Chinatowns and communities in other parts of the country. They first went to those cities where members of their family or district associations had already settled, but they showed extraordinary courage in pioneering new settlements. Chinatowns in the western mountain regions declined.

Between 1890 and 1900, although the total population of Chinese in the United States declined by 17 percent from 107,488 to 89,863 and San Francisco's Chinese community dropped from 25,833 to 13,954, New York's increased from 2,048 to 4,874 and Brooklyn's 600 doubled. The number of Chinese in Philadelphia, Boston, Chicago, Baltimore, Washington, and New Orleans tripled. Chinese appeared in ten cities where a decade before there had been none. Their means of livelihood were now restaurants, shops and laundries in the Northeast and East and groceries in the South. They avoided as much as possible any economic competition, especially in labor, with white workers.

Today there are Chinese in every state, ranging from the 170,131 in California (1970 census) to the 81,378 in New York, the 52,038 in Hawaii, and the 163 in South Dakota.

But the paradox was that, while the Chinese dispersed into communities across the nation, the number of real Chinatowns decreased. There were twenty-eight in 1940. By 1955 there were sixteen, and today only three of any size: in San Francisco, New York, and Boston. The rest are Chinese communities, where, while there may remain a small core of Chinese homes and businesses—mostly restaurants, groceries, and specialty shops—most Chinese live dispersed among other ethnic groups.

The physical structure of the old Chinatowns with their close-knit family and district organization structure has in most cases disappeared, as a result of either urban renewal or "development" or of the flight to the suburbs by middle-class Chinatown families seeking better living conditions. But, as San Francisco Chinatown shows (although thankfully the worst evils of the exclusion Chinatowns have disappeared for good), something valuable was lost in this destruction, because the Chinatowns were not only ghettoes but repositories of a sustaining folk culture and the priceless intangibles of community.

As we shall see, in both large and small towns social changes began to take place that, coupled with changes in the larger society, in the world at large, and in China, eventually ended the policy of exclusion.

NOTES

1. Howard Ah-Tye, "My Understanding of How Tongs Began," East/West, December 5, 1979.
2. Doris Muscatine, San Francisco: Biography of a City (New York: Putnam, 1975).
3. Oscar Lewis, San Francisco: Mission to Metropolis (Berkeley: Howell-North Books, 1966).
4. Mildred Crowl Martin. Chinatown's Angry Angel: The Story of Donaldina Cameron (Palo Alto: Pacific Books, 1977).
5. Interesting material can be found in the following studies: Christopher H. Edson, The Chinese in Eastern Oregon, 1860–1890 (San Francisco: R & E Associates, 1974); Kim Fong Tom, Participation of Chinese in the Community Life of Los Angeles (San Francisco: R & E Associates, 1974); Willard T. Chow, The Re-Emergence of an Inner City: The Pivot of Chinese Settlement in the East Bay Region of the San Francisco Bay Area (San Francisco: R & E Associates, 1977); Helen V. Cather, The History of San Francisco's Chinatown (San Francisco: R & E Associates, 1932); Stanford M. Lyman, "Social Demography of the Chinese and Japanese in the U.S.A., Social History (journal of Carleton University, Ottawa, Canada), vol. 3, April, 1969.

Angel Island

XVII

Why do I have to languish in this jail?
It is because my country is weak and my family poor.
My parents wait in vain for news;
My wife and child, wrapped in their quilt,
    sigh with loneliness.
Even if I am allowed to enter this country,
When can I earn enough to return to China?
Since ancient times, most of those who leave their homes
    have not been worth a damn.
Up to now how many have ever returned triumphant from this
    battle?

> A lament carved on the walls of the Angel Island
> Immigration Detention Center

ONE DAY in 1979, I joined a ferry boat filled with
people going to Angel Island in San Francisco Bay. There were bright young
people in their teens and some senior citizens so old that their children held
their elbows to help them walk. There was an attractive young community
worker in a chocolate-brown jumpsuit, glossy black hair cascading down to
her waist, the epitome of the young Chinese Americans of today, efficiently
shepherding us on our way to dedicate a monument to the thousands
of Chinese who had passed through the old immigration station on the
island.

It was one of those summer days that make living in San Francisco such
a joy. There were enchanting views on every side; the golden-brown mountains
back of the East Bay cities; the house-dotted, green hills below them; the
islands of the Bay; the fantastic bridges; the city of the Bay itself with its
soaring skyscrapers and white, house-covered hills, a picture lightly brushed
with sea mist and looking like a fairytale metropolis. The sea sparkled with
sunlight.

The old man standing next to me, a little stooped, looked fixedly at lovely
Angel Island and with the back of his hand wiped away the tears from his
eyes.

When the Exclusion Act was passed in 1882, a dilapidated old warehouse on the Pacific Mail Steamship Line's wharf in San Francisco was turned into a processing station for immigrants. Hundreds of Chinese newcomers were held here, perched precariously over the water. Conditions were abominable, and this was one of the reasons for the boycott of U.S. imports that Shanghai initiated in retaliation for the way Chinese immigrants were treated in America. Luella Miner, in her efforts to rescue her two student protegées, personally experienced conditions in the detention shed. She reported, "Suicide is common; death is not infrequent."[1] As a result of such exposures, some improvements were made in the treatment of immigrants. Funds of $200,000 were appropriated to establish an immigration station and detention facility on Angel Island. Construction began in 1905 but was interrupted by the 1906 earthquake. Angel Island was opened on January 21, 1910, when the first eighty-five Chinese immigrants entered its white-walled wooden buildings.

The immigration officers there were given the following instructions: "Upon Chinese persons claiming the right of admission to, or residence within, the United States, to establish such right affirmatively and satisfactorily . . . in every doubtful case, the benefit of the doubt shall be given to the United States government."[2] In other words, presumed guilty of fraud, the exact nature of which was often unspecified, the immigrant had to prove himself innocent while being held in detention on the islet island without bail. With such guidance, it was predictable how the facility would be run. Examinations and interrogations were traumatic events. They usually lasted two or three days but could stretch out interminably. To establish the identity of immigrants, they were asked questions relating to the minutest details of private life and were acutely embarrassing, particularly to Chinese women.

For the family-oriented Chinese, the matter of a son to carry on the family was crucial. In this matter, there was no doubt which was more important: strict observance of an unjust immigration law or a son to carry on the family. So the so-called slot racket was born. A Chinese U.S. citizen on returning after a visit to China would report the birth of a son or daughter there (and therefore a new U.S. citizen) to the U.S. authorities. This created a "slot," which someone in need of offspring could later use to bring in a child. In this way, several thousand "paper sons" were brought in, and when the ruse was exposed it became one of the main aims of the immigration service to catch these paper sons and daughters.

In the first two and a half decades of the 1900s, only one in four immigrants were allowed to land. Some immigrants languished on Angel Island as long as two years before their cases were settled. The poems carved on the walls of the barracks, including the one quoted at the beginning of this chapter and visible to this day, are poignant witnesses to the anguish endured in these wooden cells. As I peered to decipher one of them, almost obliterated with whitewash, the old man tapped it with a knuckle as if tapping at a door of memory and said, "After he carved that one, he committed suicide. He was a scholar."

Angel Island was dubbed the "Ellis Island of the West" or, as the Chinese inmates ironically translated its name, "Isle of the Immortals." Word about its conditions leaked out, but it was a long, tough struggle to get reforms. Protests were made by the Six Companies (CCBA) of San Francisco, by the journalist Ng Poon Chew, a pastor of the Chinese Presbyterian Church and founder of the Chinese daily *Chung Sai Yat Po* in 1900, by the Chinese YMCA and the Angel Island Liberty Association of detainees. Many remember the role played by the devoted Methodist Katharine Maurer, who did her best to ease the condition of inmates. She later became known as the "Angel of Angel Island." "She saved many from suicide," I was told by a woman who worked for many years as Chinese interpreter on the island. Such efforts and the changing times wrought improvements. By 1924, the waiting time between interrogations and decision had been reduced in most cases to around two to three weeks. The food was improved, and some attempts made to provide recreation and better sanitary facilities. But the basic significance of the island was not changed. It was established not to facilitate immigration but to see to it that the Exclusion Act was enforced as stringently as possible. Toward the end of its existence, the rate of rejections had dropped from 85 to 5 percent. In World War II, it was decided to close the station, and on November 4, 1940, the 144 Chinese still held there were moved to temporary facilities in San Francisco. The detention building gradually began to decay. Over on the other side of the 740 acres of the island, the U.S. army post named Fort Marshall remained sole occupant.

Angel Island went out of use when an end was put to the absurd arrangement whereby would-be immigrants were processed in the United States after crossing the ocean, and the new system was introduced of processing papers in U.S. consulates in ports of embarkation abroad.

It has been reported that by 1952 all activities begun under the Exclusion Acts had ceased, but this was not so. Evidence collected under the so-called confession program proceedings (see p. 215) was still being used against individual Chinese even in the 1960s. People whose fathers came in as "paper sons" fifty years ago are still afraid to reveal that fact.

Some Conclusions

The general public as well as politicians, diplomats, and scholars have debated the issue of Chinese immigration—indeed, any immigration—at great length. Sometimes the floods of rhetoric have threatened to obscure the facts and the simple truth so that today the same or similar misconceptions are held about the Mexicans as were held about the Chinese immigrants a hundred years ago, and the denunciations are being made in almost the same words: they are "not like us"; "they are dirty," "take away American jobs," and "keep to themselves." But when the researchers go into the matter, they find model Mexicans with a good, traditional American work ethic, hardworking, doing jobs no one else will do and becoming thoroughly American with a Mexican flavor.

The real crux of the matter is whether there should be unrestricted emigration from a country and immigration into a country and, if restrictions are necessary and justified, what sort of restrictions should there be? Those who accept the concept of one world and the essential brotherhood of humanity have no doubt that the utopian ideal of freedom of movement is worth striving for and can be attained. However, they realize that a necessary prerequisite of such freedom is the superseding of exclusive nation states by an inclusive world government and unity. But there will be no incentive for large-scale migration under such a system. With universal justice, peace, freedom, and high standards of living why should anyone wish to leave home as an immigrant? In fact, the very terms *emigrant* or *immigrant* will have lost their meaning. There will only be travelers.

However, today we are still living as in the nineteenth century, in a world of vast inequalities among states and individuals. The bold and adventurous and dissatisfied, the dissident, the fearful, the needy, the enterprising, and the desperate inevitably seek to better their lives in new homelands. Can a responsible government of an underdeveloped land be condemned as "totalitarian" or accused of violating human rights when it takes steps to prevent a "brain drain" when trained professionals are urgently needed to help build a better life for their less privileged compatriots? Can an already overcrowded state of limited means and extent be condemned for shutting its doors to an influx of strangers whom it cannot look after? Common sense answers such questions. No country will be criticized for excluding criminals, carriers of epidemic diseases, and avowedly hostile elements such as spies and terrorist agents. While we should strive to win more and more people over to the realization that the world is our common possession and to joint action on that basis, the present reality is that it is still divided into 150 nation states of varying sizes and levels of development, all of them claiming exclusive possession and government of their territories. In this age of imperialism, most of them are constantly being forced to take action to preserve and defend their rights and interests. In such a world, there is no question that the people of a sovereign state are justified in taking measures to restrict emigration and immigration and in deciding for themselves what those measures should be. It is also the right of the rest of the world community to pass judgment on the validity of the measures taken. Let the debate go on. It will only do good to discuss what kind of restrictions are justified in different situations. It is in this context, I believe, that one must realistically consider the whole tragic episode of the exclusion era and its aftermath, through which the United States and its Chinese and other ethnic minority groups are living today.

The period 1849–1943 was a time of extraordinarily rapid change in America, affecting the way of work and life of its people and their outlook. Legally, the period between 1849, when Chinese began to arrive in any numbers, and 1882 was one of almost unrestricted emigration and immigration, although, as we have seen, formidable illegal and extralegal restrictions operated, especially the growing and sustained anti-Chinese movement in the western states.

The 1868 Burlingame Treaty, the only one governing Chinese immigration up to the 1880s, was animated by lofty but also very practical considerations in a situation where the United States had ample lands for expansion and settlement for new arrivals and a great need for skilled labor to develop its newly acquired territories in the West. But the very success of the new immigrants helped to change the situation with great swiftness. Capital for development was rapidly amassed, railways were built, and the infrastructure for a booming capitalist industrial economy was created. Immigration into the United States was phenomenal. From 23 million in 1850, the population soared to 50 million in 1880 and 76 million in 1900. But the mid-1870s were a time of severe economic readjustment and depression. Competition for jobs was fierce. There was mass unemployment. The general attitude to immigration changed. Had the Statue of Liberty reflected the prevailing sentiment, she would have dropped her torch of liberty and held up the sign "Keep Out!" Some regulation of immigration was obviously necessary; what was reprehensible was the racist form it took.

It is true that many people were disturbed when brought into contact with people of another race and culture, such as Chinese dressing in a "strange" way and eating "strange" dishes. But it is also very clear from the literature of the time that such a natural feeling of strangeness was whipped up into virulent racism by demagogues with ulterior aims. A mayor of San Francisco said, "It is not a question of wealth, nor whether the wages of Chinese are higher or lower than ours. It is a question of having the Chinese at all."[3] However, the basic issue between the Chinese in America and those who inveighed against them was economic. They were attacked by those who felt threatened by their economic competition. Expediency was the reason why others supported the anti-Chinese agitation for their own ends. Conversely, expediency sometimes encouraged support for Chinese immigration. California State Senator Tingley, who was at first all for exclusion of the Chinese, later introduced a bill to bring in Chinese labor at fixed wages on ten-year contracts.

As the historical record shows, racism was quite controllable. It was a sometime thing that unscrupulous people manipulated to arouse passions and violence to gain their economic ends. It intensified when the Chinese issue was needed and faded out of the picture when the Chinese were needed for some specific task like building the transcontinental railway. Charles Crocker and Leland Stanford were anti-Chinese when they did not need the Chinese, but when Chinese were needed to build the railway they became "Crocker's Pets" and Stanford was full of praise for them. When Stanford ran for governor in 1861 and needed votes, he was anti-Chinese. The Chinese conveniently had no votes to withhold from him.

To conceal the greed and avarice that motivated their attacks on the Chinese, some found it politic to talk about the "filthy" and "unassimilable" Chinese and to assert that all Chinese were congenital liars and perjurers, depraved and unsavable.

It was a tragedy not only for the Chinese in America but also for America itself that a possibly necessary restriction of immigration took the form of racial exclusion of Chinese, "Mongolians," and Asians in general, that restrictions took racist forms pandering to the irrational fears and prejudices of a small proportion of the American people blinded by narrow regional interests and manipulated by politicians and some labor leaders cynically exploiting this situation in the name of trade unionism. The decision to restrict immigration and the manner of that restriction was not taken on legitimate socioeconomic grounds but in a spirit of racist prejudice violating the basic principles of the democracy that was the great contribution of the United States to the world. To get these restrictive racist laws passed, it was necessary to cover up something of which decent people were ashamed and had to be tricked into supporting. This led to lies, mean subterfuges, and general skullduggery that poisoned the body politic of America and had truly disastrous consequences during the next hundred years.

Not surprisingly, when in June 1920 California Governor William Stevens called for action to protect his state as the "Western outpost of Occidental civilization on the Pacific" from Asian infiltration and specifically the Japanese, he suggested exclusion acts directed against the Japanese along the same lines as those used against the Chinese.

Exclusion on the basis of race does violence to the most basic qualities of humanity, the sense of manhood, and human rights. In attempting to degrade the victim, it degrades the oppressor. If there must be restriction of immigration into a country, it should be based on nothing but the true needs of that country, the immigrants' true human worth, and evenhanded justice.

America's bad example encouraged other governments to follow suit. Anti-Chinese or racist exclusion laws were passed by Natal (1897), the Orange Free State (1899), Australia (1901), the Cape of Good Hope (1904), Transvaal (1907), New Zealand (1920), and Canada (1923).

NOTES

1. Delber L. McKee, *Chinese Exclusion v. the Open Door, 1900–1906.* (Detroit: Wayne State University Press, 1977).
2. *Ibid.*
3. *North American Review*, 173, p. 672; quoted by J. D. Phelan in "Why the Chinese Should be Excluded." See also Him Mark Lai, "*Island of Immortals:* Chinese Immigrants and the Angel Island Immigration Station," *Journal of the California Historical Society*, 57 (Spring 1978), no. 1 (special issue: "The Chinese in California").

Ending
Exclusion

XVIII

In the effort to carry out the policy of excluding Chinese laborers—Chinese coolies—grave injustice and wrong have been done by the nation to the people of China and, therefore, ultimately to this nation itself.

PRESIDENT THEODORE ROOSEVELT,
Annual Address to Congress, 1905

THE SIXTY-ONE years of exclusion, from 1882 until 1943, were tragic and shameful, and it is taking decades more to get rid of their evil consequences. They were years of insult, humiliation, and death for Chinese, not because of some crime, misdemeanor, or evil they had done but because of what they were: Chinese men and women with straight black hair, with almond eyes and golden skins, different in looks and language from their persecutors.

But America is a multilayered, pluralistic society, more varied and cosmopolitan than most because of its democratic system and antecedents, its history of reaching out to the West, constantly opening up new land and new horizons, surging forward, restless, intensely vigorous, adventurous, and, as a result, always swiftly changing. The nineteenth and twentieth centuries have been years of rapid development and transformation from a pioneer land into an agricultural and industrial giant among the great nations of the world.

Those years saw the industrialization of America, astonishing feats of canal and railway building, the introduction of the telephone and radio communications, the mechanization of agriculture and rise of agribusiness, the fantastic growth of cities—Chicago, New York, San Francisco, Los Angeles—and the emergence of America as a world power. These economic advances radically changed the outlook of its peoples, and these changes naturally affected its people of Chinese descent.

A Changed America

In the 1880s and on into the first third of the twentieth century, those who stood up for the liberal principles of American democracy and opposed exclusion of the Chinese were regarded by their opponents as, at best, slightly impractical idealists. In the second third of the century, America was fortunate to have a statesman of the caliber of Franklin D. Roosevelt, who in 1943 signed the bill repealing the Exclusion Acts. The wisdom of that repeal can be gauged by considering what the position of the United States would have been today if it had not repudiated that racist and reactionary policy. Quite simply, they would have been in the position now ingloriously occupied by racist South Africa, and they would not have had any "China card" to play in the crucial last third of the twentieth century.

In the 1880s, the United States was a developing country of 50 million people with a Chinese population of 105,000 or 0.2 percent of the total, the overwhelming majority of whom were aliens without a vote and ineligible for citizenship by naturalization. The majority population of Anglo-Saxon white Americans were persuaded that they were in danger of being swamped by succeeding and never-ending waves of peoples from eastern and southeastern Europe and from Asia, especially China. The Civil War had emancipated the black slaves but it had not solved the problem of the black Americans, who were being harried in the Reconstruction South and in the Jim Crow North. The democratic vision of its destiny that had inspired America at its birth had dimmed. The Lincolnian consciousness of itself as a great nation of nations had not yet triumphed. There was fear of the foreigner in its midst. At the same time, traditional Chinese skills, the skills of a feudal, handicraft economy that had been so useful in the 1850s, 1860s, and 1870s of the developing West, were now outdated in an industrialized, mechanized America.

Furthermore, the Chinese had been barred from learning the new machine technology. They had been technologically excluded even before they were politically excluded. They were the odd man out. It was under these circumstances that the anti-Chinese Exclusion Act was passed in 1882.

In the 1940s, America was a very different land, and so were China and the Chinese communities in America.

Changing Chinatowns

In 1943, America was looking forward to victory in the biggest and most destructive war of all time. It was a nation of 132 million people. The Chinese community had shrunk from its 1890 peak of 107,488 to a low of 61,639 in 1920. In 1943 it was a small minority of 78,000, or 0.05 percent of the population, the smallest minority of all among the major nationalities of the world represented in the American population. But now, the majority of the

Chinese communities were native-born American citizens. They were over 52 percent of all Chinese in America. Most of the others were eager to become American citizens. But there were many who for various reasons shunned any contact with the Immigration and Naturalization Service (INS). Those who did not want American citizenship had left for their homeland or other parts. In the course of World War II, this essentially new Chinese American community showed itself to be very American—and also very Chinese. America had begun to realize that in the Chinese of America it had a precious asset.

Over the turn of the century, during the exclusion years, the Chinatowns of America and the "free-floating" Chinese communities had indeed changed radically.

The numbers were smaller, to begin with. The ratio between men and women was still lopsided, three men to one woman. This meant a disproportionate number of men without wives and families.

But other significant and progressive changes had taken place. The trends that we saw in the Chinese population, and that led to the ending of exclusion in 1943, continued. In part these trends echoed those in the larger society; in part they reflected a dynamic special to the Chinese communities.

The Chinese community was now almost wholly urban. This in part followed the pattern of increasing urbanization in America as a whole. In the 1880s, America was still overwhelmingly an agricultural society, although on its way to industrialization with its inevitable movement of people to the cities. By then 28.2 percent of Americans lived in cities. At that time, 22 percent of Chinese in America lived in cities with populations of 100,000 or over. But Chinese urbanization followed its own special "law." Prejudice, law, and organized labor kept them out of many urban and industrial occupations such as the civil service, teaching, medicine, and other professions and the building trades, engineering, construction and other industries and occupations where they would normally have gone in a really open industrialized society. But they were forced to go into the cities for other reasons. In the early days of frontier life, a Chinese could get work rather readily as a cook or washer in the usually all-male bachelor mining and lumber camps or on ranches, but this type of "female" labor was gradually closed to them as the West settled down and families of settlers moved in. The Chinese therefore moved increasingly into urban areas in search of work. Those were also the times of rampant anti-Chinese agitation. While some small rural communities maintained admirable standards of American tolerance and Chinese can be found in those areas today as well-liked members of their communities, there were disgraceful pogroms in other places, and whole Chinese communities were driven out. It seemed useless simply to try their luck in another and unknown village, so they usually crowded into the Chinese urban ghettoes. In the Chinatowns, some "took in" each others' washing but quite a number scraped together sufficient capital, as we have seen, to set up industrial and commercial enterprises; hand laundries, restaurants, tailoring establishments, and shops of various kinds catering to the surrounding white communities.

As long as domestics were affordable in American households, many found employment as servants and cooks in substantial households. Others moved into market gardening around the larger cities such as San Francisco and New York to supply restaurants and homes there. By the 1890s, some 30 percent of the Chinese were concentrated in cities. Another 12.7 percent were in small urban communities, so that a total of 42.7 percent lived in cities and larger towns. The corresponding figure for America as a whole was 35.1 percent.

In 1882, perhaps a third or more of the Chinese in America were sojourners, intending to return to their homes in China as soon as possible. Because of Chinese traditional family ties and beliefs, the number of sojourners among the Chinese was somewhat larger than in other groups of immigrants, and they were naturally the first to leave when conditions worsened. The humiliations and terror caused by the exclusion agitation also forced many other Chinese to leave sooner than they wished and impelled many others to leave unwillingly. Those Chinese who remained in America had decided that, despite everything, they liked to live in the United States. They had become acclimatized and acculturated and had built up property here that made life better for them here than back home. Of course, some of those who chose to remain and make their homes here included a few who had left China because they had had to, either for perfectly good and honorable reasons or for bad. Some had struggled against the Qing tyranny and faced reprisals if they returned; others had slipped out of the country to avoid being apprehended for some wrongdoing or breach of law or custom.

Only 1 percent of the Chinese immigrants were American citizens in the 1870s. Most of these were American-born children. In 1880, the ratio of men to women in California's population was over three to one. Among the 105,465 Chinese there were only 4,779 women. Most men had no possibility of marrying Chinese women, and mixed marriages were frowned on, even though only a few states enacted miscegenation laws. Nevertheless, quite a number of men managed to marry and raise families. Their children, born in the United States, were American citizens going to American schools and getting an American education. The number of these Chinese American citizens increased steadily until by the early 1900s they were 10 percent of the Chinese population in the United States.

The social profile of the Chinese communities and Chinatowns was changed by the increasing number of Chinese going into business. Men who came here as laborers faced hard decisions when they chose to remain after exclusion. Laborers without property other than their strength and skills constantly faced the risk of deportation. They never knew when an immigration officer would stop them on the street and ask to see their papers. So more and more of them worked hard to change their status from laborer to merchant or businessman. Large numbers did this by a typically Chinese way of raising capital, bypassing the normal banking system. A group of men, say ten, formed a *hui*. Each put, for example, $50 into the *hui*, and lots were drawn to decide who should have use of the $500 available in the *hui*. A great deal of capital was not needed to set up a small shop, and in this way, a number of men with a little capital were able to change their status from excluded laborer to exempt merchant or entrepreneur with a capital of $1000 or more. Deeply motivated, frugal, noted for their sobriety, they became men of property, men of substance with families. A number of men gained merchant status by persuading established merchants to take them as partners.

This was why laundries figured so largely among Chinese occupations. It took very little capital to set up a laundry, and it made a man independent. In 1920 some 30 percent of all Chinese were engaged in laundry work. In New York City, the percentage was 37.5 percent. This was a mainstay of the Chinese until the laundry business began to use steam and machinery and later the laundromat arrived.

Outside the traditional merchant elite that had hitherto dominated the Six Companies, a new, increasingly middle-class and lower middle-class (petit bourgeois) Chinese American community was emerging. Some of them coalesced with the traditional leadership. Others challenged it. Commercial import-export enterprises supplied the needs of their own and surrounding communities. Even though most of these were small establishments, they were nevertheless sufficient to get their owners through a crucial transition, transforming them from laborers to businessmen and so enabling them to bring wives over from China and raise families. (Grocers, laundrymen, and restauranteurs were not legally "merchants," but their substantial property enhanced their status.)

This same process determined that the Chinese community in America should become not only increasingly middle-class but urban as they congregated in the cities with their better job opportunities. With few exceptions in California (such as the township of Locke, south of Sacramento on the river), the Chinese who had worked in the farms, vineyards, fisheries, and mines were bit by bit pushed or edged out and congregated in the larger Chinatowns. Here there was some safety in numbers, and it was possible to live to some extent by serving the needs of the community itself, thus avoiding confrontation with the larger outside community.

San Francisco Chinatown, first and until the 1980s largest of such communities, exhibited in the extreme both the positive and negative aspects of these peculiar habitations. Such large Chinatowns gave a coherence to Chinese community activities that was difficult to achieve in the dispersed conditions of rural life. Its area of twelve blocks and population of around 30,000 provided the critical mass needed to generate a diversity and scale of economic, social, and cultural activities that enabled it to sustain its reactions and interactions with the surrounding, larger community without losing its national cultural identity. Chinatown, San Francisco, has developed a cultural autonomy that is typically Chinese American. The great festivals of the Dragon Boat and the Ching Ming, "Clear and Bright," the yearly commemoration of the ancestors, are regularly celebrated. The Spring (New Year) Festival is a total community occasion that delights the larger society with the exotic beauty of its sounds and colors, dragon and lion dances, music, and other performances. In most U.S. cities, a film with Chinese dialogue is an event only for the intellectual elite. But San Francisco Chinatown can host Chinese-language movies as a major part of its cultural life. In 1981 it will hold the first Chinese film festival in America as part of the famed international film festival of the whole city.[2] And, while a single Chinese-style facade or roof is a curiosity, a street or block of them is an architectural ensemble that produces a Chinatown—the pride of San Francisco, one of the most beautiful cities in the world.

The fruit of these developments is the unique Chinese American culture that San Francisco Chinatown is producing today. It is neither that of mainland China, of the island province of Taiwan under Kuomintang rule, nor simply a reflection of the cultural trends of the larger society, which have a special vitality in ebullient San Francisco. It is not simply an amalgam of all these, either. It is an indigenous product—Chinese American. It is by no means homogeneous. That would not be possible in such a diverse environment as a Chinatown in America. It has its traditional wing—for instance, old and young artists making paintings in the traditional style of brush painting, with traditional themes: birds, bamboos, still lifes. It produced the art of the first generation of local Chinese artists such as Dong Kingman or Jake Lee, who emerged on the national scene as products of the realistic school of the 1930s along with such painters as Sloan or Benton. Then there are the avant garde of the abstract expressionists. All of these artists represent various aspects of the life of the Chinatowns and of the Chinese American communities of the nation. They reflect not only their Chinese background but the matrix of American society in which they grow and of which they are a part.

It was the tenacity of Chinatown, its sometimes exasperating stubbornness, its will to survive, that held the Chinese community in San Francisco together through years of troubles. When the 1906 fire and earthquake literally wiped it out and there were authoritative calls that it should relocate elsewhere, somewhere "down the Bay," it was that stubbornness that began its reconstruction right on that precise spot before the embers were cool. It also helped that many Chinese had had the forethought to take out fire insurance with eastern insurance companies rather than in San Francisco, where they might be more subject to local anti-Chinese pressures.

Of course, that stubbornness, conservatism, and clannishness also have their negative side. Because of that conservatism, the constitution of the Six Companies has not been changed for the past fifty years, and this has left that organization increasingly out of step with the needs of today. Because of that clannishness, people from Shanghai and Tientsin who speak the Shanghai dialect or Mandarin are sometimes treated like aliens in Cantonese shops or restaurants. In fact, some say that they would get better service if they forgot their natural Chinese tongue and spoke plain English. Such attitudes fuel the divisiveness that hampers Chinatown's attempts to update itself.

Nevertheless, San Francisco Chinatown has shown itself to be not only the oldest and largest but also the most progressive of the remaining Chinatowns of the nation.

Good traditions have sustained Chinatown. Animated by the traditional Chinese respect for learning that makes every Chinese household anxious to have a scholar in the family, intensified by the American urge to "get ahead," the new middle-class households send their children to American schools and colleges whenever they can, often at great cost and sacrifice to themselves. Although such families do their best to give their children, girls as well as boys, a Chinese education, including at least the basics of reading and writing in Chinese, the young products of this bilingual and bicultural education usually emerge with a pronounced tilt in their thinking toward the American elements of their training. Because of the social and economic pressures they have seen their families contend with and the conventional wisdom that "Chinese don't stand much chance in corporate management" or the state bureaucracy, most of them have deliberately gone into those fields where they could make maximum use of their individual abilities and avoid confrontation and competition with the white majority. This has led to their concentration in such scientific research fields as physics or chemistry, biology, or in education, the arts, architecture or design. Even in these days of affirmative action, relatively few Chinese work in such fields as the welfare bureaucracy, heavy industry, or the construction departments of government administration. Although, because of their work, most of these members of the new intellectual strata of the Chinese American communities live outside Chinatown and in the suburbs of New York, San Francisco, or Boston, they realize that their constituency, whether political or cultural, is largely in the Chinatowns of New York or San Francisco, which are a focus for their activities. In the old days, the Chinatowns relied for intellectual guidance on the elders of the family and district associations. These were mostly of the merchant class and, to give added legitimacy and tone to their associations, they often "imported" scholars to do clerical work for them. But these scholars were usually of the old traditional school. So the new, modern citizens of the three or four remaining Chinatowns and the peripheral "free-floating" Chinese communities in other cities found that the old associations represented their interests less and less. In fact, they seemed to be working against those interests by continuing to isolate the Chinese communities from the larger society and by stubbornly supporting such old ways as arranged marriages and the absolute subordination of the younger people to the elders with their out-of-date ideas and old-fashioned ways.

By the 1920s, the younger generation was forming its own associations in tacit if not outspoken opposition to the old. Young people such as Anna May Wong and James Wong Howe, noted cameraman, were branching out into the creative arts and boldly developing careers in the larger society. Chinatowns in the exclusion years typically communicated with the outside world through the Six Companies, the Consolidated Chinese Benevolent Associations (CCBA), and similar groupings of district and family associations. Now they began to speak in many voices directly through various new modern organizations, the Chinese Chamber of Commerce, the Chinese American Citizens Alliance, the YMCA and YWCA, the Chinese Hand Laundry Alliance, and other groups in the arts, sports, and social life and through their own press.

The organization of the Native Sons of the Golden State in San Francisco in 1895 marked the start of a new period in the history of the Chinese community in America. It was organized by the increasing number of native-born Chinese Americans determined to secure and defend their civil rights as American citizens, Chinese with votes. By 1915, under their new name of Chinese American Citizens Alliance, they had additional chapters in Chicago, Detroit, Pittsburgh, Boston, Houston, San Antonio, Albuquerque, Los Angeles, Fresno, San Diego, Salinas, Portland, and Oakland. Their newspaper, the Chinese Times, founded in 1921, had the largest circulation of any Chinese language newspaper in the country. Their 1913 success in blocking the proposal by state Senator Camminetti to disenfranchise Chinese Americans brought them prestige, but the elitist character of the organization, Republican-oriented and primarily of and for businessmen and professionals, led to its gradual decline and inability to gain a wider constituency. The 1954 formation of the Chinese-American Democratic Club in San Francisco further eroded its strength.[3]

The first major daily, the Chung Sai Yat Po, appeared in 1900. Now a dozen dailies and periodicals are published in Chinese and/or English by the San Francisco community alone, together with numerous newsletters and bulletins.

These new organizations, the churches, and influential alumni associations are at once part of the Chinese community and also linked directly with the larger society. They function not only inside Chinatown but in and as part of the larger society that surrounds and permeates Chinatown and the Chinese communities. Young voting citizens in Chinatown began to join the Republican and Democratic parties and other political groups and through their caucuses they represented a constituency that politicians felt it worthwhile to woo.

The larger society was more and more permeating Chinatown with its government bureaucracies, its religious groups, its trade unions and cultural associations, its financial and business activities. Chinatown with its new organizations was reaching out to the larger society to establish mutually beneficial contacts.

It is significant too that the new generation still takes a lively interest in events in China. Ties with families in China are as firm as ever, as reflected in the remittances that have continued to be sent regularly (except for the

1950–1970 period of severance of relations between the United States and the People's Republic of China). The early immigrants had come to America to help their families back home, and in the 1870s their remittances from California averaged $30 annually per person. By 1930 this had increased to $40, though it dropped in 1935 due to the general economic decline. The total remittances sent home to China by overseas Chinese was enough at one time to make up half of China's adverse balance of payments deficit.

The New Immigrants

A new kind of immigrant began to enter Chinese communities in the second quarter of the twentieth century. During World War I, while the great powers were preoccupied with the war, Chinese capitalist enterprises began to develop, particularly in trade and textiles, matches, cigarettes, and other light industries. A Chinese capitalist middle class grew in wealth and influence with these enterprises. Unlike the earlier elite of old China—the feudal landlord and scholar official families—they were eager to send their children to get modern educations abroad. America as well as Japan and Europe saw increasing numbers of able and ambitious young people coming to get an education and later in the post-World War II period sometimes marrying into overseas Chinese American families or setting up overseas branches of the family business or other enterprises. These young people often found the atmosphere of traditional conservative Chinatown uncongenial. They felt more at home in the larger society outside, even though at the time they faced certain discrimination in housing and in social life there.

There was a change, too, in the places from which these new immigrants came. Quite a number came from Shanghai, the most capitalist and cosmopolitan of the new cities of China, and from modern industrial and commercial Tianjin to the north. Speaking the Shanghai dialect or northern Mandarin (today the common speech of China), they could not normally understand the Cantonese dialects spoken in Chinatown. This was an additional reason why, rather than join the traditional Cantonese-speaking associations, they joined new organizations that they felt to be more congenial and in which they could take the lead.

Stranded Students

Dilution of the almost exclusively Cantonese-speaking composition of the Chinatowns has been going on steadily now for several decades. The warlord civil wars of 1911–1937 and the disturbed state of China resulting from those wars and the Japanese invasion of 1931–1945 also induced many wealthier families to send their children abroad for an education. The all-out Japanese invasion of China in 1937 and the Pacific War (1941) resulted in about 5,000 of these Chinese students staying on in the United States. Most of these "stranded students" graduated in science and technology rather than the humanities, which in the more practical atmosphere of a modernizing China had declined in popularity. Urbanized English-speaking intellectuals, they had a considerable impact on the old Chinese communities and also on the larger surrounding society. They gave that society a new, more sympathetic image of the Chinese as being "more like us."

At the time of World War I, the Chinese in America, excluded from the American political process, channeled much of their effort into the struggle for a free and democratic China, which they hoped would give them necessary support as overseas Chinese. They collected funds to help Sun Yat-sen in his revolutionary efforts, and many of them, like the young aviator Fung Joe Quey (1881–1912), returned to China to put their knowledge at the service of the progressive forces. Few were directly involved in the American war effort. But World War II witnessed a burst of patriotic and antifascist activity among Chinese Americans everywhere in the country. The Chinese Women's Patriotic Association, the Chinese Citizens Patriotic League, the Chinese Hand Laundry Alliance, and the Seamens Patriotic Association of New York with 5,000 members played a notable role in forging unity among Chinese Americans of all persuasions against the Japanese invaders and in helping defend China and America. The United China War Relief collected millions of dollars for the Chinese war effort. These were truly schools for democratic action in which hundreds of young activists grew to maturity.[4]

Before Pearl Harbor, American companies were selling scrap iron and oil to Japan, which boosted its war effort against China and ultimately against the United States. Chinese Americans, men and women, adults and youngsters, joined Chinatown parades and demonstrations against this trade and to denounce the Japanese invasion of China. For the first time, they were participating in such mass political activities alongside their American friends, urging America to recognize the danger and change course. After Pearl Harbor, large numbers of both men and women served in the armed forces and in war work. Roosevelt proclaimed that it was "only through the unity of all people that we can successfully win the war, regardless of race, color and creed." The demand for labor increased, and industrial jobs in the factories and shipyards at last became available to the Chinese.

The 13,000 Chinese in the war effort represented 17 percent of all Chinese Americans, one of the highest percentages of all ethnic groups.
They fought well in Europe and in China. Chinese seamen were in great demand in the merchant marine, and they played an heroic part manning the ships on the dangerous and vital Atlantic supply routes. At the end of the war 3,000 of them were members of the National Maritime Union (NMU). Altogether 15,000 Chinese seamen served in the U.S. merchant marine and on British ships during the war, but it is characteristic that the Chinese Seamen's Patriotic Association, which worked closely with the NMU, had to wage a real struggle to get these men the right to shore leave in American ports.

The extensive participation of Chinese women in the war effort was particularly remarkable in view of the previous reluctance of Chinese women to get into the public eye and do "men's work." They joined the women's auxiliary war services and went into nursing and many other activities on the home front, as well as into industrial war work in shipbuilding and other trades from which they as well as their men had hitherto been rigorously excluded.

These wartime activities and the camaraderie of wartime left an indelible mark on the Chinese American communities and Chinatowns. It became increasingly clear that these hard-working young men and women in the armed forces and factories would not for long continue to tolerate the second-class citizenship that the Exclusion Acts prescribed for them. They were building up public opinion against the Exclusion Acts. Those acts and their attendant attitudes were racially motivated and came of the same basic ideology that motivated the Nazis' genocidal policies. Revulsion against such racism was becoming a powerful force in all democratic communities.

These changes in Chinatowns and the Chinese American communities ensured that exclusion was on its way out.

Changing China

The anti-Chinese Exclusion Acts and resulting discrimination were predicated on the supposed inherent inferiority of the Chinese "race." But the new emerging China demonstrated to the world in World War II what the Chinese nation really was. The new China was bloodying the nose of imperial and imperialistic Japan, the honorary Aryan nation and ally of Hitler's Germany, the nation that had imposed an humiliating defeat on the old Chinese empire in 1894, humbled the Csarist Russians in 1905, and in 1941 challenged the American, British, French and Dutch colonial empires.

Shakey though it was, the united front of the two main parties, the Kuomintang led by Chiang Kai-shek, and the Kungchantang (Communist Party) led by Mao Tse-tung, was holding the Japanese at bay. By 1938, it was clear to those who watched the conflict carefully that the question was not whether Japan or China would win but when China would win. In 1882, China was a decaying and corrupt empire, semifeudal and semicolonial, the "Sick Man of Asia," the almost helpless victim of the great imperialist powers. Unable to protect itself and its citizens at home from foreign oppression, flood, famine, or foreign invasion, it was still less able to give them protection abroad.

But now, in 1940, China was standing up for itself. The decrepit feudal empire had been toppled in 1911, and a new China was emerging. Sun Yat-sen, a Guandongese who received his early schooling in Hawaii's Iolani School and had imbibed American ideas of democracy, had founded the Kuomintang Party and mobilized crucial support for his revolutionary efforts among overseas Chinese, including those in America. Now, as a result of the united front established by the Chinese Communist Party and the Kuomintang Party led by Chiang Kai-shek, China was holding down and punishing a large part of the invading Japanese army.

America was the ally of this new China in the struggle against Nazi Germany and Japan. Farsighted statesmen such as President Franklin D. Roosevelt could read the signs of the time: neither at home or abroad could Chinese for much longer be treated as an "inferior race."

Changing America in a Changing World

By 1943, it was clear that the United States and its allies would win the war against German and Japanese fascism. It was also clear that, with Europe and Japan prostrate from exhaustion and the Soviet Union faced with a massive task of rehabilitation after the Nazi occupation of much of its territory and the death of 16 million of its people, the United States, its land physically untouched by battle, would emerge as the richest and most powerful nation in the world. That position would carry with it the responsibilities as well as the prestige of leadership. One such responsibility would be to define the world's attitude to the new emerging nations arising as a result of the United Nations' pledge of self-determination for all peoples. That pledge would sound hollow indeed unless racial discrimination and racism were ended in America itself. Discrimination against and segregation of blacks, Chinese, and other ethnic minorities were especially and glaringly incompatible with that pledge. The Chinese Exclusion Acts undermined the credibility of America as a democracy, particularly in Asia and the Pacific. They gave substance to Japanese propaganda being blared throughout Asia that the American war effort was no war for freedom but a war to restore white domination over Asia, a domination that Japan was supposedly struggling to end.

Roosevelt realized that the United States was entering an era in the postwar world when, as the strongest and richest power on earth, it would have worldwide interests and commitments in Latin America, Africa, and Asia as well as Europe. Its one serious competitor in world leadership would be the Soviet Union, and the rivalry would be in terms not only of material strength but also of moral leadership. The United States would be at a serious, perhaps fatal, disadvantage if it entered that competition shackled by a policy of racial discrimination, particularly against the Chinese, the most populous nation in the world and one of the five powers with the right of veto in the United Nations. Repeal of the exclusion laws would help prepare America to deal with the complexities of the postwar world.

In his fourth inaugural address, in 1945 Franklin D. Roosevelt said, "We have learned that we cannot live alone, at peace; that our own well-being is dependent on the well-being of other nations far away. We have learned to be citizens of the world, members of the human community."

Roosevelt was responding to the new reality in the world. The struggle of the Allied Powers against the old-fashioned imperialist and racist threat of German, Japanese, and Italian fascism had resulted in a worldwide upsurge of nationalist and democratic sentiment. This was the wave of the immediate future.

Liberal and democratic America, progressive and radical labor called for repeal and backed the voices of Chinese such as Ng Poon Chew, the Chinatown journalist and lecturer who eloquently demanded repeal. Friends of China and the Chinese such as the novelist Pearl Buck, the author of *The Good Earth*, read and seen in its screen version by millions, campaigned for repeal. It was also clear to those Americans of many persuasions who looked ahead pragmatically simply in a spirit of enlightened self-interest that in the struggle already shaping up between America and the Soviet Union, the struggle for hearts and minds would be a major factor. A considerable body of opinion had formed in Congress to repeal the act. The China lobby, eager to gain prestige for Chiang Kai-shek's nationalist Kuomintang government, campaigned for repeal. Chiang Kai-shek's wife, Soong Mei-ling, a Wellesley College graduate, made a considerable impression in her role of a modern Chinese woman when she was received by President Roosevelt in the White House and addressed the Congress. Coupled with the new image of China and of Chinatown communities, all this was good publicity for the idea of repeal.

The opposition, predictably, came from a coalition of such groups as the right wing of the American Federation of Labor, still bewitched by the ghost of Samuel Gompers; the Daughters of the American Revolution; the Native Sons of the Golden West; and the Crusading Mothers of Pennsylvania.

Sentiment on the West Coast was overwhelmingly for repeal and the city board of supervisors of San Francisco reflected that sentiment in a special resolution favoring repeal.

A bill for repeal had been introduced in the House of Representatives in 1942, and in May of that year a Citizens Committee to Repeal the Exclusion Act was formed. Such AFL unions as the International Ladies Garment Workers Union and union branches in many places, including the Palo Alto Teachers Union, the Building Services Employees of Seattle, the Cafeteria Employees Union of New York, and others came out in favor of repeal. The American Legion, not usually noted for its liberal stands, also supported repeal.

Exclusion Act Repealed, 1943

The Magnuson Act "to Repeal the Chinese Exclusion Acts, to Establish Quotas and for Other Purposes" was introduced and passed with administration support in 1943. It was signed into law by President Roosevelt in December, 17, 1943. It permitted Chinese to be naturalized. This alone ended many restrictions prescribed in various laws for aliens ineligible for naturalization. It also provided for an annual quota of 105 Chinese immigrants.

There were those within the Chinese communities who did not want to or could not or found it hard to sail boldly along with the winds of change. There were those in the larger society outside who did not want, who could not, or found it hard to accept the changing communities of Chinatown and the new immigrants. But now the dominant role was being played by the new and vigorous elements among the Chinese communities seeking full integration with the larger society. They felt that once again, as in the very early days, they were welcomed. They and their supporters in the larger society outside knew that there would be many obstacles still to overcome but that postwar American society was increasingly providing them with the opportunities to develop their talents for their own good, for the good of their community, and the good of the whole society. It was an exhilarating thought. The wheel was turning full circle.

NOTES

1. Betty Lee Sung, *Mountain of Gold: The Story of the Chinese in America* (New York: Macmillan, 1967).
2. *East/West*, February 27, 1980.
3. Willard T. Chow, *The Re-Emergence of an Inner City: the Pivot of Chinese Settlement in the East Bay Region of the San Francisco Bay Area* (San Francisco: R & E Research Associates, 1977).
4. Peter Wong, *Chinatown: New York, Labor and Politics, 1930–1950* (New York: Monthly Review Press, 1979).

INTEGRATION

PART

Three

1943–1980

Today . . . the sky's the limit, regardless of race, color, or whatever. If an individual has drive and intelligence, they can go as far as their education will allow.

> MING CHANG, Chief of Staff, Carrier Group 3, U.S. Navy, in *East/West*, June 18, 1980

By establishing a Chinese Section in the San Francisco office, and understaffing that section with insensitive officers who make unreasonable demands on the petitioners, the San Francisco office has institutionalized a format which perpetuates discrimination against Chinese immigration. This fact is particularly disturbing because it exists in the district where more Chinese petitions are filed than in any other district. In one context, it can be viewed as a perpetuation of the infamous Chinese exclusion laws.

> PROFESSOR ONG HING, Golden Gate University, in *Asian Week*, June 19, 1980

Demolition, Salvage, Building

CHAPTER

XIX

"You're either a white man or a nigger here [in Mississippi].
Now that's the whole story. When I first came to the Delta,
the Chinese were classed as nigras."
"And now they are called whites?"
"That's right!"

JAMES W. LOEWEN, *The Mississippi Chinese: Between
White and Black.*

IT IS NOW thirty-seven years since the Chinese
Exclusion Act was repealed, but the nation and its Chinese Americans are
still working to end the baneful results of past discrimination.

Progress in dismantling the institutionalized structure of discrimination,
the system of laws and regulations, and the mental and attitudinal legacy of
discrimination has been slow and devious. To Chinese Americans wishing
to reunite their families and see relations between America and China develop
in friendship, that progress has been agonizingly slow. Now, of course, looking
back on those thirty-seven years, we realize that the American people have
in their own way been working out a remarkable revolutionary change in
relations between and within ethnic minorities, the Chinese Americans
included. Repeal of the exclusion acts was only a landmark in that process,
as the following list of legislation shows.

IMPORTANT FEDERAL ACTS AND DECISIONS
CONCERNING CHINESE IMMIGRATION

1943 The Magnuson Act to repeal the Chinese Exclusion Acts establishes
an annual quota of 105 Chinese immigrants, and permits
naturalization of Chinese.

1945 The War Brides Act facilitates immigration of 118,000 spouses
and children of members of the U.S. armed forces including
Chinese.

1946   The Act of August 9 puts Chinese wives of U.S. citizens on a non-quota basis.

1952   The Immigration and Nationality (McCarran-Walter) Act provides for family reunification, the immigration of persons with needed skills and the protection of the domestic labor force. It consolidates and codifies all U.S. laws relating to immigration, sets national origin quotas, and permits unrestricted numerical immigration from Western Hemisphere countries.

1953   The Refugee Relief Act admits another 214,000 refugees including some Chinese to the United States.

1965   Immigration and Nationality Act Amendments repeal national origins quota system. Eight-category preference system instituted to reunite families and admit aliens with special talents and skills on a "first come, first served" basis in each category. It provides an annual limitation of 170,000 immigrants from the Eastern Hemisphere with a limit of 20,000 per country and 120,000 from the Western Hemisphere without regard to country limitations and without preference system. Spouses and children of U.S. citizens and parents of citizens over twenty-one exempted from numerical ceilings. Requirements for labor certifications instituted to control admission of skilled or unskilled foreign workers. An annual admission of 10,000 refugees authorized.

1976   Immigration and Nationality Act Amendments end inequities between Eastern and Western hemispheres by extending the eight-category preference system to the Western Hemisphere countries, together with a limit of 20,000 per country. Priority given to people having close family ties with relatives already in the United States, those with skills needed in the United States, and refugees.

1978   Congress eliminates separate immigration for Eastern and Western hemisphere countries and replaces this with a worldwide limitation of 290,000 people annually. Naturalization made possible for anyone over fifty years of age who has been a legal permanent resident for twenty years.

Many Chinese immigrants immediately took advantage of the new right of naturalization to apply for citizenship. A relative of mine, Rupert Sancho, was one of the first civilians to take the oath of allegiance under the 1943 immigration law. But that law's Chinese quota of 105 immigrants a year was trifling, because Chinese wives and children were included in it, and priority was naturally given to them. In the next ten years, 558 Chinese were admitted, and in the next twelve years, until 1965, another 5,497 entered.

It was two years after the repeal of the Exclusion Act that the next step was taken. The War Brides Act of 1945 allowed wives and children of Chinese Americans who had served in the U.S. armed forces, into the country. This was followed by the Act of August 9, 1946, which put Chinese wives of

U.S. citizens on a nonquota basis, resulting in a small spurt in Chinese immigration.

In the next few years, 90 per cent of Chinese immigrants were women. The structure of the Chinese communities began to change. More and more American-type nuclear families emerged to challenge the authority of the district and surname (clan) associations and tongs. The bachelor society had tended to cluster for mutual support and socializing. The nuclear family could more conveniently take off on its own, out from Chinatown and into the suburbs with their better housing, schools, and other amenities, although Chinatown usually remained the social and economic focus of their lives. More families were reunited by the Refugee Relief Acts of 1953, 1957, and 1959; and President Kennedy's Executive Order of May 1962.

The McCarran-Walter Act

The McCarran-Walter Immigration and Nationality Act of 1952 is one of those pieces of legislation that have moved such authorities on immigration law as attorney Dan Danilov to state that the "immigration laws of the United States are an abysmal mess."[1] They seem to be going off in different directions at the same time. This act was supposed to consolidate and codify all laws relating to immigration into the United States. It provided for family reunification and special consideration for individuals with needed skills; it made all races eligible for immigration and naturalization, but it also set national origins quotas, permitted unrestricted immigration only from Western Hemisphere countries, and retained racial restrictions on Asian immigration. Whatever the White House or some Congressmen might think, Congress as a body still considered some races more equal than others. Flying in the face of the facts and realities, it also lumps together all the so-called communist countries, the Soviet Union, China, Romania, Yugoslavia, and the rest of eastern Europe and regards all citizens or even temporary residents in such countries as either "communists" or members of "communist front organizations" and therefore ineligible for admission to the United States, merely because they worked for any organization, school, or institution there.

The political winds had shifted again. At the end of World War II, there was a chance that China could form a Kuomintang-Communist coalition government to avoid resumption of civil war between the Kuomintang and the populist forces led by the Communist Party of Mao Tse-tung. But Chiang, assured of U.S. aid, felt no need to compromise. Civil war resumed and, defeated because of his reactionary policies and the corruption of his regime, Chiang fled to Taiwan a hundred miles off the Southeast China coast. The Truman administration continued to support Chiang Kai-shek and, when the People's Republic of China was established on the mainland, supported Chiang's continued hostility and declared policy of reconquering the mainland and overthrowing the People's Government. When the Korean conflict began and Chinese People's Volunteers entered it on the side of North Korea, China and America found themselves in an undeclared war from 1950 to 1953.

Shock waves went through the Chinese communities in America. When Japanese Americans had found themselves in a similar situation after Pearl Harbor, their citizenship and patriotism had not protected them. Under Executive Order 9066, they had been herded into concentration camps. Now, in 1950, Title II of the Internal Security Act (Emergency Detention Act) was passed over President Truman's veto, preparing the way for similar action against the Chinese of America. As part of its policy of blockading the People's Republic of China, the Truman administration had already prevented Chinese students and scholars from returning to the Chinese mainland and held them in the United States, driving at least one of them into a mental breakdown. No less a person than J. Edgar Hoover, head of the FBI and at the apex of his power, warned a House subcommittee that Chinese either coming into or living in the United States were a potential danger as enemy agents. With the justification of such advice and under the prodding of Kuomintang diplomatic representatives and their agents within the Chinese communities, an anticommunist witch hunt was launched. The Kuomintang Party used the opportunity to strengthen its hold on the Chinese communities in the United States. A favorite tactic was to denounce opponents to the Immigration Office as communists. It took one of their targets, Kwong Hai-chew, seventeen years of litigation to prevent his deportation. Every large campus with Chinese students was furnished with a Kuomintang secret agent masquerading as a student. Taking course after course and never graduating, they were known as "perpetual students." Some are still in place to this day. On my first U.S. lecture tour in 1971–1972, the same students who had prevented me from speaking from the floor at a student meeting called by the Kuomintang at Columbia University in New York were there picketing the hall in which I was to speak in Carbondale, at the University of Illinois, a thousand miles away in the Midwest, two weeks later. The meeting had not begun, but they carried placards reading "Jack Chen Tells Lies!"

To strengthen its grip on the Chinese community, the Kuomintang even appointed one member of the Six Companies in San Francisco Chinatown to a post in the Taiwan Kuomintang government. For an American citizen to serve in such a post with a foreign government is illegal, but the position, renamed, was still occupied in 1980. The witch hunt resulted in deportation of a number of "radicals" and in harassment and curtailment of the activities of groups sympathetic to the new government in Peking. It was obviously dangerous to send letters and remittances to relatives in China (U.S. dollar remittances dropped from $7 million in 1948 to $600,000 in 1949). As a result there was an increasing lack of communication with the mainland. The fog of misunderstanding and lies about China, which in part led to the Korean war involvement, deepened. The overseas Chinese, the very people in the United States who would normally have the best access to news about China, were cut off from normal contacts with China and their voices were silenced. Conditions were being prepared for American involvement in Vietnam and subsequent disasters there.

Senator Joseph McCarthy throve in this atmosphere. The Red Scare choked the expression not only of radical but all dissenting opinion inside the Chinese communities. Kuomintang Party organizations and secret agents took advantage of McCarthy's campaign to hound everyone in the Chinese communities who opposed them or their allies in the traditional organizations—the Six Companies and other benevolent associations (the CCBAs). This was the setting in which the Drumwright Report of 1955 was prepared, charging Chinese immigrants from Hong Kong with wholesale violations of U.S. immigration laws and raising the specter of Communist infiltration.

This brought the State and Justice departments into the hunt for illegal immigrants. Chinese were threatened with prosecution for passport fraud, but, far from revealing an influx of "red agents," prosecutions showed that there were a number of people who, as might be expected, did not want to live in a China moving toward a socialist economic and political setup and were desperate enough to use fraud to get into America. The intrigues of the Kuomintang-dominated Six Companies and other CCBAs now began to backfire. A federal grand jury in San Francisco attempted to subpoena membership records of the family and district associations of which the Six Companies were supposedly the head. The courts, on appeal, however, would not sanction this abuse of the power of subpoena to launch a wholesale witch hunt, a "fishing expedition," in the Chinese communities of the nation.

The matter, of course, was not allowed to rest there. A national conference of the Chinese Welfare Council, a national association of Kuomintang-oriented Chinese benevolent associations, was held in Washington the next year (1957) and adopted a resolution calling for reform of the immigration laws. The U.S. Justice Department and the CCBAs responded by devising a program whereby Chinese violators of the immigration law, then alleged to be several tens of thousands, were called on to confess to their true identities in return for immunity from prosecution and deportation. Over the next decade, some 8,000 Chinese confessed in San Francisco. But confession naturally entailed informing on others or at least giving vital clues to the identity of conniving officials, "paper fathers," "slot brokers," and other "accomplices" who had shown either avarice or compassion. The person who confessed gained immunity, but at the expense of others known or unknown. Furthermore, although he or she was not deported, they lost citizenship and had to reapply. To force confessions, people were stopped and questioned on the streets and asked for documents to prove their innocence. A wave of fear swept through the Chinese communities. Who would be next?

When the immigration authorities went after the "slot brokers" who had helped arrange the entrance of "paper sons," some were found to be in it for the money, but several turned out to be highly respected citizens acting not for money but from humane considerations. The sociologist Betty Lee

Sung recounts the story of Arthur Lem, then forty-six years old, who had entered the country as a youngster of twelve, done well at school, worked hard as a volunteer for the YMCA, was named "Man of the Year" by his fellow businessmen, and was well liked in his Long Island community. Lem had to sell his restaurant business and mortgage his home to pay his court fees and lawyer. A hung jury after a long trial did not save him. Haled into court again and financially ruined, he wished to plead *nolo contendere* but was finally forced to plead guilty to one count of conspiracy and received a token sentence. The *Daily News* report on the case ended with the query "just what is justice in the case of Arthur Lem?"[2]

A highly respected, elderly Chinese businessman in San Francisco told me, "In those days, every time I walked down the hill there on Washington Street, I wondered if something was going to hit me." At the age of twelve, he had come to America as a "paper son."

It is common knowledge that during the exclusion period many Chinese entered the country with doctored papers, but with over 60 percent of the Chinese in the country American citizens, what exactly is served by harking back to violations of unjust racist laws dating back to the last century? As Betty Lee Sung wrote, "The ghost of the past should not be allowed to haunt the Chinese in the present or in the future."

To this day, quite a number of cases of those who confessed in good faith are still unsettled.

Immigration and Nationality Acts Amendments, 1965

The Immigration and Nationality Acts Amendments of 1965 reflected further changes in the world situation and the further advance of the nationalist upsurge in the former colonies of the great powers. It also reflected the rapid advance of the civil rights movements fighting for ethnic and minority rights and opposed to racial discrimination against any ethnic minority. Spearheaded by the black minority, this movement had been building up since the early 1950s. In 1954, the U.S. Supreme Court acted against school segregation. In 1957, President Eisenhower signed the Civil Rights Act, the first since Grant's administration. In 1964, President Johnson signed the new and stronger Civil Rights Act banning segregation in all public facilities and in the trade unions. Chinese Americans took part in these civil rights struggles.

It was in this atmosphere that the 1965 Immigration Act, in a significant advance, ended the discriminatory national origins quota system and instituted the eight-category preference system to reunite families with close relatives and admit aliens with specially needed skills and talents on a "first come, first served" basis in each category. The act also provided an annual limitation of 170,000 immigrants from the Eastern Hemisphere with a limitation of 20,000 from each country. The Western Hemisphere had a limit of 120,000, with no limit as to country and no preference system. Spouses and children of U.S. citizens and parents of children over twenty-one were exempt from numerical ceilings. To control the admission of skilled or unskilled foreign workers, the act instituted requirements for labor certification. It authorized the annual admission of 10,000 refugees.[3] This legislation resulted in an increase in a new type of Chinese immigrant: men and women with high skills and intellectual attainments, of middle-class and usually affluent families from Shanghai, Tianjin, and other parts of China coming via Hongkong, or Taiwan, speaking Mandarin rather than the Cantonese dialects and usually fluent in English. Such immigrants often felt more at home in entirely American surroundings than in the Cantonese dominated Chinatowns.

This trend in the immigration laws was continued with the 1976 Immigration and Nationality Act Amendments. These ended the differences between the Eastern and Western hemispheres by instituting a 20,000 person limit for every country and extending the eight-category preference system to Western Hemisphere countries and giving priority to people having close family ties with relatives in the United States, having labor skills needed in the United States, or claiming refugee status.

The latest major legislation, passed by the 95th Congress in 1978, ended separate immigration quotas for the two hemispheres in favor of a worldwide limit of 290,000 people a year. Children of one U.S. and one non-U.S. parent are now permitted to retain U.S. citizenship without ever living in the United States. Anyone over fifty years of age and a legal permanent resident for twenty years can be naturalized. These new regulations are important for Chinese immigrants, as is the new provision governing adoption of foreign children.

Such is the current legislative framework of the Chinese American presence in America and the entry of new immigrants. Unfortunately in some cases, while the letter of the law is obeyed, its interpretation leaves something to be desired. As Danilov concludes, the immigrant laws are "very old and full of a great deal of discretion, which permits officials at the port of entry to treat people coming to our shores without a great deal of respect. Sometimes the would-be immigrants really don't have the rights they should have."[4]

Examples of this are numerous. They range from the small to the tragic. A Chinese professor going to inquire about an extension of his visa arranged through the University of Hawaii is answered by a junior official leaning back in his chair with his feet propped up on the top of his desk.

A sailor has fallen in love and jumped ship to marry his girl. At an immigration hearing, the interrogating official tells him, "You will be deported. Where do you want to be deported to?" He is about to answer truthfully, "To my native village in Guangdong" (in the People's Republic of China), but, prompted by his savvy lawyer, he replies "Taiwan." He is allowed to remain in the United States.

An elderly scholar from the People's Republic of China holds what is now the orthodox U.S. State Department opinion on the People's Republic of China, has Christian principles, and steadfastly refuses to bend the truth one iota. He just wants to be with his family and give his son an American education. He is given sixty days to show cause why he should not be deported.

When he asks under what conditions he might be allowed to remain, he is told that if he had been a "Freedom Fighter" in the People's Republic, he would have been all right. A bit confused by all this, he comments to a State Department official that the State Department and the INS seem to have two different policies in regard to the People's Republic of China. One wants to make friends with its government; the other wants to overthrow it.

"That's true!" is the reply.

And yet, despite this confusing system of limitations and quotas, bumbling officials and red tape, the United States still admits more immigrants than any other country in the world and shows astonishing generosity in admitting thousands of refugees. By natural increase and immigration the Chinese American population has increased from 117,629 in 1950 to 237,292 in 1960 to 435,062 in 1970. The estimate for 1980 is 800,000.

A better-structured system of immigration laws is expected from the recommendations made in 1980 by the Select Commission on Immigration and Refugee Policy.

NOTES

1. Dan P. Danilov, *Immigrating to the U.S.A.* (Seattle: Self-Counsel Press, 1979).
2. Betty Lee Sung, *Mountain of Gold: The Story of the Chinese in America* (New York: Macmillan, 1967). p. 107.
3. Danilov, *Immigrating to the U.S.A.*, p. xviii.
4. *Ibid.*

Some Have Made It, Some Have Not

XX

The five blocks of central [New York] Chinatown have a density exceeding the maximum of 135 dwelling units permitted under existing zoning laws. In 1960, this area had a population of 10,604. In 1970, the population was 21,796. Now, today, it is substantially higher. Some immigrants, usually those better off, elect to live in Brooklyn, Queens, or Long Island, spawning mini-Chinatowns.

THOMAS GLYNN & JOHN WANG, "Chinatown,"
Neighborhood, 1978

Every worker you talk to, they are all saving for the day when they can open their own business.

NORMAN KEE, Attorney, quoted by Bernice Chu in "Small Businesses in Chinatown," *Neighborhood*

BACK IN THE 1850s and early 1860s, the overwhelming majority of Chinese immigrants were farmers, artisans, and workers. They became miners, woodcutters, railroad hands, fishermen, farmers, ranch hands, fruit growers, cigar or boot makers, men of all trades, porters and peddlers, domestic servants and restaurant workers, cooks and laundrymen. The handful of merchants ran import-export businesses and curio and general stores. A few entrepreneurs ran hostels, restaurants, tea houses, bakeries, and herb stores; some ventured into mining or light manufacturing. There were a few diplomats, students, teachers, doctors, letter writters, and so on. The very few women were prostitutes or, still fewer, merchants' wives.

During the next thirty-five years, until the 1880s, there was not much change in this occupational pattern, although the numbers engaged in any one occupation might vary considerably. In the 1850s, for instance, around 45 percent of the 33,000 Chinese in the United States were miners. This proportion fell to 27 percent of the 63,000 Chinese in 1870.

In America, social status is closely linked with occupational status, except in the upper income brackets. Only toward the second quarter of the 1900s did Chinese Americans in larger numbers begin to master the skills of high-income money making. The first generation of American-born Chinese, American citizens with American-style educations, began to make their influence felt in the Chinese communities. Their Chinese American Citizens Alliance defeated the 1913 proposal by State Senator Camminetti to disenfranchise Chinese Americans but was unsuccessful in trying to repeal the Cable Act, which deprived of her citizenship any woman marrying "an alien ineligible for citizenship."

By the 1920s, the second generation of American-born and educated Chinese was emerging, young men and women who sometimes felt more at home in the larger society than in conservative exclusion Chinatowns. They often spoke and wrote English better than they did Chinese. They read Dewey rather than the Confucian classics. The tight little provincial world of Chinatown seemed increasingly stuffy to them, even though the more perceptive recognized its very real virtues. By 1940, they were 51.9 percent of the ethnic Chinese in the United States. Well aware that they faced a tough struggle to claim their birthright as first-class citizens, this new generation usually planned their future carefully to escape the economic constraints of Chinatown and circumvent the social barriers of discrimination. They took up scholastic careers, research, and teaching; they became doctors, lawyers, accountants, ministers, social workers, nurses, and institutional staff and took clerical and other white-collar jobs; they went into insurance, real estate, banking, and the lower grades of the civil service.

The mom and pop grocery inherited by the go-getting Americanized second generation got a face-lift and became a modern self-service store. When Thomas Foon Chew took over the Bayside Cannery his father founded in 1900 in California's fruit-rich Santa Clara County, he turned it within little over a decade into the third largest cannery in the country, on a par with Del Monte and Libby. But these early entrepreneurial efforts of the Guangdongese immigrants lacked staying power. Chinese American businessmen established the Canton Bank in 1907 and the China Mail Steamship Company in 1915, their first two large-scale American-style enterprises, but due to lack of experience they failed in 1926 and 1923 respectively. Joe Shoong, whom everyone knew in San Francisco Chinatown, was luckier and more able. He turned the little general shop he owned in Vallejo in 1928 into the National Dollar Stores, now a considerable chain with 50 outlets from the West Coast and Hawaii to Texas.

These years saw many "firsts" in the Chinese American story: Faith Sai So Leong, the first modern-trained Chinese woman dentist in the world, graduated from San Francisco's dental school in 1910. Tong King Chong was the first Chinese lawyer in America in 1912. In 1920, his wife was the first Chinese woman to cast a ballot. Their son Tom was the first Chinese to have his own radio program. His Golden Star Chinese Hour began broadcasting in Oakland in 1940. In the 1920s, Jake Lee, Dong Kingman, Anna May Wong, and James Wong Howe (1898–1975) became the first Chinese American artists to win national recognition. Howe, who launched his career as cameraman for *Drums of Fate*, starring Mary Miles Minter, was described as "the greatest stylist in the business," and won two Academy awards.

In these new occupations, the second and third generation Chinese Americans earned the same reputation for discipline, integrity, and hard work that their predecessors had earned back in the 1850s as a valued part of the California work force. They began to make a name for themselves and for Chinese Americans as a whole in modern America.

They were reinforced by four other groups of achievers who began to join them in the first and second quarters of the century and particularly as the events of World War II began to unfold: these were the "stranded students" mentioned above earlier, the new immigrants and refugee elite, Chinese American women and the new skilled working class, men and women who entered the labor force during World War II years in response to the national call for an antifascist war effort. These men and women radically changed the economic and social profile of the Chinese American community. Later, postwar political upheavals and conflicts in China and the civil war, in which the opposing sides were led by the Chinese Communist Party and Kuomintang Party, raised questions of loyalties that many found hard to resolve. Many of these men and women postponed their return to China until more auspicious times. (Large numbers have been visiting China since President Nixon's 1972 visit and normalization of relations in 1978.)

Reflecting these socioeconomic shifts in the Chinese communities and the needs of the modern middle class, new social, economic, and political organizations proliferated. Some were strictly local, such as the Cathay Club of San Francisco and the Square and Circle (a women's welfare relief group); others were affiliated with national groups such as the International Lions, the American Legion, chambers of commerce, Rotary, chapters of the Republican and Democratic parties, and many more. These took over more and more of the functions of the Chinese Consolidated Benevolent Associations, (CCBA) in defending the rights of the Chinese and organizing mutual help and education. Others, such as the Chinese American Citizens Alliance, consciously challenged the older organizations for the right to represent the Chinese communities in relations with the larger outside community.

By 1950, the number of highly professionally and technically trained Chinese Americans had risen dramatically. In 1940, there were around 900 in the United States. By 1950, there were 3,500. By then, the number of women professionals and technicians alone was almost equal to the total number of professionals in 1940. In the same decade, the number of clerical, sales, and kindred white-collar workers had risen from 8,300 to 15,400.[1]

Graph 2. Major Occupations of Chinese Americans (1950 and 1970)

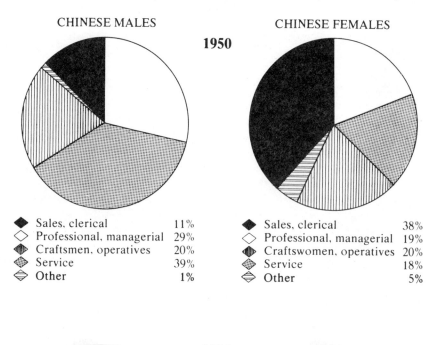

CHINESE MALES   CHINESE FEMALES

1950

◆	Sales, clerical	11%
◇	Professional, managerial	29%
◀▥▶	Craftsmen, operatives	20%
◈	Service	39%
⬗	Other	1%

◆	Sales, clerical	38%
◇	Professional, managerial	19%
◀▥▶	Craftswomen, operatives	20%
◈	Service	18%
⬗	Other	5%

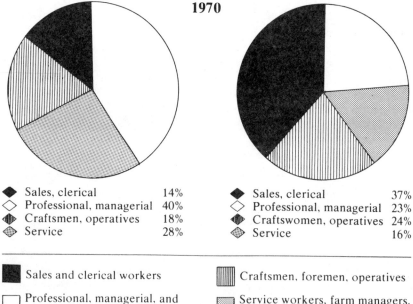

1970

◆	Sales, clerical	14%
◇	Professional, managerial	40%
◀▥▶	Craftsmen, operatives	18%
◈	Service	28%

◆	Sales, clerical	37%
◇	Professional, managerial	23%
◀▥▶	Craftswomen, operatives	24%
◈	Service	16%

■ Sales and clerical workers

▯ Professional, managerial, and administrative workers

▥ Craftsmen, foremen, operatives

▨ Service workers, farm managers, farm laborers, and other workers

Source: U.S. Census Bureau

With these social changes, there was no setting the clock back. The ghetto dwellers of the nation had come out into the mainstream of American life. From then on, supported by the 1943 repeal of the Exclusion Act and subsequent laws, the Chinese of America by direct action and political pressure have continued to press for complete rejection of exclusionist racist policies and discrimination.

Upward mobility for the Chinese Americans has not been easy. As recently as the 1960s, there were quite a number of young men and women with university degrees who found themselves "overqualified" and working as waiters and in other service trade positions in Chinatown, waiting for that long-delayed opening in their chosen field of study. Their chance came when the civil rights movement in the mid-1960s peaked with the Civil Rights Act of 1964, spearheaded by the black communities, banning segregation and making discrimination more difficult to maintain.

This native-born Chinese community elite and the enforced immigrant elite were reinforced by a number of highly trained professionals in the arts, sciences, management, business, and industry who had left China because of the seemingly endless civil war between the Chinese Communist and Kuomintang Parties. These men and women had little difficulty adapting themselves to the American scene and, given the necessary experience, rising swiftly to the top of their professions and into the upper-income brackets. Many were already in the high-income class even before they came. In recent years, quite a number of Kuomintang senior civil servants and businessmen have similarly settled themselves and their wealth in the United States to ride out the expected changeover of power in Taiwan. There has been a similar movement of Hong Kong businessmen and capital.

Many of these new immigrants are not Guangdongese, that is, not from the rural areas and petit bourgeois towns of Guangdong like the older immigrants but Mandarin-speaking intellectuals and businessmen from capitalist and middle-class families of Shanghai, Tianjin, and other cities. Gradually a rough stratification of Chinese Americans has emerged, from the small businessmen of the Chinatown Guangdong communities to the more geographically dispersed business and intellectual elite of Shanghai and other non-Guangdongese immigrants, settled in San Francisco, New York, and Los Angeles as well as in Hawaii and big university and industrial centers.

Dr. M. C. Chang, co-discoverer of the birthcontrol pill; Chinn Ho, the Hawaiian real estate developer, owner of the landmark Ilikai Hotel; I. M. Pei, son of a Cantonese banker, the architect and designer of the Kennedy Memorial Library and the new wing of the National Art Gallery in Washington, are typical of this intellectual and professional elite. It is their earning power that has pushed the median income of the Chinese American community to its present high level.

Graph 3. Comparison of National and Chinese American Incomes (1970)

INDIVIDUAL

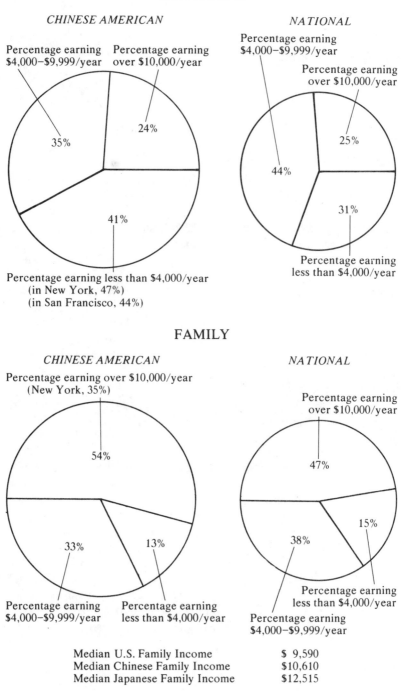

CHINESE AMERICAN

Percentage earning $4,000–$9,999/year

Percentage earning over $10,000/year

24%

35%

41%

Percentage earning less than $4,000/year
(in New York, 47%)
(in San Francisco, 44%)

NATIONAL

Percentage earning $4,000–$9,999/year

Percentage earning over $10,000/year

25%

44%

31%

Percentage earning less than $4,000/year

FAMILY

CHINESE AMERICAN

Percentage earning over $10,000/year
(New York, 35%)

54%

33%

13%

Percentage earning $4,000–$9,999/year

Percentage earning less than $4,000/year

NATIONAL

Percentage earning over $10,000/year

47%

38%

15%

Percentage earning less than $4,000/year

Percentage earning $4,000–$9,999/year

Median U.S. Family Income	$ 9,590
Median Chinese Family Income	$10,610
Median Japanese Family Income	$12,515

Source: U.S. Census Bureau

Some Have Made It

The 1970 census and the continuing upward trends show that as a whole the Chinese American community of 437,000 (it is now probably around 800,000) has done well by itself and by America. With a labor force of 190,000 (120,000 males and 70,000 females in 1970) it has the highest median family income of any minority ethnic group except the Japanese. But that high median family income of $10,610 for a family of four (in 1970 prices) or $1,000 above the national median income, hides as much as it reveals. The earning power of the intellectual and professional elite and of the 50 percent of Chinese women earning wages pushes the median up. It is the average of the high-income earners (24 percent or just under the national average) and the many low earners (41 percent compared with the 31 percent national average).

The overall bright picture has some serious problem areas.[2] While the rate of poverty among all Chinese families (10 percent) is lower than the whole U.S. rate (11 percent), the poverty rate for New York City Chinese is much higher—15 percent.

Nationwide, 24 percent of Chinese males make over $10,000 (in 1970) per annum, but the comparable figure for San Francisco is only 15 percent and for New York, 12 percent. Overall, 41 percent earn less than $4,000 per annum. The two big Chinatowns are definitely problem areas.

Those who have "made it"* as they say in Chinese, acquire the status symbols of success. A lot of the highly paid technicians, scientists, professors and other professionals live and work in suburban areas and on university campuses. Although, as a result of the Chinese immigrant tradition, they do not usually go in for ostentatious consumption, their offices, homes, automobiles, and annual holidays spent in foreign travel reflect the affluent American way of life. These are families of successful businessmen, managers of firms, university professors and professionals, doctors, lawyers, senior civil servants, engineers, accountants, architects, trade, and other professionals, many concentrated in such high-technology and growth industries as electronics. Their annual incomes range from $20,000 into six-digit figures for a few. The proportion of Chinese males in professional and managerial (mostly self-employed) occupations—some 40 percent—is higher than for any other ethnic group. By 1970, twenty-four percent of Chinese American men had college degrees—double the U.S. average and higher than any other ethnic group.

Economically, these men and women have "made it," but a surprising number admit that discrimination still dogs their footsteps. It is a statistical fact that they receive lower salaries than non-Chinese doing comparable work. A leading businessman in the $50,000 income bracket in a West Coast city

---

* The Chinese phrase *Chu to-la* is not a value judgment. It means a person whose "head has surfaced."

admits ruefully that "it's still there, but in more subtle forms." A community activist and a "joiner," he belongs to the local chamber of commerce, the Shriners, and half a dozen other community groups, but the doors of the country club have remained closed to him. "I could probably get in," he says, "but why should I give the few racists there the chance to blackball me? And, say that I did get accepted, why should I play the role of token Chinese?"

This should not be looked at from the viewpoint of an individual Chinese having to overcome a last barrier to integration. The implications are deeper than that. It is a reflection of the attitude of dominant elements of society. It is dangerous to have such hard-core racial prejudice in the ranks of those who wield great power in defining the policies of this country. It may be regrettable but it is not tragic that some affluent Chinese may not be getting the full salary that they are entitled to or have not attained the social status that should by rights be theirs or failed to get into the country club of their choice. But, if the past is anything to go by, they will make it here too. It is just a matter of time.

It is commonly said among Chinese Americans that "you have to be at least half as good again." Parents tell this to their sons and daughters as a matter of course, to urge them to do their homework. The traditional respect for learning is reinforced by competition. More Chinese American male citizens have a higher education than in any other ethnic group: 25 percent of the men and 16.5 percent of the women. In deciding what to major in or what line of work to go in for, the inevitable question is still how much discrimination may be encountered. Rightly or wrongly, for instance, it is generally felt that a Chinese stands a better chance of advancement if he or she works in a job such as research where he or she does not have to deal with personnel problems or that a Chinese will find the going tough in such a job as personnel manager in a big corporation or as a pastor in a white community. As a matter of fact, there is no such person as a Chinese pastor in a predominantly white community.

In comparison with its size—one of the smallest ethnic minorities in the United States—and bearing in mind its checkered history, the Chinese American community has produced a notable number of outstanding men and women in many fields who have overcome great difficulties to reach levels of high responsibility in their professions. Well known are the physicists Yang Chen-ning and Tsung Dao Lee, the 1957 Nobel Prize laureates, and Wu Chien-shiung, the outstanding woman physicist who worked on the Manhattan (atomic bomb) Project. Ten years ago, there was only a short list of such Chinese contributors to the expanding fields of American science and culture. Today there is a whole roster of names in mathematics (such as Shing-shen Chern, of the University of California at Berkeley), biochemistry (Professor Li Chao-hao, famous for his work on the pituitary gland and its products), electronics (An Wang, creator of the "memory chip" and of a multi-million dollar electronics corporation) and other fields. Close to 2000 distinguished Chinese American scholars are teaching in colleges and universities. Any contemporary *Who's Who* is studded with Chinese names in the academic world.

March Fong Eu, the able secretary of state of California, is spoken of with warm respect in California, but quite a number of "old hands" echo the opinion that she "has got about as high as she can go," not because of any lack of ability to go "higher" in the governmental sphere but because she is a woman and a Chinese. I personally do not believe they are right. The time is ripe for a Chinese American woman of ability and dedication to seek high office. It is evident, however, that Chinese of either sex must continue to work with the progressive segments of society to overcome prejudice of any kind, particularly the baleful racial prejudice that lingers on.

Some Have Not

These handicaps must be measured against the progress made over the decades, which explains why Chinese have chosen to stay in this country and emigrate to it to the limit of their allotted quota.

The affluent elite will undoubtedly get what they currently regard as their rights in incomes and in status. The middle-income citizens will have their difficulties and their ups and downs, but what should be of deepest concern is the fate of those members of the Chinese American community who have not "made it"—the disadvantaged. These can be seen any day in the parks and alleys of such Chinatowns as San Francisco or New York. They are the ones who battle with the often crushing disabilities of old age, youth, inexperience, lack of salable skills, and inadequate knowledge of English.

It might be said that Chinese are barred from integration into the larger society more by economics than by ideology. But this is only partly true. Their low income results from the fact that as Chinese they still suffer from past discrimination and from disadvantages in education and occupational opportunity. A telling fact is that 11 percent are illiterate, a percentage seven times greater than whites and three times greater than blacks.

As the oldest and second largest Chinatown, San Francisco can serve as an example of the plight of these disadvantaged. The casual visitor or tourist wandering its streets will be intrigued or delighted by its little, crowded shops or bazaars, its wonderful variety of eating places, its temples and buildings with colorful designs and Chinese-style touches in decorations and rooftops. After being dazzled by the jewelry shops and the bumper-to-bumper line of cars parked by the sidewalks, an observant visitor will notice the grime on the pavements and the many signs that this is a community working hard to make a living and struggling hard to deal with many longstanding and intractable problems.

Penetrate, if you can, into the crowded tenements, and you will find families of four, five, and six living, working, playing, and sleeping in a single room. Pots, pans, and food must be taken to a community kitchen shared with other families. Privacy is a sometime thing. These facts speak for themselves: for all its gaiety, good humor, and indomitable spirit, this area suffers from widespread poverty, high unemployment, substandard and overcrowded housing, inferior public services and facilities, and resulting grave health problems. Sixty-eight thousand people live within a mile of the heart of Chinatown. In Chinatown proper, 63 percent of the population of around 58,696 (1970) is under eighteen or over sixty-five. Senior citizens number 10,000. Population density is 228 people per acre, the second highest in the nation after some parts of Manhattan. Sixty percent of the housing is substandard. Twenty-four percent of inhabited apartments, many of them one-room, are grossly overcrowded and mostly substandard. The federal government recommends 90 square feet of park and recreational space per capita. Chinatown can barely manage 10 square feet.[3] The only place where housing conditions are worse is in the area of the Western Addition, an area of stranded low-income black families who arrived here during the war to work in wartime industries. Under such conditions, it is no wonder that tuberculosis and suicide rates were among the highest in the city and the nation. For far too many, the question is not how to enjoy life but how to survive.

The Rumford Act, making discrimination in housing illegal in California, was passed just sixteen years ago, and since then, steady, although slow progress has been made in housing. For those who have "made it," housing is no big problem now, nor is health or education for their children. For those who have not made it, all of these are serious problems. In part, they face the usual difficulties of anyone of their economic standing of any ethnic group in American society today, but they also face special difficulties resulting from the history of Chinese immigration. Nationwide, a fifth of all Chinese housing is overcrowded. In New York, that figure rises to 33 percent, with more than one person per room in a third of all housing units.[4] In New York dormitories for bachelors, several men will share a room, sleeping in bunk beds caged with wire to prevent theft.

Chinese families in the middle and upper income brackets and therefore with the means to move out of crowded Chinatown, are making homes in the Richmond and Sunset districts and in the suburban East Bay cities where twenty years ago they would have found it difficult to find a house. But the basic difficulties remain for the disadvantaged. With two-bedroom homes in El Cerrito selling for $80,000 (1979 prices) and mortgage rates at 11 percent, it is impossible for a family earning even $10,000 a year to buy or rent a suburban home there. Even lower-middle-income families are priced out of that market.

A complicating factor is that San Francisco Chinatown is on prime central-city real estate. The average cost of Chinatown land (in the early 1970s) was around $40 to $60 a square foot (certainly an underestimate at this date in 1980) compared to $15–$30 in other places.* Investors are looking eagerly for a chance to buy any part of it to develop into high-profit deals. Owners of land are under great pressure to raise rents or sell to developers. All that restrains them is the fact that a number of key sites are owned by family and district associations and families rooted in the area and that every attempt to "redevelop" the area according to outside criteria has met with stubborn community resistance. A landmark case is the International Hotel block on Kearny Street, where the developer, even after evicting its low-income dwellers in 1977, was still not able to build after three years, and the Mayor's Citizen's Advisory Committee was appointed to devise a plan of development including low-income housing.

There have been several attempts to relocate Chinatown. Back in 1884 and again in 1900, under the pretext that it was filthy and a "plague spot," city plans were afoot to move its inhabitants out and rebuild it. When the 1906 earthquake and fire flattened it, official plans were again afoot to move it to a more southerly location on the Bay. Rapid rebuilding by the Chinese community foiled this scheme. Its people know what happens when such an area is "developed." St. Louis Chinatown also occupied prime land near the heart of the riverside city, just a block or two from City Hall and where the main inner city redevelopment is going on. That development leveled Chinatown, which is now buried under the grand stadium arena and its parking lot. The Chinese community there no longer exists as a cohesive community. Its people are scattered around the city. With their dispersal, the localized community, the neighborhood and all that signifies, disappeared.

Chinatowns in San Francisco, New York, and, to a lesser degree, Boston, with their shops and restaurants and colorful signs, festival parades, and community gatherings, are more than just the sum of their numbers. San Francisco Chinatown, more than any other, has attained that "critical mass" that generates real community activity. It is no accident that San Francisco Chinatown attracts delighted tourists from all parts of the nation and world with its special character, foods, and shops and can sustain cultural activities that are impossible for any other Chinese community in the country: dance and musical groups, singers and choruses, a first-rate children's orchestra, an outstanding group of artists, and a thriving Chinese Culture Foundation that has mounted the largest exhibition to date on the Chinese Americans and with the Chinese Historical Society of America hosted the 1980 national conference on Chinese American studies.

It is to preserve this special quality that the community is cudgeling its brains for a solution of immediate and long-term problems. Some problems are crucial. Every year, as the opportunity crops up, rents are raised and old, established shops and businesses are forced to relocate or close. Every solution so far proposed to create new housing seems fraught with new

* In San Francisco's downtown business area on the edge of Chinatown, land costs were over $200 a square foot in the early 1970s. In New York, a similar inflationary land squeeze sent land values for the same period up to $210 a square foot in Chinatown.

problems. Rezoning to permit high-rise construction would inevitably increase the density of population, with its attendant problems. Lateral expansion is increasingly difficult because of soaring real estate values throughout San Francisco. Some say designation of the area as a historical site can save it. But that would entail a lot of problems too.

The story of the village of Locke, south of Sacramento on the river, is a miniature of what is involved.

The Locke Story

Locke is the last remaining village in the nation inhabited mainly by Chinese. Tin Sin Chan built the first building there in 1912 on a corner of the estate of the Locke family. Chan had the same surname I have (Chen), although he spelled it differently, and he came from Zhongshan in Guangdong, where my family also comes from. A few other houses were built, and then, in 1915, the Chinese settlement in Walnut Grove burned down and the people from Zhongshan who were living there decided to rebuild in Locke. Locke grew swiftly. This was the time of the "asparagus boom." Chinese, Japanese, and Filipino laborers followed the crops in the Sacramento Delta: vegetables, pears, and other fruit. Locke was a recreation center for them, a "home port" to which they returned from their work forays. Locke throve in prohibition days when, as an unincorporated township, it was a "wide-open" settlement. Whites came in to open speakeasies and bordellos, and soon gambling dens were crowded with footloose men playing fantan and pai-chiu and tempting fate on slot machines. As many as 1,500 people lived there in its heyday. It had a post office, a lodge, a theater, six restaurants, five hotels and roominghouses, two saloons, a poolroom, five grocery stores, two cigar stands, a shoe repair shop, a bakery, a dentist, and a church.

Then Locke began to decline. Prohibition ended, and the speakeasies and all they brought with them went out. The asparagus boom moved south to the San Joaquin Delta. The educated Chinese youngsters had hopes beyond field work and moved out to San Francisco and Sacramento. By early 1979, only fifteen Chinese families were left, and the two main establishments were the Chinese-owned Yuen Cheng Market and Al the Wop's steakhouse. Gone were the men who had once helped to build the railways and levees and settled Locke in the first place. Their sons who had followed the harvests were now old men doing a bit of fishing on the river and tending their vegetable gardens on the flat land behind the levee.

All told there were only 150 people living permanently in Locke in 1970: Chinese and a few Caucasians and Filipinos. It had and has a casual air. Most of the buildings are empty and unlocked. Visitors wander through the empty street back of the levee, and no one pays any attention to them. Rose bushes, untamed, proliferate in back gardens. Bees buzz around their sweet-smelling blossoms.

Locke was gently dying when in 1977 a Chinese investor from Hong

Kong named Wu Tou-tai and his wife Fancy bought Locke—lock, stock, and barrel—from the original Locke estate. The Wu's Asian City Development Corporation announced big plans for Locke. It would construct 400 houses of Chinese design, with a nearby Tin Hau Temple and Giant Buddha; world fair-style pavilions representing Japan, Taiwan, Korea, the Philippines, Hong Kong, and Thailand; a floating restaurant on the Sacramento River, a shopping center, hotel, country club, and facilities for Dragon Boat races. As a taste of things to come, a public telephone booth was built at the entrance of the village in glass with vermilion-painted wood trim and a little conical roof with turned-up eaves.

Luckily the announcement of this plan appeared in a Hong Kong newspaper and caught the eye of someone in Sacramento and the Sacramento County Board of Supervisors promptly slapped a twelve-month building moratorium on the entire area. Currently Wu has shelved plans for future development; the Sacramento Housing and Redevelopment Agency, the state parks and recreation department and a number of conservation groups are locked in a discussion of what to do with Locke. Somehow, they all agree, Locke must be preserved as a living community. But how? As far as the Locke residents are concerned, all they want is to be allowed to live and die in peace. No one has yet come up with a solution as to how this can be achieved and Locke be preserved. As it is, the many tourists who have been attracted to Locke by its new notoriety are a constant hazard to its safety and environment.

Locke is now an issue larger than itself. How it is treated will indicate how mature society has become and how wise. Its senior citizens certainly want to live out their days in peace, but that does not mean being kept like performers in a sideshow for tourists to gape at and trample over their gardens. Its young people want to have Locke as their home as long as their homes are there. What happens after that is a matter for the whole community in and outside Locke. At the very least, Locke should be preserved as a living reminder of the past, treated with respect and left in dignity.

The Chinese of America have come through some searching tests in the past. Problems such as these will test their mettle anew. Is it likely that they will respond to these new challenges any less sturdily than their ancestors did in the past?

MARCH FONG EU

A second-generation, native-born American citizen, March Fong Eu is the first Asian American and the first woman to be elected California's secretary of state, the highest elected office now held by a Chinese American. She came to that position the hard way, through grueling election contests. Winning the Oakland assembly seat in 1966, she was reelected in 1970 and 1972 and so demonstrated her mettle and competence that she won her bid for the post of secretary of state by the biggest majority of votes in such an election.

Born in Oakdale, California, in cramped quarters behind a hand laundry and raised behind another in the tough Richmond area, she knew poverty or near poverty throughout her youth. She had to work her way through school, like so many of the second-generation Chinese who realized that education and professional training was one accessible way out of the ghetto. She set her goals early and worked hard to realize them.

The circumstances of Chinese American youth in the 1940s and 1950s spurred her ambitions. "I have always been the kind of person who wanted to change the world, to improve it for future generations . . . yes, even as a kid. Also, being Chinese probably has been a driving force, being aware that your ancestors have not enjoyed first-class citizenship in a country of which they considered themselves part."

That drive motivated her on her way through school and university. She finished her education as a dental hygienist with a masters degree from Mills College and a doctorate from Stanford. Working as a dental hygienist for Oakland schools kept her alive to the tough social realities of the times, and she gained administrative experience through her work as the first Asian-American president of her national professional association and on the Oakland school board. From there she went to the state assembly and then to the job of secretary of state.

Her upbringing has made her uncompromising in matters of principle. In 1978, although a would-be candidate in a primary election was a personal and long-standing friend, because he had filed late she refused to certify him. She defended her action all the way to the state supreme court. That might not have made her popular, but it is one of the things that have made her respected in her present post.

Her horizons have broadened. She says, "I represent the needs, wishes, and aspirations of all the population, not just one tiny segment. But by virtue of the fact that I am by ancestry Chinese, there is a significant impact to Californians of Chinese ancestry and other minorities in terms of a role image."

She has supported the Equal Rights Amendment, and women worked hard in her 1974 campaign committees for her election, but feminist support was not the decisive factor in her victory. She won on much broader grounds. But whether or not that is her aim, she stands as a symbol of the way Chinese American women have broken out of the stereotype forced on them for so long. The conservative, all-male Chinese American Citizen's Alliance made her their first woman member.

Ten years ago San Francisco—with the nation's largest Chinatown—did not have a single Chinese American in an elected office. Now it has five, and March Fong Eu, a woman, holds the most senior post among them. This is symptomatic of a considerable change. There are some 65,000 Chinese Americans in the city today and they make up about eight percent of the population. They are becoming increasingly integrated in all San Francisco *neighborhoods and are showing greater political awareness and activity. They have produced a modern, educated professional middle class willing and able to assume the responsibilities of political office. They have a lively younger generation of civic-minded activists who are matured politically and are able to function effectively in the political system. March Fong Eu is a typical product of this new Chinese American community, of this new San Francisco, California, and America.*

NOTES

1. Betty Lee Sung, *Survey of Chinese-American Manpower and Employment* (New York: Praeger, 1976).
2. *A Study of Selected Socio-Economic Characteristics of Ethnic Minorities Based on the 1970 Census.* Office of Planning and Evaluation. HEW Publication No. (OS) 75-121. July 1974.
3. *Sharing the Abundant Life* (San Francisco: Donaldina Cameron House, 1979).
4. *A Study of Selected Socio-Economic Characteristics*, p. xi.

Problems
and Issues

There are ten thousand to twelve thousand Chinese members of the International Ladies Garment Workers Union. They do not get union scale. And how many members of the Board of Directors of the ILGWU are Chinese?"

> AUGUSTINE CHUA, Immigrant Social Service Agency, New York, *Neighborhood*, 1978

Chinatown is experiencing a golden age of business prosperity, but the problems that have surfaced are spurring concerned Chinese to think and plan for the future.
Prosperity is meaningless without improved social conditions.

> BERNICE CHU, "Small Business in Chinatown, New York," *Neighborhood*

THE BIG Chinatowns of America, San Francisco and New York, with their large concentrations of 60,000 and more Chinese in a contiguous area, are not urban Lockes, but to some extent their problems are similar. They too face problems of conservation, preservation, and development that clearly go beyond themselves and demand the attention and will require the efforts of the whole urban community of which they are a part. Boston and the smaller Chinatowns of Los Angeles, Seattle, and Chicago face problems of a similar kind, but on a smaller scale. Their destinies are now the subject of many discussions and experiments. What is already clear is that they are determined to retain their identity as Chinese American communities with their special characteristics and values in their present locations. And if the past is any indication of the future, their stubborn Cantonese character, which has carried them through so many difficulties in the past, will assuredly carry them through present and future trials too.

If the present study focuses largely on California and New York, this is because 39 percent of all Chinese Americans live in California, primarily in the San Francisco and Los Angeles areas; 27 percent live in the northeastern states (with 20 percent in New York state); and 12 percent live in Hawaii.[1]

The Census Bureau describes the two big city Chinatowns as special cases and Hawaii's Chinese community as a special case of a different kind.

The main problems and issues of San Francisco Chinatown are those left by years of exclusion and segregation—inadequate housing, inadequate sanitation, lack of social amenities. The tuberculosis and respiratory disease rate in Chinatown is four times greater than in the rest of the city. This is closely linked with housing. Two to four persons sharing a bedroom is common. Only 2 percent of families own their own homes. Over 30 percent live in flats, sharing a kitchen or bathroom. Life expectancy is shorter in Chinatown. Of all Chinese, 68 percent live in inner cities; 25 percent live in suburbs.

Better housing, expansion of public health programs, and better sanitation are crying needs. The difficulties are not small. A 1974 study in New York by the Department of Housing, Education, and Welfare showed that a third of all New York residences are overcrowded.[2] A fifth of all residences have inadequate plumbing. San Francisco Chinatown faces a similar situation. A considerable infusion of local, state, and federal aid is needed here, as well as good planning. Such projects as the Confucius Plaza in New York and the Ping Yuen housing complex in San Francisco help, but much remains to be done. Provision of additional low-rent housing will solve many other problems of both young and old, because it is now understood that proper housing must go hand-in-hand with provision of recreation and playground space—and jobs.

There must also be a special drive for better health facilities and health delivery services to people who, because they have to count every cent of the money they spend, fear doctors' bills.

Senior Citizens

One of the saddest aspects of life in disadvantaged communities is the fate of the old. Thousands of old men and women, couples or singles, are living in one-room apartments of so-called "hotels," often in dilapidated surroundings from which sunlight and fresh air are both excluded. Their main recreation is the daily outing in crowded Portsmouth Square: doing their exercises—usually forms of Tai Chi Chuan or "shadow boxing"—playing checkers or go, or simply sunning themselves on the benches with an assortment of drunks. Various community organizations near the Square, including the churches and the Chinese Culture Center, try with insufficient funds to provide the elderly with social services, entertainment, and aid, but the inadequacy of all this is tragically demonstrated by suicide figures. Although new programs for the elderly have reduced Chinatown's suicide rate, it is still above the average for the city of San Francisco as a whole.

Existing community efforts, such as Self Help for the Elderly, set up in 1966 to deal with this situation, must be applauded, but no one thinks enough has been done. Even when the housing problem is solved, there is a need of more of the special services for the elderly provided by the three On Lok centers: recreation, entertainment, health and community get-togethers to take the place of the family life that is or should be the normal environment of the old. On Lok has been a national model in providing longterm day-care for the elderly.

Because of the nature of current Chinese immigration, most of the new Chinese immigrants are young people, men and women in the prime of life, so the percentage of elderly among Chinese nationwide is 9 percent, lower than that for the nation as a whole. But because of the nature of past Chinese immigration, there is a disproportionate number of elderly in the old Chinatowns: While nationally 28 percent of all Chinese elderly are poor, in San Francisco the figure is 31 percent and in New York 40 percent. Most elderly Chinese (58 percent) are males and most live alone, a sad legacy of the old days of exclusion politics. A lot of light is thrown on the social attitude of Chinese Americans by the fact that the number of Chinese families living in poverty is larger than the number receiving welfare: 2.8 to 1.[3]

Garment Sweatshops

Another area of prime concern is sweatshop conditions in the garment industry, the single largest industry that remains in New York and San Francisco Chinatowns. This has long been a scandal, but so far all attempts to deal with it have failed. New York seems to have the worse problem.

Although there are a number of modern, well-run enterprises, a 1972 federal report on the industry in New York stated that in 52 of 200 garment workshops investigated, women were working as much as fifty hours a week at from $0.65 to $0.75 an hour. A 1978 article in *Neighborhood*,[4] the organ of the New York Urban Coalition, showed that New York Chinatown had approximately 400 garment workshops employing 12,000 workers, one-sixth of the Chinatown population, and nearly 10 percent of the 125,000 workers in the New York garment work force. Now there are about 500 workshops.

These workshops employ mostly women. Wages are low: the ILGWU contract stipulates hourly wages of from $3.65 to $4.65, with overtime over the thirty-fifth hour; the federal minimum wage is $3.10 an hour. But a 1970 report reveals the following: Wah Ching (not his real name) works as a presser in a New York shop. He works fifty hours a week with no overtime pay at a wage of $2.56 an hour. A woman in the same shop gets $1.30 an hour as a threadcutter, again without overtime. One firm, which would not let its name be used, excused itself for violating the law by stating: "Chinese women like to work more than eight hours a day—that only gives them $24 a day. But we can't afford to pay them overtime."

The 1978 *Neighborhood* survey revealed that the New York Chinatown wage is more likely to be $0.30 to $1.30 a piece for a sewing machine operator with no overtime, and even less for pressers, and $0.05 to $0.08 per piece for a thread cutter who might well be in her sixties or seventies. That works out to $1.30 an hour, or less than half the federal minimum wage.

Because of the continuously expanding immigrant pool in New York an increase of 4,000–5,000 a year—there is actually keen competition for these sweatshop jobs. This is no small problem.

San Francisco Chinatown has around 200 garment workshops, and conditions there are not much different. A 1979 state investigation spotted labor violations in 90 percent of San Francisco and Oakland's garment manufacturing plants and workshops, and 500 citations were issued. Half were for technical violations such as not posting regulations, but the rest concerned the minimum wage, child labor, and illegal at-home piece work. Only 26 of 228 garment workshops had no violations. The firms cited owed $40,000 in unpaid wages to their workers. More than half that sum was owed by two workshops, employing in one case 74, and in the other 20, workers. One owner justified his failure to pay overtime rates by claiming that his women workers liked to go on working while they waited for their husbands to pick them up and that he allowed this as long as it was not counted as overtime (*San Francisco Chronicle*, April 12, 1979).

The unions must bear a large share of the responsibility for this state of affairs. In New York, 90 percent of the garment workers are ILGWU members, paying dues of $80 a year for benefits such as medical care and unemployment insurance. Investigations have revealed widespread finagling to make it appear that federal, state, and union regulations are being observed.

It is said that the neighborhood women, who comprise the majority of the garment work force, have few other choices of work. Many have no knowledge of English and are untrained for other work. They believe that they are not getting too bad a deal because of the absence of strict work controls, they can drift in to work after seeing their husbands and children off to school. They can take time out to do shopping and pick up the children. They can even bring their small children to play in the workroom or in the street outside, and if they want to do extra work they can take it home at piece rates (which is illegal) or even do it in the workshop while they wait for their husbands.

Because the women believe all this, sporadic attempts to unionize them in San Francisco have been only very partially successful and unionization in New York has hardly improved working conditions. Those who know say that it would need a joint community, union, and federal effort to achieve desired results. There is no insuperable difficulty in unionizing the shops and retaining those features of working conditions that suit the women working there by adding proper health and welfare facilities, such as day-care centers, on a modest scale. What is an essential ingredient, however, is solidarity among the workers. Garment workshops in and near Chinatown are operating as subcontractors to the big downtown New York or San Francisco apparel manufacturers, but, while these larger concerns pay reasonable wages to their own employees under union and government pressure, they lower the prices they pay to their Chinatown subcontractors, who in turn press their women workers to accept sweatshop wages and conditions.

One writer says, "There are no easy answers to this problem. The contractors are in as much of a bind as the workers; indeed, it might seem as if they were the ones who need a union to protect themselves against the manufacturers who play them off against each other." As the figures indicate, these contractors are owners of rather small enterprises.

The Chinatown garment factory owner in most cases does not have enough reserves of capital to withstand much pressure from the main contractors who play subcontractors off against each other. Something must be done to give the owner extra clout. His employees usually know little about trade unionism and the techniques of collective bargaining or even their simple rights under the law. They are usually part of the incoming flow of new immigrants hungry to get a job, any job, and afraid to lose that job when they get it. Successful unionization would require more than a one-shot, several weeks' effort. It would have to include prolonged education and training to show the Chinatown garment worker how to achieve and maintain good working conditions and reasonable benefits and would also have to back the Chinese subcontractors, many of whom are former garment workers themselves.

The Chinatown garment workers are being exploited as if they were a colony of the industry. Other ethnic groups working in the trade are better organized and enjoy better conditions than their Chinese colleagues. Failure thus far to organize cooperative workshops should not be taken as definitive. Something must be done. The industry is of prime importance to the community: it makes more than half of all the blouses and sportswear in New York, and brings in some $40,000,000 in annual revenue to the New York community, where 12,000–14,000 people are employed in it. In San Francisco's Chinatown (figures are hard to get here, too) there are over 160 workshops with over 3,500 workers and a $12 million payroll, part of a $400 million garment industry in northern California, states one private 1980 survey.

The Food Industry

The food industry and restaurants are other major employers in both San Francisco and New York Chinatowns. There are over 300 Chinese restaurants in San Francisco and over 400 in New York, whose Chinatown has 900 businesses in the twelve blocks south of Canal, north of Worth, east of Baxter, and west of the Manhattan Bridge. Although many establishments are well run and serve excellent food, sweatshop conditions are common here, too. In New York, waiters work a 72-hour week for $50 in wages. But tips in a good season can average $150–$200 a week. In many places, there are no fringe benefits such as sick leave, medical insurance, retirement pensions, job security, overtime, or vacations. Good chefs are always in great demand and can make from $1,000 to $1,800 a month.[6]

To get all restaurants to look after their employees adequately, strict observance of labor laws should be enforced. Licenses to operate should depend on real observance of proper labor conditions and wage laws.

One difficulty in the way of enforcing proper conditions is the reversal of the 1950 situation when the Chinese community was over 50 percent native American-born citizens. Between 1960 and 1970, the Chinese population in the United States increased by 84 percent, mainly from new immigration. Thus, 67 percent of the Chinese in New York are now foreign born, and the comparable figures for San Francisco and Los Angeles are 52 percent and 54 percent respectively. It is not surprising that aliens are not as insistent as citizens in demanding their rights. Their first priority is survival; then, to make good and leave their low-paying jobs and inferior housing for the newcomers, while they go on to something better.

Shops and Services

The third main economic activity in New York and San Francisco Chinatowns are the shops and services catering to the local and tourist trade. These also face urgent problems. The influx of "flight capital" from Taiwan and Hong Kong (where the British lease on part of the territory runs out in 1999) and inflation creates intense competition for real estate, whose price has soared. Although the family and district associations and some larger concerns own their own places, most premises in the Chinatowns are rented. Every year, old, established Mom-and-Pop stores are faced with steeply rising rents, and many have been forced to close. Further closures will change the nature of Chinatown irreparably, dislocating lives and causing great suffering. Here too, the only viable solution seems to be concerted local, state, and federal action with intelligent use of the principle of eminent domain as a means of preservation.

The various community organizations that the work, wages, and salaries of San Francisco Chinatown help to support include a variety of artistic and cultural activities in a wide range of styles. The angry confrontations and rhetoric of a few years ago when the younger modern generation was first trying out its wings seem to have calmed down somewhat, and public opinion seems now to accept the fact that soft-spoken Jade Snow Wong, a talented writer and ceramicist of the older generation, is as much an authentic Chinese American artist as is Frank Chin of the strident school of brutal realism.

Conflicts

Two special types of inner conflict afflict Chinatown communities in New York, San Francisco, and a number of other cities: one is the political struggle between Peking- and Taiwan-oriented groups, and the other is provincialism and rivalry between the earlier Guangdongese immigrants and the later immigrants from other parts of China, especially Shanghai, speaking the Shanghai dialect or Mandarin (*putong hua* or *guo yu*), which is now the official common speech of China.

Even in late 1979, the Peking-Taiwan issue caused violent clashes on the streets. Now it is muted because the partisans of Taiwan know that by rioting at this time of rapprochement between the United States and China they risk official U.S. displeasure. Furthermore, the majority of Chinatown residents are restoring ties with their relatives in the home country and are disinclined to become embroiled in old Communist-Kuomintang animosities, particularly when the People's Republic of China (PRC) government is bending over backward to be conciliatory. Vociferous and violent support of Taiwan is clearly opposed to Washington administration policy and the congressional majority. There is criticism that immigration practices in 1980 still treat Chinese from different places differently—maintaining, for instance, colonial status quotas for Chinese coming from Hong Kong and Macao.* Chinese American families trying to get close relatives over from the PRC to reunite families find it difficult to do so. Residents of the PRC wishing to emigrate to the United States have found that support of the PRC does not expedite their applications, currently held up behind a big backlog of cases.

Provincial Rivalry

The old provincial rivalry between Shanghai and the Northerners on the one hand and the Guangdongese on the other still makes itself felt in uncomfortable rather than crucial ways. If one wants good service in quite a number of Chinatown establishments, one had better speak Cantonese or English rather than Mandarin. Shanghaiese will probably just elicit a blank stare. Such attitudes carry over into the larger sphere of business as well. As recently as 1979, no less than three rival groups in New York Chinatown were raiding each other's offices and tossing furniture into the street.

It is therefore an encouraging sign when all groups or most of them can get together in joint projects that serve the community as a whole rather than any one faction. The Chinese Culture Center in San Francisco is a good example of this. Community influence installed it on the third floor of the Holiday Inn, a twenty-seven-storey skyscraper next to the supermodern TransAmerica pyramid, the symbol of San Francisco's business district. But it is linked directly to Chinatown's Portsmouth Square by a bridge with lanterns over the busy thoroughfare of Kearny Street. In the square and on the bridge every fine day, senior citizens of Chinatown gossip on the benches and children play on the jungle gym. The center hosts meetings and performances for Head Start; it packs its auditorium with Chinatown residents at performances

---

* Immigration quotas of 600 a year (recently up from 200 a year) are allotted Chinese citizens of Hong Kong and Macao. Yet citizens of Britain's and Portugal's colonies are not allowed to use the unused quotas allotted to their "mother" countries.

of Chinese movies, singers, musicians, martial arts and lion dancers, poetry readings and Asian American musical comedies like *The Avocado Kid.* The only such center in the nation, it also mounts major exhibitions of paintings, sculpture, and ceramics and hosts lectures by top-rank scholars. It is a center of community art groups from modern dancers to calligraphers to photographers.

Maintaining such a center fostering Chinese American cultural activities and knowledge of the Chinese cultural heritage is quite beyond the capacities of any smaller community. The only possible exception is New York, where, unfortunately, feuds between various groups keep that community from the sort of unified effort that can alone generate the funds and talent needed for such a major cultural effort. And yet a seemingly highly sophisticated modern intellectual visiting the center one day said to me disparagingly, "What is the use of Chinatown?" Fools have short memories. This attitude did considerable harm to the Chinese Culture Center at one time. Conflict between elitism and populism and between Shanghai and Cantonese provincialisms threatened to split the members' ranks. Some wanted to give priority to sophisticated scholarly and esthetic activities at the expense of the community-oriented projects that had been the original impetus of the center. Fortunately, wiser counsels have prevailed.

Tongs and Youth Gangs

The tongs that caused such havoc in the Chinatowns in exclusion times are today shadows of their former selves, but a few are operating more than charter trips to Las Vegas or Atlantic City for their members. With a better balanced ratio of males and females, prostitution is no longer profitable. And opium is a vice of the past. Gambling, however, continues to flourish, and this links the tongs and the youth gangs produced by recent, increasing teenage delinquency.

Chinatown juvenile delinquency and youth gangs partly reflect conditions in the larger society and partly reflect the breakdown of the old family traditions and the influx of new immigrants, especially from such places as Hong Kong, where the crime problem is even more serious than in New York. San Francisco in the second half of the 1970s experienced a wave of youth crimes, muggings, and "shake downs" that culminated in the murderous outburst of shooting when the Joe Boys attacked the Wah Ching at the Golden Dragon restaurant and a number of innocent bystanders lost their lives. But in New York, gang-related crime appears to be more serious, overall, than in San Francisco. There the Hip Sing and On Leong tongs have made a comeback. Battening on the economic upturn in the area, their gambling operations have increased. In the 1970s $600,000 are said to have changed hands there in a week over gambling deals. The tongs recruited youth gangs as guards and enforcers. The Black Eagles worked for the On Leong and the Flying Dragons for the Hip Sing, but the youth gangs, having tasted power and easy money, grew greedy and struck out on their own in shakedown rackets that even threatened their tong sponsors. Ten gambling operations are said to have provided the gangs with $5,000 a week per operation. In addition, they regularly collected money from 90 percent of the shopkeepers, restaurants, and other businesses in the area. Gang battles for these spoils involving the fancifully named White Eagles and Black Eagles, the Flying Dragons and Ghost Shadows terrified Chinatown but led to a decline in gang activities. As in San Francisco, a series of vicious shootouts took place. In 1977, there were over thirty gang-related killings in Chinatown alone, and, despite increased police activity, not a single conviction. Witnesses were too terrified to testify in court. Only when the unofficial "mayor of Chinatown," M. B. Lee, was almost stabbed to death was a real drive launched to find the would-be murderer. Chik Keung Pang was arrested and convicted in March 1978.

Just as in San Francisco, the audacity of the New York gangs has been curbed, but it would be naive to believe that the problem has been solved. The roots of this problem are now well-known: a high level of youth unemployment, reflecting conditions in the larger society, the generation gap, overcrowded tenements, lack of recreational facilities, school dropouts, the erosion of old family traditions, the influx of new young immigrants without salable skills or enough English—any social worker can recite these causes and possible ways of dealing with them through home and community action with the cooperation of federal, state, and local authorities. But it remains puzzling that members of these youth gangs can appear on television and name the adult leaders of known tongs as the ones who recruited them for criminal activities, and yet apparently nothing is done about this.

Chinatown cannot handle this problem by itself. Law enforcement agencies must take more energetic measures against the youth gangs, but it is clear that much more than this is needed. The problem demands a concerted attack through positive programs dealing with youth unemployment, education and vocational training, English language teaching, recreational facilities, and, more important, community action.

Sociologist Betty Lee Sung, however, in a recent study in New York, gives reassuring evidence that juvenile delinquency is not as widespread in the Chinese community as a few sensational events and stories in the press seem to indicate. She points out that, out of the 20,000 or so Chinese youngsters in the five New York City burroughs, there are no more than 200 to 300 gang members, and less than that in the hard-core groups. Chinese children show an outstandingly high level of discipline, and problem children are a small minority. The relatively low level of delinquency despite poor environmental conditions in New York and San Francisco is clearly linked to the stability of traditional Chinese family relations. In this group, the number of husband and wife families is larger than in any other ethnic group in the nation—a healthy 89 percent.

A significant shift has occurred in the Chinese American community. In the early years and until the 1950s the majority of immigrants and residents went into trade, service trades, or farm or industrial work. After 1965, professionals, managers (of shops, restaurants, trading companies, and factories), and technicians made up the bulk of the community (40 percent in 1974), with a smaller percentage in the service trades (24 percent). Now a further shift is taking place: a larger middle-class group is going into more varied types of business. Where before men were concentrated in a narrow range of professions such as medicine, research, law, and education and women in clerical jobs and there was a sharp division between a high-income elite of professionals and a low-income group in the service trades, now a more diversified occupational pattern is developing, with a larger middle-income stratum. The Americanization of the Chinese American community is continuing, and a more normal occupational pattern is developing. Conspicuously rare, however, is the Chinese American industrial worker and farmer. Ninety-eight percent of Chinese Americans are urbanites or suburbanites. The financial situation of new immigrants, however, remains precarious and hard. As of now, it is mostly these who staff the restaurants and garment workshops.

Conclusions

America is one of the most ethnically and culturally pluralistic countries in the world. Seeking national unity, national leaders and the dominant public opinion once held that America could be forged into some kind of homogeneous all-American alloy by a process of more or less pressured fusing of its diverse elements and expulsion of "unassimilable" entities. That "melting pot" concept is now rejected by Chinese Americans and other ethnic groups as a guide to national policy. In fact, it is harmful in this day and age. National cohesion can now only come about by a frank recognition of America's pluralism and a voluntary joint effort to legitimize cultural democracy and diversity. Only in this way can the full economic and cultural potential of the nation's last remaining Chinatowns and its Chinese communities be developed and the special aptitudes of its Chinese American and all other citizens be fostered for the good of themselves and their families and of the nation and all its parts. Cultural democracy among ethnic groups will strengthen their political unity.

Hindsight reveals the defects of the strategy used by the Chinese American traditional leadership in the struggle against exclusion. The conservative leadership of the merchant elite of Chinatown adopted a "siege strategy" when the Chinese withdrew into their Chinatowns under racist pressure. But that conservatism played into the hands of the opposition, which pointed to the clannishness and unassimilability of the Chinese, their differences, their avoidance of contact, and their "inscrutability," and which used such pretexts to demonstrate the necessity of expelling such an obviously alien element. The defensive strategy should have been complemented by a consistent strategy of sorties—economic, cultural, and social—to bring the Chinese out from the ghetto strongholds into contact with broader and friendly elements of the larger society. This in fact was done over the ensuing years but not as a conscious policy of the whole community and its leadership. In fact, it had to be done in large part in opposition to the traditional leadership of the Six Companies and other CCBAs by the new generation of leadership in the Chinatowns and the Chinese communities, by young Chinese Americans, born in the United States as U.S. citizens, speaking English as well as Chinese and regarding themselves as American Chinese, confident in their education and proficiency, often feeling more at home in the larger community than in Chinatown, and impatient with the conservative traditionalism of the old leadership.

This new younger generation set up new organizations that bypass the district and family associations: the Chinese Democratic Club, the Republican Party groups in the Chinese communities, the Chinese American Citizens Alliance (CACA), the chambers of commerce, the YMCA and YWCA, sports associations, various cultural groups, social clubs, and religious groups— Methodist, Presbyterian, and Baptist. These new groups work closely with their counterparts in the larger society and provide activists who compete in that larger society. Out of these groups emerged such political figures as Ng Poon Chew (d. 1931), journalist and lecturer; former Senator Hiram Fong of Hawaii, and March Fong Eu, present Secretary of State of California.

Other Chinese Americans have been promoted to high and responsible posts in the judiciary and the armed forces. Thomas Tang is a judge of the U.S. Court of Appeals, Ninth Circuit. Captain Ming Chang of the USS *Coral Sea*, born in Shanghai and schooled in Brooklyn and Fairfax, Virginia, is chief of staff and second in command of Carrier Group Three of the Seventh Fleet in the western Pacific and Indian Oceans, one of the most powerful naval units afloat. Major General Dewey Lowe of the U.S. Air Force is a former lawyer and active service pilot with 6,000 flying hours; commander of the Sacramento Air Logistics Center, he is responsible for worldwide support of Air Force aircraft, space and missile equipment, and communications-electronic-meteorological systems and equipment. He assumed his present command after seeing active service in World War II, serving in several headquarters posts, and winning a string of military decorations and awards. Together with creative artists, writers, researchers, and businesspeople—a talented professional, technical, and cultural intelligentsia—they have created a new public image of the Chinese community as modern, progressive, and innovative.

These outstanding individuals and the groups they represent reflect the acceptance of democratic pluralism among Chinese Americans. The old, paternalistic, sometimes benevolent and often heavy handed dominance of the CCBAs has ended. They are now only part of the network of organizations representing various interests and trends of thought that has been developed to run the affairs of the Chinese communities in these complex modern times. These groups have in recent years been joined by still newer groups, such as the Organization of Chinese Americans (OCA), with 3,000 members, and the National Association of Chinese Americans (NACA), which have mainly been organized by the free-floating communities of intellectuals and businesspeople outside the Chinatowns. All these organizations as well as those such as Head Start, the Chinatown Planning Council, the Chinese for Affirmative Action, the Asian-American Legal Defense and Education Fund, the Chinese Newcomers Center, and many more handling day-to-day activities and needs, make the Chinese American community in the Chinatowns approximate more closely to the pluralistic pattern of American society as a whole.

The obvious success of these new organizations and their growing prestige in the larger society has forced the traditional leadership to take a grudging pride in their achievements. The old CCBA leadership in both New York and San Francisco hangs back consistently, even today. They backed the Truman, Eisenhower, Kennedy, Johnson and earlier Nixon administrations' policies of supporting the Kuomintang Party in its civil war against the revolutionary forces of the Chinese people led by the Chinese Communist Party, and they have been the last to switch when, following the disasters of the Korean and Vietnam Wars, the American establishment under President Nixon's leadership began to switch to more realistic policies regarding the People's Republic of China and signed the Shanghai Communique in 1972.

The younger leadership of the Chinese American community, however, played a progressive leadership role in these latest events, even helping to pressure the Ford and Carter administrations into going ahead with the normalization of relations, which was finally brought about in February 1979. Still in step, although now a bit hesitantly, with the Kuomintang Party, the CCBAs have begun to split and gradually begun to switch allegiances.

While the general direction of development is more or less the same, the degree of development varies greatly between New York and San Francisco Chinatowns. New York Chinatown is still heavily influenced by older, conservative, provincial, and parochial attitudes. Businesses are proliferating, but the struggle for survival absorbs the energies of the underprivileged majority. Most residents are newcomers; the question of "identity" is not pressing for them. Parochial and factional attitudes represented by the CCBA impede the advance of the newer, younger forces. San Francisco Chinatown takes its cue from the rest of the ebullient City by the Bay with its thriving cultural life. A few years ago the question of cultural identity was a burning issue for its young people, evoking strident rhetoric. That is so no longer. Young people have matured beyond that, recognizing that there are many ways to a Chinese American identity, although it may not be easy to find the exact way that is right for each.

In San Francisco Chinatown, the younger group of political workers of the NACA, the Organization of Chinese Americans, Chinese for Affirmative Action (who carried on a campaign against the Hollywood resurrection of Charley Chan), and other more radical though smaller groups regard all of the older leadership groups, even the CACA, as essentially conservative and out of date, although in differing degrees. Conscious of its slipping prestige, the CACA has bestirred itself to aid a campaign for voter registration. The newer groups are working energetically within the larger society as well as within the Chinese communities. More and more they are emerging as a Chinese American caucus or pressure group of Chinese American voters, although because of their relatively small numbers they do not, of course, have the same clout that the black, Irish Catholic, or Jewish caucuses, for example, have. But they have come a long way in the last ten years.

The oldest of the grass roots neighborhood organizations, the Chinatown Park and Recreation Committee, was formed in 1970. Like many such popular organizations, it was conceived in response to a threat to the neighborhood, in this case the elimination of the Chinatown Playground on Sacramento Street, which they saved. Soon after that the Chinatown Coalition for Better Housing was founded, and their new low-income highrise housing project, conceived in a joint effort with Presbyterian Church activists, is finally being built at Stockton and Sacramento Streets. In 1977, these two groups combined with the Ping Yuen Tenants' Association, the Chinatown Transportation Improvement Project, and the Chinatown Neighborhood Center to open the Chinatown Neighborhood Improvement Resource Center. They believe that their combined efforts will enable them to tackle larger problems related to planning, zoning, and in general improving the quality of life in Chinatown. They have already begun to prove their point with successful applications for federal, state, and city funding and with new bus lines, low-income housing, and street improvement projects.

Those Chinese Americans who grew up in the days of anti-Chinese exclusion and blatant discrimination see life in very different terms from those coming to maturity in the 1970s and those who came to America in the postexclusion period as part of the affluent "new immigrant" elite. Most of the early newcomers were poor and came to get rich; the typical "new immigrants" arrive rich or established, and their bearing shows it.

In the 1960s and 1970s, the "identity crisis" of quite a number of ethnic Chinese citizens and permanent residents, particularly among the youth, was summed up in the question "Am I Chinese or American?" Now a growing majority find the answer "I am Chinese American" entirely adequate. It is said with a sense of pride. It has a special meaning. And it does not require the validation of a bureaucrat to give it that special meaning.

This self-image is validated by history, by the courage of those early immigrants of the mid-1880s, who crossed the ocean in fetid holds, washing themselves in rain from the heavens; who dug wealth out of the ground for America; who toiled to build a new, united nation; who washed its clothes and fed it delicious meals, exotic or simple, made of fish caught fresh in San Francisco Bay and vegetables and fruit grown on former marshlands and deserts that they had helped to tame; who built roads and houses and a railroad spanning the continent; who cleared and farmed its fields and labored in its vineyards, shod its feet, made its clothes and cigars; who suffered cruelly for their pains but, indomitable, emerged from the shadows to defend their new homeland from the most serious threat it ever faced, and, after victory, smiled again, planning and building and toiling, raising the new generation— eager, black-haired, black-eyed American children of Han, as American as apple pie, pizza, or chop-suey.

The people of Chinatown and the Chinese communities are reaching out to share with others their rich store of folklore and culture and also to mine the inexhaustible Golden Mountain of knowledge and cultural riches, both Chinese and American, that is their heritage as Chinese Americans.

Their story of welcome, rejection, and acceptance has shown that America is great when it provides conditions for all its many peoples to flourish, enabling them to develop their talents and abilities for their own and the general good; and that discriminatory oppression and exploitation of any of those peoples is a cancer corrupting the democratic foundations of American society.

Chinese Americans along with all Americans today face the puzzling problems of the 1980s. Domestic problems are inextricably meshed with international problems. Inflation is inseparable from exports and alliances; the problem of energy and the automobile as a generator of waste and pollution is part of the Middle East problem; the gasoline crunch is linked with the dangers of Soviet expansionism. In all these equations, the factor of China looms large. It is essential therefore that America should have a truer understanding of that country and vice versa. Because of their unique character and connections, Chinese Americans can play a significant role in enhancing that understanding and so facilitate solutions to the problems of today.

America has an enormous asset in her Chinese and other minorities. This fact is insufficiently realized and greatly underestimated.

NOTES

1. *A Study of Selected Socio-Economic Characteristics of Ethnic Minorities Based on the 1970 Census*. Office of Planning and Evaluation. HEW Publication No. (OS) 75–121. July 1974.
2. Cited in *Neighborhood* (New York Urban Coalition), 1, no. 3.
3. *A Study of Selected Socio-Economic Characteristics;* see also *The Forgotten Minority: Asian Americans in New York City*, Report of the New York State Advisory Committee to the U.S. Commission on Civil Rights (Washington: U.S. Commission on Civil Rights, 1977).
4. Antony Tom, "The Return of the Sweatshop," *Neighborhood* (New York Urban Coalition), 1, no. 3 (1978).
5. *Ibid.*, p. 38.
6. Bernice Chu, "Profile of a Chinese Chef," *Neighborhood* (New York Urban Coalition), 1, no. 3 (1978).
7. Betty Lee Sung, *Transplanted Chinese Children* (New York: City University of New York, 1979).

Chinatowns and -Chinese American Communities

SOME 20 million ethnic Chinese live overseas, and of this number around 800,000 now live in the United States in the two large Chinatowns of San Francisco and New York; in the much smaller Chinatowns in Boston, Los Angeles, Chicago, and Seattle; and in the more dispersed Chinese communities of Detroit and other cities and the Hawaiian Islands. But Chinese can be found today in every state of the Union in small communities and family groups.

Back in the 1850s, 1860s, and 1870s, there were many small Chinatowns, nearly all of them in the West Coast states and mining country. At Chinese Camp in the Mother Lode country east of Stockton, only a few ruins and the lacy Trees of Heaven that the Chinese loved to plant remind one of the 5,000 Chinese miners who once lived there in 1856. Virginia City, Auburn, and Sonora once had large Chinese populations—as did Butte, Montana, among its 50,000 people. Some went into railroad work and moved on. Others, from preparing lunch pails for wifeless white miners, went into the restaurant business, tailoring, laundrywork, and other locally needed occupations. Chinese herb doctors are remembered as being skilled in curing venereal disease. But gradually, as the mining and local populations of English, Irish, French Canadians, Italians, Slavs and others settled down and brought in their families, the need for such Chinese services diminished. The anti-Chinese exclusion movement drove many of them out to return to China or seek safety in the larger Chinatowns. The driving out was not universal. Good communities protected their Chinese neighbors, and scattered pockets of Chinese remained in several towns. Not long ago I had a meal with a Chinese family, the Leongs, who have lived, highly respected, in Auburn, northeast of Sacramento, for five generations. The last Chinese resident of several hundreds died in Fiddletown to the south in 1965. The Chinese community remains in Locke on the Sacramento River to this day.

Map 5. Chinese American Population by States (1970)

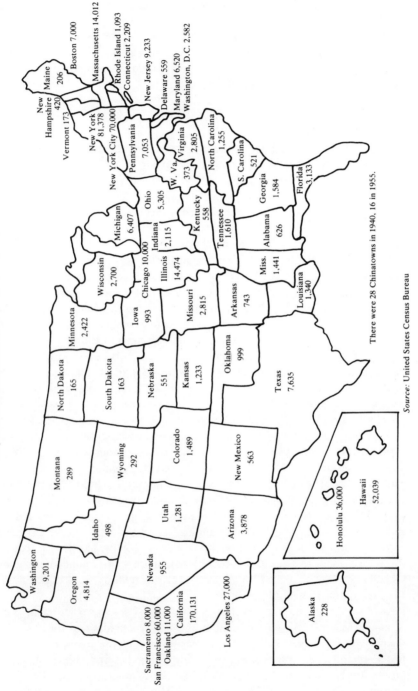

Washington 9,201
Oregon 4,814
California 170,131
San Francisco 60,000
Oakland 11,000
Sacramento 8,000
Los Angeles 27,000
Nevada 955
Idaho 498
Utah 1,281
Arizona 3,878
Montana 289
Wyoming 292
Colorado 1,489
New Mexico 563
North Dakota 165
South Dakota 163
Nebraska 551
Kansas 1,233
Oklahoma 999
Texas 7,635
Minnesota 2,422
Wisconsin 2,700
Iowa 993
Missouri 2,815
Arkansas 743
Louisiana 1,340
Michigan 6,407
Illinois 14,474
Chicago 10,000
Indiana 2,115
Ohio 5,305
Kentucky 558
Tennessee 1,610
Miss. 1,441
Alabama 626
Georgia 1,584
Florida 3,133
S. Carolina 521
North Carolina 1,255
W. Va. 373
Virginia 2,805
Pennsylvania 7,053
New York 81,378
New York City 70,000
Vermont 173
New Hampshire 420
Maine 206
Boston 7,000
Massachusetts 14,012
Rhode Island 1,093
Connecticut 2,209
New Jersey 9,233
Delaware 559
Maryland 6,520
Washington, D.C. 2,582

Hawaii 52,039
Honolulu 36,000

Alaska 228

There were 28 Chinatowns in 1940, 16 in 1955.

Source: United States Census Bureau

Of the major California Chinatowns, only those in San Francisco and Los Angeles survived exclusion. Los Angeles Chinatown, however, succumbed to that city's renewal program. The present Chinatown on Broadway was built as a new entity, a sort of Broadway version of what a Chinatown should look like. After a decline in numbers during the exclusion era, the present Chinese community of 52,000, dispersed among the general population there, has now become the third largest in the country.[1]

San Francisco

San Francisco Chinatown is the oldest and second largest Chinese American community. Over 35,000 people live in its core area of twenty-four blocks bounded by Columbus, Montgomery, California, Powell, and Broadway, a mixed residential and commercial zone with some light industry, mainly garment making and food processing. Although it is the second most densely populated area in the United States outside of parts of Manhattan, its attraction to new immigrants is what it has always been. Here a newly arrived FOB (fresh-off-the-boat) immigrant hears his or her native tongue—mostly various dialects of Guangdongese spoken in shops, places of work, and recreation. He or she can buy any of a dozen newspapers and magazines published locally in Chinese or in Chinese and English. Excellent restaurants give a wide choice in food, from Guandongese to Beijingese, from Shanghaiese to Sichuanese. If you want to do your own cooking, you can buy live fish, fresh meat, poultry, vegetables, and fruit in a score of shops and Chinese delicacies as varied as one might find in shops in China. The unique character of this community and its shops crowded with Chinese wares makes it a delight to the tourist.

Herbal stores sell Chinese medicines. Acupuncturists, masseuses, and orthopedists treat patients in traditional Chinese medical ways. Buildings with Chinese-style decorations house offices and meeting rooms of the old Six Companies and other associations. A dozen tongs maintain an open, friendly existence, but at least two are still secret and engage in illegal activity. While the Six Companies and family associations still have considerable influence, most of their functions have been taken over by a large number of new federal, state, and community organizations ranging from Social Security, to the Visitors and Convention Bureau, to Self-Help for the Elderly (which sharply reduced the suicide rate), to a dozen business and trade associations and the Chinese Chamber of Commerce, which among its other activities organizes the annual Miss Chinatown Beauty Pageant.

A directory of the traditional organizations of Chinatown fills eight pages of names in small type: In addition to the Six Companies and thirty-four district and forty-six clan (family) associations and eleven tongs, there are five Veterans' Posts, thirty social clubs, forty churches and church-related groups, twelve trade associations, including the Chamber of Commerce, and community groups like the Chinatown Neighborhood Improvement Resource Center and institutions such as the Intersection Theatrical group and the

Map 6. Downtown San Francisco, Including Chinatown

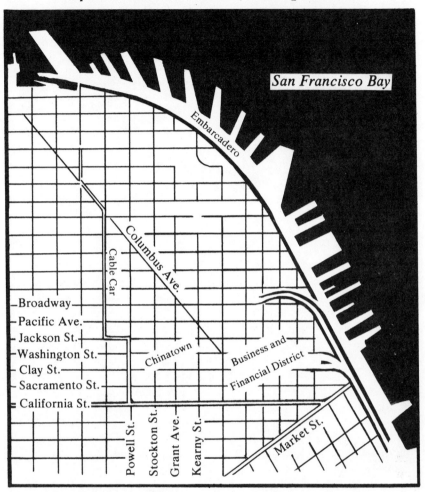

Kearny Street Workshop, a group of avant-garde photographers.

These organizations include a number of modern political groups, local chapters of such organizations as the veteran Chinese American Citizens Alliance, the China Democratic Club and Republican party group, the National Association of Chinese Americans, and the Kuomintang Party.

There is no known Chinese American communist organization, but a group calling itself the Revolutionary Communist Party, Marxist-Leninist, led by Robert Avakian, has made Chinatown a special focus of its activities. In the name of "Maoism," a term which Mao himself rejected, it pickets functions in which representatives of the People's Republic of China participate. It is said to be supported by the Albanians and its Chinese members are mainly middle-class and college youth. Most Chinese Americans appear to accept

Graph 4. Organizational Structure of San Francisco Chinatown

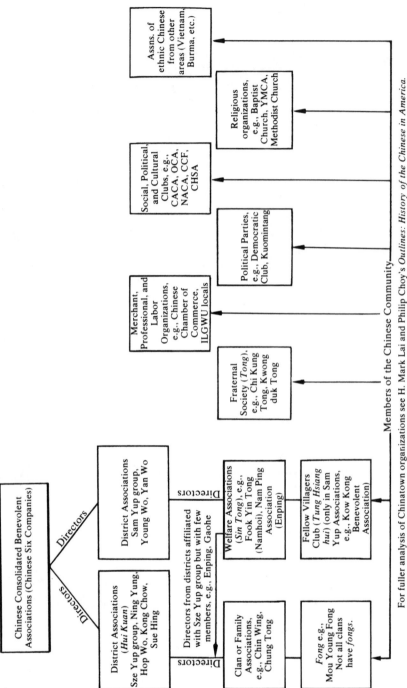

For fuller analysis of Chinatown organizations see H. Mark Lai and Philip Choy's *Outlines: History of the Chinese in America.*

the premises of the present American quasi-capitalist-socialist system and, like most mainstream Americans, look to its continued evolution in answer to their needs. There is likewise no known group of socialists, although it would be hard to believe that no one in Chinatown is interested in socialist ideas of any kind.

If a free poll of adults were taken on the question of pro–People's Republic of China or pro-Taiwan sympathies, the overwhelming majority would probably

Map 7. San Francisco Chinatown

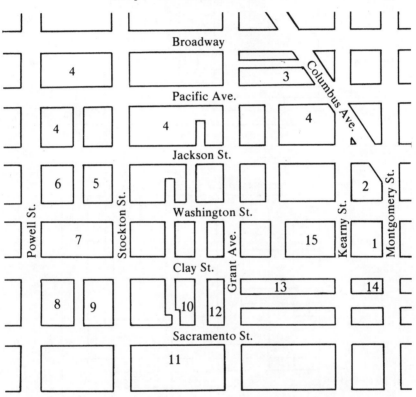

Legend:
1. Chinese Culture Center
2. International Hotel site
3. Chinese Historical Society of America
4. Ping Yuen Houses
5. Chinese Hospital
6. Cumberland Church
7. Commodore Stockton School
8. YWCA
9. Donaldina Cameron House
10. Chinese Playground
11. YMCA
12. Chinese Newcomer Center
13. East/West Newspaper
14. Kearny Street Workshop
15. Portsmouth Square

This core area of Chinatown contains the meeting rooms of the family and district associations and the *tongs*, political and social groups; scores of shops, business houses, restaurants, and garment workshops; residential highrises and hotels and apartments houses.

Graph 5. Chinese American Population in Major Cities (1970)

Chinese Population in Major Cities and as a Percentage of Total Chinese Population (1970)

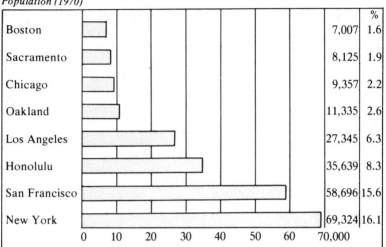

		%
Boston	7,007	1.6
Sacramento	8,125	1.9
Chicago	9,357	2.2
Oakland	11,335	2.6
Los Angeles	27,345	6.3
Honolulu	35,639	8.3
San Francisco	58,696	15.6
New York	69,324	16.1

0   10   20   30   40   50   60   70,000

Chinese Population as a Percentage of Cities' Total Population (1970)

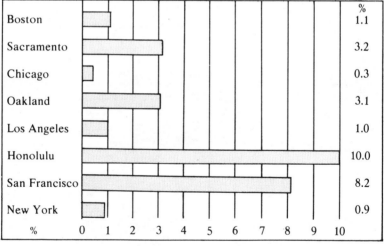

	%
Boston	1.1
Sacramento	3.2
Chicago	0.3
Oakland	3.1
Los Angeles	1.0
Honolulu	10.0
San Francisco	8.2
New York	0.9

%   0   1   2   3   4   5   6   7   8   9   10

Source: U.S. Census Bureau

tilt to the PRC and most of them for the simple reason that they want to maintain ties with their relatives in Guangdong. Family ties remain strong in the community. The practice of marrying within the group still predominates, but there is an increasing tendency for the younger generation to intermarry with other peoples.

Chinatown is a vital center not only for those who live in it and would feel lost if wrenched away from it but also for the tens of thousands more who live outside it in the Richmond and Sunset or other districts on the San Francisco side of the Bay (where together they form 10 percent of the city's population) or across the bridges in Marin County or in East Bay cities.

Chinese lived in Oakland in the 1850s, but Oakland's present-day Chinatown developed shortly after the 1906 earthquake. It now has a Chinese population of 11,335 (1970), clustered southwest of Lake Merritt and spread across the Oakland hills. There are Chinese living in Berkeley (4,035); Albany (305); El Cerrito (761), where I myself live; and Richmond (635). On weekends, Chinatown is crowded with Chinese Americans journeying there to do their shopping or at night to party or find entertainment in its restaurants, movie houses, or community groups. Chinatown has its social and cultural groups, its lovers of painting and ceramics, its literary coteries, its dance groups—its youth gangs and elderly gang leaders, its few pimps and prostitutes.

In a word, Chinatown is a city, a community within a community, an ethnic neighborhood of a particularly vital kind in that sparkling, lively metropolis of San Francisco.

The Bay Area Chinese American community of over 100,000 is the largest in the United States and, with the arrival of ethnic Chinese from Vietnam, Burma, and Cambodia, probably the most diverse.

Changing Patterns of Chinatowns: The Northwest

From the 1850s till today, Chinatowns have displayed a changing pattern not only in their nature but in geographical location.

Chinese communities spread to the northwestern states of Washington and Oregon at an early date as the lumber industry, mining, and salmon canneries developed there in the early and mid-1850s. In the 1860s and 1870s, they moved to Idaho and Montana to work in the mining industries. All the smaller Chinatowns disappeared during the exclusion period. Only the larger ones in Portland and Seattle have survived. In the lumber areas, Chinese were mainly cooks and storekeepers.

The numbers of Chinese miners were not large. In 1870, there were 7,740 in the four states, with 234 on the Columbia River. A young Chinese named Chin Chun Hook arrived in Seattle in 1860 and in 1868 opened a general goods store by the waterfront. This was the beginning of Seattle's Chinatown,[3] which grew in numbers when coal mining and the railway came to the area. They worked in the Yesler Saw Mill and followed their usual occupations as laundrymen, domestics, restaurant and hotel keepers, and cigar makers. As in California, when the economy faltered in 1873 and 1875, the Chinese became the scapegoats and were driven out of most northwestern towns. In Seattle, of the 350 forced out of their homes, 196 were shipped to San Francisco on the *Queen of the Pacific* on February 7, 1886. A week later, 110 were shipped out on the *George W. Elder*. Federal troops stopped the riot there.

But the growing Northwest needed labor and the Chinese had their defenders. Chinatown managed to hold on. Chinese worked on the Alaska-

Graph 6. Geographic Concentration of the Chinese Population

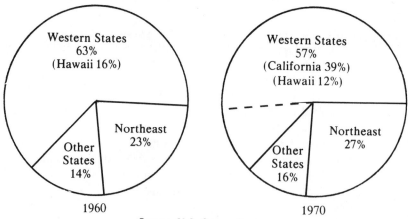

1960

Western States
63%
(Hawaii 16%)

Northeast
23%

Other
States
14%

1970

Western States
57%
(California 39%)
(Hawaii 12%)

Northeast
27%

Other
States
16%

Source: U.S. Census Bureau

Yukon Pacific Exposition in 1909 and the Lake Washington Ship Canal in 1910–1915. Seattle Chinatown had a single Overseas Chinese Benevolent Association uniting people of all districts and family names. The community grew back to over 7,500 in the 1970s and more modern types of social organizations were formed.

As restrictive housing was eliminated in the civil rights struggles of the 1960s, Chinese family groups moved out of Seattle Chinatown. They are now found scattered around the city with the original downtown Chinatown remaining mainly as a social and community center. Redevelopment plans, however, threaten its existence. A new stadium and facilities are planned for the site, around Washington Street between 2nd and 4th Avenues. Portland, as a port of entry, early had a Chinatown, which still exists.[4]

The Sierra and Rocky Mountains

The Chinese spread from western California to the areas between the Sierra and the Rockies—eastern California, Utah, Wyoming, Colorado—in the later 1850s and 1860s. They reached Nevada in 1855. In 1856, 50 of them were hired to dig the canal from the Carson River to Gold Canyon, and they stayed on to mine gold near Dayton (then called China Camp). More came through with the building of the first transcontinental railway (1864–1869) and other lines. Some stayed on to mine coal in Utah and Wyoming and work on the borax beds at Columbus, Nevada, and Searles Lake, California. When the mines in Oro Fino were largely abandoned by the white miners in 1864, Chinese were allowed to take over their claims. The first big demonstration against the Chinese in Nevada was in 1869. The last violent anti-Chinese riot was in 1903. From a high of 3,132 in 1870, their numbers declined to under 900 in 1910. They have gradually returned in recent years to establish mostly restaurant businesses in the larger towns. The newspapers yield some curious facts: In 1894 Ah Yu enlisted in the U.S. Navy and in 1903 he returned to Nevada with military honors and a government pension of $30 a month. In 1898, Sing Boo, a servant of 25 years with the Charles Schultz family, petitioned the Governor for permission to cook and to fight with the Nevada Volunteers in the Spanish-American War.

The Southwest

Groups of Chinese came for the first time into Texas, Arizona, New Mexico, and Oklahoma with the railways they were building, and some settled down in the 1870s in such railway towns as El Paso.[5] San Antonio owes most of its present Chinese population of over 1,000 to the 427 Chinese who had helped supply stores to General Pershing's 1916–1917 expedition against Pancho Villa in Mexico. The Chinese were having a hard time in the heat of the nationalist fervor that then gripped Mexico, and they were glad to accompany the American force when it withdrew. At Pershing's request, a special act of Congress granted them residence in the United States. There are over 8,000 Chinese in Texas today, 4,000 of them in Houston. Most of them operate or work in grocery stores and restaurants. A few have prospered directly from the Texas oil bonanza. Some are professionals in the aerospace and petrochemical industries.

Arizona has had a Chinese community since the time the Chinese came there to work at stagecoach stations or as community photographers and miners. Others came in on the Southern Pacific Railway they helped to build and that crossed the Colorado River into Arizona on September 30, 1877.[6] They suffered the usual misfortunes of the exclusion era. As late as 1900, only 7 percent of them were women. Tombstone, Prescott, and Bisbee were especially notorious as centers of anti-Chinese sentiment. At one time, anti-Chinese Leagues paraded down the streets once a week with brass bands. Merchants were commended by the newspapers for firing their Chinese help. Gradually, however, Americanization prevailed. The Chinese abandoned their queues, symbols of subservience to the Manchu emperor, and drew closer to their neighbors. In World War I, they bought $10,000 worth of war bonds. The larger community reciprocated in a spirit of brotherhood. The state today has a community of some 4,000 Chinese Americans.

The Eastern States

When Chinese immigrants reached New York in the 1870s in any numbers, they also reached Massachusetts, New Jersey, Philadelphia, Baltimore (present Chinese population over 5,000) and Washington, D.C. (over 8,000). The first Chinese laundry opened in Philadelphia in 1870; the first Chinese restaurant opened in 1880. Philadelphia's Chinatown was greatly reduced in size when its main street was incorporated into a freeway leading to the Benjamin Franklin Bridge, which connects the city to New Jersey. Later a slum clearance program took away more of what remained. The Chinese community of 1,000 was reduced to 200, but has subsequently recovered to over 5,000, ten percent of whom live in Chinatown. By taking the initiative in an urban development plan for Chinatown, the Chinese community, through its nonprofit Chinatown Development Corporation, has ensured the continued existence of Chinatown in Philadelphia. Among the development schemes was the construction of a lively Chinese cultural and community center built by volunteers from eleven trade unions.

New York

The New York *Herald* on July 10, 1847, reported the arrival of thirty-five Chinese in New York,[7] the crew of the *Keying*. The first permanent Chinese resident in the city was Quimpo Appo, a tea merchant who arrived in the late 1840s or early 1850s.[8] In 1858, a Cantonese with the same surname as my grandfather, Ah Ken, opened a cigar store on Park Row and lived on Mott Street. A small group of Chinese arrived from the West Coast in 1869 after completion of the trancontinental railway. It included Wo Kee, who opened a general store at 8 Mott Street, and Chu Fung Wing, a founding member of the New York Consolidated Chinese Benevolent Associations. An association of 60 district and family associations, it is still dominated by Kuomintang Party members and sympathizers. When I was appointed Consultant on Chinese Studies to the New York State Education Department in 1972, they sent a letter to Governor Nelson Rockefeller informing him that I was not really Jack Chen at all, but Chen Pei-hsien, a top-level Chinese Communist Party functionary, who was formerly head of political affairs for all Eastern China and is now again in a senior government post.

After West Coast anti-Chinese violence broke out in the 1870s and 1880s, a thousand more Chinese arrived in New York. During the exclusion period, the population grew to 10,000, mainly at the expense of San Francisco and other, smaller Chinatowns that were abandoned. Wholesale and retail trade, restaurants, laundries, and garment making became and remain the main occupations. In the years since repeal of the Exclusion Act in 1943, the population has grown to around 200,000 in the whole New York metropolitan area and 117,000 in Manhattan.[9]

The Consolidated Chinese Benevolent Associations, which once aspired to speak for the whole New York Chinese community, is now only one of several civic organizations answering the needs of the community. Others are the Hamilton-Madison House social service agency with an eighty-year history that runs such projects as Head Start, day-care for children, mental health centers, and senior citizens' programs. The Chinatown Planning Council, a multipurpose social service agency, runs similar projects and helps with housing, legal aid, and employment. There are also a variety of more

Map 8. New York Chinatown

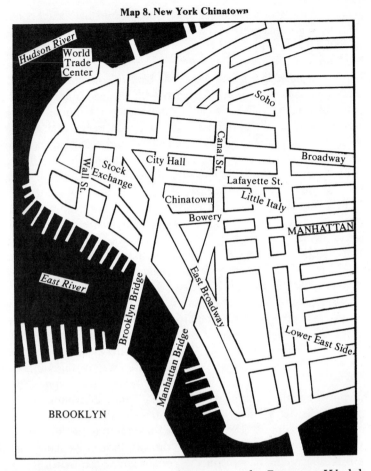

specialized organizations such as student groups; the Basement Workshop, a cultural group on Lafayette Street; Asian Americans for Equal Employment; and, of course, political groups similar to those in San Francisco. Chinatown New York, like San Francisco, is gradually cutting its political ties with the Kuomintang. The number of registered and actual voters is low. This has spurred organization of the reform-minded United Democratic Organization, which now challenges the older established Democratic Club. No less than nine newspapers are published in the New York area in Chinese or in Chinese and English. The Immigrant Service Society provides off-the-street aid, especially to young people. The Better Chinatown Project, drawing like the others on local, state, and federal funds, provides somewhat similar counseling services and training programs.

The Chinatown median income is below that of New York State as a whole: $7,344 compared with $10,607 (1970 figures). Unemployment is high, running 3.4 percentage points above the national average. A Department of Health, Education and Welfare field study in the 1970s showed 15 percent of families living below the poverty level, but a surprisingly low figure of 3.4 percent receiving public assistance. (The comparable national figures are 11 percent and 5.3 percent.)

New York Chinatown has been described as "a thriving area with problems." A decade ago, it had just a few banks. Now there are eight commercial banks and three savings banks with thirteen branch offices and total assets of over $2 billion, 80 percent belonging to Chinese. Greater Chinatown has some 900 enterprises, with over 700 in the core area. There are 500 garment workshops, 150 restaurants, and 64 retail shops and wholesale businesses; banks and other enterprises make up the remainder. One of the biggest problems is housing, despite such projects as the Confucius Plaza. Another is soaring rent and real estate values due to inflation and flight capital from Taiwan and Hong Kong. As these figures show, the area has considerable resources with which to handle its problems, but a big difficulty is that it, like San Francisco and Los Angeles, is a port of entry for new immigrants, and these naturally go into Chinatown at the rate of 4,000–5,000 a year, straining housing, educational, and health facilities.

In the face of these problems, a grave responsibility faces those who "have made it" in Chinatown: its professionals, lawyers, and businesspeople, who can give much-needed support to public-spirited social workers in their efforts to deal with the old and constantly new problems that history brings.

Boston[10]

Some of the Chinese brought into North Adams, Massachusetts, in 1870 as strike breakers (see Chapter 10) later drifted into Boston and settled near the South Railway Station. They were soon joined by a group brought straight from the West Coast on contract to build the Pearl Street telephone exchange. This was the beginning of what in the 1970s became the fourth largest Chinatown in the nation, with 6,758 people.

In the late 1830s, the site of this Chinatown, centered on Beech Street, was marshland being reclaimed for building houses. But when the railroad tracks were laid the middle-class Americans who lived there began to move out, and their abandoned homes became a low-rent enclave quickly taken over by Chinese immigrants, most of whom were poor. By 1890, some 250 Chinese lived in Boston, four-fifths of them in Chinatown. In 1920, they numbered 1,000 and in 1950, 1,600. During exclusion days, Boston's Chinese clustered tightly in this segregated Chinatown where even in the 1960s, around 80 percent of them could not speak English. This was mainly a bachelor society with few families. Laundry and restaurant work were the principal occupations. Work days were long, twelve or more hours. In 1875, the various family groups combined to form the Chinese Consolidated Benevolent Association, which until the middle of the twentieth century was their unofficial spokesperson and which mediated problems within the community. By then, it included the Chinese Merchants Association, which functioned as an embryo chamber of commerce. It also ran a school for Chinese children that gave an eighth-grade traditional Chinese education in classes from 4 to 6 P.M. daily and on Saturday mornings. A small office provided an essential service: sending remittances back to China.

World War II brought major changes to Boston Chinatown. Quite a number of Chinese seamen joined the crews ferrying men and munitions over the Nazi U-boat infested Atlantic. Other young Chinese joined the U.S. armed forces or did war work, especially in the Boston Naval Shipyard, the South Boston Naval Yard Annex, and the Watertown Arsenal. Repeal of the Exclusion Act in 1943 and increasingly progressive immigration legislation increased the Boston Chinatown population. Families were reunited, more women immigrants arrived, new families were formed, and a new generation of native-born Chinese American citizens grew up. Among the problems that arose was a generation gap between tradition-bound Chinese-speaking parents and English-speaking and U.S.-educated Chinese children. A complicating factor was that many immigrants in the 1950s, 1960s, and 1970s were from Hong Kong and other places with very cosmopolitan ways. This created problems typical of many other Chinese American communities.

These developments posed opportunities as well as problems, but a serious threat occurred when, under Boston redevelopment plans, the building of the Southeast Freeway halved the Chinatown area at a time when its population was doubling. A further threat was the planned extension of the Tufts New England Medical Center into Chinatown. The community reacted sharply and received veto power from the city authorities over any "outside" developers eyeing the area from Essex to Kneeland Streets, part of the central business district, and from Kneeland to Tai Tung Village. Such a "memorandum of understanding" may be a useful model for other Chinatowns threatened by redevelopment.

Chinese Americans can be found today in every section of Boston, but, although only 10 percent of them live there, Chinatown remains a focal point for community social and business activities. It is a small but vital community center for Boston Chinese with its two language schools, two movie theaters, bookstores, and print shops; its newspaper, community center, and arts center promoting Chinese culture; its restaurants offering excellent Chinese food, grocery stores, gift shops; its family associations; and its lively younger generation of Chinese Americans.

The Midwest and Chicago

Three Chinese from the West Coast reached the Midwest in 1860. They came to Morgan County in southern Illinois, and one remained there until 1870, by which time there were two more in Chicago.[11]

Ten years later, in 1880, when more Chinese were leaving the West Coast at the height of the anti-Chinese campaign to "end the flood of Chinese pouring into the United States," there were 209 of them in Illinois, all but

5 in Chicago. They congregated in a one-block Chinatown at Clark and Van Buren Streets south of the downtown area, but on the advice of the Chinese ambassador, Wu Ting-fang, they spread out as much as possible to keep "a low profile." Their main occupations then and on into the mid-1900s were laundries, restaurants, and grocery and curio stores.

Most immigrants came from Taishan in Guangdong, and they brought their familiar family associations—mainly Moy, Chan, and Fong—and two tongs, the Hip Sing Tong and On Leong Tong. In 1910, due to rising rents, the need for expansion, and conflict between the two tongs, the On Leong Tong led an exodus to a second Chinatown five miles away, encompassing ten blocks centered on Cermak and Wentworth Streets. This area is now known as Chinatown. New black neighborhoods are on its south, and the Italians, Swedes, and Croatians who once lived in the area have prospered and moved out. The Chinese, however, began buying homes and improving them in the 1940s when the second generation of American-born gave up

Map 9. Chicago Chinatowns

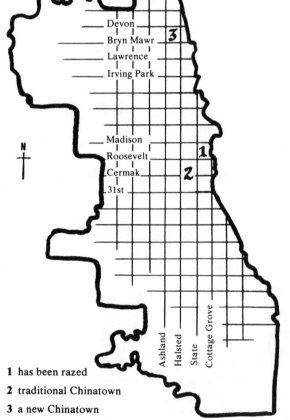

1 has been razed

2 traditional Chinatown

3 a new Chinatown

the sojourner mentality of so many of the first generation of immigrants and began to consider America their home. By then there were well over 100 families.

While these developments were taking place, the first Old Chinatown was razed under an area development plan in 1972 and moved to a third Chinatown uptown on Argyle and Broadway Streets where some Chinese already lived. This is twelve miles from the second Chinatown, in a rather seedy district. However, it appears to be prospering and because of its cheap rents is now filling up with ethnic Chinese Vietnamese refugees.

In the 1970s, when Chicago had over 12,000 Chinese Americans, the more affluent, college-educated white-collar workers, professionals, and managers in the Chinatowns were following the exodus to the suburbs, but recently a new trend has started: they are remaining in Chinatown and thereby benefiting it with their knowledge, skills, and community spirit.

Chinatown remains a supportive center, but new organizations are taking over and expanding the services once provided by the traditional organizations. A modern community center sponsors a senior citizens' program giving medicare, nutritional aid, translation services, and other help. A senior citizen low-income housing project was completed in 1979, and there are special programs such as English and naturalization classes for new arrivals and day-care centers to help working mothers. Working conditions are said by local community workers to be "reasonable" in the thirty restaurants and thirty or more groceries and gift shops. The crime rate is the lowest in the city. A need now is felt for some organizational center to serve and foster the cultural needs of the new generation of Chinese Americans as an ethnic group with a unique heritage in the midwestern metropolis.

Chinese reached Detroit in the 1870s. Today they live dispersed among the other ethnic groups. Minneapolis had a small Chinatown in the 1920–30's, just a cluster of families living above their shops and an eating house on Third Avenue between 7th and 8th Streets.[12]

Chinese arrived in Minnesota in the late 1870s. Here they tried to avoid competition and conflict with other races by setting up small businesses such as laundries, hotels, novelty shops, restaurants. Just before World War II, they numbered 1,000 (with just 100 women). Now they number around 3,500 with several active community groups. In Pennsylvania, Pittsburgh's Chinatown was obliterated by the building of a modern expressway.

The South

The Chinese in the Mississippi Delta were among those who first arrived in the southern states of Arkansas, Tennessee, Louisiana, Alabama, and Georgia. Following the Civil War and the emancipation of slaves, southern plantation owners hoped to replace their slaves with Chinese labor. Chinese were contracted to work the cotton fields, but because of harsh conditions, all left as soon as their contracts ended. Most of them went on to the Illinois area or back to the West. The rest stayed in the area to open grocery stores. Those in the Mississippi Delta became one of the most prosperous communities in the area.[13] The 1970 census showed their numbers in various regions of the South to range from several hundred to 1,600.

Twenty-five Chinese coming from Indianapolis arrived in Augusta, Georgia, on November 4, 1873, to work on the Augusta Canal, which brings water from the Savannah River to the city.[14] Eventually several score were working on the project, and their work was highly praised by the press. They were able to live on about $7 a month, saving what remained of their wages. When the canal was completed in 1875, Chinese stayed on to form the largest Chinese community in the South, outside of New Orleans. Many settled in the black district and set up laundries and grocery stores. In 1915, these numbered fifteen and twenty-nine respectively.

Augusta Chinese raised funds for Chinese war relief in World War II, bought war bonds, and served in the U.S. armed forces. After the war, many family grocery stores here as elsewhere lost out to the chain stores. The seventy-five listed in 1948 were reduced to twenty-five in 1973, but by this time the younger generation was going into the professions. The 1970 census showed 1,528 Chinese in Augusta.

The decline in the number of Chinatowns that exclusion caused has not been reversed. In 1940, just before the end of exclusion, there were twenty-eight Chinatowns. By 1955, there were only sixteen. Today there are only two real, self-sustaining Chinatowns: San Francisco, and New York, now the largest. Boston's is hardly more than a mini-Chinatown. Only strenuous efforts on its part will develop it.

The occupations engaged in by the Chinese of America show a pattern of geographic distribution. I have already described at length the diverse occupations of the early immigrants in the West. During the major part of the exclusion period (1882–1943), when they were segregated in the urban areas, they were concentrated in domestic work, laundries, restaurants, and the garment industry. Some continued in agriculture, raising flowers and vegetables. Those who moved to the Midwest supported themselves mainly with laundry work and restaurants. In the Southeast and Southwest, grocery stores were their economic mainstay.

Today, with the third generation of American-born and educated young people entering the labor market, these patterns are changing, but not only because Chinese are taking up new activities. Even in the 1960s many a young Ph.D. found that, despite his diploma, discrimination barred him from work in his chosen field. But one by one the barriers are being battered down by the equal opportunity movement of all ethnic groups backed by the law of the land. Among Chinese Americans, more and more are going into the professions and managerial work, into large-scale business activities of their own, and into scholarly pursuits. There is a concentration in the fields of technology, and a trend away from the service trades into white-collar jobs.

Hawaii

Hawaii repeats the pattern of a handful of pioneering Chinese arriving to be followed by larger groups of sojourners and settlers.[13] Captain George Vancouver noted the presence of Chinese in the Hawaiian Islands as early as 1794. They were said to be crewmen from European vessels trading sandalwood from Hawaii to Canton. Hence the Chinese name for Hawaii—the Sandalwood Mountains. Other Chinese came later to start the sugar industry. Some of the earliest were Wong Tse Chun, who arrived in 1802 with a stone mill and boilers to make sugar on Lanai; Achung and Atai, who set up the Hung Tai Company in 1828 on Maui; and Aiko, who ran a sugar mill in Kohala and later on Hilo in 1841. The first contract laborers arrived in 1852. From 1854 to 1864, over 700 Chinese were working on the sugar plantations mainly operated by white planters.

The sugar industry is peculiar in that it is very seasonal and labor intensive. The cane has to be cut, hauled, and crushed in less than three days to prevent the cane juice from turning sour. Moreover, the process of plowing, planting, and cultivating the canes is long. Native Hawaiians were unaccustomed to such a work style. Therefore, and because the native population declined catastrophically, from 300,000 in 1779 to 130,000 in 1832 and 30,000 in 1900, the mainly white Planters Society in 1864 arranged for a board of immigration to recruit laborers from abroad. The Chinese, who were preferred as workers (earning the nickname "planters' pets"), usually came under a five-year contract at a starting wage of $4 a month, with passage, room, and board. The workday lasted from 4:00 A.M. to sundown. Men slept six to forty per room in barracks. Some Chinese arrived under independently negotiated contracts, and a number of younger men took jobs as domestics.

At first things seemed to go well, but the harsh terms of work and the brutality of some plantation owners and their overseers led to Chinese strikes. Many men refused to renew their contracts; they took off for the towns to engage in business as shopkeepers or peddlers or leased land for rice farming, both to satisfy local needs and to export to California with its growing Chinese population. By 1880, Chinese, many of them Hakkas, made up 50 percent of the plantation work force. By 1884, the 18,254 of them comprised 22.6 percent of the population of Hawaii and were engaged in many trades. Hitherto, it had been the planters and businessmen who had supported Chinese immigration; now, Chinese began to compete with business interests, and anti-Chinese agitation, which had begun in 1875, increased.

Various restrictive measures were taken. In 1884, with the Workingmen's Union organizing an anti-Chinese drive, ships were limited to carrying only twenty-five contract laborers each, and passports which they had to carry with them were issued to all Chinese in Hawaii. An Anti-Chinese Union was set up in 1888. By 1890, Chinese were only 10 percent of the plantation work force. When Hawaii was annexed to the United States in 1898, the Chinese Exclusion Act of the mainland was extended to the Islands.

Anti-Chinese agitation culminated in the total destruction of Honolulu's Chinatown by fire in January 1900.

The fire had been set to rid the area of bubonic plague, but it had "gotten out of control." No advance notice had been given to residents, and of forty-one sanitary fires set, only one, that in Chinatown, "got out of control." Between 1900 and 1910, the Chinese population in Hawaii dropped by over 4,000.[15]

By this time, those that remained were beginning to regard themselves as permanent residents. When rice farming declined due to competition from California and lack of labor, more and more Chinese went into the towns and took up such occupations as laundering, cooking, tailoring, shopkeeping, and trade. Chinese quickly dominated wholesale and retail distribution and their restaurants did exceedingly well. An official attempt was made to fill the depleted ranks of labor with Japanese. Until 1900, the twenty-five acres of Chinatown had been home to 40 percent of the Chinese in Honolulu. After that they lived dispersed among the rest of the population, but Chinatown remained home to quite a number and continued to be a prime center for business, shopping, and socializing.

Chinatown played a key role in the lives and survival of the contract laborers in the early days. It had developed the familiar pattern of family and district associations and tongs, and its shops and trade agencies maintained close contact with the homeland villages of the immigrants where normal postal services did not exist. By this means, immigrants sent home the remittances on which their families depended.

It was also the means by which the Chinese Hawaiian immigration played a key role in the revolutionary transformation of China that was taking place at the turn of the century. Sun Yat-sen, the "Father of the Chinese Revolution" had received his early education in Hawaii when he lived with his uncle. Here he learned English and made his first acquaintance with those ideas of democracy and republicanism that later developed into his famous Three People's Principles: "nationalism, democracy, and the people's livelihood." He revisited Hawaii in 1894 at the age of twenty-nine and established his first overseas revolutionary organization, the Xing Zhong Hui or China Reviving Society. On his fifth visit in 1910, he established the Tung Min Hui, the forerunner of the Kuomintang or National People's Party, and the newspaper that is still published in the islands. The next year, the Qing dynasty was overthrown and China became a republic, with Sun Yat-sen as president (1912). Hawaiian Chinese, like San Francisco Chinese, played a notable role as supporters of the nationalist movement in China that finally freed the country from foreign domination. They also battled fiercely against the racist exclusion laws. They gave financial and moral support to the boycott movement in China of the 1900s that led to a slight liberalization of exclusion regulations under President Theodore Roosevelt.

But as the years went by Chinatown's importance declined. In 1884, 75 percent of the 5,000 Chinese in Honolulu lived in Chinatown. In 1900, the

9,000 who lived there were only 40 percent of the Chinese population, and by 1960, only 5 percent of 38,119 Chinese in Honolulu lived in Chinatown. The same sort of changes were going on among the Chinese of Hawaii as were going on in the United States. They were becoming increasingly urbanized (over 94 percent in 1960) and middle class. In 1882, of 17,648 Chinese in Hawaii, 28.5 percent were plantation workers—49 percent of the labor force in Hawaii. By 1932, Chinese made up only 1.4 percent of the farm labor force. Eighteen percent of Chinese men are now in the professions. They made up 10 percent of the lawyers and 20 percent of the doctors by 1950 and they have the highest percentage of college-educated adults of all ethnic groups in Hawaii. In 1910, they spent three times as much on education in proportion to income as did Caucasians. By that time, the second- and third-generaton Chinese were growing up as native-born American citizens and going into such fields as education, finance, and politics. Hawaii elected the first Chinese U.S. senator, Hiram Fong, in 1959.

The somewhat jocular self-assessment is that fourth generation Chinese are absolute "bananas": yellow outside and white inside. In their new occupations, a number of Chinese made spectacular gains in real estate, tourism, and insurance. Chinn Ho, the well-known developer, whose monument is the Ilikai Hotel in Waikiki, is reputed to have a personal fortune of $15 million. Many others moved from middle- to upper-middle-class status. In 1970, 36 percent of all Chinese males in Hawaii earned more than $10,000 a year, while the figure for all Chinese in the United States was 24 percent. Only 27 percent (just under the U.S. average) made less than $4,000, compared to 41 percent for U.S. Chinese as a whole. Only 6 percent of Hawaiian Chinese families were rated poor; 7 percent (or half the U.S. average) earned less than $4,000. Median Chinese family income there was $14,936, the highest among all Asian groups in the state and double that among New York Chinese.[16]

In 1970, Hawaii's 52,000 ethnic Chinese (11 percent of them foreign born) were 6 percent of its population, 12 percent of all Chinese Americans.

The success of the Chinese of Hawaii stems largely from the diligence, sobriety, capacity for hard work, family solidarity, and similar "ethnic characteristics" for which they are noted. But they enjoyed certain advantages in comparison with their compatriots on the mainland. The polyglot population of Hawaii (Hawaiians, Caucasians, Chinese, Portuguese, Japanese, and Filipinos) is remarkably harmonious. With Caucasians in a minority, the Gompers-type leaders of white labor were not able to stir up the sort of anti-Asian, anti-Chinese virulence that disgraced the mainland labor movement. Because they were not segregated in an exclusion ghetto—as in San Francisco, for instance—they were able to seize the opportunities offered by the rapidly expanding Hawaiian economy. Furthermore, the so-called Big Five *haole* (Caucasian) corporations that have traditionally dominated the Hawaiian economy and still do, were less hostile to their Chinese Hawaiian competitors than to the Japanese, particularly in the 1910–1945 period.

Table 3. Total and Chinese Population in the U.S. (1850–1880)

Year	U.S. Population	Chinese in America
1850	23,191,876	
1860	31,443,321	34,933
1870	39,818,449	63,199
1880	50,155,783	105,465
1890	62,947,714	107,488
1900	75,994,575	89,863
1910	91,972,266	71,531
1920	105,710,620	61,639
1930	122,775,046	74,954
1940	131,669,275	77,504
1950	150,697,361	117,629
1960	179,323,175	237,292
1970	203,235,298	435,062
1980		(est.) 800,000

Table 4. U.S. Population, Distribution by Race (1970)

	White	Black	Indian	Japanese	Chinese	Others
Urban	128,773,240	18,367,318	355,738	523,651	418,779	886,204
Rural	48,975,735	4,212,971	436,992	67,639	16,283	177,376
TOTAL	177,748,975	22,580,289	792,730	591,290	435,062	1,063,580

NOTES

1. Kim Fong Tom, *Participation of Chinese in the Community of Los Angeles* (San Francisco: R & E Research, 1974).
2. Victor Nee and Brett de Bary, *Longtime Californ'* (New York: Pantheon, 1973) and Him Mark Lai and Philip P. Choy, *Outlines: History of the Chinese in America* (San Francisco: Chinese-American Studies Planning Group, 1973).
3. Doug Chin and Art Chin, *Uphill: The Settlement and Diffusion of the Chinese in Seattle* (Seattle: Shorey Publications, 1974).
4. Nelson Chai-chi Ho, *Portland's Chinatown, History of an Urban Ethnic District* (Portland: Bureau of Planning, 1978).
5. Edward Rhoads, *The Chinese in Texas* (Austin: Texas State Historical Society, 1977) and Nancy Farrar, *The Chinese in El Paso*, Southwestern Studies, Monograph No. 33 (El Paso: Texas Western Press and Texas University Press, 1972).
6. Laurence Fong, *The Chinese Experience in Arizona and Northern Mexico, 1870–1940* (Tucson: Arizona Historical Society, 1979).
7. I Hsuan Julia Chen, *The Chinese Community in New York, 1920–1940* (Washington, D.C.: American University, 1941); *The Forgotten Minority: Asian Americans in New York City*, Report by the New York State Advisory Committee to the U.S. Commission on Civil Rights (Washington, D.C., 1977); Victor Marrero, ed., *Chinatown: Street Revitalization* (New York: Dept. of Planning, 1976); and Betty Lee Sung, *Transplanted Chinese Children* (New York: HEW Administration for Children, Youth and Family, 1979); and *Neighborhood*, no. 3 (1978).

8. Lai and Choy, *Outlines.*
9. Sung, *Transplanted Chinese Children.*
10. *Chinatown* (Boston: Boston 200 Neighborhood History Series, 1976).
11. Susan Lee Moy, "Chinese in Chicago" (Unpublished paper). Chicago, 1980.
12. *Chinese in Minnesota* (Minnesota Historical Society). Information Leaflet.
13. James W. Loewen, *The Mississippi Chinese: Between White and Black* (Cambridge, Mass.: Harvard University Press, 1971).
14. Sally Ken, *The Chinese Community of Augusta, Georgia, 1873–1971* (Augusta, Ga.: Richmond County Historical Society, 1971) and Eileen Law and Sally Ken, *Study of Chinese Communities* (Augusta, Ga.: Richmond County Historical Society, 1971).
15. Tin Yuke Char, *The Sandalwood Mountains* (Honolulu: University Press of Hawaii, 1975).
16. Department of Health, Education and Welfare, *Study of Selected Socio-Economic Characteristics.* (Washington, D.C., 1970).

Index

Some topics discussed in this book are so central that they surface on almost every page: California, Chinatowns, Chinese Americans, etc. To index such topics in detail would require another volume; therefore only a few significant entries are included here. Consult the Table of Contents for somewhat broader areas of discussion.